Decision Support Systems and Industrial IoT in Smart Grid, Factories, and Cities

Ismail Butun
Chalmers University of Technology, Sweden & Konya Food and Agriculture University, Turkey & Royal University of Technology, Sweden

A volume in the Advances in Computational Intelligence and Robotics (ACIR) Book Series

Published in the United States of America by
    IGI Global
    Engineering Science Reference (an imprint of IGI Global)
    701 E. Chocolate Avenue
    Hershey PA, USA 17033
    Tel: 717-533-8845
    Fax: 717-533-8661
    E-mail: cust@igi-global.com
    Web site: http://www.igi-global.com

Library of Congress Cataloging-in-Publication Data

Names: Butun, Ismail, 1981- editor.
Title: Decision support systems and industrial IoT in smart grid,
   factories, and cities / Ismail Butun, editor.
Description: Hershey : Business Science Reference, 2021. | Includes
   bibliographical references and index. | Summary: "This book offers
   contributed chapters focusing on artificial intelligence and machine
   learning concepts as they apply to IoT systems and their decision
   support mechanisms which are leading to a better, sustainable, liveable,
   automated, and safer world"-- Provided by publisher.
Identifiers: LCCN 2021009747 (print) | LCCN 2021009748 (ebook) | ISBN
   9781799874683 (hardcover) | ISBN 9781799874690 (paperback) | ISBN
   9781799874706 (ebook)
Subjects: LCSH: Decision support systems. | Internet of things--Industrial
   applications.
Classification: LCC T58.62 .D4285 2021 (print) | LCC T58.62 (ebook) | DDC
   658.4/03--dc23
LC record available at https://lccn.loc.gov/2021009747
LC ebook record available at https://lccn.loc.gov/2021009748

This book is published in the IGI Global book series Advances in Computational Intelligence and Robotics (ACIR) (ISSN: 2327-0411; eISSN: 2327-042X)

British Cataloguing in Publication Data
A Cataloguing in Publication record for this book is available from the British Library.

For electronic access to this publication, please contact: eresources@igi-global.com.

Advances in Computational Intelligence and Robotics (ACIR) Book Series

ISSN:2327-0411
EISSN:2327-042X

Editor-in-Chief: Ivan Giannoccaro, University of Salento, Italy

MISSION

While intelligence is traditionally a term applied to humans and human cognition, technology has progressed in such a way to allow for the development of intelligent systems able to simulate many human traits. With this new era of simulated and artificial intelligence, much research is needed in order to continue to advance the field and also to evaluate the ethical and societal concerns of the existence of artificial life and machine learning.

The **Advances in Computational Intelligence and Robotics (ACIR) Book Series** encourages scholarly discourse on all topics pertaining to evolutionary computing, artificial life, computational intelligence, machine learning, and robotics. ACIR presents the latest research being conducted on diverse topics in intelligence technologies with the goal of advancing knowledge and applications in this rapidly evolving field.

COVERAGE

- Brain Simulation
- Fuzzy Systems
- Natural Language Processing
- Heuristics
- Computer Vision
- Artificial Life
- Robotics
- Automated Reasoning
- Cognitive Informatics
- Adaptive and Complex Systems

IGI Global is currently accepting manuscripts for publication within this series. To submit a proposal for a volume in this series, please contact our Acquisition Editors at Acquisitions@igi-global.com or visit: http://www.igi-global.com/publish/.

Titles in this Series

For a list of additional titles in this series, please visit: http://www.igi-global.com/book-series/

AI Tools and Electronic Virtual Assistants for Improved Business Performance
Christian Graham (University of Maine, USA)
Business Science Reference • © 2021 • 300pp • H/C (ISBN: 9781799838418) • US $245.00

Transforming the Internet of Things for Next-Generation Smart Systems
Bhavya Alankar (Jamia Hamdard, India) Harleen Kaur (Hamdard University, India) and
Ritu Chauhan (Amity University, India)
Engineering Science Reference • © 2021 • 173pp • H/C (ISBN: 9781799875413) • US
$245.00

*Handbook of Research on Machine Learning Techniques for Pattern Recognition and
Information Security*
Mohit Dua (National Institute of Technology, Kurukshetra, India) and Ankit Kumar Jain
(National Institute of Technology, Kurukshetra, India)
Engineering Science Reference • © 2021 • 355pp • H/C (ISBN: 9781799832997) • US
$295.00

Driving Innovation and Productivity Through Sustainable Automation
Ardavan Amini (EsseSystems, UK) Stephen Bushell (Bushell Investment Group, UK) and
Arshad Mahmood (Birmingham City University, UK)
Engineering Science Reference • © 2021 • 275pp • H/C (ISBN: 9781799858799) • US
$245.00

Examining Optoelectronics in Machine Vision and Applications in Industry 4.0
Oleg Sergiyenko (Autonomous University of Baja California, Mexico) Julio C. Rodriguez-
Quiñonez (Autonomous University of Baja California, Mexico) and Wendy Flores-Fuentes
(Autonomous University of Baja California, Mexico)
Engineering Science Reference • © 2021 • 346pp • H/C (ISBN: 9781799865223) • US
$215.00

701 East Chocolate Avenue, Hershey, PA 17033, USA
Tel: 717-533-8845 x100 • Fax: 717-533-8661
E-Mail: cust@igi-global.com • www.igi-global.com

Editorial Advisory Board

Table of Contents

Section 1
DSS for LPWAN, LoRaWAN, and Wireless Technologies

Chapter 1
    Åke Axeland, Chalmers University of Technology, Sweden
    Henrik Hagfeldt, Chalmers University of Technology, Sweden
    Magnus Carlsson, Chalmers University of Technology, Sweden
    Lina Lagerquist Sergel, Chalmers University of Technology, Sweden
    Ismail Butun, Chalmers University of Technology, Sweden & Konya
        Food and Agriculture University, Turkey & Royal University of
        Technology, Sweden

Chapter 2
    Olof Magnusson, Gothenburg University, Sweden
    Rikard Teodorsson, Chalmers University of Technology, Sweden
    Joakim Wennerberg, Chalmers University of Technology, Sweden
    Stig Arne Knoph, Chalmers University of Technology, Sweden

Chapter 3
    Joar Blom Rydell, Chalmers University of Technology, Sweden
    Oliver Otterlind, Chalmers University of Technology, Sweden
    Amanda Sjöö, Chalmers University of Technology, Sweden

Section 2
Decision Support Systems and Industrial IoT in Smart Grid, Factories, and Cities

Section 3
DSS for Vehicular Networks

Section 4
DSS Applications From Various IoT Domains

Detailed Table of Contents

Section 1
DSS for LPWAN, LoRaWAN, and Wireless Technologies

Chapter 1
> *Åke Axeland, Chalmers University of Technology, Sweden*
> *Henrik Hagfeldt, Chalmers University of Technology, Sweden*
> *Magnus Carlsson, Chalmers University of Technology, Sweden*
> *Lina Lagerquist Sergel, Chalmers University of Technology, Sweden*
> *Ismail Butun, Chalmers University of Technology, Sweden & Konya*
> *Food and Agriculture University, Turkey & Royal University of*
> *Technology, Sweden*

With the contrast of limited performance and big responsibility of IoT devices, potential security breaches can have serious impacts in means of safety and privacy. Potential consequences of attacks on IoT devices could be leakage of individuals daily habits and political decisions being influenced. While the consequences might not be avoidable in their entirety, adequate knowledge is a fundamental part of realizing the importance of IoT security and during the assessment of damages following a breach. This chapter will focus on two low-powered wide area network (LPWAN) technologies, narrow-band iot (NB-IoT) and long-range wide area network (LoRaWAN). Further, three use cases will be considered—healthcare, smart cities, and industry—which all to some degree rely on IoT devices. It is shown that with enough knowledge of possible attacks and their corresponding implications, more secure IoT systems can be developed.

   Olof Magnusson, Gothenburg University, Sweden
   Rikard Teodorsson, Chalmers University of Technology, Sweden
   Joakim Wennerberg, Chalmers University of Technology, Sweden
   Stig Arne Knoph, Chalmers University of Technology, Sweden

LoRaWAN (long-range wide-area network) is an emerging technology for the connection of internet of things (IoT) devices to the internet and can as such be an important part of decision support systems. In this technology, IoT devices are connected to the internet through gateways by using long-range radio signals. However, because LoRaWAN is an open network, anyone has the ability to connect an end device or set up a gateway. Thus, it is important that gateways are designed in such a way that their ability to be used maliciously is limited. This chapter covers relevant attacks against gateways and potential countermeasures against them. A number of different attacks were found in literature, including radio jamming, eavesdropping, replay attacks, and attacks against the implementation of what is called beacons in LoRaWAN. Countermeasures against these attacks are discussed, and a suggestion to improve the security of LoRaWAN is also included.

   Joar Blom Rydell, Chalmers University of Technology, Sweden
   Oliver Otterlind, Chalmers University of Technology, Sweden
   Amanda Sjöö, Chalmers University of Technology, Sweden

Many techniques for wireless positioning have existed for years, but with emerging technologies like 5G and ultra wideband, wireless positioning is becoming more accurate than ever. On the one hand, improved accuracy implies increased usefulness. It will open up new application areas and lead to advances in areas like internet of things (IoT), self-driving cars, and contact tracing. Furthermore, decision support systems can benefit from better positioning techniques. On the other hand, the ability to track connected devices with sub-meter precision brings some privacy and security concerns. This chapter aims to review indoor and outdoor positioning technologies and how they can be used for contact tracing. It then further discusses some of the data management, privacy, and security concerns that follow. To that end, this chapter studies the main techniques for wireless positioning, cellular-based positioning using 5G, and their use to contact tracing. Finally, the authors provide some insight into how 5G and UWB might help the area of positioning and contact tracking in the future.

Section 2
Decision Support Systems and Industrial IoT in Smart Grid, Factories, and Cities

Chapter 4

Suresh P., Kongu Engineering College, India
Keerthika P., Kongu Engineering College, India
Sathiyamoorthi V., Sona College of Technology, India
Logeswaran K., Kongu Engineering College, India
Manjula Devi R., Kongu Engineering College, India
Sentamilselvan K., Kongu Engineering College, India
Sangeetha M., Kongu Engineering College, India
Sagana C., Kongu Engineering College, India

Cloud computing and big data analytics are the key parts of smart city development that can create reliable, secure, healthier, more informed communities while producing tremendous data to the public and private sectors. Since the various sectors of smart cities generate enormous amounts of streaming data from sensors and other devices, storing and analyzing this huge real-time data typically entail significant computing capacity. Most smart city solutions use a combination of core technologies such as computing, storage, databases, data warehouses, and advanced technologies such as analytics on big data, real-time streaming data, artificial intelligence, machine learning, and the internet of things (IoT). This chapter presents a theoretical and experimental perspective on the smart city services such as smart healthcare, water management, education, transportation and traffic management, and smart grid that are offered using big data management and cloud-based analytics services.

Chapter 5

Ismail Butun, Chalmers University of Technology, Sweden & Konya Food and Agriculture University, Turkey & Royal University of Technology, Sweden
Alparslan Sari, University of Delaware, USA

The internet of things (IoT) has recently brought major technological advances in many domains, including the smart grid. Despite the simplicity and efficiency that IoT brings, there are also underlying risks that are slowing down its adoption. These risks are caused by the presence of legacy systems inside existing infrastructures that were built with no security in mind. In this chapter, the authors propose a method for early-stage detection of cyber-security incidents and protection against them through applicable security measures. This chapter introduces security techniques such as anomaly detection, threat investigation through a highly automated decision support system (DSS), as well as incident response and recovery for smart grid systems. The introduced framework can be applied to industrial environments such as cyber-threats targeting the production generator as well as the electricity smart meters, etc. The chapter also illustrates the framework's cyber-resilience against zero-day threats and its ability to distinguish between operational failures as well as cyber-security incidents.

Chapter 6

A warehouse is an indispensable part of the logistics. A warehouse management system (WMS) is designed to improve efficiency in warehouses to increase their throughput and potential. The rise of IoT and its commercialization enabled 'smart things' to be widely adopted by hobbyists and companies. Cheap sensors and smart devices triggered better automation opportunities. Many devices and sensors that are being deployed in the industry and warehousing are affected by this trend. A well-designed WMS is needed to connect devices and humans in a heterogenous warehouse environment. This chapter introduces a prototype of a WMS powered by a decision support system (DSS) based on real-life requirements. In order to have fast, reliable, and efficient decision making in warehousing, the importance of employing DSS in the WMS is emphasized. Warehouse-related IoT technology is briefly introduced, and its security considerations are discussed thoroughly. The main contribution of this chapter is to show how warehouse operations can be modeled in business process model notation and executed in a DSS.

Section 3
DSS for Vehicular Networks

Chapter 7

Smart vehicles have introduced many services which can be categorized by their functionality (infotainment, comfort, ADAS, OEM services). Introducing new services increases the risk of compromising security. A mobile app used by drivers to connect the vehicle could be infected with malware and spread to the vehicle. Forging remote starting signals enables an attacker to start the vehicle without a key. Security implications of these services should be investigated and addressed thoroughly. This chapter investigates such problems and provides an overview of vulnerabilities, attacks, and mitigations related to these services along with findings including software bugs and insecure protocols. The mitigations for these attacks include strengthening the security protocol of the vehicle CAN bus and incorporating security protocols such as TLS and IPsec. It is hard to say that all connected vehicles are secured. In conclusion, security cannot be neglected, and best practices like sufficient logging (e.g., IDS), reviewing, security testing, and updating of software and hardware should be used.

Chapter 8

Dennis Dubrefjord, Chalmers University of Technology, Sweden
Myeong-jin Jang, Chalmers University of Technology, Sweden
Oscar Carlsson, Chalmers University of Technology, Sweden
Hayder Hadi, Chalmers University of Technology, Sweden
Tomas Olovsson, Chalmers University of Technology, Sweden

The automotive industry has seen remarkable growth in the use of network and communication technology. These technologies can be vulnerable to attacks. Several examples of confirmed attacks have been documented in academic studies, and many vehicular communications systems have been designed without security aspects in mind. Furthermore, all the security implications mentioned here would affect the functionality of decision support systems (DSS) of IoT and vehicular networks. This chapter focuses on in-vehicle security and aims to categorize some attacks in this field according to the exploited vulnerability by showing common patterns. The conclusion suggests that an ethernet-based architecture could be a good architecture for future vehicular systems; it enables them to meet future security needs while still allowing network communication with outside systems.

Section 4
DSS Applications From Various IoT Domains

Chapter 9

Çağlar Akman, Havelsan, Turkey
Tolga Sönmez, Havelsan, Turkey

The motion capture (MoCap) is a highly popular subject with wide applications in different areas such as animations, situational awareness, and healthcare. An overview of MoCap utilizing different sensors and technologies is presented, and the prominent MoCap methods using inertial measurement units and optics are discussed in terms of their advantages and disadvantages. MoCap with wearable inertial measurement units is analyzed and presented specifically with the background information and methods. The chapter puts an emphasis on the mathematical model and artificial intelligence algorithms developed for the MoCap. Both the products from the important technology developers and the proof-of-concept applications conducted by Havelsan are presented within this chapter to involve an industrial perspective. MoCap system will act as a decision support system in either application by providing automatic calculation of metrics or classification, which are the basic tools for decision making.

Chapter 10
Luis Eduardo Villela Zavala, Cinvestav Unidad Guadalajara, Mexico
Mario Siller, Cinvestav Unidad Guadalajara, Mexico

Internet of things (IoT) systems are taking an important role in daily life. Each year the number of connected devices increases considerably, and it is important to keep systems working appropriately. There are some options related to decision support systems to perform IoT systems tasks such as deployment, maintenance, and its operation on environments full of different connected devices and IoT systems interacting among them. For the decision-making process, the authors consider the complexity nature observed in IoT systems and their operational context and environments. In this sense, rather than using grain and fixed control rules/laws for the system design, the use of general principles, goals, and objectives are defined to guide the system adaptation. This has been referred to as guided self-organization (GSO) in the literature. The GSO design approach is based in evaluating the system entropy to reduce the emergence and enable self-organization. Also, in this chapter, a series of study cases from different IoT application domains are presented.

Foreword

I am pleased to write this foreword for this very interesting book, *Decision Support Systems and Industrial IoT in Smart Grid, Factories, and Cities*. The editor of this book, Dr. Ismail Butun, is a well-known researcher with impactful contributions in wireless communications, computer networks, and network security for the past several years. He published more than 50 scientific articles which were noticed by the research community. His publications have already received more than 1,750 citations along with an H index of 17. He demonstrates his knowledge in this edited book. I find this book very useful for academicians and practitioners in the industry.

As the industrial revolution (a.k.a. Industry 4.0) continues at full pace, it is indispensable to include all the benefits offered by artificial intelligence, as it is also evolving at a very fast pace. Moreover, as the autonomous robots are being implemented on the factory floors at a rapid pace, they constitute another fleet of things in the IoT to be wirelessly connected to each other and to the control center. Additionally, after several decades of design and development, the smart grid and microgrid technologies have evolved from the traditional electric grid to the point where they include remote monitoring and control, along with smart meters, sending gigabytes of information per hour to the control center. Further, using the 4G/5G cellular and Low Power WAN wireless technologies, the Internet of Things (IoT) such as NB-IoT and LoRaWAN are more flexible, deployable, scalable, and reachable than ever before. With all these advances, the Industrial IoT (so-called IIoT) concept is evolving and comprises the primary focus of this book along with decision support system integrations.

This book is not only for academicians, researchers, and experts in the field, but also for the beginners and practitioners in the industry. It introduces all the recent technologies devised for the industrial networks, IoT, and IIoT domains, from factory floor deployments to in-house applications.

This book covers a wide range of topics, including but not limited to, the digital twin, IoT-based industrial indoor/outdoor lighting systems, decision support systems (basics and advanced topics), vehicular communications (challenges and opportunities), industry best practices, wireless communications challenges and opportunities, decentralized computing, fog/edge/cloud computing, data streaming, cyber-security, and intrusion detection.

I am certain that the readers will enjoy the contents of the book, enjoy and learn a great deal about this emerging technology

Ian F. Akyildiz
Broadband Wireless Networking Lab, School of Electrical and Computer
Engineering, Georgia Institute of Technology, Atlanta, USA
May 2021

Preface

Recently, the interest of various stakeholders (government, industry, academia, and citizens) in building smart environments such as grids, factories, cities, etc. have grown exponentially. Various governments have a plan to initiate more than 1,000 smart city projects by 2025. One of the key challenges for the success of any smart city project is the assurance of the security and the privacy of the citizens in an efficient way. The concept of the smart city can be realized using a wide range of interconnected cyber-physical systems such as ZigBee, RFID, WiFi, Bluetooth, VANETs, etc. With the help of these heterogeneous systems, data is processed and exchanged between multiple stakeholders. This phenomenon introduces large and complex attack surfaces, which cannot be handled with traditional security solutions.

According to Frost & Sullivan, the global smart cities market is projected to reach $1.56 trillion by 2020. Security in a smart city is one of the major challenging issues as discussed recently in various major conferences held by ACM and IEEE such as RSA, CCS, Security and Privacy, etc. Currently, there are not many books available in the market which discuss the privacy and security issues of a smart city in a comprehensive manner. This book tries to fill this gap by providing recent advances in smart city security and privacy. It will help the researchers and engineers to design and implement a safe, secure, and reliable smart city project.

A Decision Support System (DSS) is software that aids the decision-making process for a given task based on analyzing massive amounts of unstructured (or structured) data. Usually, a DSS should have at least the following components: Model Management System (models will be used to fit the given data to make informed decisions), User Interface (to help end-user), Knowledge Base (collected information from both internal or external sources). This book presents the DSS integration with the Internet of Things (IoT) and its place during the technological revolution, which is taking place now to bring us a better, sustainable, automated, and safer world.

This book also covers the challenges being faced such as relations and implications of IoT with existing communication and networking technologies; applications like practical use-case scenarios from the real world including smart cities, buildings, and grids; and topics such as cybersecurity, user privacy, data ownership, and information handling related to IoT networks. Additionally, this book focuses on the future applications, trends, and potential benefits of this new discipline.

This edited book, *Decision Support Systems and Industrial IoT in Smart Grid, Factories, and Cities*, aims at presenting the discussion on recent security frameworks, solutions, and challenges of a smart environment. For this book, 26 chapter proposals were submitted by the researchers and students. The 10 chapters were finally accepted for inclusion in this book. The acceptance rate was 38%. The contributed chapters in this book cover a broad range of security topics related to Decision Support Systems and Industrial IoT, including:

Section 1 discusses DSS for LPWAN, LoRaWAN, and Wireless Technologies. LoRaWAN (Long Range Wide Area Network) is an emerging technology for the connection of IoT devices to the Internet, and can as such be an important part of DSS. In LoRaWAN, IoT devices are connected to the Internet through gateways by using long-range radio signals. Hence, wireless positioning technologies are also of interest in this book. Overall, this section consists of 3 chapters, details of which are provided as follows:

Chapter 1 presents the cybersecurity and privacy issues, threats, and challenges of various technologies used in Low Power Wide Area Network (LPWAN), Narrow-Band IoT (NB-IoT), and LoRaWAN systems. It also identifies the application areas which are more vulnerable to security threats and needs more protection. This chapter also presents solutions that can be used to increase the privacy and security of LPWAN systems. Three use cases will be considered: Healthcare, Smart Cities, and Industry which all to some degree rely on IoT devices. It is shown that with enough knowledge of possible attacks and their corresponding implications, more secure IoT systems can be developed.

Chapter 2 presents a survey which has summarised research of attacks such as Radio Jamming Attack, Beacon Attacks (Malicious wake-up times, Faking GPS-coordinates, Forcing a class change), Eavesdropping, Replay Attack, Wormhole Attack, Rogue Gateway Attacks, and defenses on LoRaWAN gateways in protocol version v1.1 and suggested some improvements. These improvements are based on the theoretical analysis of an important feature of LoRaWAN, which is the long battery life of the end devices. The current implementation of beacons leaves it open for anyone with a radio transmitter, capable of sending out messages to the network, to impersonate a gateway and drastically reduce the performance and downlink availability of an end-device while at the same time heavily impacting the battery lifespan.

Chapter 3 aims to review the indoor and outdoor wireless positioning technologies and how they can be used for contact tracing. It then further discusses some of the data management, privacy, and security concerns that follow. This chapter also studies the main techniques for wireless positioning, cellular-based positioning using 5G, and their use to contact tracing. Furthermore, DSS can benefit from better positioning techniques. Finally, the chapter provides some insight into how 5G and UWB might help the area of positioning and contact tracing in the future.

Section 2 discusses DSS for Smart Grid, Factories, and Cities. As such, the application of DSS along with cloud-based big data analysis has the prime importance, especially in this new era of smart cities and smart everything. Moreover, the section also discusses the applicability of DSS for addressing advanced issues for instance a) in the early detection of cyber-events at the smart grid applications, and b) warehouse management systems to efficiently manage and govern warehouse assisting IoT devices. This section consists of 3 chapters, details of which are provided as follows:

Chapter 4 discusses the vulnerabilities of smart grid and EPES systems. Since these need to be protected against cyberattacks, therefore, robust algorithms are needed for the efficient intrusion detection system (IDS). This chapter presents the classification of IDSs according to the source of audit data and detection methodologies. It also proposes a method for early-stage detection of cyber-security incidents and protection against them through applicable security measures. Moreover, security techniques such as anomaly detection, threat investigation through a highly automated DSS as well as incident response and recovery for smart grid systems are introduced. The proposed framework can be applied to industrial environments such as cyber-threats targeting the production generator as well as the electricity smart meters etc. The chapter also illustrates the framework's cyber-resilience against zero-day threats and its ability to distinguish between operational failures as well as cyber-security incidents. With respect to these classification methods, an overview and problems of existing schemes are presented. Industry best practices are also provided as part of Security information and event management (SIEM).

Chapter 5 presents a case study of integrating a DSS and a smart environment (warehouse). A warehouse is a crucial and strategic element in logistics. A warehouse management system (WMS) is designed to improve efficiency in warehouses to increase their throughput and potential. The rise of IoT and its commercialization enabled 'Smart Things' to be widely adopted by hobbyists and companies. Cheap sensors and smart devices triggered better automation opportunities. Many devices and sensors that are being deployed in the industry and warehousing are affected by this trend. A well-designed WMS is needed to connect devices and humans in a heterogenous warehouse environment. This chapter introduces a prototype of a WMS powered by a DSS based on real-life requirements. In order to have fast, reliable, and efficient decision-making in warehousing, the importance of employing DSS in the WMS is emphasized. Warehouse-related IoT technology is briefly introduced and its security considerations are discussed thoroughly. The main contribution of this chapter is to show how warehouse operations can be modeled in business process model notation and executed in a DSS.

Chapter 6 presents cloud-based big data analysis tools and techniques towards sustainable smart city services. Machine learning and data mining are useful tools for both data management and sensing data to extract meaningful insights. Thus, it is possible to avoid resource wastage and system failures in smart cities utilizing such tools and techniques.

Section 3 discusses DSS for Vehicular Networks, especially for which the services being used would benefit from it. Moreover, the behavior of internal signaling mechanisms such as CAN bus, under the possibility of cyber incidents are also discussed and presented thoroughly. This section consists of 2 chapters, details of which are provided as follows:

Chapter 7 presents the services in connected vehicles which is especially a topic of interest under Vehicular IoT. Introducing new services increases the risk of compromising security. Therefore, security risks and their countermeasures constitute the cybersecurity-related part of the chapter, which is also an appealing topic for the audience. For instance, a mobile app used by drivers to connect the vehicle could be infected with malware and spread to the vehicle. Another example would be forging remote starting signals enabling an attacker to start the vehicle without a key. This chapter investigates such problems and provides an overview of vulnerabilities, attacks, and mitigations related to these services along with findings including software bugs and insecure protocols. The mitigations for these attacks include strengthening the security protocol of the vehicle CAN bus and incorporating security protocols such as TLS and IPsec.

Chapter 8 aims to provide readers with a comprehensive understanding of automotive security vulnerabilities, especially of in-vehicle communication. The methodology used is a study of recent research related to the topic which is categorized and summarized. The chapter scope is restricted to in-vehicle communication which excludes communication between the vehicle and its surroundings. Within in-vehicle communication, the chapter focuses on currently existing technologies such as the CAN bus and Local Interconnect Network (LIN) bus, FlexRay, and Automotive Ethernet. The chapter also provides an analysis of attacks in different communication technologies in a sequence: categorized automotive security attacks; explanations about major attacks' implementations; technical limitations in major vehicle communications; expected or reported negative consequences; and solutions. Furthermore, all of the security implications mentioned here would affect the functionality of DSS in the IoT and Vehicular networks. Finally, this chapter focuses on in-vehicle security and aims to categorize some attacks in this field according to the exploited vulnerability by showing common patterns.

Section 4 discusses DSS Applications from various IoT domains such as wearable devices for virtual reality systems towards Guided Self-Organization (GSO) systems for Autonomic Computing. Overall, this section consists of 2 chapters, details of which are provided as follows:

Chapter 9 represents a strong background on the Motion Capture (MoCap) systems along with the mathematical model and artificial intelligence algorithms developed for the MoCap. Within the chapter, an overview of MoCap utilizing different sensors and technologies is presented and the prominent MoCap methods using inertial measurement units and optics are discussed in terms of their advantages and disadvantages. The chapter emphasizes the mathematical model and artificial intelligence algorithms developed for the MoCap. Both the products from the important technology developers and the proof of concept applications conducted by Havelsan Inc. are presented within this chapter to involve an industrial perspective. The MoCap system will act as a DSS in either application by providing automatic calculation of metrics, classification which are the basic tools for decision making. Overall, the chapter has a strong foundation and merits for wearable device-related literature.

Chapter 10 presents an overview on the use of decision-making processes to support DSS under uncertainty based on GSO within IoT systems oriented to application domains such as Smart Cities or Industry 4.0. Points of view of different authors, antecedents, and previously carried out works are covered, and the topics are linked to each other to reach the basis of a proposal that is currently being prepared to obtain completely autonomic IoT systems that can make decisions considering the uncertainty of the system. The GSO design approach is based on evaluating the system entropy to reduce the emergence and enable self-organization. Also, in this chapter, a series of study cases from different IoT Application Domains are presented.

Finally, it is worth mentioning that this book addresses researchers, academicians, and industry professionals who are working in the domain of DSS for IoT. It provides insight into state-of-the-art research to various graduate-level academic departments such as electrical and computer engineering, computer science, etc.

The editor of this book hopes that, with covered topics in-depth from IoT domain such as vehicular to smart grid systems, wearable technologies to cloud-assisted data analysis, cybersecurity to warehouse management systems, the book covers all possible applications of DSS while assisting in the decision-making process of the IoT networks.

Ismail Butun
Chalmers University of Technology, Sweden & Konya Food and Agriculture
University, Turkey & Royal University of Technology, Sweden
31 May 2021

Acknowledgment

First and foremost, I would like to express my appreciation to our assistant editor Mr. Alparslan Sari for his endless and tremendous support on this book project.

My special thank goes to Prof. Ian F. Akyildiz (Georgia Institute of Technology, Atlanta, Georgia, USA) for reviewing my book and providing his valuable feedback along with the Foreword section he has written.

Other special thanks go to board members of this book, Assoc. Prof. Tomas Olovsson (Chalmers University of Technology, Gothenburg, Sweden) and Assoc. Prof. Robert Lagerström (Royal University of Technology, Stockholm, Sweden).

I would like to convey my gratitude to all contributors including the chapters' authors, and reviewers. Special thanks to the following people who participated in the reviewing process:

Alparslan Sari (Ph.D. Candidate), University of Delaware, Newark, DE, United States

Tolga Sönmez (Ph.D.), Havelsan Inc., Ankara, Turkey

Dennis Dubrefjord, Chalmers University of Technology, Göteborg, Sweden

Joar Blom, Chalmers University of Technology, Göteborg, Sweden

Kazi Masum Sadique, Stockholm University, Stockholm, Sweden

Stig Arne Knoph, Chalmers University of Technology, Göteborg, Sweden

Suresh P. (Ph.D.), Kongu Engineering College, Erode, India

Onur Ülgen (Ph.D.), King's College London, London, United Kingdom

Yasin Çelik (Ph.D.), LinkedIn, Mountain View, California, United States

Acknowledgment

My special thanks to the IGI development team for their assistance in formatting, designing, and marketing the book. Special thanks to Ms. Jan Travers, Katelyn McLoughlin, and the ever-patient Assistant Development Editors.

Last, but not least, this book is dedicated to all our families and friends, who have never given up on supporting us even during COVID-19 times.

Section 1

DSS for LPWAN, LoRaWAN, and Wireless Technologies

Chapter 1
Implications of Cybersecurity Breaches in LPWANs

Åke Axeland
Chalmers University of Technology, Sweden

Henrik Hagfeldt
Chalmers University of Technology, Sweden

Magnus Carlsson
Chalmers University of Technology, Sweden

Lina Lagerquist Sergel
Chalmers University of Technology, Sweden

Ismail Butun
iD https://orcid.org/0000-0002-1723-5741
Chalmers University of Technology, Sweden & Konya Food and Agriculture University, Turkey & Royal University of Technology, Sweden

ABSTRACT

With the contrast of limited performance and big responsibility of IoT devices, potential security breaches can have serious impacts in means of safety and privacy. Potential consequences of attacks on IoT devices could be leakage of individuals daily habits and political decisions being influenced. While the consequences might not be avoidable in their entirety, adequate knowledge is a fundamental part of realizing the importance of IoT security and during the assessment of damages following a breach. This chapter will focus on two low-powered wide area network (LPWAN) technologies, narrow-band iot (NB-IoT) and long-range wide area network (LoRaWAN). Further, three use cases will be considered—healthcare, smart cities, and industry—which all to some degree rely on IoT devices. It is shown that with enough knowledge of possible attacks and their corresponding implications, more secure IoT systems can be developed.

DOI: 10.4018/978-1-7998-7468-3.ch001

INTRODUCTION

Technology is steadily emerging with our everyday lives. People are more connected now than ever and the prediction for mobile connected devices is expected to increase from 50 billion in 2020 to around 125 billion by 2030. This is due to several factors like the adoption of 5G, the continuously increasing number of people connected to the internet, adoption of IoT devices in the homes and in the enterprise world (Brent, 2020). For these IoT devices to be able to operate as intended they need to communicate via a gateway. This is often done by using cloud infrastructure with an IoT communication protocol. Which protocol to use boils down to several factors such as environment, hardware, and energy requirements (Hasan, 2020).

IoT devices located in private homes often run on the electrical grid and communicate over Wi-Fi granting a high supply of energy and bandwidth. The communication range is seldom a problem given that conventional network routers can cover an entire home. However, there are IoT devices that need to operate without these conveniences since they are usually running on batteries and communicate over a long-range communication network.

This is where the Low-Powered Wide Area Network (LPWAN) protocols come into play. With these protocols, we solve the problem of range and power by compensating with reduced bandwidth (Butun, Pereira, 2019). A system implementing LPWAN technologies should therefore be a system that only requires a handful of light-weight transmissions a day. This trade-off enables LPWAN connected devices to have longer battery life (> 10 years).

Two of the currently most popular LPWAN technologies are Long-Range Wide Area Network (LoRaWAN) and Narrow-Band IoT (NB-IoT), which will be the ones that this chapter focuses on (Lora Alliance, 2017), (GSM Alliance, 2020). NB-IoT is an LPWAN standard that focuses on specifically low-cost, energy-efficient, and indoor coverage. The challenges, opportunities, and research trends showed LPWAN communication mechanisms and functionalities targeted in low-end devices (IoT) are deployed widely and LoRaWAN (a subset of LPWAN) is known to be secure for most of the known cyber-attacks (Sari, 2020). However, recent research has presented some of the possible attacks that threaten these protocols and how to stay protected from them.

This chapter builds upon this research; however, it will not present any new vulnerabilities. Instead, the goal is to extend the knowledge these papers bring by analyzing possible resulting practical implications of security breaches from various vulnerabilities. This is done by matching real-world examples of actual security breaches to present vulnerabilities of the papers.

Decision Support Systems (DSS), sometimes also referred to as Expert Systems, are strategically located at the heart of a network or a management system, in which the decisions related to -management of the network and/or -operation of some (or all) of the critical components (end users/devices). DSS comprises the heart of an IoT network in complicated scenarios such as in the case of smart city, smart grid, and IIoT applications (Butun, 2020). Cybersecurity of the DSS systems is not secluded from the technologies that they are operating on. One of the prominent communications and networking technologies of IoT networks is LoRa.

As such, the objective of this chapter is to provide an insight into the importance of analyzing possible implications that may follow breaches in IoT systems, especially the LoRa-based IoT networks.

BACKGROUND

This section will provide a fundamental explanation about IoT, general information about NB-IoT and LoRaWAN, and some fundamental knowledge about the Confidentiality, Integrity, and Availability (CIA) model and cyber-attacks.

IoT is about embedding computers and communication technologies into devices to empower industry and society using the Internet. It has a wide span of applications: health care, industries, homes, and cities. IoT also allows for the possibility to remotely manage countless numbers of automated networked devices.

Due to urbanization, the focus on improved quality of life and the development of cities in a sustainable manner has been brought to light. And with it, the concept of *Smart Cities* has grown by utilizing IoT technologies (Theodoridis, 2013). When connecting the infrastructure of a city to the Internet, real-time data can constantly be collected and open doors for new smart city applications. The definition of Smart Cities is, according to the European Commission: "Cities using technological solutions to improve the management and efficiency of the urban environment" (European Commission, 2020).

Another attractive area of application for IoT is in health care. The services it can provide are expected to increase the quality of life for patients through medical applications. In 2015, real-time monitoring was used to provide early diagnosis and alert in medical emergencies. This shows how medical applications can be aided by the use of wireless technologies (Islam, 2015). An example of real-time monitoring is a wearable LPWAN smart monitor. It was developed to create an understanding of how to predict heart failure. The monitor measured the patient's skin temperature, the surrounding temperature, and the patient's GPS location (to quickly get there in the event of illness or fall) (Catherwood, 2018).

Cities and health care are not alone in adopting IoT to improve their sectors with new fields of applications. The term Industrial Internet of Things (IIoT), is a revolution for industrial manufacturing since it has improved efficiency and productivity while at the same time, reducing costs. By connecting sensors, devices, and instruments to an LPWAN, data can be collected and analyzed to improve the production line. An example of this is a factory that utilizes NB-IoT to connect high-precision screwdrivers with motion sensors to predict when they need to be calibrated or lubricated. The connected devices send a continuous stream of data that can be analyzed to make improvements faster than before. Also, errors and inefficiencies can be dealt with faster than if a human had to gather all the information.

In June 2016, 3GPP released their completed standardization of the narrow-band radio technology for the Internet of Things, NB-IoT. It uses existing licensed frequency bands and can coexist with Global System for Mobile communications (GSM) and Long-Term Evolution (LTE). GSM is, in short, the standard for digital mobile communications that is widely used by mobile phone users and LTE provides wireless broadband Internet access. Even though NB-IoT is designed based on existing functionalities from LTE and they both are LPWAN technologies for low-bandwidth IoT applications, they have their differences. The choice between the two technologies depends largely upon the amount of data that will be used and how much latency is acceptable for the application. NB-IoT is focused on very low data rates and is ideal for simpler sensor applications while LTE supports devices that need to communicate in real-time.

NB-IoT can coexist with GSM and LTE by being deployed in three operation modes: stand-alone, guard-band, and in-band. In the first mode, NB-IoT can occupy one GSM channel. In the second and third modes, there is an existing LTE carrier of which NB-IoT utilizes either unused resource blocks within the carrier's guard band or resource blocks within the carrier. In 2018, GSM Alliance wrote that in the future there could be another possible operation mode where the 5G core network could support NB-IoT with radio access (GSM Association, 2020). NB-IoT offers long-distance communication (up to 10 km) and a device battery life of 10 or more years (Sinha, 2017).

The second LPWAN technology, LoRa, is a proprietary physical layer protocol. By using a modulation technique called Chirp Spread Spectrum, long-distance communication up to 20 km is supported and is energy efficient with 10 or more years of battery life (Butun, 2018). LoRaWAN is the upper layer protocol that defines the system architecture, and, unlike NB-IoT, it operates in the non-licensed frequency bands. It was first standardized in January 2015 by LoRa-Alliance.

The architecture of the LoRaWAN network is made up of end devices (ED) that are connected to one or more Gateways (GW) in a single hop. The GWs then forward the data over IP to a Network Server (NS) which in turn routes the message to an Application Server (AS). Since its release, several vulnerabilities have been discovered and a few are presented in the upcoming section on attacks.

The later version of LoRaWAN, v1.1, was released in October 2017 and has had its fair share of scrutiny. It is deemed more secure and most of the vulnerabilities that existed in LoRaWAN v1.0 have been addressed. However, new vulnerabilities were found after its publication (Eldefrawy, 2019), (Butun, Pereira, 2019).

Security implications of IoT and sample case studies are described in Butun et al.'s work (Butun, Sari, 2019). Industry 4.0 and IoT hardware and communication technologies (including LPWAN), along with security implications, challenges, and solutions ahead are thoroughly explained in Sari et al. (2020).

In the field of cybersecurity, the CIA model is often referred to when categorizing the different threats and attacks posed to a system. CIA stands for Confidentiality, Integrity, and Availability. If an adversary breaks confidentiality, it means that the content of the data is no longer secret between the parties who were supposed to take part in the data exchange. If an adversary is taking part in communications meant for someone else, without anyone's knowledge, is usually termed 'eavesdropping'. Integrity is breached when the content of the message is altered in any way or form. An example of this would be to scramble the data so it does not make sense or to change crucial content like the amount of money to be transmitted over a transaction. Finally, availability is tarnished when the devices cannot reach a certain node in the system that is crucial for communication.

Cyber-attacks are often categorized into subgroups where the intent of the attack is common, but the different attacks vary. Examples of these are Denial of service attacks (DoS), Man-in-the-middle attacks (MITM), and side-channel attacks, which are briefly explained below. DoS attacks aim to reduce the availability in a system, often by keeping it busy with garbage data or to overload the network so packets are lost in transmission. This is a very common attack over the internet and one that often does not require sophisticated knowledge of the system that is targeted.

The second category, Man-in-the-middle attacks, is a type of threat that exists between two or more parties. An example is where an adversary poses as one of the parties and takes part in the communication without their knowledge, which breaks the confidentiality or integrity of the data. These attacks can be hard to detect since the goal of the adversary is to be transparent to the entities. It is down to the cryptography techniques used in the system to prevent these kinds of attacks. Side-channel attacks are a broad type of threat and are often the hardest to protect against since the adversary deduces information from a system without impacting system performance. A threat is categorized as a side-channel whenever an adversary can compromise the contents of a system without having to break it first. For example, the noise of a system can reveal when it is working harder and the transmission time could expose the byte length of the transmitted data.

Systems that have helped management and business make structured decisions from collected data are Decision Support Systems (DSS). These systems are often used in businesses, corporations, or organizations to support decisions through data collected in various processes. Industries that rely on IoT systems inherently contain plenty of funnels for data to be collected through and could turn guesswork into decisions based on reality-bound data.

ATTACKS, BREACHES, AND IMPLICATIONS

Attacks

This section starts with a description of the core problem with IoT security and proceeds to summarize several discovered attacks on NB-IoT and LoRa from recent research that can exploit the networks in hand. To get a deeper knowledge about the attacks it is advised to look further into the relevant referenced papers. Later on, these attacks will be referred back to when we discuss the potential consequences that can follow a breach.

IoT Security

Security in IoT is and has long been questioned. The reason for this is the limitations in the hardware that comes with the utility of the devices. For devices to be useful in many areas, developers rely on microchips which perform specialized tasks rather than on more powerful computers. This is beneficial for IoT networks since smaller microchips have lower power usage and cost less which make them more suitable for scaling. The disadvantages, however, is the reduced memory and computation power which leads to a more vulnerable device. Another problem linked to IoT security is to prevent physical access to a device. This stems from the fact that they are often spread out over a large area to perform their tasks and not locked inside of a server farm. This makes it harder to prevent an adversary from tampering with a device.

Jamming Attacks

A type of DoS attack called jamming attack can be targeted at the LoRa system. It is called a jamming attack when an adversary transmits large volumes of garbage data on the same frequency as the EDs and thereby interferes with the actual data sent. Protection against these types of attacks can be difficult and since the technologies are transmitting with low bandwidth and power, the adversary does not need to perform sophisticated jamming attacks. The only need is a high-powered signal to transmit, which will out-compete the communication.

A possible defense against jamming attacks is to have multiple GWs, which is advised in LoRa. With several GWs, an ED has more routes to choose from when communicating over the network. Therefore, the adversary must jam multiple instances which is more costly. This in turn reduces the threat and brings some defense against jamming (Coman, 2019).

However, one clear problem with the implementation of LoRa is the lack of GWs enterprises use in their infrastructure. Usually, one or two GWs are used which reduce the fault tolerance and the robustness of the system significantly (Butun, Pereira, 2019).

Classic IP Attacks

Since NB-IoT is a cellular network that can handle ordinary IP datagrams, classic spoofing and scanning threats exist. Examples of these are port scanning, Address Resolution Protocol (ARP) spoofing, and Domain Name System (DNS) spoofing. Port scanning is a technique where the adversary sends packets to different ports on a computer to extract information about the system. This is the first step in finding vulnerabilities in a system and could be used to detect software running on the computer like the operating system. An adversary performing ARP spoofing could fool the local network to redirect the data to the IP address of the adversary. This is done by changing the associated Media Access Control address to IP address in the local network so that the outgoing data is transmitted to the adversary. Finally, the DNS spoofing attack poisons the DNS cache in the name server and alters the IP records causing the data to flow to the attacker instead of the intended recipient.

Another threat is the possibility for an adversary to drain an ED of its battery life. An attacker can send a flood of Internet Control Message Protocol (ICMP) messages to an ED which due to the low bandwidth would be overwhelmed. The ED would try replying to the messages forcing it to transmit and receive more data than intended which in turn would reduce the longevity of the device.

Physical Attacks

Physical attacks are done directly on the hardware including stealing the device, uploading new firmware, or alter the device for instance. The classic IP attacks described in section 3.3 could for example be performed if an adversary gets a hold of an ED in an NB-IoT network. This is because the EDs in such a network are usually connected with each other in a private network.

Physical attacks against LoRa can be performed either by getting access to a GW or an ED. By removing a GW there is no communication route between the ED and the NS. Since backup GWs usually do not exist, the system collapses. Another possibility is if an adversary gets hold of an ED which is transmitting some arbitrary type of data. This data can become corrupt by causing physical manipulations to the device. For example, heating up a temperature sensor could trigger an alarm or destroy it, making a sensor send corrupted data (Butun, Pereira, 2019).

MITM Attacks

A MITM vulnerability was found in LoRa v1.0 which remains in the later version, v1.1. The vulnerability resides between the NS and the AS and is a threat to the communication between these. The attack is called ''bit-flipping attack'' and an adversary who successfully performs this attack can change the content of the data and compromise the whole system. This attack is rather sophisticated since the adversary has to perform a MITM attack in the back-haul network which can be run over Ethernet, Wi-Fi, or mobile network. However, if performed, all headers and data in the packet can be altered which results in various complications for the network. The packet can be rejected due to (i) the counter field being changed, (ii) the ED id being changed (which makes the AS believe the data originated elsewhere), or (iii) the core payload being changed (which either could make the data bogus or malicious) (Butun, Pereira, 2019).

Side Channels

Since the protocols used in LoRa and NB-IoT are made for infrequent transmissions of small packets, an adversary can deduce that any activity from an ED will most certainly contain data of significance. This can be exploited by an adversary, for example by triangulating where an ED is located, then by the position and placement of the device to find out what kind of sensor it is producing the transmitted data. This knowledge can let the adversary draw conclusions even without decrypting any of the data (Butun, Pereira, 2019).

Implication of Breaches

The application of the attacks in the previous section will result in several consequences which impact the system performance, infrastructure, and the usage of the data. This section will discuss these impacts in relation to the presented attacks in three use cases of LPWAN. The first being in the context of a health care application used to monitor people's heart rates or act as a fall detection device (Catherwood, 2018). The second being in the context of sensors in Smart Cities and the third bringing up IoT in industries (LoRa Alliance, 2020). The consequences will be split into three threat categories with different consequences according to the CIA model.

The first category regards threats that compromise the confidentiality of a system, the second consists of threats related to jeopardized integrity with the third being threats that impact the system availability. Please refer to Figure-1 for an overview of the implications of security breaches in LPWANs.

Figure 1. Implications of security breaches in LPWANs[1]

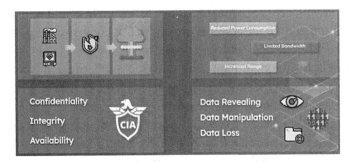

Threats: Confidentiality

A threat to confidentiality results in the revealing of otherwise secret data to an adversary. The consequence of such a reveal depends heavily on the data itself as the system performance often is not affected. The data might contain direct private information like medical journals or second-hand information that does not seem private at first glance but could be used to draw privacy-infringing conclusions. In the scope of LPWAN, this type of security breach can be the result of physical attacks where the confidentiality of an ED is breached through re-programming. Another possibility is the use of MITM attacks which reveal the data to an adversary before passing it along to its destination. To acquire a better understanding of the implications following this category of attacks, the cases will now be reviewed in their respective context.

In the health care application case, the data being sent over the communications link is people's heart rates and other values used to detect falls. This type of information can be regarded as direct private as it is directly connected to the health of individuals. An eavesdropping adversary could monitor and log the data being sent. This data history could reveal second-hand information by analyzing patterns of heart rates to determine exercise routines, social interactions, sleeping routines, etc. In reality, a criminal could use this data to know when a person is away from home or asleep revealing the perfect conditions under which criminal activities could be performed.

In Smart Cities, most data might not directly reveal exact information about individuals but instead, show location conditions and behavior of people at these locations. It may also reveal the current state of the infrastructure such as traffic situations, sewage systems, building and location security, etc. A potential adversary could for example analyze the data from security system sensors to get the best conditions to perform a robbery.

In the last case regarding IIoT, a compromise in confidentiality could result in devastating consequences for a manufacturer. An example would be if an adversary intercepts information about a secret project that a company is developing. The information could then be sold to a competitor in the same field, resulting in a significant backlash to the victim company. This would affect the company's reputation and worker morale as all the time and effort spent on the project was in vain. Not to mention the exhaustion of financial resources. Further, internal communication of a company could be breached to reveal information about the login credentials of workers. This information could then be used by an attacker to hijack robots on the manufacturing line or to gather additional confidential company data.

Threats: Integrity

Abusing an integrity vulnerability could be used to change the data to produce biased results or to provide invalid data, possibly disabling the system. The performance of a system could possibly be measured by the added transmission time of having the data stopover at an adversary. In LPWAN, a typical example of an integrity breaching attack would be a MITM attack. This could be done with or without the compromise of confidentiality, although if only integrity is breached, the altered encrypted data would likely just decrypt to a mess. In the previous section, *MITM Attacks,* such an attack could be seen made possible by a bit-flipping attack. The review cases will now be examined in the context of integrity breaches.

In the health care case, an adversary could alter the heart rate being sent which would provide an invalid picture of that person's health. One strategy is making small adjustments over a period of time to corrupt the person's health journal. Further, a more direct approach is to adjust the heart rate to invoke a sudden response from the receiving party. Possibly by increasing the sent heart rate severely to indicate a heart attack or decreasing it, faking a person's death. The same could be done in reverse by always adjusting the sent value to indicate normal conditions when in reality, the person is experiencing severe physical stress.

The following case, as previously mentioned, might handle data connected to people in certain locations which in turn could be the basis for some major political decisions regarding the location e.g., infrastructure expansion, regulations, budget provisioning, etc. A connected traffic system could also be influenced by altering system control data to direct traffic which could lead to delayed transports of wares and individuals or even mass collisions.

In the IIoT case, tampered data could lead to the destruction of property and equipment or worse, individuals getting hurt or killed. The following is an example of an attack where the intent was to cause an explosion. In 2017, hackers successfully compromised several controllers in a petrochemical plant in Saudi Arabia. These controllers regulate pressure, temperature, and voltage around the plant to keep the equipment running safely. If not for a bug in the hacker's code, the compromised controllers would have triggered an explosion in the plant causing several human casualties. Since the same controllers are used at over 18 000 other plants all around the globe, the same technique could be used anywhere.

Threats: Availability

By losing availability, access to data is lost. Again, depending on what data is being transferred, this could be anything from an inconvenience to a catastrophe. This means that an adversary could, by making use of some vulnerability, perform a DoS attack resulting in the disabling of a system for a period of time. These types of attacks have the greatest impact on system performance as they can be halted in their entirety. As previously mentioned, a DoS attack could have a wide range of implications, it could disable just a single service or an entire system. We have discussed the possibility of jamming attacks which can impact the wireless transmission of data from an ED. The transmission range is a key factor in pinning down a jamming device which can make it very hard in an LPWAN. The solution can be adjusting transmission parameters, but it could as well require re-positioning of EDs or GWs.

Figure 2. Implications of availability for LoRaWAN and NB-IoT networks[2]

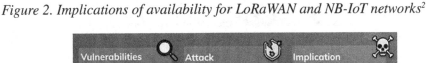

Vulnerabilities	Attack	Implication
Physical Access	Physical harm *L/N*	No Service
Physical security to device.	Physically destroy a device.	Hazards may be arise as a result of the missing data.
Infrastructure	Jamming *L*	Sensors in industry might regulate crucial systems.
Fragile communication paths.	Block wireless signal.	
Protocol Weakness	Ping Flood *N*	Health care might rely on sensors to monitor a patient.
Utilizing bugs as entry point for an attack.	Abusing IP by sending ping messages.	

L = LoRa, N = NB-IoT

Other types of attacks have been highlighted in LPWAN such as physical attacks, where an adversary sabotages a device by destroying, stealing, or re-programming it. There is a possibility the data is then re-routed to the adversary while denying the original recipients. Further, in the section, *Classic IP Attacks*, a wide range of IP vulnerabilities are shown which can be used to leak device information and halt it from performing as expected. Please refer to Figure-2 for the implications of availability for LoRaWAN and NB-IoT Networks.

When reviewing the first case (healthcare, refer to Figure-3) once again, the importance of availability is clear. If the heart rate monitor device falls victim to an availability-compromising attack, it might become disabled or have data prevented from reaching the destination. As IoT devices are heavily dependent on data transmission, this means the device will no longer serve its purpose which was to monitor a person's heart rate or detect falls. In short, the recipients would not be able to find out if there is a dangerous fluctuation in the heart rate or if the person has taken a fall. In contrast to integrity threats, an availability attack could be easier to detect as the recipients could notice that data no longer is being sent from a device.

Figure 3. Implications of availability-breach in health care[3]

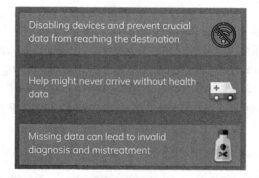

In Smart Cities, availability is again of great importance. Many sectors depend on collecting data to support political decisions. Public transport infrastructure development is one of these sectors which can use sensors on vehicles to collect various data e.g. number of passengers at different times, which locations usually infer transport delays or how often the bus has to break suddenly. An availability flaw could allow an adversary to deny city information on selected locations, giving the public transport data a large bias towards other locations and thus influencing decisions to be made by a city.

In IIoT, the availability of continuous data streams from connected IoT devices is important for the manufacturer since it can be analyzed to increase financial profits, efficiency, and productivity. A disruption in availability could damage instruments and machines if information regarding service or maintenance never reaches its destination. Considering the case with screwdrivers, if the information about when to calibrate and lubricate them is lost, the result could be poorer precision and damage to the products.

Countermeasures

To the authors' envision, the cyber-security of LoRaWAN will be improved by addressing the problems listed as the ones in this paper and likewise publications. For instance, recently (Mårlind, 2020) has provided an enhancement to the OTAA session of the LoRaWAN v1.1. This solution improves the overall network cyber-security by the inclusion of the Public Key Cryptography (PKC) to allow flexible key distribution to the end-users. So, rather than a renewal of the root keys by in-person application to the network authority, end-users can renew them remotely owing to the PKC-adapted key renewal scheme that Mårlind offered.

Ethics in IoT

As the use of connected IoT devices is predicted to continuously increase in organizations and people's everyday life, it is important that security can be guaranteed. Two key ethical issues in IoT are privacy and accuracy (Brous, 2020). The first issue concerns what information can be revealed without consent and the second issue concerns who carries the responsibility if there are modifications or errors in the information being sent (AboBakr, 2017). In May 2018, the General Data Protection Regulation (GDPR) was applied to the members of the European Union to give the citizens control over their personal information. Since IoT collects and analyzes information from users it is within the orbit of GDPR.

Consider the first ethical issue: privacy. How can the two protocols NB-IoT and LoRaWAN be used to exploit user's privacy? An attack against the medical application case of the previous section might enable an adversary to draw conclusions about the person's health based on the information the monitor is sending. This could lead to a privacy breach if the adversary can guess some of the content in that person's medical journal which is supposed to be confidential (1177 Vardgiuden, 2020). Also, according to GDPR Article 4, information such as location (recall the GPS-location being sent from the monitor) is included in GDPR and should therefore have a high level of privacy protection as well. In Smart Cities, people's privacy could be compromised by locating people or to watch, listen or even record activities of individuals through surveillance systems. Privacy, which includes the protection of people's health, could clearly be compromised in the IIoT case described in section

Threats: Integrity where hackers could have triggered an explosion resulting in multiple human casualties.

It is now clear that user privacy can be compromised due to attacks on current LPWAN technologies. Moving on to the second ethical issue: accuracy. Who should be held responsible if there are modifications or errors in transmitted data? This is an important question to be addressed in organizations using IoT devices to gather and process information that could be used to harm others. It is essential that there are no mistakes where the responsibility of the data lies throughout its life cycle.

FUTURE RESEARCH DIRECTIONS

While the importance of security in LPWANs was shown in this chapter by highlighting implications, further areas of research remain. Examples of implications were merely shown in this chapter, an attempt could be made at ranking such implications to produce an order of priority for patching vulnerabilities. Further, this chapter reviewed two LPWANs leaving implications in other IoT networks such as Sigfox, Bluetooth, and Wi-Fi open for future research.

CONCLUSION

LPWAN is an evolving technology and as connected IoT devices are increasing, it is of great importance that security evolves with it. In future revisions of the LoRaWAN and NB-IoT, vulnerabilities in the protocols might be patched. Although, even as the protocols get more secure, new vulnerabilities will certainly emerge. As we have seen, only part of the vulnerabilities is based on the protocols. Poor physical security or hardware issues in infrastructure will remain to be addressed through other measures.

As vulnerabilities persist, so will the implications that follow. These implications could be small software annoyances, but it is shown that even a small bug can lead to devastating consequences such as human casualties. With this in mind, the IoT networks must strive for solid security, not only for the continued efficiency of IoT in industry or data collection in Smart Cities but for the future security of the people in our society.

ACKNOWLEDGMENT

We would like to give a special thanks to anonymous reviewers for sharing their improvement suggestions and wisdom.

This research was supported by Chalmers University of Technology.

REFERENCES

AboBakr, A., & Azer, M.A. (2017). Iot ethics challenges and legal issues. *2017 12th International Conference on Computer Engineering and Systems (ICCES)*, 233–237.

Brent. (n.d.). *By 2030, each person will own 15 connected devices — here's what that means for your business and content*. https://www.martechadvisor.com/articles/iot/by-2030-each-person-will-own-15-connected\-devices-heres-what-that-means-for-your\-business-and-content

Brous, P., Janssen, M., & Herder, P. (2020). The dual effects of the internet of things (iot): A systematic review of the benefits and risks of iot adoption by organizations. *International Journal of Information Management*, *51*, 101952. doi:10.1016/j.ijinfomgt.2019.05.008

Butun, I., Lekidis, A., & dos Santos, D. R. (2020). Security and Privacy in Smart Grids: Challenges, Current Solutions and Future Opportunities. In ICISSP (pp. 733-741). Academic Press.

Butun, I., Pereira, N., & Gidlund, M. (2018). Analysis of lorawan v1.1 security. *Proceedings of the 4th ACM Mobi Hoc Workshop on Experiences with the Design and Implementation of Smart Objects*, 1–6.

Butun, I., Pereira, N., & Gidlund, M. (2019). Security risk analysis of lorawan and future directions. *Future Internet*, *11*(1), 3. doi:10.3390/fi11010003

Butun, I., Sari, A., & Österberg, P. (2019, January). *Security implications of fog computing on the internet of things*. Academic Press.

Carron, X., Bosua, R., Maynard, S., & Ahmad, A. (2016). The internet of things and its impact on individual privacy: An australian privacy principle perspective. *Computer Law & Security Review*, *21*(1), 4–15. doi:10.1016/j.clsr.2015.12.001

Catherwood, P. A., Rafferty, J., McComb, S., & McLaughlin, J. (2018). Lpwan wearable intelligent healthcare monitoring for heart failure prevention. *Proceedings of the 32nd International BCS Human Computer Interaction Conference 32*, 1–4. 10.14236/ewic/HCI2018.126

Check Point. (n.d.). *What is a cyber attack?* https://www.checkpoint.com/cyber-hub/cyber-security/what-is-cyber-attack/

Chi-Chun, L., & Yu-Jen, C. (1999). Secure communication mechanisms for gsm networks. *IEEE Transactions on Consumer Electronics*, *45*(4), 1074–1080. doi:10.1109/30.809184

Coman, F. L., Malarski, K. M., Petersen, M. N., & Ruepp, S. (2019, June). Security issues in internet of things: Vulnerability analysis of LoRaWAN, sigfox and NB-IoT. In *2019 Global IoT Summit (GIoTS)* (pp. 1-6). IEEE.

Davis, G. (2018). 2020: Life with 50 billion connected devices. *2018 IEEE International Conference on Consumer Electronics (ICCE)*, 1–1. 10.1109/ICCE.2018.8326056

Eldefrawy, M., Butun, I., Pereira, N., & Gidlund, M. (2019). Formal security analysis of lorawan. *Computer Networks*, *148*, 328–339. doi:10.1016/j.comnet.2018.11.017

European Commission. (2020). *Smartcities*. https://ec.europa.eu/info/eu-regional-and-urban-development/topics/cities-and-urban-development/city-initiatives/smart-cities_en

Frost, S. (n.d.). *Growing industry applications of lpwan technologies*. https://rfdesignuk.com/uploads/9/4/6/0/94609530/murata_lpwan_study.pdf

GSM Alliance. (2020). *Mobile IoT Deployment Map*. https://www.gsma.com/iot/deployment-map/#deployments

GSM Association. (2018). *Mobile iot in the 5g future – nb-iot and lte-m in the context of 5g*. https://www.gsma.com/iot/resources/mobile-iot-5g-future/

Hossain, M. M., Fotouhi, M., & Hasan, R. (2015). Towards an analysis of security issues, challenges, and open problems in the internet of things. *2015 IEEE World Congress on Services*, 21–28. 10.1109/SERVICES.2015.12

Islam, S. M. R., Kwak, D., Kabir, M. H., Hossain, M., & Kwak, K. (2015). The internet of things for health care: A comprehensive survey. *IEEE Access: Practical Innovations, Open Solutions*, *3*, 678–708. doi:10.1109/ACCESS.2015.2437951

Kitchin, R. (2016). The ethics of smart cities and urban science. *Philosophical Transactions - Royal Society. Mathematical, Physical, and Engineering Sciences*, *374*(2083), 20160115. doi:10.1098/rsta.2016.0115 PMID:28336794

Latre, S., Leroux, P., Coenen, T., Braem, B., Ballon, P., & Demeester, P. (2016). City of things: An integrated and multi-technology testbed for iot smart city experiments. *2016 IEEE International Smart Cities Conference (ISC2)*, 1–8.

Lora Alliance. (2017). *LorawanTM1.1 specification.* https://lora-alliance.org/resource-hub/lorawanr-specification-v11

LoRa Alliance. (2020). *Smartcities.* https://lora-alliance.org/lorawan-vertical-markets/cities

Mårlind, F., & Butun, I. (2020, October). Activation of LoRaWAN end devices by using Public Key Cryptography. In *2020 4th Cyber Security in Networking Conference (CSNet)* (pp. 1-8). IEEE.

Mekki, K., Bajic, E., Chaxel, F., & Meyer, F. (2019). A comparative study of lpwan technologies for large scale iot deployment. *ICT Express, 5*(1), 1–7.

Navani, D., Jain, S., & Nehra, M. S. (2017). The internet of things (iot): A study of architectural elements. *2017 13th International Conference on Signal-Image Technology Internet-Based Systems (SITIS),* 473–478.

Perlroth, N., & Krauss, C. (n.d.). A cyberattack in saudi arabia had a deadly goal, experts fear another try. *The New York Times.*

Rouse, M. (2020). *Confidentiality, Integrity, and Availability (cia triad).* https://whatis.techtarget.com/definition/Confidentiality-integrity-and-availability-CIA

Sanchez, J. J., Morales-Jimenez, D., Gomez, G., & Enbrambasaguas, J. T. (2007). Physical layer performance of long term evolution cellular technology. 2007 16th IST Mobile and Wireless Communications Summit, 1–5. doi:10.1109/ISTMWC.2007.4299090

Sari, A., Lekidis, A., & Butun, I. (2020). Industrial Networks and IIoT: Now and Future Trends. In *Industrial IoT* (pp. 3–55). Springer. doi:10.1007/978-3-030-42500-5_1

Seo, J., Kim, K., Park, M., & Lee, K. (2017). An analysis of economic impact on iot under gdpr. *2017 International Conference on Information and Communication Technology Convergence (ICTC),* 879–881. 10.1109/ICTC.2017.8190804

Sinha, R. S., Wei, Y., & Hwang, S.-H. (2017). A survey on lpwa technology: Loraand nb-iot. *Ict Express, 3*(1), 14–21. doi:10.1016/j.icte.2017.03.004

Theodoridis, E., Mylonas, G., & Chatzigian-nakis, I. (2013). Developing an iot smart city framework. *InIISA, 2013,* 1–6.

Trend Micro. (n.d.). *Industrial internet of things (iiot).* https://www.trendmicro.com/vinfo/us/security/definition/industrial-internet-of-things-iiot

Vardgiuden. (2020). *Din journal.* https://www.1177.se/sa-fungerar-varden/sa-skyddas-och-hanteras-dina-uppgifter/din-journal/#section-18299

Wireless, S. (2018). *Lte-m vs. nb-iot: What are the differences?* https://www.sierrawireless.com/iot-blog/lte-m-vs-nb-iot/

Xueying, Y. (2017). *Lorawan: vulnerability analysis and practical exploitation.* Delft University of Technology.

KEY TERMS AND DEFINITIONS

Denial of Service Attacks (DoS): In this type of cyber-attack, targeted victim (server, service, etc.) is overwhelmed by the fake requests (such as fabricated user queries), so that it is prevented from serving the legit requests (such as the queries resulting from real users).

LoRa: A proprietary Long-Range LPWAN radio communication technology which uses CSS (Chirp Spread Spectrum) modulation and offers communications up to 100 kms and a battery lifetime of 10 years.

LPWAN: Low-Powered Wide Area Network, which allows long-range networking for low-powered IoT devices.

Man-in-the-Middle Attacks (MITM): In this kind of cyber-attack, an attacker intercepts the incoming transmission (data, or packets) to a victim node, fulfills the desired task (copying or altering the data) and then re-transmits the data to the intended victim.

Narrow-Band IoT (NB-IoT): Uses existing licensed frequency bands and can coexist with GSM and LTE. It is focused on very low data rates and is ideal for simpler sensor applications while LTE supports devices that need to communicate in real-time.

Public Key Cryptography (PKC): Also known as asymmetric cryptography, is a class of cryptographic algorithms that uses pairs of keys: A public key that everyone can know and a private key that is only known by one entity.

ENDNOTES

[1] Icons in this figure were made by Freepik from www.flaticon.com
[2] Icons in this figure were made by Freepik from www.flaticon.com
[3] Icons in this figure were made by Freepik from www.flaticon.com

Chapter 2
A Survey on Attacks and Defences on LoRaWAN Gateways

Olof Magnusson
Gothenburg University, Sweden

Rikard Teodorsson
Chalmers University of Technology, Sweden

Joakim Wennerberg
Chalmers University of Technology, Sweden

Stig Arne Knoph
Chalmers University of Technology, Sweden

ABSTRACT

LoRaWAN (long-range wide-area network) is an emerging technology for the connection of internet of things (IoT) devices to the internet and can as such be an important part of decision support systems. In this technology, IoT devices are connected to the internet through gateways by using long-range radio signals. However, because LoRaWAN is an open network, anyone has the ability to connect an end device or set up a gateway. Thus, it is important that gateways are designed in such a way that their ability to be used maliciously is limited. This chapter covers relevant attacks against gateways and potential countermeasures against them. A number of different attacks were found in literature, including radio jamming, eavesdropping, replay attacks, and attacks against the implementation of what is called beacons in LoRaWAN. Countermeasures against these attacks are discussed, and a suggestion to improve the security of LoRaWAN is also included.

DOI: 10.4018/978-1-7998-7468-3.ch002

INTRODUCTION

Nowadays, more and more devices are being connected to the Internet. The term Internet of Things (IoT) is used to describe this phenomenon. These devices are typically small with a very specific purpose. They range from sensors in homes, to infrastructure, agriculture, and more. In 2019, there were 26 billion active IoT devices, and this number is expected to increase to 35 billion by 2021 (Maayan, 2020).

As IoT devices become increasingly more common, so does the need to facilitate their connection to the Internet, especially when placed in remote locations with limited access to conventional methods of Internet connections (such as 4G, Wi-Fi, or similar). To enable connection of IoT devices in these circumstances, multiple technologies have been developed, which serve devices in a wide area using low power, but with limited bandwidth. These technologies go under the umbrella acronym LPWAN, which stands for Low-Power Wide-Area Network (Wedd, 2020).

One such technology is called LoRa (**Lo**ng **Ra**nge) and is a physical-layer network protocol which enables communication with IoT devices over a wide area (10+ km) with low power consumption and low bandwidth. There are several upper-layer protocols on top of the LoRa physical layer, one of which is LoRaWAN. The physical layer protocol enables access, while the upper-layer protocols define how the network is accessed and secured.

The first version of LoRaWAN, version 1.0, was released in 2015 (LoRa Alliance, 2015). Much research has been done regarding this version and it has been discovered that it suffers from several security vulnerabilities, concerning data confidentiality, message integrity and network availability. Many of these issues were fixed when version 1.1 of the protocol was released in 2017 but, as this paper will show, not all of them.

Emerging network protocols require thorough analysis to guarantee their security. Flaws in network protocols enable attacks on connected devices, which can include extraction of poorly secured data, impersonation of devices, usage of botnets in distributed denial-of-service (DDoS) attacks, etc. It is therefore of paramount importance to secure network protocols against attacks like these.

In (Lambrinos, 2019) the author shows that a LoRaWAN network can be used to gather information from different sensors for a Decision Support System (DSS) in agriculture and smart farming. Similarly, (Cui et al, 2018) uses LoRaWAN to monitor a lake brine pump with the help of a DSS as a method to detect pump failures. In both cases the transmitted information, including weather, crop and pump voltage data, needs to be reliably and securely transmitted to facilitate quality decisions in order to, for example, optimise harvests and detect pump failures.

This paper surveys research done on attacks and defences against LoRaWAN gateways, i.e. connection points for IoT devices to the Internet, and is structured as follows. The introduction continues with an overview of previous work followed by a description of LoRaWAN and its limitations. Section II surveys different attacks related to gateways and in Section III the authors summarise those attacks and possible countermeasures. The authors end the survey in Section IV, with a conclusion and suggestions for improving the security in LoRaWAN and lastly give directions for possible future work.

BACKGROUND

Although several research institutions have analysed the LoRaWaN protocol regarding security, there is limited research focusing on building a systematic review of the potential security issues with the LoRaWAN gateways.

Tomasin et al. (2017) investigated the join procedures critical security issues in LoRaWAN and described the vulnerabilities in the protocol. This concerns using a random number in the join procedure and attack strategies by generating malicious traffic to make resources unavailable. The paper shows the result of the current implementation inaccuracies and the potential vulnerabilities to denial-of-service (DoS) attacks. Furthermore, the papers (Aras et al., 2017; Ingham et al., 2020; Krejčí et al. 2017) discuss the LoRaWAN vulnerabilities regarding jamming, eavesdropping and key distribution and propose their conclusions of possible vulnerabilities. However, the papers do not cover all possible attacks and do not propose any ideas of defences in regard to these attacks. This is a problem as there could be unknown risks in the LoRaWAN application that could provide a window for more potential attack vectors. The authors think, in addition, by identifying the current attacks and defences to the LoRaWAN gateway it will serve a good template, which could be used as a complement when testing the protocol in a more practical context.

A notorious problem with the LoRaWAN networks is that the protocol's security requirements are not discussed based on its architecture. It is essential to form discussions regarding the structure of the given system. This concerns which devices are used in the system, and what information is the most important to protect. There could also be devices that have data which does not need to be encrypted, as this could accelerate the performance within the IoT system. Sundaram et al. (2019) points to similar issues where applications in the system may require Network and Application keys to be independent, and the Network Session Key to be confidential from the application server.

Butun et al. (2019) performed an extensive risk assessment and security analysis of the current state of LoRaWAN 1.1. Some attacks related to gateways are discussed but only a few suggestions on solving them are given. Eldefrawy et al. (2019) conducted a formal security analysis of the LoRaWAN protocol using

Scyther, a formal security analysis tool, and found that it is cryptographically secure. Although the protocol itself is found to be secure, the authors highlight that there may be other security vulnerabilities, related to cryptographic primitives, keys and trust to the LoRa infrastructure.

The previous research emphasises the security hazards of LoRaWAN with clear examples. However, an in-depth analysis of the current attacks and defences towards gateways has not been done. In this project, the authors will fill this gap by investigating which types of defences that could potentially solve different attacks against the LoRaWAN gateway.

LORAWAN PROTOCOL AND SECURITY

This section begins with introducing the LoRaWAN protocol, both how it works and the network structure. Following, different attacks towards it, and defences and mitigations against these attacks are explained. Lastly, the found issues and problems with the protocol are discussed.

The LoRaWAN Protocol

The LoRaWAN protocol is defined by the LoRaWAN v1.1 specification and is maintained by the LoRaWAN Alliance (LoRa Alliance, 2017). LoRaWAN v1.1 was released in October 2017, and is a continuation of the initial version, v1.0, which was released in January 2015.

Topology

The LoRaWAN network has a star-of-stars topology, where end-devices are connected to gateways using radio signals. Gateways are in turn connected to a network server with the purpose of forwarding messages, enabling end-devices to connect to the Internet using long-range radio signals. The network layout can be seen in Figure 1.

At the left in the figure are different types of end-devices that connect to the LoRaWAN network. The first connection is made through gateways, which in turn connect to the backhaul Network Servers (NS). The three types of NS are used for, for example, roaming, serving and forwarding of messages. To the far right are the Join Server (JS) and the Application Server (AS) which take care of devices joining the network and sending data from and to different applications that the end-device uses.

Figure 1. The architectural layout of LoRaWAN v1.1
Adapted from Butun et al. (2017)

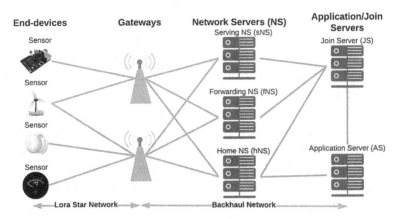

Join Procedures

End devices must perform a join procedure in order to connect to the LoRaWAN network. LoRaWAN has two join procedures, Over-The-Air-Activation (OTAA) and Activation By Personalisation (ABP). An end device can use either of these procedures to connect.

OTAA is performed by having the end-device send a join-request, consisting of the fields (*join ID, device ID, device nonce*), where the nonce has to be unique for each join ID. This message is sent to a network server via a gateway which responds with a join-accept message if the device is accepted into the network. This join-accept message is sent out with a delay, and contains the fields (*join nonce, network ID, device address, downlink settings, latency, network parameters*). The nonce in the join-accept message is used to derive the keys used in the session and is incremented for every join-accept message.

ABP on the other hand is performed by having the session information stored in the devices directly. That means, the session keys and the address have already been stored in the end-device, completely bypassing the OTAA procedure.

Device Classes

An end-device can operate as one of three different classes: class A, B and C (LoRa Alliance, 2017). Each class specifies how the end-device operates, e.g. when and how often it can receive downstream connections and messages.

A class A end-device is the most basic class and offers limited bi-directional communication. The device can at any time create an uplink transmission and send messages, but it can only receive downlink messages once it opens its receive window. This happens two times shortly following the uplink transmission. A device that rarely makes an uplink will also rarely receive any messages, and a server needing to contact it will have to wait. The main benefit of this is the very low power-usage since the device is idle most of the time.

Class B devices are a slight upgrade compared to a class A device. In addition to the limited downlink availability, it also opens receive windows at scheduled times, allowing for lower-latency downlinks. The scheduling is done by a gateway that sends a time-synchronised Beacon to the end-devices in range. The beacon contains information about when and how often a receive window should be opened.

Lastly, class C devices offer almost continuous availability for downlink communication by keeping receive windows always open, except when transmitting. The cost of this is a much higher energy consumption.

Class B Beacons

In LoRaWAN v1.1, a beacon frame consists of some headers together with a payload (LoRa Alliance, 2017), as shown in Table 1.

Table 1. Example of a beacon payload

Field	RFU	Time	CRC	InfoDesc	lat	long	RFU	CRC
Value Hex	000000	CC020000	7EA2	0	002001	038100	00	D450

The *RFU* field is always equal to zero. Following that is a *Time* field containing the current GPS time, modulo 2^{32}, to synchronise the end-devices' internal clocks with the gateway and network servers to prevent messages being sent and received out-of-sync. *InfoDesc* can be a value between 0-255 and describes the content in the following field (in the table this field is *lat* and *long*, but it differs). If it is zero, one or two, the following two fields give the coordinates of the gateway's first, second or third antenna, respectively.

Lastly, to protect the integrity of the beacon payload the RFU and the Time fields are protected by a 16-bit cyclic redundancy check (CRC). The same is done for the InfoDesc, lat and long fields, giving the last CRC value.

Limitations

This survey focuses on research done on LoRaWAN gateways and does not cover any attacks done on the backhaul network unless a gateway plays a part in the attack. The purpose of this limitation is to focus on the security of the gateways specifically, as these are an important part of the LoRaWAN network.

Furthermore, any attacks done at the layer between the gateways and the backhaul networks will not be covered. This should be covered by conventional IP security analysis and does not strictly apply to LoRa technologies.

This survey mainly focuses on research done on LoRaWAN v1.1, and research relating to v1.0 is out of scope. This is because v1.1 has many security improvements from v1.0, so it is difficult to know if the attacks are still applicable to v1.1. Therefore, the research done on the security of v1.0 is mostly outdated, although some information in these papers is still relevant to discuss in this survey.

Research on LoRaWAN Gateway Security

As mentioned in earlier in the chapter, and as shown in Figure 1, the LoRaWAN network consists of end-devices, gateways and servers. The gateways are responsible for receiving and transmitting messages and sending out periodic beacon messages to keep end-devices in sync. The whole network relies on the gateways to function properly, and attacks towards them can have a big impact.

A malicious gateway enables a range of different attacks that can be difficult to detect, especially if the end-devices connected to it have no other alternative gateway in range. The gateway can, for example, drop certain messages from or to the end-device or send fake beacon data, to make them open receive windows much more frequently, resulting in a heavily reduced battery life on the end-devices.

In the following sections a few different attacks relating to gateways will be discussed, along with a discussion on possible countermeasures. It should be noted that there might be more attacks possible than the attacks listed in this paper, but in this case, there is little to no research on these attacks.

Radio Jamming Attack

A major security problem with LoRaWAN gateways is the susceptibility to radio jamming attacks, which are denial-of-service attacks targeting the physical layer of LoRaWAN. End devices communicate with LoRaWAN gateways using radio signals, which can be disrupted by malicious hardware. Radio jamming attacks can be seen in many types of wireless communication, and research on it has been applied on LoRaWAN architecture as well.

Aras et al. (2017) demonstrated several types of radio jamming attacks, which were carried out on cheap hardware consisting of a microcontroller and a radio module. First, a triggered jamming attack was demonstrated, which is a jamming attack that activates when there is activity on a channel. Then, a selective jamming attack was demonstrated, which works by conditionally jamming the channel when a specific type of LoRaWAN packet is detected on it. Triggered jamming attacks are easier to detect because it disrupts communication to all devices connected to a gateway, while selective jamming attacks are harder to detect because it may only disrupt communication when some of the connected devices try to communicate on the channel. Due to the inexpensiveness of the hardware required to perform this attack and its relatively high potential for disruption, it could pose a problem in the future.

Jamming attacks can be efficient on their own, but also be part of a more complicated attack. In (Tomasin et al., 2017), jamming was used to reduce the randomness of a random number generator, resulting in a more predictable cryptography nonce during the join procedure. This attack was carried out in LoRaWAN v1.0 and has been addressed in v1.1 (Eldefrawy et al., 2017), but it still shows that security analysis must consider the possibility of jamming used in conjunction with other attacks. Future research should therefore be carried out in this area.

Some defences have been investigated to counter radio jamming attacks. For example, Danish et al. (2018) investigated algorithms to detect radio jamming attacks, and that found one with 98% detection rate. However, while radio jamming attacks are a widely researched subject in many wireless technologies, little research exists in this subject in the LoRaWAN domain.

Since radio jamming attacks are the wireless equivalent of physically cutting a network cable, it is not possible on the protocol layer to completely prevent such attacks. The most that can be done in this case is to mitigate the effects of such an attack. For example, with an intrusion detection system, radio jamming attacks can be detected and averted through physical means.

Beacon Attacks

What is important to note from Table 1 is that a CRC is only good to protect against radio channel noise and random bit-flips in the beacon transmission, not as a protection against modification (Yang et al., 2018). CRCs are linear and can easily be calculated and sent out by anyone.

An important feature of the end-devices is their long battery lifetime. Class B end-devices use a trade-off between long battery life (class A) and high availability for the reception of messages from servers (class C). Since gateway beacons are sent to the end-devices to schedule receive windows, and that they are not secured, leaves it open for an attacker to modify beacon messages, sent from the gateway to the end-devices, or for a malicious gateway to perform different attacks. Butun et al. (2019) speculate that since class B beacons are not secured, there might be a security problem wherein a rogue gateway sends false beacon transmissions, causing packet collisions or messages being received out-of-sync. This would effectively lead to a denial-of-service. More specific, the attacks are:

1. **Malicious Wake-Up Times**: a gateway sending a beacon controls an end-device's scheduled receive windows. First, sending a beacon that schedules excessively many receive windows causes the end-device to quickly drain its battery. Secondly, it can schedule the receive windows to be out-of-sync with the actual downlink messages from the server causing it to not receive them.

2. **Faking GPS-Coordinates**: a beacon message contains a timestamp and the GPS-coordinates of the gateway (LoRa Alliance, 2017), where the timestamp is used to synchronise the internal clock of the end-device while the GPS-coordinates can be used by the device to let the AS (and the device's owner) know its geographical position. The coordinates are also used by the NS (when the device performs an uplink transmission) so that it knows which gateway is closest to it that should forward downlink messages (LoRa Alliance, 2017). A malicious gateway faking these coordinates can both trick the end-device into thinking it has moved location (Yang et al., 2018) (and cause confusion for its owners), but also the NS that then sends messages to the wrong gateway, causing downlink communication to be unavailable until the next uplink from the end-device.

3. **Forcing a Class Change**: if a gateway refrains from sending beacons it will, as per specification (LoRa Alliance, 2017), force the end-devices in its range to switch back to being a class A device. The result is that the end-device has to inform the NS that it is no longer a class B device and try to switch back to class B. This attack is only possible if there is a single gateway in range of the end-device and it mostly involves more work for the end-device and NS while having a possibility to disrupt the communication between them.

Butun et al. (2019) propose introducing keys for beacon transmissions, so that rogue gateways cannot send false beacon transmissions. So far, no proof of concept of this attack has seemingly been published.

Yang et al. (2018) argues that replacing the CRC with a MIC (message integrity code), using the network session key, would solve the problem. As they state, the argument against this is that only one device can verify the beacon (the one with the same network session key), and it would require the gateway to send out n beacons, one for each end-device in its range. This is highly inefficient, and the authors instead claim that signing the beacon frame using public-key cryptography would be better, at the cost of setting up a public key infrastructure (PKI) and distributing the gateway's public key to each end-device.

Eavesdropping

A fundamental problem that is widely discussed in wireless communication is the passive attack called eavesdropping. The attack occurs in the physical layer of the network, where an attacker in most cases is using a rogue gateway for receiving radio signals from the end-device (Yang et al., 2018). One implementation issue regarding the security for LoRaWAN is that the protocol is using AES in counter mode. More specifically, a packet counter (counting the number of packets sent) is used as input to the block cipher. Instead of using a nonce as an input, the block cipher will, in turn, recreate the same key material if the packet counter (or device) resets and uses the same value. This will cause duplicate packets in the network. Yang et al. (2018) demonstrate a way of exploiting this based on the assumption that a plaintext P is combined through an exclusive OR with a keystream to obtain the ciphertext C. Given that the two messages P_1 and P_2 are encrypted under the same keystream K, it gives $P_1 \oplus K = C_1$ and $P_2 \oplus K = C_2$. A rogue actor could, in this case, have the possibility to eliminate the secret key, as shown in the following equation:

$$C_1 \oplus C_2 = \left(P_1 \oplus K\right) \oplus \left(P_2 \oplus K\right) = P_1 \oplus P_2 \oplus \left(K \oplus K\right) = P_1 \oplus P_2$$

This leaves an XOR of the two plaintexts, which then can be extracted to their original form (Griffing, 2006). Yang et al. (2018) propose two different solutions to this attack. The first is the use of nonces instead of the packet counter as input to the block cipher. This drastically increases the security since it is almost impossible for an attacker to guess an almost random value from a cryptographically secure pseudo-random number generator. The other suggestion is that all the key material (session keys) is rekeyed upon a device reset, or when the packet counter reaches its limit and would flip over to zero. Then, although the same counter value is used as input, all the keys have changed, so $C_1 \oplus C_2 \neq P_1 \oplus P_2$.

Replay Attack

One efficient yet simple attack on a LoRaWAN gateway is the replay attack, which mainly focuses on detecting the data transmission to delay or repeat the information to the receiving system. This method articulates that the potential attacker is fooling the system to believe that it is an authorised user by replaying data to the system.

Similarly to the previously discussed attack *Eavesdropping*, a rogue attacker uses the highest counter value to repeat this message to the device. With this consideration, these messages could cause the device to change its session key for the message to be retrieved (Gresak & Voznak, 2018). An essential thing in this process is that when the device is flooded with entries it will force the device to be automatically restarted as the resource becomes unavailable. This opportunity creates the window for a potential attacker to find that particular device which has been overflowed with traffic. Butun et al. (2019) proposed the use of an additional randomised number (DevNonce), which could be included in the message by the end-device in order to prevent duplication and to avoid the replay-attack during the Join-Request. The setup of how the communication should be established between the server and the client without inferring in the performance could be a bit challenging regarding constrained devices.

Wormhole Attack

A wormhole attack is where an attacker captures or records a packet and re-transmits it at another location in the network (Basu et al., 2020). This attack is not an attack to the contents of the captured package, but instead to the LoRa-network's underlying routing mechanism. Similar to faking GPS-coordinates in the previously explained Beacon attack, this attack causes downlink messages to be routed to the wrong location.

The wormhole attack is possible even though the end-device's message has full integrity and authenticity since no check is done at the receiving server of where the message came from (Basu et al., 2020). Hu et al. (2003) propose packet leashes to detect against the attack. By setting an upper bound to the number of hops that a message in normal cases should take it is possible to detect a wormhole attack if the message traverses a longer path on its way to a LoRaWAN server. However, this is of limited use in LoRaWAN since the route from an end-device to a Network Server is at most two hops away (one to the gateway and the next to the NS). Each gateway in range of the end-device will forward the message so it is required that an attacker also blocks the message from being received by any of the gateways.

Rogue Gateway Attacks

Another set of relevant attacks in literature are rogue gateway attacks. As previously stated, gateways are not authenticated in any way and are assumed in the protocol to not be malicious. However, there are attacks that show that rogue gateways can cause problems in LoRaWAN. One usage of rogue gateways has already been covered in *Beacon Attacks*, relating to rogue gateways sending false beacons.

Another, more subtle, attack that is similar to the Wormhole attack is when a malicious gateway is set up or captured and which drops certain packets (selective forwarding). Unless there are other GWs in range of the end-device, there is no way for the NS to receive the packet unless the ED retransmits it. This is illustrated in Figure 2, where the rogue GW can selectively drop packets and send fake Beacon messages to end-devices in its range.

Figure 2. Rogue gateway attack

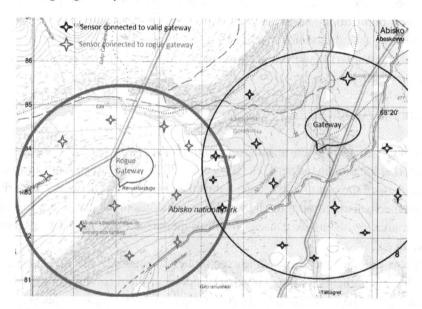

Butun et al. (2019) have also found attacks related to gateway impersonation. Firstly, a rogue gateway can impersonate a real gateway and find out network addresses of connected end-devices. Then, multiple rogue gateways can find the exact physical location of an end-device.

As previously stated in *Beacon Attacks*, gateway authentication has been suggested by Butun et al. (2019). The same countermeasures can be applied here in order to prevent rogue gateways.

Issues, Controversies, Problems

LoRaWAN has gathered significant interest from the community where much research has been conducted with surveys and empirical studies. Still, there are wide issues when IoT devices are becoming increasingly more common and need to be connected to the internet. Previous research has shown several vulnerabilities and emphasise on security hazards with implementation accuracies. Tomasin et al. (2019) demonstrated the join procedure problem and described the attack strategies by generating malicious traffic. Other papers, e.g. Butun et al. (2019), performed security analysis of the current state of LoRaWAN gateway. The authors show that security problems in regard to IoT devices are often generated by cryptographic primitives. Several studies, e.g. Kirk et al. (2019), Killgallin et al. (2019), have shown that IoT devices have weak RSA keys which indicates that key factoring will be much easier on devices with limited computational power.

The public-key infrastructure needs to be revisited in design, key management, and operation Kirk et al. (2019). Especially with LoRaWAN, the authors argue that the keys on the devices need to be renewed on a regular basis and that a well-suited authentication protocol needs to be implemented to isolate rogue gateways. There have been discussions regarding how a blockchain could be a technique to build trusted LoRaWAN sharing servers to solve the problems with rogue gateways Butun et.al (2020). However, one could argue that adding more techniques to the existing ones could provide another layer of complexity on the devices. This indicates that simplicity must be taken into consideration when designing systems and that the hardware and software need to be integrated in such a way that bottlenecks are avoidable.

SOLUTIONS AND RECOMMENDATIONS

A starting point for research would be to apply general IoT and wireless network research on the LoRaWAN domain. IoT security covers aspects on the application layer, network layer and hardware layer. Khan et al. have generalised attacks that may be applicable on IoT protocols (Khan & Salah, 2018). Especially since IoT technologies have many common characteristics, it may make them susceptible to attacks that are similar in nature. Hence, it is important to verify whether general IoT or wireless attacks work in LoRaWAN v1.1 or future LoRaWAN protocol versions.

Moreover, LoRaWAN shares concepts with other LPWAN technologies, so it is possible that research done on other technologies have not yet been applied on LoRaWAN. It would be useful to investigate whether research on cybersecurity and other LPWAN technologies can be applied on LoRaWAN too.

Another area of interest would be verifying the countermeasures that were discussed in this paper. Many of the countermeasures stated here are theoretical ones, as the authors did not have time to implement or execute them. Consequently, research verifying whether the suggested countermeasures are viable and live up to the required standard of security is needed. Proof of concepts are left for future research.

The problem with the Beacon attacks is that an end-device has no idea which gateway actually broadcast the beacon message.

As in Yang et al. (2018) suggests, adding public key cryptography to the gateways is a nice idea that solves these attacks by signing the beacon message with the gateway's private key.

Taking this one step further, the authors introduce and suggest the use of *trusted gateways*, which will now be explained further.

1. **A public and private key pair should be created for each gateway and end-device**. The gateway's public key should be shared with the LoRa Network Servers. The NS can then have a pair of *public keys, gateway~ID* for each gateway.

2. **When an end-device performs a Join-request to a NS**, the NS knows which gateway the device connects to and where it should send the response message. In this Join-accept response message the NS includes the public key of the gateway. The end-device now has everything it needs to ''trust'' the gateway.

3. **The end-device can periodically generate a unique session key,** (using, for example, AES), encrypt it using the gateway's public key and send it in a message signed with the gateway's public key to the gateway. When the gateway receives this message, it can decrypt it and extract the session key.

So, whenever a beacon message is received by the end-device it can check whether it was signed by one of its ''trusted gateways''. If it was not, the message can simply be discarded. To send a message, the end-device encrypts it with the session key and transmits the message as usual. The difference is that only the gateways with the corresponding key can decrypt and forward the message to the NS. An alternative is that the NS includes the public keys of all the gateways in-range of the end-device. The end-device can then do step three to several of the gateways, using the same symmetric (session) key for each one. This adds more reliability in case one of them goes down since any of them can receive and decrypt the message.

In this way, this solves both the Beacon attacks (by signing the beacon messages) and the Wormhole attack (no other gateway than the trusted ones can forward the message). It would be possible to not use the session key and only use public key cryptography, but that would require more work for the end-device as AES is much faster than, for example, RSA (Singh, 2013). The authors argue that using one algorithm for the whole system is not the solution either, as it could provide attack windows when using the same arithmetic for both the encryption and decryption phase.

Lastly, this survey has shown that a LoRaWAN network is a good candidate for Decision Support Systems that require transmitted information to be secure over long distances. The solution with trusted gateways that this paper provides, together with a DSS, can facilitate quality decisions to e.g., detect malicious traffic or IoT device failures in order to optimize, for example, harvests or other functionality used in the field.

FUTURE RESEARCH DIRECTIONS

A malicious gateway enables a range of different attacks that can be difficult to detect, especially if the end-devices connected to it have no other alternative gateway in range. The gateway can, for example, drop certain messages from or to the end-device or send fake beacon data, to make them open receive windows much more frequently, resulting in a heavily reduced battery life on the end-devices.

The underlying problems is that gateways are not authenticated in any way and are assumed in the protocol to not be malicious. However, there are attacks that show that rogue gateways can cause problems in LoRaWAN. One usage of rogue gateways has already been covered in *Beacon Attacks*, relating to rogue gateways sending false beacons.

The authors of this paper have proposed a way to eliminate such hazards with the use of trusted gateways. However, the authors believe that this proposal of trusted gateways needs to be tested in a more practical environment to explore the full potential of the idea. Therefore, the authors suggest for future research that more analysis needs to be done empirically in regard to key distribution and management, especially when malicious gateways are starting to be a global phenomenon.

CONCLUSION

This survey has summarised research of attacks and defences on LoRaWAN gateways in protocol version v1.1 and suggested some improvements. These improvements are based on the theoretical analysis where the authors discover one important feature of LoRaWAN, which is the long battery life of the end-devices. The current implementation of beacons leaves it open for anyone with a radio transmitter, capable of sending out messages to the network, to impersonate a gateway and drastically reduce the performance and downlink availability of an end-device while at the same time heavily impact the battery lifespan. As such, it is important to tamper-protect a gateway's beacon messages, but also to make it difficult for someone to fake a gateway beacon.

Other attacks, like radio jamming, are more challenging to predict, and it is not possible to completely prevent these attacks as it is hardware dependent. However, it is possible to reduce the impact of the radio jamming attacks by using counter measurements such as intrusion prevention systems to block the signals. One important note is that this method has its adverse effect by introducing additional latency in the system where it is active listening to prevent incoming radio jamming. To successfully set up these systems, forensics needs to be done in the identification, collection, and examination process in order to build these systems as efficiently as possible.

The authors recommend that adding countermeasures to these discussed flaws will be important in the future as IoT devices will become more frequently used in today's computer systems. In order to increase the viability of large-scale deployment of LoRaWAN, security issues must be addressed in advance. Every sound physical security system is built up of both locks and surveillance and in this perspective a system to spot tampering attempts is of great importance, even more so because of the difficulty to anticipate what an attacker is able to do. Even if the communication is strongly encrypted to the degree the public opinion considers it to be safe this does not mean you can trust it to 100 percent. One way to address these problems could be to let every end device communicate with more than one gateway and compare received packages. Any differences should then sound the alarm and a more meticulous investigation performed. The important point the authors would like to draw is that more research should be done in this area.

ACKNOWLEDGMENT

Special thanks to Ismail Butun for ideas and support to help the authors develop this paper.

REFERENCES

Aras, E., Ramachandran, G. S., Lawrence, P., & Hughes, D. (2017, June). Exploring the security vulnerabilities of LoRa. In *2017 3rd IEEE International Conference on Cybernetics (CYBCONF)* (pp. 1-6). IEEE. 10.1109/CYBConf.2017.7985777

Aras, E., Small, N., Ramachandran, G. S., Delbruel, S., Joosen, W., & Hughes, D. (2017, November). Selective jamming of LoRaWAN using commodity hardware. In *Proceedings of the 14th EAI International Conference on Mobile and Ubiquitous Systems: Computing, Networking and Services* (pp. 363-372). 10.1145/3144457.3144478

Butun, I., & Österberg, P. (2020). A Review of Distributed Access Control for Blockchain Systems towards Securing the Internet of Things. *IEEE Access: Practical Innovations, Open Solutions.*

Butun, I., Pereira, N., & Gidlund, M. (2019). Security risk analysis of LoRaWAN and future directions. *Future Internet, 11*(1), 3. doi:10.3390/fi11010003

Chaudhari, B. S., Zennaro, M., & Borkar, S. (2020). LPWAN technologies: Emerging application characteristics, requirements, and design considerations. *Future Internet, 12*(3), 46. doi:10.3390/fi12030046

Cui, Y., Liu, H., Zhang, M., Stankovski, S., Feng, J., & Zhang, X. (2018). Improving Intelligence and Efficiency of Salt Lake Production by Applying a Decision Support System Based on IOT for Brine Pump Management. *Electronics (Basel), 7*(8), 147. doi:10.3390/electronics7080147

Danish, S. M., Nasir, A., Qureshi, H. K., Ashfaq, A. B., Mumtaz, S., & Rodriguez, J. (2018, May). Network intrusion detection system for jamming attack in lorawan join procedure. In *2018 IEEE International Conference on Communications (ICC)* (pp. 1-6). IEEE. 10.1109/ICC.2018.8422721

Eldefrawy, M., Butun, I., Pereira, N., & Gidlund, M. (2019). Formal security analysis of LoRaWAN. *Computer Networks, 148,* 328–339. doi:10.1016/j.comnet.2018.11.017

Gresak, E., & Voznak, M. (2018, September). Protecting gateway from abp replay attack on lorawan. In *International Conference on Advanced Engineering Theory and Applications* (pp. 400-408). Springer.

Ingham, M., Marchang, J., & Bhowmik, D. (2020). IoT security vulnerabilities and predictive signal jamming attack analysis in LoRaWAN. *IET Information Security, 14*(4), 368–379. doi:10.1049/iet-ifs.2019.0447

Khan, M. A., & Salah, K. (2018). Iot security: Review, blockchain solutions, and open challenges. *Future Generation Computer Systems, 82,* 395–411. doi:10.1016/j.future.2017.11.022

Kilgallin, J., & Vasko, R. (2019, December). Factoring RSA Keys in the IoT Era. In *2019 First IEEE International Conference on Trust, Privacy and Security in Intelligent Systems and Applications (TPS-ISA)* (pp. 184-189). IEEE. 10.1109/TPS-ISA48467.2019.00030

Kirk, J. (n.d.). *Study: IoT Devices Have Alarmingly Weak RSA Keys*. Technical report, bankinfosecurity.

Krejčí, R., Hujňák, O., & Švepeš, M. (2017, November). Security survey of the IoT wireless protocols. In *2017 25th Telecommunication Forum (TELFOR)* (pp. 1-4). IEEE. 10.1109/TELFOR.2017.8249286

Lambrinos, L. (2019). Internet of Things in Agriculture: A Decision Support System for Precision Farming. In 2019 IEEE Intl Conf on Dependable, Autonomic and Secure Computing, Intl Conf on Pervasive Intelligence and Computing, Intl Conf on Cloud and Big Data Computing, Intl Conf on Cyber Science and Technology Congress (DASC/PiCom/CBDCom/CyberSciTech) (pp. 889-892). IEEE. doi:10.1109/DASC/PiCom/CBDCom/CyberSciTech.2019.00163

Lora Alliance. (2015). *LoRaWAN 1.0 Specification*. Author.

Lora Alliance. (2017). *LoRaWAN 1.1 Specification*. LoRa Alliance Technical Committee.

Singh, G. (2013). A Study of Encryption Algorithms (RSA, DES, 3DES and AES) for Information Security. *International Journal of Computers and Applications*, *67*(19).

Sundaram, J. P. S., Du, W., & Zhao, Z. (2019). A survey on lora networking: Research problems, current solutions, and open issues. *IEEE Communications Surveys and Tutorials*, *22*(1), 371–388. doi:10.1109/COMST.2019.2949598

Tomasin, S., Zulian, S., & Vangelista, L. (2017, March). Security analysis of LoRaWAN join procedure for Internet of Things networks. In 2017 IEEE Wireless Communications and Networking Conference Workshops (WCNCW) (pp. 1-6). IEEE. doi:10.1109/WCNCW.2017.7919091

Wedd, M. (2020, June). *What is LPWAN and the LoRaWAN Open Standard?* Technical report, iotforall.

Yang, X., Karampatzakis, E., Doerr, C., & Kuipers, F. (2018, April). Security vulnerabilities in LoRaWAN. In *2018 IEEE/ACM Third International Conference on Internet-of-Things Design and Implementation (IoTDI)* (pp. 129-140). IEEE. 10.1109/IoTDI.2018.00022

ADDITIONAL READING

Adelantado, F., Vilajosana, X., Tuset-Peiro, P., Martinez, B., Melia-Segui, J., & Watteyne, T. (2017). Understanding the limits of LoRaWAN. *IEEE Communications Magazine, 55*(9), 34–40. doi:10.1109/MCOM.2017.1600613

Butun, I., & Österberg, P. (2020). A Review of Distributed Access Control for Blockchain Systems towards Securing the Internet of Things. *IEEE Access: Practical Innovations, Open Solutions.*

Butun, I., Pereira, N., & Gidlund, M. (2019). Security risk analysis of LoRaWAN and future directions. *Future Internet, 11*(1), 3. doi:10.3390/fi11010003

Haxhibeqiri, J., De Poorter, E., Moerman, I., & Hoebeke, J. (2018). A survey of LoRaWAN for IoT: From technology to application. *Sensors (Basel), 18*(11), 3995. doi:10.339018113995 PMID:30453524

Marais, J. M., Abu-Mahfouz, A. M., & Hancke, G. P. (2020). A Survey on the Viability of Confirmed Traffic in a LoRaWAN. *IEEE Access: Practical Innovations, Open Solutions, 8,* 9296–9311. doi:10.1109/ACCESS.2020.2964909

Ngo, T. D., Ferrero, F., Doan, V. Q., & Van Pham, T. (2021). Industrial LoRaWAN Network for Danang City: Solution for Long-Range and Low-Power IoT Applications. In *Research in Intelligent and Computing in Engineering* (pp. 65–75). Springer. doi:10.1007/978-981-15-7527-3_7

Sornin, N., Luis, M., Eirich, T., Kramp, T., & Hersent, O. (2015). Lorawan specification. *LoRa alliance.*

Yang, X., Karampatzakis, E., Doerr, C., & Kuipers, F. (2018, April). Security vulnerabilities in LoRaWAN. In *2018 IEEE/ACM Third International Conference on Internet-of-Things Design and Implementation (IoTDI)* (pp. 129-140). IEEE. 10.1109/IoTDI.2018.00022

KEY TERMS AND DEFINITIONS

Authentication: The act of proving or verifying that, for example, a system is who it says it is.

Beacon Message: A time-periodic message sent out from a gateway to synchronise all end-devices in its range.

End-Device: A source device that connects to the LoRaWAN network and sends and receives data to support IoT applications.

Gateway: The connection point of an end-device to the LoRaWAN network. The gateway transmits, broadcasts and relays data.

Malicious: A malicious gateway has intent to cause harm or disturbance in the network traffic or operation of end-devices.

Packet: Data in a network transmission. A packet contains a header (routing information) and a payload.

Public-Key Cryptography: Used in a cryptographic system where each sender/receiver has a public and a private key pair. The public key is public to everyone and the private key is known only to the holder of it. A sender can, for example, use the public key of the recipient to encrypt the data transmission and the receiver uses his own private key to decrypt it.

Session Key: A symmetric encryption/decryption key used for a shorter period of time during a communication session. Switched out after a period of time or after a certain number of messages.

Chapter 3

A Review of Wireless Positioning From Past and Current to Emerging Technologies

Joar Blom Rydell
Chalmers University of Technology, Sweden

Oliver Otterlind
Chalmers University of Technology, Sweden

Amanda Sjöö
Chalmers University of Technology, Sweden

ABSTRACT

Many techniques for wireless positioning have existed for years, but with emerging technologies like 5G and ultra wideband, wireless positioning is becoming more accurate than ever. On the one hand, improved accuracy implies increased usefulness. It will open up new application areas and lead to advances in areas like internet of things (IoT), self-driving cars, and contact tracing. Furthermore, decision support systems can benefit from better positioning techniques. On the other hand, the ability to track connected devices with sub-meter precision brings some privacy and security concerns. This chapter aims to review indoor and outdoor positioning technologies and how they can be used for contact tracing. It then further discusses some of the data management, privacy, and security concerns that follow. To that end, this chapter studies the main techniques for wireless positioning, cellular-based positioning using 5G, and their use to contact tracing. Finally, the authors provide some insight into how 5G and UWB might help the area of positioning and contact tracking in the future.

DOI: 10.4018/978-1-7998-7468-3.ch003

INTRODUCTION

The number of wirelessly connected devices increases by the minute, with more people having access to them while at the same time more everyday objects are being connected (Ahmed, 2020). With all of these wireless devices, more possibilities to position them arise. Cellular networking and Global Positioning Systems (GPS) are the two most common location systems in smartphones and have been around for many years (Liu, 2007). Apart from these two, the use of Bluetooth and Wireless Local Area Network (WLAN) increases by the minute. Consequently, this means that most people walk around with a device that can be used for positioning purposes but can be subjected to tracking.

As with all technology, advances are being made continuously, and newer positioning systems are emerging. For instance, 4G is being replaced by 5G to deliver improvements in all areas, such as throughput, latencies, and capacity (Koivisto, 2017). Ultra Wideband (UWB) is a proximity technology similar to Bluetooth but has much higher throughput, lower energy consumption, and more advanced positioning techniques. This makes UWB ideal for proximity tracking, e.g., contact tracing (Liu, 2007).

At the same time, as technologies get more accurate, more areas of use emerge. One new area is applications that aim to reduce the spread of COVID-19 (Ahmed, 2020). However, many have later questioned these applications' privacy and security concerns because they share user and location information. This, in turn, has opened up a discussion on the trade-offs between the usefulness of a system and the privacy and security aspects for the end-users. This is a trade-off that is important to discuss in all applications using positioning systems.

Compared to the used reference papers (i.e., Liu 2007, Koivisto 2017, and Ahmed 2020), this chapter introduces more aspects on the topic of wireless positioning, explaining the basic metrics and algorithms used. It further gives an overview of the most popular wireless positioning systems and discusses security and privacy issues that can arise when used in various tracking applications (contact tracing). This layout makes it possible to understand some parts of a wireless positioning system on an introductory level and explain how these can be applied in applications.

The remainder of this chapter is structured as follows. In Section 2, the authors summarize the fundamental techniques used in positioning systems. Section 3 summarizes the different systems used for positioning and which kinds of techniques each uses, respectively. In Section 4, the authors look at one area of use for these systems, namely COVID-19, and present what privacy and security concerns arise from different system architectures used in such applications. Section 5 discusses the reality of implementing these systems, particularly the emerging 5G and UWB, in terms of potential future use cases and how this can affect the outcome of these systems becoming a reality. Finally, the authors conclude the chapter in Section 6 with some thoughts on what to expect in the future.

POSITIONING TECHNIQUES

To understand how the different wireless locating systems works, the first step is to learn about the underlying techniques that calculate an estimated location. It is challenging to accurately assess a device's position using only signal measurements within a wireless network. Various characteristics related to wireless signals, e.g., multipath and attenuation, affect the signal measurements and make it challenging to create an accurate radio propagation model (Liu, 2007). There does not exist an ideal method for location estimation. Instead, several exist, each more or less suitable depending on the specific network environment's conditions in question. However, all of them share the same restriction, where they are bound to work with information/measurements either received or calculated from wireless signals received from Base Stations (BS) (Liu, 2007).

First, the authors would refer the reader to the definition section at the end of the book chapter that explains essential terms related to wireless signals. The first subsection (2.1) will detail how a few important radio signal measurements can be retrieved through calculations and radio signal measurement. The last subsections (2.2-2.5) will present a few different positioning techniques widely used in all sorts of larger systems. The authors further refer the reader to Liu *et al.'s* paper (Liu, 2007) for extended coverage of the following notions, summarized in this section. Additional references will be stated.

Radio Signal Measurements

The types of measurement obtained from radio signals related to positioning techniques are the distance between two nodes and the angle at which a signal arrives at the transmitter, called Angle of Arrival (AoA). This part will start with a closer look into AoA and how this measurement can be retrieved. After that, three different methods of estimating distance will be presented. These three methods being Received Signal Strength (RSS), Time of Arrival (ToA), and Time Difference of Arrival (TDoA).

Angle of Arrival (AoA)

Most of the existing AoA estimation techniques rely on sensor arrays at the base stations. The sensor array has multiple sensors spaced by a few wavelengths, deployed in a specific geometric arrangement. When a signal is impinging on the array, it will be received by different sensors at slightly different times (Munoz, 2009). Array processing techniques are then used to interpret all signal outputs to estimate the Angle of Arrival information.

The significant advantage of using AoA is that no time synchronization between the network nodes is required. However, at the same time, this method has several disadvantages. Firstly, when the signal is not in Line-of-Sight (LOS), the sensor array will be misled by the multipath signals and, therefore, estimate the wrong angle (Porretta, 2008). The method is also relatively expensive due to the complex hardware requirements. Lastly, as the distance increases between Up-Link (UP) and BS, minor errors in angle estimation will result in a less accurate positioning estimation (Porretta, 2008).

Received Signal Strength (RSS)

The received signal strength method takes advantage of signal attenuation. It uses a path-loss model to translate the difference between the transmitted signal strength and the received signal strength into a distance estimation. In a short-range network environment with LOS, higher accuracy can be obtained with the use of RSS. This method also does not require any time-synchronization within the network, which is an essential advantage since the implementation difficulty is drastically reduced. However, the disadvantage is that the power control used in the system can affect the measurements' accuracy (Porretta, 2008).

Time of Arrival (ToA) and Time Difference of Arrival (TDoA)

In the ToA method, the propagation time of the signal traveling from a transmitter to a receiver is measured. The propagation time is directly proportional to the distance (assuming Line-of-Sight) and can be calculated by multiplying the total propagation time with the speed of light. One main challenge with ToA is that all transmitters and receivers must be precisely synchronized to get accurate results. The TDoA method is similar to ToA, but with the addition that it calculates the time difference between the signals arriving at the base stations.

Both methods are considered to be very accurate. Unlike angulation methods and signal attenuation methods, ToA and TDoA are not prone to lower accuracy for longer distances between receivers and transmitters. However, some disadvantages do exist. One drawback is that both methods require the system to be time-synchronized (Porretta, 2008). Similar to the other signal measurement methods, NLOS (Non-Line Of Sight) condition and multipath will result in faulty calculations.

Trilateration

With all of these positioning techniques, it is assumed that a piece of User Equipment (UE) is to be located and a set of base stations to use. For all these positioning techniques, it is also essential that the base stations' coordinates are known. Specific for trilateration, the UE's position can be found if the distance to at least three BSs can be obtained. First, assume that the UE is connected to a single BS. If the distance to this BS is known, by drawing a circle around the BS with the distance's radius, it is possible to see all the UE's locations. Next, it is assumed that the UE finds another BS and can determine its distance. The UE needs to be located at the points where the two circles intersect. If two BSs are used, there should be two possible locations where the UE can be. Lastly, if a third BSs is added in the same way, only a single point exists where the UE can be located. See Figure 1 for an illustration of how this works.

Figure 1. Trilateration visualized. The user device can be found where the circles from at least three base stations intersect.

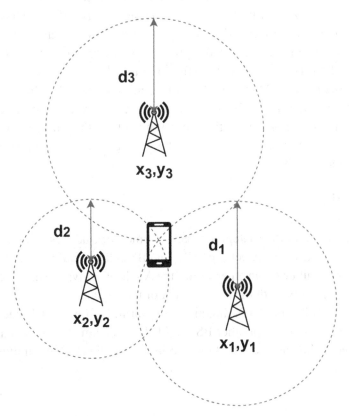

To conclude, three known BSs can be used to estimate a UE's position in two dimensions. It is also possible to estimate location in three dimensions with the addition of a fourth BS. However, it is not easy to obtain accurate distance measurements in practice, often resulting in an estimated location rather than an accurate one. But adding more than the three necessary BSs can help pinpoint the actual location more accurately and therefore try and alleviate these problems.

There also exists an extended version of trilateration called Multilateration, where instead of imagining circles around the BSs, spheres are used. With multilateration, it is, therefore, possible to go from 2D positioning to 3D positioning. However, to find the exact position of the UE, the addition of a fourth known BSs is required. Multilateration works similarly to trilateration. The distance from the BSs to the transmitter of the UE needs to be calculated as done in trilateration, but with the additional fourth BS creating the 3D sphere. There are several ways of doing this by using measurements from the radio signal. The most common measurements are the ones mentioned previously in Section 2.1.2 and 2.1.3. For further information on how these different measurements are used to calculate the distance, the authors refer the reader to those sections.

Some disadvantages with trilateration and multilateration are that the result will depend on how accurate the distance measurements will be. These distance measurements will, in turn, significantly depend on the specific network environment. For example, the mentioned radio signal measurements in Sections 2.1.2 and 2.1.3 are used for trilateration and require LOS to calculate an accurate result. For an indoor environment, having LOS is often not the case. Another property the methods share is that they will calculate more accurate results the more BSs they have access to. Therefore, an optimal environment for the trilateration technique would be outside, with few obstacles blocking the LOS and many BSs that can be used as reference points.

Triangulation

In triangulation, similar to trilateration, basic geometric principles are used. However, instead of using the distance between UEs and BSs, this technique uses the signal's angle at the transmitter. Or, in other words, the Angle of Arrival. In the case of having a UE and a single BS, with the known AoA of the signal, it is possible to imagine a line from the BS in the UE's direction. Similar to before, the UE needs to exist somewhere on this line. If another BS is added and one more line is imagined, the UE is located at the intersection of the two lines. See Figure 2 for an illustration of how this works.

Figure 2. Triangulation visualized. The distance to the user equipment can be calculated with trigonometry if at least two base stations know the angle of arrival to the user equipment.

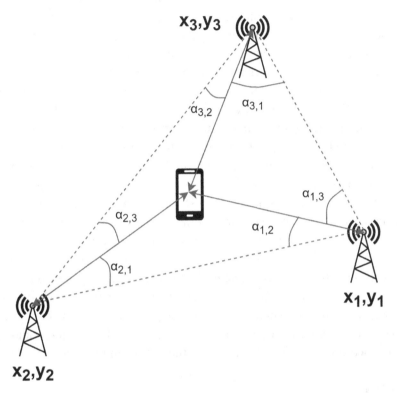

This technique uses at least two known reference points and the two measured angles of arrival to derive the UE's position. For more information on how to determine the incidence angle of a signal, see subsection 2.1.1. This positioning technique's advantage is that only two reference BSs are needed to determine the UE's position. It also requires no time synchronization within the system. On the other hand, expensive hardware is necessary to do the AoA estimations. NLOS and multipath could lead to distorted results, and lastly, estimation of the AoA measurement will degrade when the distance between UEs and BSs increases.

Scene Analysis

Scene analysis in Radio Frequency (RF) refers to the type of algorithms that first collects features of a scene called fingerprints and then estimates a device's location by matching online measurements with the most similar location fingerprints collected. Location fingerprinting is the technique that matches some location-dependent characteristic of a signal to the fingerprint. Location fingerprinting is performed in two stages, an offline and an online stage (or run-time stage). In the offline stage, a chosen site is analyzed based on the signal measurement selected. A fingerprint for this location is created by combining the site's measured signal values from nearby base stations. All fingerprints are stored for future matching. An example of how the offline stage could work in practice could be like the following. First, let us assume that the location scene analysis should be performed in is an office environment. It has a corridor, several rooms along the corridor, and a few wireless routers placed in different office areas. Then by going around various parts of the office and capturing and measuring the signals at the different locations, these measurements will then be stored as fingerprints mapped to the position at where they were taken.

In the online stage, a location fingerprinting-based positioning algorithm uses the currently observed signal measurements and the previously collected fingerprints to estimate the device's location. One standard signal measurement used for fingerprinting is RSS, but other measurements can be used as well. With scene analysis, it is possible to perform wireless positioning even in environments where the signal conditions are bad, and another positioning technique could lead to inaccurate results. This property makes scene analysis suitable for indoor wireless positioning, where the signal is characterized with high attenuation, path loss, shadow fading, and interference. On the other hand, since fingerprints are not updated in real-time, a change in the environment, e.g., passing people or refurnishing, could change the signal measurements for a location and thus could end with inaccurate results.

Proximity

With proximity, instead of finding the exact location of a device, it can be settled by finding the closest BS and using its position as an approximation (del Peral-Rosado, 2017). See Figure 3 for an illustration of how proximity works. In some use cases, the exact location is not needed. The goal is satisfied if the area in which a device is located can be pinpointed. Proximity is relatively simple to implement and can be the right choice when exact positioning is not required. The technique is already well established in cellular systems, where the Cell Identification (Cell-ID) or Cell Of Origin (COO) method is used. This method uses proximity by determining which cell site the device is connected to at a given time. Additional signal measurement calculations are not required for this use case since the target device will automatically be connected to the cell with the best signal strength. However, if proximity is used outside the cellular system, optional ways of determining the closest BS are using RSS, ToA, or TDoA to determine the distance to every BS and then pick the closest one. But, there could arise situations where the UP is approximated to another BS, for example, if some large obstacle blocks off the signal from a closer BS.

Figure 3. Proximity visualized. The user equipment finds the closest base station and approximates its location to that of the base stations.

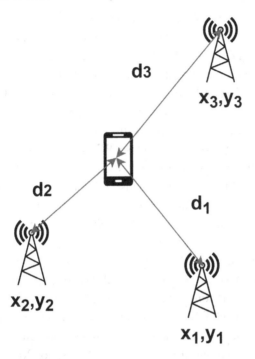

POSITIONING SYSTEMS

Today, connected devices use many different technologies to give them their desired functionality. Some examples are cellular 4G/5G that allows us to browse the internet, send text messages and make phone calls. Other examples are WLANs that make it possible to connect to private networks, or Bluetooth, that can connect to other local devices, e.g., headphones and speakers. Everyone does not know that many of these technologies are also used for wireless positioning purposes, much like the more obvious system GPS.

There exist quite a few positioning systems in a single device. The scale of the systems ranges anywhere from large GPS to smaller local systems used in homes (WLAN), all to provide positioning services wherever the user is. In the following section, the authors will summarize the standard systems used for these purposes and which techniques mentioned in the previous section each of them uses.

Wireless Local Area Network

Wireless local area network (WLAN) is the standard IEEE 802.11 WLANs. This collective standard operates in various bands depending on the type: the 2.4-GHz (IEEE 802.11b/g/n) and 5-GHz (IEEE 802.11ac/ax). These bands that the standards operate at are unlicensed, meaning that different WLANs will interfere with each other to some extent (Khalajmehrabadi, 2017). The availability of WLAN is widespread, and it is supported by almost all mobile phones. RSS fingerprinting is common when it comes to positioning schemes within WLAN.

Three approaches are available to use WLAN for positioning: Trilateration, geometric, and fingerprint matching (del Peral-Rosado, 2017). All of these approaches use RSS in some way, but the latter two also rely on fingerprinting. See Table 1 for some of the traits of WLAN. Fingerprint matching, or Wi-Fi fingerprint matching, stores RSS fingerprints as raw data in a database. Advanced pattern recognition algorithms then use the fingerprints to derive a UE's location based on the given raw RSS fingerprint value (del Peral-Rosado, 2017).

The geometric approach uses pre-recorded RSS fingerprint values for each base station, where each pre-recorded value represents a distance. When a base station gets an RSS value from a UE, it can estimate its location by looking at pre-recorded values. The closer a measured value is to a pre-recorded value, the distance will be roughly that of the pre-recorded value (del Peral-Rosado, 2017).

Trilateration is also a viable method for WLANs to locate UE. Trilateration has been used in combination with RSS in, for example, the RADAR system. The RADAR system uses signal propagation modeling and empirical RSS measurements to derive a UE's location; this is then compared to fingerprint matching performance (del Peral-Rosado, 2017).

Table 1. The traits of the different systems. Table values are taken from (Decawave, 2019). The ranges are only theoretical. In practice, these are lower due to various factors like obstacles or signal interference, for example.

System	Accuracy	Range	Used	Availability
Bluetooth	1-5m	Theoretically 100m	Usually indoors	Deployed on a major scale
GPS	5-20m	N/A	Outdoors	Deployed on a major scale
UWB	Centimeter	Theoretically 250m	N/A	N/A
WLAN	5-15	Theoretically 150m	Indoors	Deployed on a major scale

Bluetooth

Bluetooth, and Bluetooth Low Energy, is a common positioning system due to its presence in many hardware kinds. Operating at the same 2.4GHz frequency spectrum as WLAN (Liu, 2007), its difference is in the range and throughput, which is substantially lower. Combined with using the basic technique RSS mentioned in Section 2.1.2, Bluetooth may seem non-competitive compared to other systems. However, its strong point is the commonality out in society, and with the use of RSS, locating other nearby devices makes it useful for proximity tracking (Liu, 2007). See Table 1 for some of the traits of Bluetooth.

Global Positioning System

The GPS is a satellite-based navigation system that is available globally. It is considered the primary technology for positioning due to its global coverage and high accuracy (del Peral-Rosado, 2017). However, for environments where satellite signals lack accessibility, i.e., urban and indoor environments, cellular-based positioning is a complementary solution (del Peral-Rosado, 2017). The system itself contains a few different segments—the space segment, which is the satellites, the control segment, and the user segment.

The space segment consists of 24 active satellites and a few more inactive backups. The 24 satellites are located around the earth in four groups, where the four satellites occupy one of the six orbital planes (Khalel, 2010). With this configuration, a user device can, at any time, detect between four to eleven GPS satellites. Within an interval, the GPS satellites transmit a signal containing the current time and data about its position (Khalel, 2010). Using the TDoA-method (see Section 2.1.3), it is possible to determine the distance between the user device and the signal.

To control that the GPS satellites transmit the correct information, the control segment will monitor all satellites and their transmissions and, if needed, inform satellites to make time or position-information changes (Khalel, 2010). To have high accuracy in the system, the timing of all components is crucial. For this reason, the GPS satellites are equipped with atomic clocks that will be controlled by the control segment (Khalel, 2010).

The last part of the system is on the user side. Every device that wants to use GPS needs to have a GPS receiver. With the receiver, the device obtains the information sent by the satellites and can retrieve information about the place and time the signal was sent (Khalel, 2010). By measuring the TDoA, the device can calculate each satellite's distance. When the device has obtained the distance to at least four different GPS satellites, it can then use trilateration to estimate its position in 3D space (Khalel, 2010). See Table 1 for some of the traits of GPS.

GPS is well-established and widely used in many different devices. However, it works best when the satellites have LOS to the target device; thus, the accuracy decreases in indoor environments (Liu, 2007). To potentially overcome this limitation of GPS, a technology called wireless assisted GPS (A-GPS) has been developed. In A-GPS, the cellular network facilitates the search for GPS satellites by providing information on their location and shortening down the initial steps of finding the four required GPS satellites (Liu, 2007). A task that otherwise would be time-consuming.

Ultra Wideband

UWB is a technology that has been around for quite some time, primarily for radar, but has, in recent years, gained more interest in common areas due to its robust characteristics. UWB uses different techniques depending on the variation of location type used, i.e., 2-D or 3-D location (Liu, 2007). The basics of UWB is that it is a pulse pattern radio-based technology that sends ultrashort variable energy pulses in a broad frequency spectrum compared to other wireless technologies. Operating at 500 MHz for a single channel, UWB uses frequencies ranging from 3.1 to 10.6 GHz on the spectrum to transmit data (Liu, 2007). As a result of this, UWB operates within the same frequency spectrum as WLAN and microwaves, which may seem problematic. However, due to the nature of UWB using ultrashort pulses when transmitting, the wide channel bandwidth combined with the low power usage yields no interference with other kinds of signals. See Table 1 for some of the traits of UWB.

Furthermore, the signals are not easily affected by obstacles such as walls (Liu, 2007). This makes UWB ideal in urban places where many different signals operate at different frequencies that can interfere with one another and pass through buildings. UWB can be used as a positioning system because of the time-based method ToA described in Section 2.1.3. Depending on how an object should be positioned in space, i.e., 2-D or 3-D positioning, different methods that originate from ToA can be used (Liu, 2007). For 3-D positioning, the TDoA variant is most commonly used. Combining both TDoA and AoA, the number of sensors required is less than when only using TDoA—thus reducing the amount of hardware needed for implementing UWB for 3-D positioning (Liu, 2007).

Cellular

Almost every decade for the last 50 years, a new generation of cellular radio has been presented, resulting in five generations of cellular networks. The different generations' primary purpose has mainly been communication, but positioning with cellular networks has been around since the first generation (1G). By using the difference of arrival time, signal strength, and time delay, vehicles could be positioned already with 1G. Today solutions like TruePosition, Qualcomm-AFLT, and RFPM-Polaris Wireless all support localization with 2G, 3G, and 4G/LTE (del Peral-Rosado, 2017). The accuracy for the different positioning schemes can be seen in Table 2.

Trueposition has two approaches. First is an approach that utilizes Uplink-TDOA (U-TDOA) to derive a location from the time it takes for a signal to go from a UE to location measuring units. The sent signal emulates a voice call similar to an emergency 911 call. The second approach is a combination of their U-TDOA and A-GPS, where the location that is returned is the one with the highest accuracy (del Peral-Rosado, 2017).

Qualcomm Scheme Advanced Forward Link Trilateration (AFLT) utilizes distances from several cell towers. Qualcomm also has a hybrid approach that, similarly to Trueposition, uses A-GPS. Their A-GPS/AFLT location exploits the GPS satellite's constellation and the terrestrial wireless network (del Peral-Rosado, 2017).

The Technology Radio Frequency Pattern Matching (RFPM) by Polaris Wireless, compares mobile measurements (time delays, RSS, signal-to-interference ratios) against a geo-referenced database for the active operator's radio environment (del Peral-Rosado, 2017).

Table 2. Accuracy of the different cellular positioning methods. The accuracy below is with 67% positioning error, which means that in 67% of the cases, the positioning methods will result in X meters or less than X meters accuracy (del Peral-Rosado, 2017).

Company	Technique	Indoor	Accuracy	Networks
Trueposition	U-TDOA	False	Dense urban: — Urban 57.1 m Suburban: 28.4 m Rural: —	2G, 3G, 4G/LTE
Trueposition	U-TDOA/A-GPS	False	Dense urban: — Urban: 48.8 m Suburban: 20.5 m Rural: —	2G, 3G, 4G/LTE
Polaris wireless	RFPM	False	Dense urban: 116.7 m Urban: 198.4 m Suburban: 232.2 m Rural: 575.7 m	2G, 3G, 4G/LTE
Qualcomm	A-GPS/AFLT	True	Dense urban: 155.8m Urban: 226.8 m Suburban: 75.1 m Rural: 48.5 m	2G, 3G, 4G/LTE

5G Used as a Positioning System

Compared to other communication systems, 5G networks will supposedly be more energy-efficient, have better latencies, bigger capacity, support more connected devices, and improve positioning accuracy. This will be achieved using flexible radio access solutions and advanced antenna technologies (Koivisto, 2017). To fulfill these traits of 5G, it is expected that network density will play a significant role. Ultra-dense networks could contain base stations placed in lamp posts or having several of them placed in rooms indoors. This would result in the distance between the base stations going from a few meters to a few tens of meters. Combined with the base station's technical specifications, like potential use of higher frequency bands and antenna arrays supporting Multiple-Input Multiple-Output (MIMO) techniques, it will lead to accurate time of arrival estimates. Base stations equipped with multi-antennas would make it possible for transceivers to perform the difference of arrival of the LOS-path from the up-link reference signals. Whether conformal or planar arrays are used, cylindrical or circular antenna arrays could be used to estimate the azimuth arrival angles and elevation. This, in turn, could result in the possibility to enable 3D positioning (Koivisto, 2017).

With the expectation that 5G will operate at relatively short radio frames, frequent location information about a transmitting UE will be possible. With Ultra-dense networks, using the network's denseness to figure out which base stations are in LOS to the UE can be vital because it can estimate clock-offsets and directional parameters of the LOS path. This improves the accuracy of positioning UE (Koivisto, 2017).

With the specifications mentioned above, 5G can track UE's locations continuously. By adding different algorithms, the movement of UE can be stored and predicted. This is also in interest for 5G since this would allow for improvements in 5G when it comes to the high density of UEs and provides high throughput for UEs in movement. This could be achieved using sophisticated spatial interference mitigation and geometric beamforming (Koivisto, 2017).

ARCHITECTURES USED IN POSITIONING APPLICATIONS

With these different kinds of positioning techniques and the various technologies that utilize them, there are numerous use cases that they can be used for. One use case that lies in our time of 2020 and 2021 is the tracking of COVID-19 (Ahmed, 2020). Applications can use the techniques and systems mentioned in Sections 2 and 3, respectively, and track the virus's spread. These kinds of applications are at their core the same due to them using some of the mentioned systems. The difference is how they are used and how the applications handle the users' data.

Moreover, due to user information being collected and used in these applications, several privacy and security concerns emerge. These two aspects are essential to understand since they will know information about the user, albeit unidentifiable or encrypted when using these kinds of applications. However, suppose they are compromised or built in a bad way. In that case, the user's private information and location history (where the user has been geographical) can be leaked to the public or used by a malicious user. This is why it is essential to understand the differences between architectures and how they handle users' private information between the user and the systems' servers.

The authors refer the reader to Ahmed *et al.'s* paper (Ahmed, 2020) for extended coverage of how these kinds of applications handle these factors, summarized in this section.

Functionality and Concerns

There needs to be an underlying system architecture that binds together the functionality of the application and the positioning systems to implement tracking applications. The most commonly used types are centralized architecture, decentralized architecture, or hybrid architecture. From a user interface experience, all three of them are more or less the same. The difference lies in how they communicate with the server and other devices and how the data flow between them.

Centralized Architecture

Having a centralized server means that the server handles most of the tasks from data management to the registration phase between a user device and the server. In short, how an application based on this architecture could work is that the server creates encrypted identifiers for each device and then sends them to the respective device. When devices with this application installed are close to each other, they send their identification to other devices. Both the device proximity and the transfer of identification are done using Bluetooth. If an individual using this application is tested positive for COVID-19, that user can agree to let the application send all the users' encounter identifications to the server. The server can then calculate and map all the encounters using RSS and timestamps values in the encounter messages and Tx Power (the measured energy in the signal) to generate a proximity approximation. This is then sent out to individuals letting them know whether there has been a potential at-risk contact.

There are three types of phases from a data management perspective, where data is being collected and stored during the application's operation. Firstly, the registration phase, where the initial setup between a server and user device is performed. Secondly, the operation phase, which is the normal operating mode of the application. Lastly, the positive case identification phase in which data related to positive cases is being stored. What should be noted is that all three of these phases relate to all three architectures. Now with the way that centralized architectures work, the registration phase is all done by the server. Here, user data or Personally Identifiable Information (or PII, which is all the data related to the user) is being stored on the server-side, so nothing on the user device. However, when it comes to the normal operation phase, the server generates and stores all users' identifications while the user device stores its identification and encounters. Finally, when there is a potential at-risk case, the server stores all details of the positive cases and those who have been in close contact with reported cases.

The data itself can be classified into three categories seen from a privacy perspective. PII is the primary one, and another is contact advertisement messages, which are the different pseudonyms exchanged between devices when in proximity to each other. The last one is social/proximity graphs, which are data generated from the interactions with other users they come in contact with. As for the centralized architecture, the problem lies in the fact that all data is centralized. Meaning that if there is a security breach at the server, then user data can be accessed, resulting in user integrity being compromised. Therefore, it is crucial to have security mechanisms in place for authentication and access to the server.

Decentralized Architecture

A decentralized architecture places more emphasis on the user device when it comes to responsibility. By moving more tasks to the user device, privacy can be improved since no third party handles user information. The decentralized architecture's identifiers differ from the centralized in that it is randomly generated (called seeds). This seed is then used in conjunction with the current time to create so-called chirps that have a minimal lifespan. They are what is exchanged with other devices nearby. This seed generation is moved to the user device, as well as the mapping calculations. The only thing the server does is advertise individual seeds to other users. This is because when an individual is tested positive in the decentralized case and chooses to upload their seed, only theirs and no other encounters are uploaded to the server. The application downloads the newly added seeds from infected users and performs a reconstruction of the downloaded seeds using the chirps to perform proximity tracing. If there are matches, then based on RSS -and timestamp values collected via Bluetooth, the applications perform a risk analysis to determine whether the user has been close to an infected individual.

When it comes to the data management for the decentralized architecture, there are differences compared to the centralized. There is no registration phase, therefore limiting the amount of PII data. This is the primary reason decentralized privacy enhances privacy since the user device has more responsibility. During the operation phase, the user device stores and generates their seeds and chirps, with the chirps and RSS values from proximity encounters. The server has no role in this phase; it only stores the seeds in the third phase, i.e., the seeds from at-risk individuals. In this phase, the user devices' downloaded seeds from the server, and the generated chirps based on these seeds, are stored on the user device used for reconstruction.

Having this kind of architecture does have its challenges. Even though PII data is limited, access to the server can be done by anyone since there is no registration phase between the server and user device. Although seeds can be downloaded from the server, the chirps are still needed to perform the reconstruction. However, network traffic sniffing attacks can result in unauthorized access of necessary data to reconstruct or even to only identify users who have been tested positive for COVID-19.

Hybrid Architecture

As for the hybrid system architecture, functionality from both centralized and decentralized is combined. The server's responsibility is to compute the risk assessment and send these out to individuals. The generation of the identifiers remains on the user devices for privacy reasons. Since both the server and user devices play an essential role in the hybrid case, the challenge is to keep the registration and operation phases as secure as possible while still not storing any PII data. Cryptography -and privacy enhancement methods are adopted in the hybrid architecture regarding how the data flows between devices to mitigate potential replay attacks. In the registration phase, unique device identifications are generated and stored on the device using cryptographic methods and sent to the server. Similar kinds of chirps as the decentralized architecture are generated and encrypted on the device during the operation phase. These chirps are then shared via Bluetooth. When a device receives this, it creates two Private Encounter Tokens (PETs) stored locally along with the received RSS values. As for the case of a user being positive, the user's PET is uploaded and stored on the server, which then performs the risk assessment.

DISCUSSION

Up until now, a few techniques and applications that are present and deployed out in society today have been summarized. However, how they stand against each other when it comes to real-life implementation is an important aspect. Furthermore, there are still advances to be made using the mentioned emerging technologies 5G and UWB and how they can be used for other application use cases. Based on the author's understanding, they will now further explore these areas.

The Future of Wireless Positioning

5G is the new hot topic for the future of cellular, but it is still not deployed on a significant scale, meaning that the general public is still in need of using 4G and LTE. Manufacturers of various electronics are starting to get their eyes on UWB thanks to its powerful traits. However, looking briefly at the big smartphone manufacturers, only four high-end smartphones and one smartwatch have a UWB chip as of writing, meaning that there will not be any applications that will utilize them in the near future. Nevertheless, if it is imagined that they were deployed today, there are many ways that UWB and 5G could improve today's contact tracing and positioning tracking.

In (Zhang, 2019), Zhang *et al.* have created a system where Bluetooth and UWB could work together to improve fingerprinting capabilities for improved indoor localization. Although Zhang *et al.* have created a whole system with separate Bluetooth and UWB scanners and beacons (Zhang, 2019), by utilizing their respective strengths in the form of sensor fusion and only using the chips in the devices, the implementation would become easier to do but also more cost-efficient. This could then affect making UWB more commercially available and, therefore, more attractive for applications to implement support for it. Because this is the main problem today, that it is such a new technology for commercial products, which leads to it being expensive and only present in five high-end devices mentioned earlier.

Another use case could be to combine 5G and UWB to get better positioning accuracy. In (Adebomehin, 2016), Adebomehin *et al.* talk about how UWB could be used together with 5G to mitigate the NLOS and LOS problem. As discussed previously, cellular is not suited for indoor positioning, and although 5G will be better at this than its predecessors, it will not be perfect. Furthermore, since UWB is not susceptible to interference for many kinds of obstacle materials, it is ideal in multipath scenarios like in urban locations. By varying the pulses' energy output, ranges of up to 200 meters are achievable in theory, making it suitable for enhancing 5Gs positioning possibilities.

More Use Cases for Wireless Positioning

With all the mentioned systems, there are many more types of applications that these systems can be used for. One area of use where improved wireless positioning is applicable is for self-driving vehicles. When the new 5G network is deployed in urban areas, access to more BSs will make it possible to achieve very high accuracy for positioning, using any of the previously mentioned methods. A big part of an actual self-driving car is, of course, that it will be aware of its position. Apart from this prominent area where improved positioning helps, several other aspects also exist related to traffic.

One example could be distance estimation from a car to a pedestrian where the pedestrians UE could communicate its position to vehicles and infrastructure. This could make it possible for vehicles to avoid potential collisions or for a crossing point to notice when a pedestrian wants to cross the road automatically. Features like this could be extra helpful for people with disabilities like blindness or impairment of hearing. However, to make this viable, sub-meter positioning would be required, and the positioning for the UE needs to be very reliable. Otherwise, there could be a possibility of a vehicle avoiding a non-existing pedestrian. With 5G and UWB, this could be possible. Although more complicated situations like vehicles avoiding pedestrians, they probably need to rely on more than just the estimated position to be safe.

Another example could be determining the positions of other vehicles in the area. Using UWBs potential extensive area coverage, it could be used with a vehicle-to-vehicle (V2V) protocol to communicate with other vehicles. Furthermore, with UWB's high throughput, many kinds of data can be shared between the vehicles in real-time, making it reliable in crucial situations. Another possible use-case for positioning could be in large companies or factories. By continuously tracking their employees and devices, a company can store information on where everything moves. This data can then be used to change how devices move and adjust the layout if necessary to avoid chokepoints and make production run more efficiently. However, using methods like this to track and examine every employee's move would probably open up a discussion on usefulness versus privacy.

Apart from the traffic-related use cases, further exploration within the theme of Section 4 will most definitely happen in the future. The use case described in that section, COVID-19, is only one use case for such a tracking application, and the described system architectures are common within all kinds of systems found in many areas. Although the specific use case described in that section is for tracking purposes, the core functionality in the centralized, decentralized, and hybrid architectures are the same. Payment systems, voting systems, data servers, to mention a few, are all at their core, most likely one of the three systems. V2V protocols mentioned earlier are, for example, a distributed system. It is how they are adapted for a specific purpose they differ from each other.

Since COVID-19 has impacted the world's society in such a profound way, the post-COVID-19 era will probably never be the same. However, that does not necessarily have to be a bad thing. The concept of tracking the spread of a disease such as COVID-19 using modern all-day technology like smartphones has never been done in public before. Nevertheless, with emerging technologies like 5G and many different kinds of IoT devices, COVID-19 has sparked many new potential use cases. In Siriwardhana *et al.'s* paper (Siriwardhana, 2020), the authors discuss many different areas that can benefit from these new technologies and system architectures.

Although no one wants a new pandemic, contact tracing, and applications where users opt-in to say if they are sick can help in even the mildest of sicknesses like a cold. To check in on people who need to self-isolate, Unmanned Aerial Vehicles (UAV) can monitor their conditions at a long and safe distance thanks to 5G connectivity.

Another benefit of using 5G for connecting BLE and IoT devices used for contact tracing (or any other kind of service that requires network connectivity) is massive Machine Type Communications (mMTC) services. This can be used to enhance the architectures mentioned in section 4, where a Multi-access Edge Computing / Mobile Edge Computing (MEC) server can be deployed directly at the BS. This means that the data can be handled and processed locally and then forwarded to dedicated cloud servers. Compared to, for example, a centralized server, where instead of the data being relayed through many gateways or servers and then finally to the government. Having a dedicated server used for contact tracing purposes directly at the BS adds privacy and security since it is integrated with its connection. This is important since mMTC and MEC are prominent network technologies and servers to be used to create smart cities around the world for 5G-connected IoT devices.

Lastly, following this book's theme, Decision Support System (DSS) can benefit significantly from improved wireless positioning. The agriculture sector is an area that has adopted DSS for improved precision when it comes to crop production. Having improved positioning capabilities, the deliverance of water or pesticides to exact locations will reduce waste since it will only use the amount needed at the area that needs it. This, in turn, leads to farmers being able to produce the same or even more amount of crops but using less water and pesticides.

CONCLUSION

This chapter surveys different kinds of positioning systems used for indoor and outdoor localization using numerous techniques. A summary of the most used techniques (i.e., trilateration, triangulation, scene analysis, and proximity) and systems (i.e., WLAN, Bluetooth, GPS) that exist today are provided, along with an insight into how they can be used in actual applications. For instance, it can help the fight against COVID-19 by providing individuals with the ability to track where positive cases have been and see if there is an at-risk for other users. The authors also discussed why 5G and UWB systems are the future of positioning and contact tracing, what they can potentially bring to the table, and possible future application use cases like self-driving cars, pedestrian safety, and the agriculture sector using DSS.

FUTURE RESEARCH DIRECTIONS

Considering what the future might hold, from what the authors discussed in Section 5, 5G and UWB will bring significant improvements to the area of wireless positioning. Their powerful traits will open up many more potential use cases in the future than the ones mentioned in this chapter. As they become more available to the general public, more discussions and topics related to them will emerge, which will help spark ideas for even more potential use cases. In time, both systems will function as a crucial part of connecting many different kinds of devices, including IoT. With this said, the authors hope that they have successfully provided an introduction to the area of wireless positioning and how it works.

REFERENCES

Adebomehin, A. A., & Walker, S. D. (2016). Enhanced ultrawideband methods for 5g los sufficient positioning and mitigation. *2016 IEEE 17th International Symposium on A World of Wireless, Mobile and Multimedia Networks (WoWMoM)*, 1–4.

Ahmed, N., Michelin, R. A., Xue, W., Ruj, S., Malaney, R., Kanhere, S. S., Seneviratne, A., Hu, W., Janicke, H., & Jha, S. K. (2020). A survey of covid-19 contact tracing apps. *IEEE Access: Practical Innovations, Open Solutions*, 8, 134577–134601. doi:10.1109/ACCESS.2020.3010226

De Los Santos, H., Sturm, C., & Pontes, P. (2015). Introduction to Radio Systems. Springer. doi:10.1007/978-3-319-07326-2_1

Decawave. (2019). *Our Technology*. https://www.decawave.com/technology1/

del Peral-Rosado, A. J., Raulefs, R., Lopez-Salcedo, J., & Seco-Granados, G. (2017). Survey of cellular mobile radio localization methods: From 1g to 5g. IEEE Communications Surveys & Tutorials, 20(2), 1124–1148.

Khalajmehrabadi, A., Gatsis, N., & Akopian, D. (2017). Modern wlan fingerprinting indoor positioning methods and deployment challenges. *IEEE Communications Surveys and Tutorials*, 19(3), 1974–2002. doi:10.1109/COMST.2017.2671454

Khalel, M. H. A. (2010). Position location techniques in wireless communication systems. Blekinge Institute of Technology Karlskrona, Sweden.

Koivisto, M., Hakkarainen, A., Costa, M., Kela, P., Leppanen, K., & Valkama, M. (2017). High-efficiency device positioning and location-aware communications in dense 5g networks. *IEEE Communications Magazine, 55*(8), 188–195. doi:10.1109/MCOM.2017.1600655

Liu, H., Darabi, H., Banerjee, P., & Liu, J. (2007). Survey of wireless indoor positioning techniques and systems. *IEEE Transactions on Systems, Man and Cybernetics. Part C, Applications and Reviews, 37*(6), 1067–1080. doi:10.1109/TSMCC.2007.905750

Munoz, D., Bouchereau Lara, F., Vargas, C., & Enriquez-Caldera, R. (2009). *Position location techniques and applications.* Academic Press.

Porretta, M., Nepa, P., Manara, G., & Giannetti, F. (2008). Location, location, location. *IEEE Vehicular Technology Magazine, 3*(2), 20–29. doi:10.1109/MVT.2008.923969

Siriwardhana, Y., De Alwis, C., Gür, G., Ylianttila, M., & Liyanage, M. (2020). The Fight Against the COVID-19 Pandemic With 5G Technologies. *IEEE Engineering Management Review, 48*(3), 72–84. doi:10.1109/EMR.2020.3017451

Zhang, Q., D'souza, M., Balogh, U., & Smallbon, V. (2019). Efficient ble fingerprinting through uwb sensors for indoor localization. *2019 IEEE SmartWorld/SCALCOM/UIC/ATC/CBDCom/IOP/SCI Conference*, 140–143. 10.1109/SmartWorld-UIC-ATC-SCALCOM-IOP-SCI.2019.00065

ADDITIONAL READING

Bruno, L., & Robertson, P. (2011). WiSLAM: Improving FootSLAM with Wi-Fi. *Proc. Int'l. Conf. In indoor Positioning and Indoor Navigation (IPIN)*, pp. 1–10.

Kanaan, M., & Pahlavan, K. (2004). A comparison of wireless geolocation algorithms in the indoor environment. *Proc. In IEEE Wireless Commun. Netw. Conf.*, vol. 1, pp. 177–182. 10.1109/WCNC.2004.1311539

Kela, P., Costa, M., Turkka, J., Koivisto, M., Werner, J., Hakkarainen, A., Valkama, M., Jantti, R., & Leppanen, K. (2016). *Location Based Beamforming in 5G UltraDense Networks.* Proc. In IEEE 84th Vehicular Technology Conference (VTC2016-Fall), Montréal, Canada.

Kela, P., Turkka, J., & Costa, M. (2015). Borderless Mobility in 5G Outdoor Ultra-Dense Networks. In IEEE Access, vol. 3. doi:10.1109/ACCESS.2015.2470532

Koivisto, M., Costa, M., Werner, J., Heiska, K., Talvitie, J., Leppänen, K., Koivunen, V., & Valkama, M. (2017). Joint Device Positioning and Clock Synchronization in 5G Ultra-Dense Networks. *IEEE Transactions on Wireless Communications*, *16*(5), 2866–2881. doi:10.1109/TWC.2017.2669963

Li, G., Geng, E., Ye, Z., Xu, Y., Lin, J., & Pang, Y. (2018). Indoor positioning algorithm based on the improved RSSI distance model. In Sensors, vol. 18, no. 9, p. 2820. doi:10.339018092820

Sand, S., Dammann, A., & Mensing, C. (2014). *Positioning in Wireless Communication Systems* (1st ed.). John Wiley & Sons Ltd. doi:10.1002/9781118694114

KEY TERMS AND DEFINITIONS

Azimuth Angle: The azimuth angle is the compass direction from which the sunlight is coming.

Multipath Propagation: When a signal is propagated from a sender, it will be transmitted in many directions. The signals will then travel in separate ways, bounce on objects, and spread. The signals that reach the same receiver can have taken different routes but still ended up at the same end destination. This is called multipath. The problem with this is that if two signals are sent simultaneously from the sender and take different routes and end up at the same receiver, they will probably reach the destination at different times. This can make it hard to interpret the signal sent from the beginning.

LOS/NLOS: Line Of Sight (LOS) vs. Non-Line Of Sight (NLOS) explain whether the sender of a signal and the receiver of a signal have an unobstructed vision of another. For wireless signals, having a line of sight between the sender and the receiver will, for the most part, lead to the best performance.

Path Loss: Another term for signal attenuation. See its definition.

Shadow Fading: The fluctuation of the signal envelope due to large objects obstructing the propagation paths between the transmitter and the receiver.

Signal Attenuation: Signal attenuation means that the signal strength will become weaker the further the signal travels. The degree of attenuation depends on the frequency and the surrounding environment of the signal. However, attenuation will occur. For situations where the signal has a line of sight, the attenuation is more predictable.

Signal Propagation: This is the movement of radio waves from a transmitter to a receiver. When the waves travel (propagate) from one point to another, they are, like light waves, affected by different phenomena such as light reflection, absorption, or scattering.

Section 2
Decision Support Systems and Industrial IoT in Smart Grid, Factories, and Cities

Chapter 4
Cloud–Based Big Data Analysis Tools and Techniques Towards Sustainable Smart City Services

Suresh P.

iD https://orcid.org/0000-0001-9815-2982

Kongu Engineering College, India

Keerthika P.

Kongu Engineering College, India

Sathiyamoorthi V.

iD https://orcid.org/0000-0002-7012-3941

Sona College of Technology, India

Logeswaran K.

iD https://orcid.org/0000-0001-8161-7376

Kongu Engineering College, India

Manjula Devi R.

Kongu Engineering College, India

Sentamilselvan K.

iD https://orcid.org/0000-0002-2486-5127

Kongu Engineering College, India

Sangeetha M.

Kongu Engineering College, India

Sagana C.

Kongu Engineering College, India

ABSTRACT

Cloud computing and big data analytics are the key parts of smart city development that can create reliable, secure, healthier, more informed communities while producing tremendous data to the public and private sectors. Since the various sectors of smart cities generate enormous amounts of streaming data from sensors and other devices, storing and analyzing this huge real-time data typically entail significant computing capacity. Most smart city solutions use a combination of core technologies such as

DOI: 10.4018/978-1-7998-7468-3.ch004

computing, storage, databases, data warehouses, and advanced technologies such as analytics on big data, real-time streaming data, artificial intelligence, machine learning, and the internet of things (IoT). This chapter presents a theoretical and experimental perspective on the smart city services such as smart healthcare, water management, education, transportation and traffic management, and smart grid that are offered using big data management and cloud-based analytics services.

INTRODUCTION

Information and Communications Technologies (ICT) are successfully used in smart cities for data communication to increase the quality and efficiency of civil services, reduce resource usage, and include interactive apps and active services with citizens. ICT applications and the widespread use of digital objects such as sensors, actuators, and mobile phones are primarily useful in achieving smart city growth (Yin et al., 2015). Data collection and storage, information processing, networking, and security decision making are all contributing to the infiltration of urban life. Digital infrastructure is primarily needed in smart cities for water and waste management, smart health care, smart governance, power management, transportation and traffic management (Arasteh et al., 2016).

Cloud and big data technologies are shaping the evolving business computing landscape, which holds a lot of promise for a new era of collective applications. Many companies can benefit from the integration of Big Data analytical capabilities with cloud services because it will save them money and time while also simplifying valuable insights that will provide them with a variety of competitive advantages (Wieclaw et al., 2017). Big Data with cloud as a service can ease the implementation of sophisticated analytic features over the bigger and heterogeneous data sources that business organizations need to handle and get benefit of the useful insights derived from it (Quwaider, Al-Alyyoub, & Jararweh, 2016). Data Analytics as a Service (DAaaS) is an advanced platform that provides cloud-based analytical capabilities over a variety of use cases and industries (Güemes, Janeczko, Caminel, & Roberts, 2013). From a practical standpoint, this approach encompasses an analytical solution's end-to-end features, such as data collection, data visualization, reporting, and user interaction. It also extends to innovative concepts, like Analytical Apps and Analytical Appstore (A. M. S. J. F. G. C. S. Osman, 2019).

Nowadays, a vast amount of data is generated and stored in smart city data repositories in both structured and unstructured formats. The collected data have the possibility to be shared and openly accessible by the potential clients in either private or public sector. Fog-to Cloud computing (F2C) is the recent technology for data management for smart city that combines the benefits of centralized and distributed data management. Hierarchical distributed data management also can be used as it has various advantages such as reduced communication latencies for real-time or essential services, reduced network data traffic, and the application of various policies (Sinaeepourfard, Krogstie, & Petersen, 2018).

Generally, smart cities are enabled with IoT infrastructure that often produces a huge volume of data which is called as big data (Tragos et al., 2014). Valuable insights and correlations can be retrieved by using big data tools and techniques on this massive amount of data. Despite the fact that big data analytics is one of the primary enabling technologies for smart cities, it is complicated by a number of issues, including the need for cross-thematic applications (e.g., electricity, transportation, water, and urban), multiple data sources offering various types of data and data reliability. Cloud based big data analytics (BDA) tools and technologies can provide solutions to facilitate storing, manipulating, and analyzing the data for information and knowledge extraction with Artificial Intelligence (AI) techniques (Mohammadi & Al-Fuqaha, 2018).

Figure 1. Smart city services with cloud based big data technology

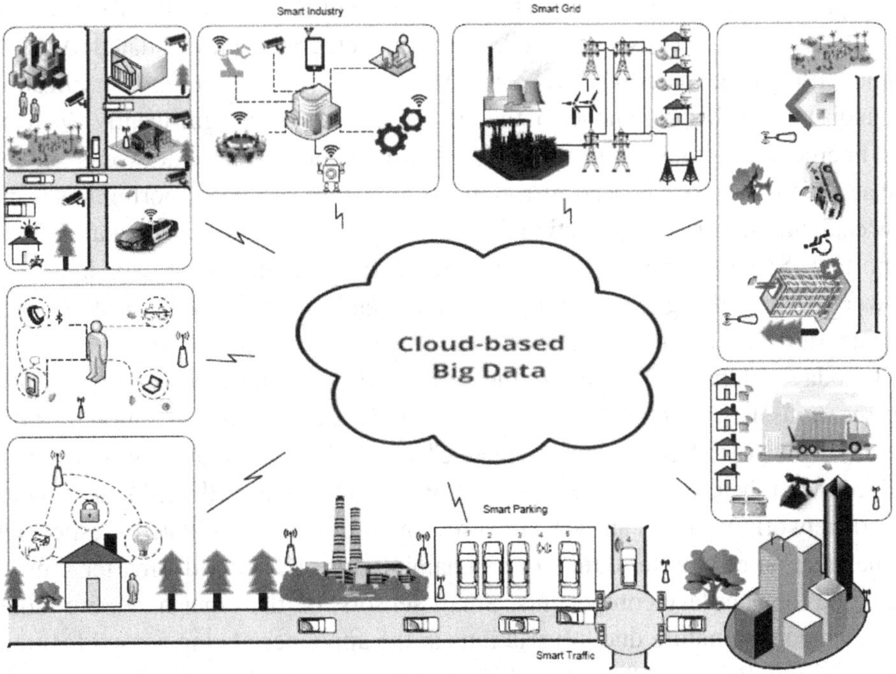

Figure 1 depicts the landscape of a sample smart city with cloud based big data technologies. With the help of the two emerging technologies like big data and cloud computing, many smart applications like smart home, smart waste management, smart parking and smart grid can be implemented. This book chapter presents some exciting new perspectives on using cloud computing services for large-scale smart city data analytics. It provides a comprehensive overview of the various cloud-based big data analytics services available for sustainable smart cities in fields such as smart healthcare, smart water management, smart education, smart transportation, and smart power grid. The next section provides comprehensive review about recent technologies for sustainable smart city development.

RECENT TECHNOLOGIES FOR SMART CITY DEVELOPMENT

Smart City (SC) is a new idea aimed at addressing the issues that have arisen as a result of rapid urbanization. To address these issues, government decision-makers fund SC initiatives that aim for long-term economic growth and improved quality of life for common people. ICT can be effectively utilized for smartening in urban development. Both city policy makers and residents will benefit from useful knowledge and information resources if spawned big data are integrated and evaluated (A. M. S. Osman, Elragal, & Bergvall-Kåreborn, 2017). With the growth of industrialization and industry 4.0, the prominence of the IoT and IIoT has risen significantly. With the vast interconnected devices of the IIoT, cyber protection of those networks and the privacy of their users has become a significant feature, as new opportunities bring new challenges. Intrusion detection for industrial networks like IIoT is particularly important. Since the research is moved from the cloud to the fog for industrial networks to provide agile response, data streaming is a viable choice, as it provides the benefit of fast intrusion detection (Sari, Lekidis, & Butun, 2020).

In today's global ICT scenario, the number of powerful devices such as smart phones, household appliances, sensors and RFID devices increase global traffic volume. Things as a Service or also called Cloud of Things is created by aggregating and abstracting heterogeneous resources according to customized thing-like semantics. Sensor networks will play an even larger role in future Internet initiatives, especially in the creation of smarter cities. In a dynamic future ICT world, smarter sensors would be the ancillary components. Smart sensors, on the other hand, are rather heterogeneous in nature due to variations in the appliances being sensed (Mitton, Papavassiliou, Puliafito, & Trivedi, 2012).

Big data analysis with cloud infrastructure paradigm for smart cities can utilize the MapReduce using Hadoop framework. Some case studies are done using real data from Montevideo, Uruguay's transportation system such as a QoS assessment using historical bus location data, and mobility estimation of passenger using ticket sales data from smartcards. The experimental results show that the model is capable of efficiently processing large amounts of data (Massobrio et al., 2018).

Smart city applications are vital for better urban governance as urban population continues to grow. These solutions are motivated by ICT technologies on the one hand, and on the other, by a desire to improve cities' ability and capacity to address environmental, economic growth, and development challenges. The challenge is to make it easier for the general public to obtain the right contextual knowledge in order to be more efficient, creative, and capable of making appropriate decisions, as well as environmental and economic sustainability. Hence cloud is used to store and process large amounts of data while also producing intelligent contextual information (Khan & Kiani, 2012).

In smart cities, cloud enabled car parking projects are implemented which follows the top down design pattern. It includes locator service, supervision service, information service, GIS/GPS services, license plate patrolling service, tracking service, etc. It enables anytime-anywhere-anyhow communication in smart cities (Ji, Ganchev, O'Droma, & Zhang, 2014). Big data will radically transform city populations at various levels. Furthermore, a potential big data business model for smart cities can be developed in order to address the business and technical research challenges (Hashem et al., 2016).

The widespread adoption of the IoT is facilitating smart city projects and initiatives across the globe. Electronic devices and protocols are being added to everyday objects in order to have the secured communication over the Internet. According to a new Gartner report, smart cities will have 50 billion linked items by 2020 (Hammi, Khatoun, Zeadally, Fayad, & Khoukhi, 2017). Wireless sensor networks have become increasingly important sources of massive quantities of data. The recent implementation of wireless sensor networks in Smart City infrastructures has resulted in massive amounts of data being produced every day across a wide range of domains, including environmental monitoring, healthcare monitoring, and transportation monitoring (Gaur, Scotney, Parr, & McClean, 2015). With the help of IoT and cloud, smart cities will be able to create innovative and improved facilities using vast volumes of data stored in the cloud and processing it (Formisano et al., 2015). As shown by the advent of global government clouds, cloud computing has become a strategic path for e-government initiatives (G-Cloud). Cloud computing has enough potential to develop smart city projects (Clohessy, Acton, & Morgan, 2014).

The term "smart city" is a relatively new idea in the world of urban planning. A smart city uses ICT to improve the efficiency of its urban areas and civilian population. One of the most important characteristics of a smart city is the ability to use data from its ICT infrastructure to enhance city services and features like connectivity and sustainability (Carter et al., 2020). Cyber-attacks have increased in smart cities in recent years, especially against infrastructure less networks like IoT. In most botnet attack variants, the tiniest micro devices at the network's lower spectrum are becoming valuable botnet participants, allowing more complex attacks against infrastructure networks to be carried out. As a result, the fog systems must be protected from cyber-attacks, with respect to both software and hardware alterations and manipulations (Butun, Sari, & Österberg, 2020).

Fog computing and IoT integration is effectively used to provide many opportunities for researchers, especially when developing cyber-security solutions for smart city projects. Despite the fact that this integration appears to be difficult and time-consuming, the advantages outweigh the risks (Butun, Sari, & Österberg, 2019). Interfacing smart cities with cyber-physical systems strengthens cyber infrastructures while also implementing security vulnerabilities that, if not handled properly, can lead to serious issues such as device failure, privacy violations, and/or data integrity issues (Butun & Österberg, 2019). Given the safety consequences of potential threats, detecting intrusions in IIoT systems is all the more relevant, given the growing threat surface of industrial networks as a result of distributed, IoT based system architectures. Data streaming can be used to benefit future industrial networks, especially their Intrusion Detection Systems (IDSs), by decoupling semantics from deployment (Butun, Almgren, Gulisano, & Papatriantafilou, 2020).

A smart city effectively employs information technology to incorporate and operate social, physical, and business infrastructures in order to deliver better services to residents while maximizing the use of available resources. In order to provide a safe communication channel, a security system can be used that combines blockchain technology with smart devices (Biswas & Muthukkumarasamy, 2016). Big data analytics holds a lot of promise for improving smart city services. Data processing has resulted in the accumulation of massive quantities of data that can be used in a variety of useful application domains as digitization has become an integral part of daily life. In several market and utility domains, including the smart city domain, effective analysis and use of big data is a major factor for success (Al Nuaimi, Al Neyadi, Mohamed, Al-Jaroodi, & Applications, 2015). Cloud computing will provide the support for the transformation of the volume, velocity, variety and veracity into values of big data that can be used for local to global digital earth science and applications (Yang, Huang, Li, Liu, & Hu, 2017). The next section describes the architectural design for smart city applications with cloud and big data technologies.

ARCHITECTURAL DESIGN FOR SMART CITY WITH CLOUD-BASED BIG DATA ANALYTICS

Figure 2 represents the data management infrastructure using cloud and big data computing in smart cities. The raw data is collected from various data sources of monitored area and stored in cloud environment. Then, the big data analytics tools and techniques are applied to extract valuable insights from large amount of data. For data analytics, various techniques such as statistical modelling, machine learning and tools such as RapidMiner and R combined with Hadoop MapReduce framework can be applied to generate knowledge (Susmitha, Jayaprada, & Technology, 2017).

Figure 2. Data management infrastructure with big data and cloud computing in smart cities

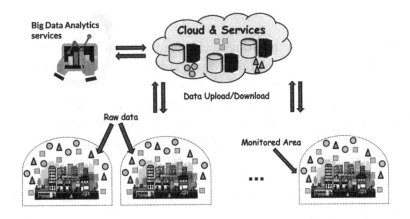

The most important objective is to develop a completely new holistic environment which supports the following:

- Collect and organize the data from multiple dispersed sources
- Manage and organize data streams
- Integrate heterogeneous data into coherent databases
- Implement preprocessing and transformation of data
- Manage extracted models and patterns
- Evaluate of the quality of the extracted models and patterns
- Visualize and explore behavioral patterns and models
- Perform simulation of the mined patterns and models
- Exploitation of the results for decision support and service provision

Figure 3. Proposed architectural design

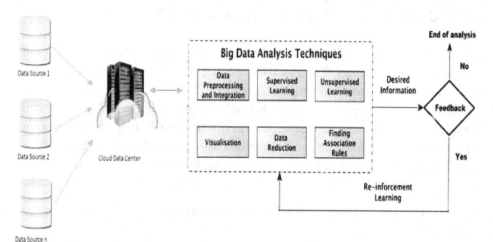

Figure 3 represents the proposed architectural design model for urban data management and services. Cloud data center collects big data from multiple data sources and store them with enough security measures. Figure 4 depicts the various data pre-processing techniques. Data preprocessing is a data mining technique that entails converting raw data into a usable format. Usually, data collected from real world is often incomplete, unreliable, and deficient in specific habits or patterns, as well as containing numerous errors. Preprocessing data is a tried and true way of addressing such problems. Since data is likely to be unreliable, inconsistent, and redundant, it cannot be used directly in the data mining process. The data preprocessing stage allows us to process data by adapting it to the needs of each data mining algorithm (Roy, Cruz, Sabourin, & Cavalcanti, 2018).

Big data refers to the scale, velocity, abundance, variability, sophistication, availability, changeability, and use of data in a variety of fields of activity that exceeds the computational and analytical capabilities of traditional software applications and traditional database infrastructure (Suma, Mehmood, & Albeshri, 2017). As a result, big data includes tools such as classification, clustering, and regression algorithms, as well as techniques such as data mining, deep learning, and predictive analysis, as well as technologies such as Hadoop, HBase, and MongoDB that work to extract useful information from massive amounts of data for timely and accurate decision making and practical insights.

BDA is the often dynamic method of analyzing big data to discover knowledge that can help companies make better business decisions, such as hidden patterns, correlations, industry dynamics and consumer preferences (Suciu et al., 2013). Data analytics tools and techniques on a wide scale offer a means of analyzing data sets and

Figure 4. Data preprocessing techniques

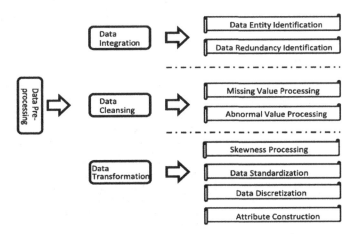

taking away fresh knowledge that can help companies make better business decisions. BDA requires cost-effective, innovative data processing, analysis, and data management for improved decision-making because of high-volume, high-variety, and high-velocity nature of big data (Strohbach, Ziekow, Gazis, & Akiva, 2015). Table 1 represents the various analytics techniques that can be applied on the big data. It covers the different techniques such as supervised learning, unsupervised learning, correlation and dimensionality reduction. Although in the sense of smart sustainable cities, there is no canonical or conclusive definition of big data, the term can be used to define a colossal amount of urban data usually to the degree that its handling, study, management and communication pose significant computational, analytical and logistical coordinating challenges. Smart cities data are invariably marked with spatial and temporal labels, streamed mainly from different types of sensors, and produced mostly automatically and routinely. In addition, big data solutions require advanced technology to skillfully process vast amounts of data from numerous sources, in unparalleled quantities and rapidly (Aljumah, Kaur, Bhatia, & Ahamed Ahanger, 2020).

Users of big data analytics are embracing Hadoop Data Lake which acts as the key storehouse for inward streams of raw data. Hadoop cluster or processing engine like Spark can be used to analyze the data. Streaming analytics is becoming more popular in big data as users seek real-time analytics on data fed into Hadoop systems through stream processing engines like Spark, Flink, and Storm. Big data systems were initially implemented on-premises, mostly in large organizations where vast volumes of data are collected, organized, and analyzed. However, cloud platform providers such as Amazon Web Services (AWS) and Microsoft Azure have made it much simpler. Cloudera-Hortonworks, for example, is a Hadoop supplier that supports the delivery of the big data platform on the AWS and Microsoft Azure

(Sinaeepourfard, Krogstie, Petersen, & Ahlers, 2019). The next section provides an implementation of smart healthcare using cloud enabled big data techniques.

Table 1. Data analytics techniques

Category	Algorithm	Description
Supervised Learning	Decision Tree	A decision tree is a graphical structure in which each internal node represents a "test" on an attribute, each branch represents the test's result, and each leaf node represents the class mark.
	Naïve Bayes	Nave Bayes algorithm is based on the Bayes theorem which is used to solve classification problems. It is simple and most powerful classification algorithms for developing fast machine learning models capable of making quick predictions.
	Support Vector Machine Classifier	It is a supervised learning algorithm used for both classification and regression problems. Face recognition, image classification, text categorization, and other tasks can be accomplished using the SVM algorithm.
	K- Nearest Neighbor	The k-nearest neighbours (KNN) algorithm is a straightforward supervised machine learning algorithm that can be used to solve classification and regression problems.
	Random Forest	It is an ensemble learning method for classification, regression, and other tasks that works by training a large number of decision trees and then outputting the class that is the mode of the classes.
Unsupervised Learning	K-means clustering	It is an iterative clustering algorithm which is used to find the highest value for iteration.
	Hierarchal clustering	Hierarchical clustering creates a network of clusters. It starts with all of the data, which is allocated to their own cluster. Two close clusters would be in the same cluster in this case. When there is only one cluster remaining, the algorithm terminates.
	Principal Component Analysis	It aids in minimizing the dimensionality of the dataset, which consists of several variables that are often associated with each other, either heavily or lightly, while maintaining the variance present in the dataset to the greatest extent possible.
Correlation	FP growth algorithm	FP growth algorithm is an improvement of Apriori algorithm. It is used for finding frequent itemset in a transaction database without candidate generation. It represents frequent items in frequent pattern trees or FP-tree.
	Apriori Algorithm	It is used for frequent itemset mining and association rule learning over relational databases.

SMART HEALTHCARE USING CLOUD BASED BIG DATA

Smart healthcare can be provided as a service using cloud, big data and IoT devices to the common people in the smart cities (Gill, Arya, Wander, & Buyya, 2018). It enables efficient management of data about the patients that are coming from IoT sensors. This data will be helpful to diagnosis the health status to identify the different diseases of the patients (Quwaider, Jararweh, & Theory, 2015).

Figure 5. Smart healthcare architecture with IoT enabled cloud based big data computing

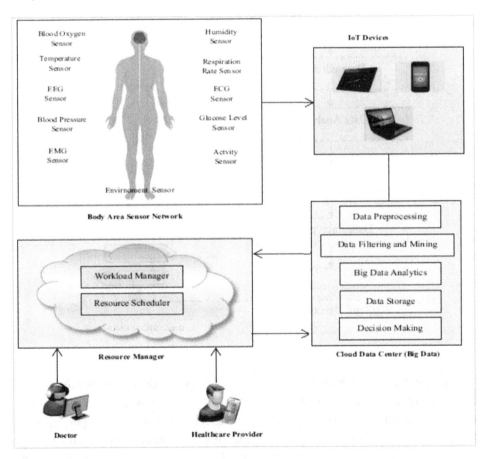

Figure 5 depicts the architecture of smart healthcare system which is enabled with IoT devices, cloud data centers and BDA techniques in order to provide meaningful insights from huge amount of data with easy store and retrieval features. Body area sensor network module consists of sensors that sense the data from patient and transfer to attached IoT devices. IoT devices collect the data from different sensors and forward the data to cloud data center for storing and retrieving the data with security. Resource manager module consists of two sub modules such as workload manager and resource scheduler. Workload manager handles the patient data in terms of bulk of workloads and maintains a workload queue for processing of data based on emergency. Resource scheduler schedules the provisioned cloud resources for processing of cloud workloads.

Figure 6. Process flow diagram

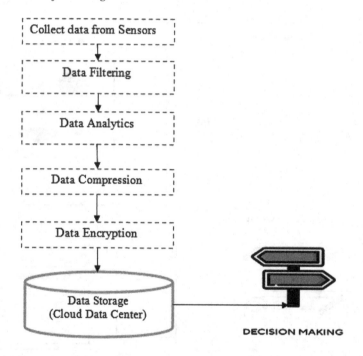

The cloud data center component is enabled with big data tools and techniques that perform the processing of patient data. Figure 6 depicts the process flow diagram for smart health care system. While executing workloads, it performs the data pre-processing in order to convert the huge amount of data into desired format. Next, data filtering is performed to process data of only specific users using data analytics. Filtered data is classified into two categories such as text and image. Then, the text data is compressed using Huffman coding that uses frequency of characters to assign variable-length codes to characters to reduce the volume of data and the images are compressed using set partitioning in hierarchical trees algorithm and encrypted using singular value decomposition method with the goal of discovering the status of health of patients. Based on the patient's health status, a decision is taken automatically to recommend medication and suitable check-up based on the continuous opinion of healthcare providers and doctors and stores their status into database for further purpose. Smart water management system using cloud and big data is described in the next section.

Smart Water Management Using Cloud Based Big Data Analytics

Nowadays, the surface water is also heavily polluted, with nearly 70% of it believed to be unfit for consumption. In addition, almost 40 million liters of waste water reach the rivers and other bodies of water every day just a fraction of which is properly treated. This is a major challenge which compounds the water crisis and further affects its already declining supply of freshwater (Jiang et al., 2020). The current scenario highlights the need for a long-term, oriented and strategic approach to water management, particularly in cities (Kumar, Askarunisa, Kumar, & Microsystems, 2020).

When designing and implementing smart water and waste water management systems in smart cities, there are several factors to be considered. The strategy must be systematic and durable, capable of overcoming today's specific problems while planning for tomorrow's needs and contingencies. The challenges are accessibility and optimum resource use, predicting potential demand and compensating for the effects of climate change (Chen & Han, 2018). At present due to the Covid-19 pandemic, it is being witnessed periodic sanitization drives in factories and workplaces, regular cleaning in households, and increased hand-washing. It is estimated that a family of five needs 100 to 200 liters of water per day just to wash their hands. This would result in the production of about 200 litres of waste water every day which would raise the demand for water and the generation of waste water from human settlements by 20 to 25 percent. During these times, it is therefore important to drink water carefully and judiciously (Gopinath et al., 2019).

For smart cities, smart water management is developed using cloud-based big data analytics, which includes the implementation of sustainable technology that can help the city stay 'water-positive' in all seasons. This approach is an intelligent and integrated system for water supply, distribution, waste water and treatment in the entire system. It also focuses on the proliferation of recycling facilities that facilitate and enable the repeated use of resources before disposal (Leccese et al., 2018). It then includes the features of driving the responsible use of water by intelligent monitoring systems that track individual use, alerting individuals when their use exceeds prescribed or predetermined limits. This will guarantee greater transparency for individuals and inculcate disciplined use of resources. This strategy not only focuses on energy conservation, but also on the extensive use of renewable sources of energy to ensure that these strategies remain sustainable. Then, it includes features that encourage responsible water use by monitoring individual use and alerting people when their use exceeds prescribed or predetermined limits. This would increase individual responsibility and disciplined resource use. This approach is not only energy efficient, but it also makes extensive use of renewable energy sources, ensuring that these solutions are long-term. In the end, they want to recycle and restore more electricity than they use (Harshadeep & Young, 2020).

Figure 7 depicts the architecture of smart water management system which is enabled with cloud based big data analytics techniques in order to utilize the water resources efficiently and monitor the water usages. It includes the major components such as intelligent pumping system, remote management and monitoring, mapping network infrastructure, advanced treatment systems and wastewater treatment and removal unit. Intelligent pumping systems are pumping systems are smart, IoT-enabled, and digitally connected pumps are fixed with sensors that automatically track and control the flow and pressure of water. Such solutions can provide real-time insights and help prevent and predict leaks, thus improving reliability and performance.

Remote management and monitoring allows remote management and cloud-based monitoring of pump installations. It can process and analyze data from smart pumps, sensors, meters and pump controllers that can be accessed through a central server from any device which is enabled with internet connection. Mapping Network infrastructure includes new instruments, such as dynamic 3D water utility applications, exploit data to provide a comprehensive and analytical view of the entire infrastructure of the network. Data-driven intelligence would be the foundation for

Figure 7. Architecture of smart water management with cloud based big data

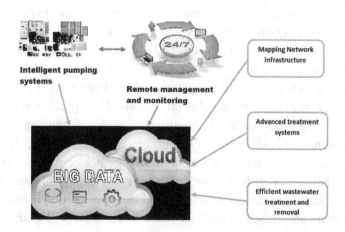

decision-making and prioritizing such as the estimation of losses and failures, the assessment of system performance and the prediction of water losses and failures, the assessment of system performance and the production of pipe replacement plans.

Advanced treatment systems has the provision of safe and adequate water sources is inextricably related to the management of wastewater and treatment systems are an important part of the treatment of wastewater. In addition to simply filtering waste, genuinely advanced filtration systems often extract essential nutrients from waste water, such as phosphorous and nitrogen, which can then be used in other applications. Effective treatment and removal of wastewater system produces large quantities of sludge, another obstacle to address in the design of smart cities. The use of carefully calibrated devices and procedures, such as lifting stations, pre-fabricated pumping stations, water pressure control submersible pumps, and proven techniques to ensure the safe removal of leftover sludge, requires efficient wastewater treatment.

Maintenance activity data in a computerized maintenance management system (CMMS), real-time data in a supervisory control and data acquisition (SCADA) system, regulatory data in a laboratory information management system (LIMS), and customer complaint data from a consumer information system (CIS) are all common datasets created by water management systems. Figure 8 represents smart water management scheme representation which includes different phases such as data collection, dissemination, data integration, modeling and analytics, visualization, management and control and decision support process. The next section describes the smart education system.

Figure 8. Smart water management scheme representation

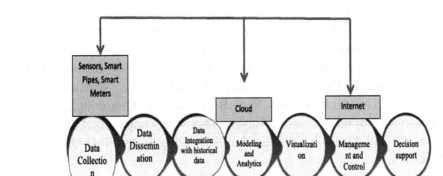

SMART EDUCATION USING CLOUD BASED BIG DATA ANALYTICS

A main ingredient in smart city growth is smart education. A smart city is characterized by strengths in basic education, technical training and certification, universities and community colleges, e-learning facilities, lifelong learning and innovation in educational technology. Different innovations have been applied in education in the past century, but not all technologies have been effective in the classroom (Martín, Alario-Hoyos, & Kloos, 2019). They were also teacher-centered tools intended to operate in combination with conventional teaching approaches that did not require new generations of students moving up the digital adoption curve rapidly. The creation of a smart education environment today requires the more intelligent application of digital technologies. Educators should shift to developments based on student and teacher-student collaboration to allow more productive use of classroom technology (Sathiyamoorthi et al., 2020).

Smart education is a learning paradigm tailored to new generations of digital natives. Smart education is an interactive, collaborative and visual model compared to conventional classroom teaching models, designed to enhance student participation and enable teachers to adapt to the skills, desires and learning preferences of students (Nikolov et al., 2016). Smart classroom technology facilitates the professionalization of the teaching process, empowering teachers to better plan and enrich their lectures and to adapt flexibly to the needs of students and classroom conditions, resulting in improved productivity and improved performance of teaching. The teacher is no longer an authoritarian figure in this student-centric sense, but a guide, a learning partner, in what is essentially a bi-directional phase. The vast volumes of data that can be obtained from cloud are one of the advantages of smart education (Waqas et al., 2017). Smart education system is used to make predictions about students' behavior or to develop security measures to detect network intrusions (Zhong, Zhu, Xu, & Cui, 2018). This system uses data acquisition and analysis techniques like Decision Tree, Random Tree, Random Forest, Artificial Neural Network (ANN), Convolution Neural Networks (CNNs), Naïve Bayes, K-means Clustering, k-Nearest Neighbor (K-NN) and others including Bayesian Network, Graph-based Clustering, and Multimedia and Agents based Question Answering System (MAQAS) (Shi, Xu, & Li, 2017).

To provide more economical, stable, and efficient education services, cloud computing has attracted a lot of interest in the education sector. Cloud-based smart education framework for e-learning content services delivers and distributes different enhanced types of educational content. The framework consists of six main features required for the implementation of cloud-based educational content services: 1) a cloud platform that provides a cloud-based educational media service environment

Figure 9. Cloud based big data enabled smart education system

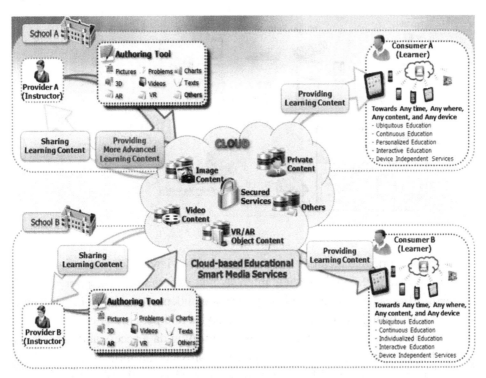

infrastructure, 2) a compatible file format that allows media content to be distributed across various types of devices, 3) an authoring tool that allows teachers to build various types of media content 4) a content viewer that shows various types of media on multiple channels, 5) an inference engine that offers individualized learning content to students, and 6) a protection mechanism for secure educational content services that handles privileged user access and data encryption in the cloud (Jeong, Kim, Yoo, & Engineering, 2013).

Figure 9 represents the proposed cloud-based big data enabled smart education system for smart media content services. It provides delivery and sharing of a diversity of enhanced educational contents and services by integrating a number of features required for the deployment of a cloud-based educational media service environment. Teachers in schools are able to use an authoring tool provided by the framework to create different types of learning material, including text, photographs, video, 3-dimensional (3D) objects, and virtual scenes based on virtual reality (VR) and augmented reality (AR). The content is handled in the cloud in a compliant common file format. Various platforms, such as personal computers (PCs), notebooks, laptops, smart TVs and smart phones, are supported by the device.

Figure 10. Content viewer of smart education system

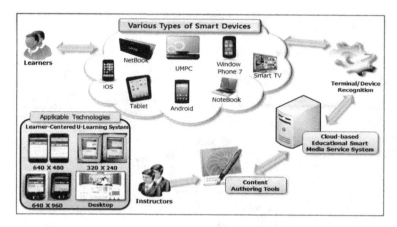

The framework also includes a content viewer for viewing learning content and an inference engine, based on their interests and experience, to support content personalized to each individual student. To provide students with customized learning content by analyzing their interests, learning styles and patterns of content use an inference engine is included. Moreover for controlling data access and encryption in the cloud, a security framework is given. It provides an infrastructure for the implementation of a cloud-based big data enabled educational media service environment by applying many IT and cloud computing technologies, such as data synchronization, virtualization, service provisioning, and multi-sharing services.

Content viewer is used to display media on multiple platforms. Figure 10 shows a sample content viewer that supports number of devices. Authoring tool creates contents that are saved in the XML-based common file format. Inference Engine incorporates an inference engine to provide customized learning information to

Figure 11. Learner's profile and characteristics

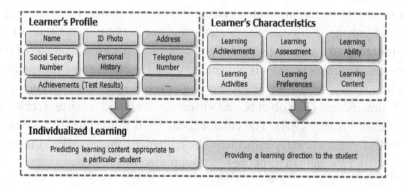

students by examining their interests, modes of learning, and patterns of use of content. The system stores each student's learning material, learning patterns, and learning achievements in databases to achieve customized learning services relevant to the characteristics of each student and analyses them to infer learning elements correlated with the characteristics of each student.

Figure 11 represents the managed user information for estimating the students' learning characteristics. It includes data mining techniques to assess the magnitude of the correlation between students and learning material, including the Proportional Reporting Ration (PRR), Reporting Odds Ratio (ROR), Bayesian Statistics, and Knowledge Component (IC) methods. The next section provides a detailed description of smart transportation and traffic control using cloud based big data analytics.

SMART TRANSPORTATION AND TRAFFIC CONTROL USING CLOUD BASED BIG DATA ANALYTICS

Smart transportation is one of the key ways in which smart cities transform citizens' everyday lives and promote sustainability. The growth and development of an area is accelerated by the proper movement of people, goods and services. For every community, a well developed and efficiently operated transport network is a must. One of the key objectives of smart transport systems is to minimize dependency on private vehicles, increase the attractiveness of private transport and enable residents of the city and tourists to move from private to public transport. Smart transport systems, for instance, can restrict private cars to certain routes and reserve priority lanes or even whole roads for other modes of transport (Wang & Li, 2016).

Figure 12 illustrate the landscape of smart transportation and traffic control system. It includes the technologies such as advanced tracking system, sensing technologies, video vehicle detection, traffic light system and E-call vehicle service. Advanced tracking system enables the most of vehicles are now equipped with in-vehicle GPS. The GPS system provides two-way communication to help traffic professionals locate cars, monitor vehicles for speeding, and provide emergency services (Sharif et al., 2017). In tracking them, knowing road quality, traffic density and identifying various routes and locations, smart phones, mobile apps and Google maps have become useful tools.

Advanced sensing technologies include smart sensors in both the car and road infrastructure sectors. Intelligent beacon sensing systems and Radio Frequency Identification (RFI) ensure the safety of drivers in cities around the world. Inductive loops are designed with road reflectors, helping to manage traffic and drive safely, particularly during the night. In a specific time frame, they can also say about the vehicle density and can distinguish vehicles at both slow and high speeds.

Figure 12. Landscape of smart transportation and traffic control system

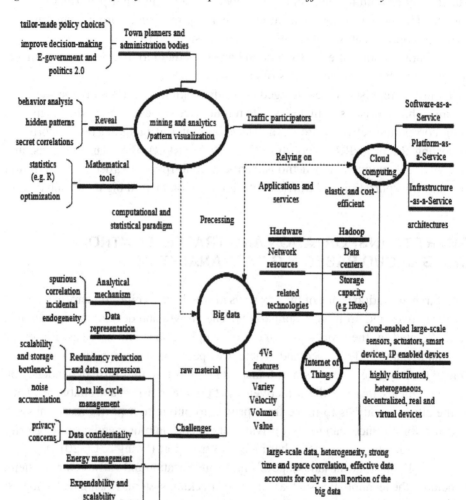

Figure 13 depicts the smart transportation and traffic control system which is enabled with cloud and big data technologies. Advanced video vehicle detection helps traffic managers using video cameras or CCTV monitoring. Strategic places and prime junctions video footage will assist operators in monitoring traffic flow, detecting any emergency situation or congestion on the lane. Automatic number plate detection in installed vehicle sensors helps to keep a check on vehicles for safety purposes. Advanced traffic light system is enabled with Radio Frequency Identification (RFID) to identify traffic lights. And when extended to several lanes,

Figure 13. Cloud based big data enabled smart transportation and traffic control system

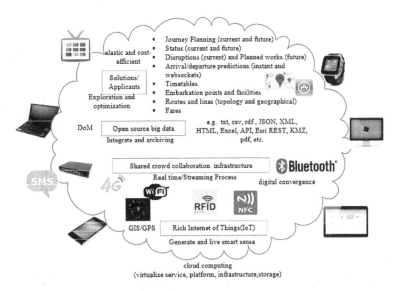

road junctions and cars, the technology provides accurate algorithms and databases. Without any manual presence, such lights can change themselves during critical and peak hour traffic situations. E-Call vehicle service uses in-vehicle sensors to create communication with the nearest emergency centre in emergency situations such as collisions or other mishap. The e-call will help the driver communicate with the qualified operator and also directly relay crucial information to the centre, such as time, location, vehicle direction and identification of vehicles. The next section describes the smart power grid used in smart cities.

SMART POWER GRID USING CLOUD BASED BIG DATA ANALYTICS

A large range of algorithms and technologies for data analytics are being applied, focusing on smart grid data processing. The key goal of smart grid big data analytics is to derive useful knowledge from historical data and to prepare future operations and maintenance (Zhang, Huang, & Bompard, 2018). By using the Cloud Computing (CC) model, computational requirements for Smart Grid applications can be fulfilled. In modern industrial systems, data analytics now plays a more important role. An information layer is now added to the traditional electricity transmission and distribution network for data collection, storage and analysis with the aid of

Figure 14. Communication infrastructure for smart power grid

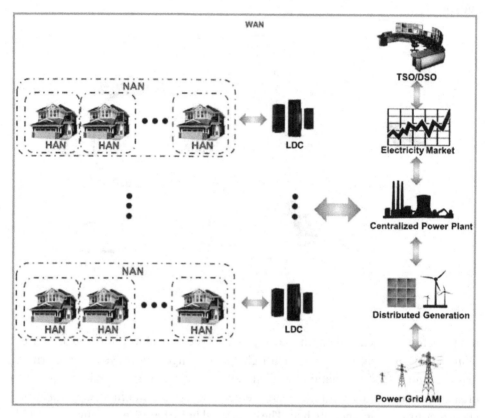

a large installation of smart meters and sensors, powered by the advancement of information and communication technology (Ye, Qian, & Hu, 2017). Traditional fossil fuels are facing the issue of decline in the power grid and de-carbonization allows the power sector to reduce carbon emissions. In order to accelerate the pace of electrification of human society with high penetration of renewable energy sources, smart grids and super grids are successful solutions. Renewable energy forecasting approaches focused on data analytics are a hot research subject for better regulation and dispatch planning in such situations. In distribution systems, conventional electricity meters only contain a limited amount of data that can be manually collected and processed for billing purposes. While the vast amount of data obtained from two-way communication smart grids at various time resolutions now involves sophisticated data processing to obtain useful information not just for billing information, but also for the electricity network status. For instance, for consumer behavior analysis, demand forecasting and energy generation optimization, high-resolution user usage data can also be used (Butun, Lekidis, & dos Santos, 2020).

Figure 14 represents the communication infrastructure of the smart grid which is composed of three types of networks: home area network (HAN), neighborhood area network (NAN) and wide area network (WAN). By attaching a modulated carrier signal to the power cables, power line communication (PLC) is a wired communication technology and has already been successfully introduced in the power grid. ZigBee, WALN, wireless communication, WiMAX, PLC, etc. are among the current communication technologies.

Figure 15. Architecture of big data enabled smart grid

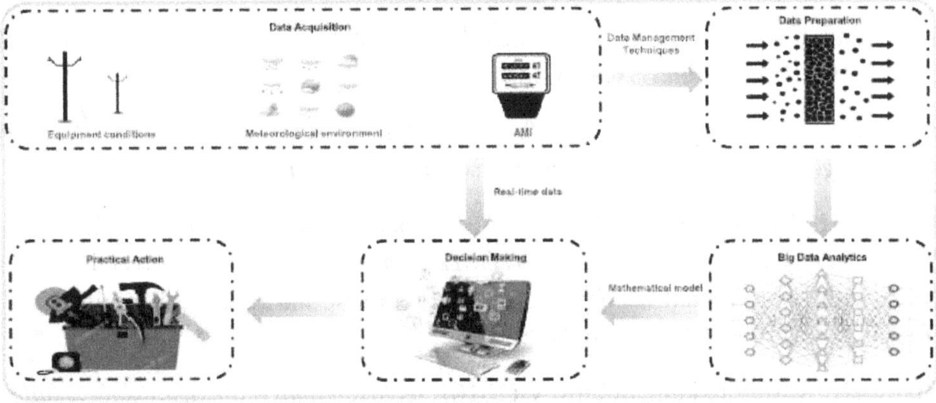

Figure 15 shows the architecture of big data enabled smart power grid which uses data mining or machine learning algorithms are usually categorized as supervised or unsupervised learning depending on whether there is a label attached to each item in datasets. Big data in smart grid and the related state-of-the-art methods of analysis have been analyzed. Smart meters mounted in the power grid, energy sector, GIS, meteorological information system, social media, etc. are used to collect data that can contain useful information. In order to discover possible regulations, the goal of advanced ICT technology in the power system is to connect the typical physical parameters in the power system with external variables.

CONCLUSION

Big data and cloud computing are inevitable technologies in smart city services. Development of smart cities mainly relies on creating communities that are technologically supported and processed. Several smart city services have been established with IoT devices, cloud and big data technologies. Services such as healthcare, water management, smart education, smart transportation and traffic control and smart power grid makes use of cloud and big data. This chapter identified the methodologies that are adopted to build these services effectively. Machine learning and data mining as well as big data analytics are useful tools for both data management and sensing data to extract meaningful insights. Thus it is possible to avoid resource wastage and system failures in smart cities.

REFERENCES

Al Nuaimi, E., Al Neyadi, H., Mohamed, N., & Al-Jaroodi, J. (2015). *Applications of big data to smart cities.* Academic Press.

Aljumah, A., Kaur, A., Bhatia, M., & & Ahanger, T. (2020). *Internet of things-fog computing-based framework for smart disaster management.* Academic Press.

Arasteh, H., Hosseinnezhad, V., Loia, V., Tommasetti, A., Troisi, O., Shafie-khah, M., & Siano, P. (2016). *Iot-based smart cities: A survey.* Paper presented at the 2016 IEEE 16th International Conference on Environment and Electrical Engineering (EEEIC). 10.1109/EEEIC.2016.7555867

Biswas, K., & Muthukkumarasamy, V. (2016). *Securing smart cities using blockchain technology.* Paper presented at the 2016 IEEE 18th international conference on high performance computing and communications; IEEE 14th international conference on smart city; IEEE 2nd international conference on data science and systems (HPCC/SmartCity/DSS). 10.1109/HPCC-SmartCity-DSS.2016.0198

Butun, I., Almgren, M., Gulisano, V., & Papatriantafilou, M. (2020). Intrusion Detection in Industrial Networks via Data Streaming. In *Industrial IoT* (pp. 213–238). Springer. doi:10.1007/978-3-030-42500-5_6

Butun, I., Lekidis, A., & dos Santos, D. R. (2020). *Security and Privacy in Smart Grids: Challenges, Current Solutions and Future Opportunities.* Paper presented at the ICISSP. 10.5220/0009187307330741

Butun, I., & Österberg, P. (2019). Detecting intrusions in cyber-physical systems of smart cities: Challenges and directions. In *Secure Cyber-Physical Systems for Smart Cities* (pp. 74–102). IGI Global. doi:10.4018/978-1-5225-7189-6.ch004

Butun, I., Sari, A., & Österberg, P. (2019). *Security implications of fog computing on the internet of things.* Paper presented at the 2019 IEEE International Conference on Consumer Electronics (ICCE). 10.1109/ICCE.2019.8661909

Butun, I., Sari, A., & Österberg, P. (2020). *Hardware Security of Fog End-Devices for the Internet of Things*. Academic Press.

Carter, E., Adam, P., Tsakis, D., Shaw, S., Watson, R., & Ryan, P. (2020). *Enhancing pedestrian mobility in smart cities using big data*. Academic Press.

Chen, Y., & Han, D. (2018). *Water quality monitoring in smart city: A pilot project*. Academic Press.

Clohessy, T., Acton, T., & Morgan, L. (2014). *Smart city as a service (SCaaS): A future roadmap for e-government smart city cloud computing initiatives*. Paper presented at the 2014 IEEE/ACM 7th International Conference on Utility and Cloud Computing. 10.1109/UCC.2014.136

Formisano, C., Pavia, D., Gurgen, L., Yonezawa, T., Galache, J. A., Doguchi, K., & Matranga, I. (2015). *The advantages of IoT and cloud applied to smart cities*. Paper presented at the 2015 3rd International Conference on Future Internet of Things and Cloud. 10.1109/FiCloud.2015.85

Gaur, A., Scotney, B., Parr, G., & McClean, S. (2015). *Smart city architecture and its applications based on IoT*. Academic Press.

Gill, S. S., Arya, R. C., Wander, G. S., & Buyya, R. (2018). *Fog-based smart healthcare as a big data and cloud service for heart patients using IoT*. Paper presented at the International Conference on Intelligent Data Communication Technologies and Internet of Things.

Gopinath, M., Tamizharasi, G., Kavisankar, L., Sathyaraj, R., Karthi, S., & Aarthy, S. (2019). *A secure cloud-based solution for real-time monitoring and management of Internet of underwater things (IOUT)*. Academic Press.

Güemes, C., Janeczko, J., Caminel, T., & Roberts, M. (2013). *Data analytics as a service: unleashing the power of cloud and big data*. White paper.

Hammi, B., Khatoun, R., Zeadally, S., Fayad, A., & Khoukhi, L. (2017). *IoT technologies for smart cities*. Academic Press.

Harshadeep, N. R., & Young, W. (2020). *Disruptive Technologies for Improving Water Security in Large River Basins*. Academic Press.

Hashem, I. A. T., Chang, V., Anuar, N. B., Adewole, K., Yaqoob, I., Gani, A., . . . Chiroma, H. (2016). *The role of big data in smart city*. Academic Press.

Jeong, J.-S., Kim, M., & Yoo, K. (2013). *A content oriented smart education system based on cloud computing*. Academic Press.

Ji, Z., Ganchev, I., O'Droma, M., & Zhang, X. (2014). *A cloud-based intelligent car parking services for smart cities.* Paper presented at the 2014 XXXIth URSI General Assembly and Scientific Symposium (URSI GASS). 10.1109/URSIGASS.2014.6929280

Jiang, J., Tang, S., Han, D., Fu, G., Solomatine, D., & Zheng, Y. (2020). *A comprehensive review on the design and optimization of surface water quality monitoring networks.* Academic Press.

Khan, Z., & Kiani, S. L. (2012). *A cloud-based architecture for citizen services in smart cities.* Paper presented at the 2012 IEEE Fifth International Conference on Utility and Cloud Computing. 10.1109/UCC.2012.43

Kumar, D. S., Askarunisa, A., & Kumar, R. (2020). *Embedded processor based automated assessment of quality of the water in an IoT background.* Academic Press.

Leccese, F., Cagnetti, M., Giarnetti, S., Petritoli, E., Luisetto, I., Tuti, S., . . . Bursić, V. (2018). *A simple takagi-sugeno fuzzy modelling case study for an underwater glider control system.* Paper presented at the 2018 IEEE International Workshop on Metrology for the Sea; Learning to Measure Sea Health Parameters (MetroSea). 10.1109/MetroSea.2018.8657877

Martín, A. C., Alario-Hoyos, C., & Kloos, C. D. (2019). *Smart education: a review and future research directions.* Paper presented at the Multidisciplinary Digital Publishing Institute Proceedings. 10.3390/proceedings2019031057

Massobrio, R., Nesmachnow, S., Tchernykh, A., Avetisyan, A., & Radchenko, G. (2018). *Towards a cloud computing paradigm for big data analysis in smart cities.* Academic Press.

Mitton, N., Papavassiliou, S., Puliafito, A., & Trivedi, K. S. (2012). *Combining Cloud and sensors in a smart city environment.* SpringerOpen. doi:10.1186/1687-1499-2012-247

Mohammadi, M., & Al-Fuqaha, A. (2018). *Enabling cognitive smart cities using big data and machine learning: Approaches and challenges.* Academic Press.

Nikolov, R., Shoikova, E., Krumova, M., Kovatcheva, E., Dimitrov, V., & Shikalanov, A. (2016). *Learning in a smart city environment.* Academic Press.

Osman, A. (2019). *A novel big data analytics framework for smart cities.* Academic Press.

Osman, A. M. S., Elragal, A., & Bergvall-Kåreborn, B. (2017). *Big Data Analytics and Smart Cities: A Loose or Tight Couple?* Paper presented at the 10th International Conference on Connected Smart Cities 2017 (CSC 2017), Lisbon, Portugal.

Quwaider, M., Al-Alyyoub, M., & Jararweh, Y. (2016). *Cloud support data management infrastructure for upcoming smart cities.* Academic Press.

Quwaider, M., & Jararweh, Y. (2015). *Cloudlet-based efficient data collection in wireless body area networks.* Academic Press.

Roy, A., Cruz, R. M., Sabourin, R., & Cavalcanti, G. (2018). *A study on combining dynamic selection and data preprocessing for imbalance learning.* Academic Press.

Sari, A., Lekidis, A., & Butun, I. (2020). Industrial Networks and IIoT: Now and Future Trends. In *Industrial IoT* (pp. 3–55). Springer. doi:10.1007/978-3-030-42500-5_1

Sathiyamoorthi, V., Suresh, P., Jayapandian, N., Kanmani, P., & Janakiraman, S. (2020). *An Intelligent Web Caching System for Improving the Performance of a Web-Based Information Retrieval System.* Academic Press.

Sharif, A., Li, J., Khalil, M., Kumar, R., Sharif, M. I., & Sharif, A. (2017). *Internet of things—smart traffic management system for smart cities using big data analytics.* Paper presented at the 2017 14th international computer conference on wavelet active media technology and information processing (ICCWAMTIP).

Shi, H., Xu, M., & Li, R. (2017). *Deep learning for household load forecasting—A novel pooling deep RNN.* Academic Press.

Sinaeepourfard, A., Krogstie, J., & Petersen, S. A. (2018). *A big data management architecture for smart cities based on fog-to-cloud data management architecture.* Academic Press.

Sinaeepourfard, A., Krogstie, J., Petersen, S. A., & Ahlers, D. (2019). *F2c2C-DM: A Fog-to-cloudlet-to-Cloud Data Management architecture in smart city.* Paper presented at the 2019 IEEE 5th World Forum on Internet of Things (WF-IoT). 10.1109/WF-IoT.2019.8767226

Strohbach, M., Ziekow, H., Gazis, V., & Akiva, N. (2015). Towards a big data analytics framework for IoT and smart city applications. In *Modeling and processing for next-generation big-data technologies* (pp. 257–282). Springer. doi:10.1007/978-3-319-09177-8_11

Suciu, G., Vulpe, A., Halunga, S., Fratu, O., Todoran, G., & Suciu, V. (2013). *Smart cities built on resilient cloud computing and secure internet of things.* Paper presented at the 2013 19th international conference on control systems and computer science. 10.1109/CSCS.2013.58

Suma, S., Mehmood, R., & Albeshri, A. (2017). *Automatic event detection in smart cities using big data analytics.* Paper presented at the International Conference on Smart Cities, Infrastructure, Technologies and Applications.

Susmitha, K., & Jayaprada, S. (2017). *Smart cities using big data analytics.* Academic Press.

Tragos, E. Z., Angelakis, V., Fragkiadakis, A., Gundlegard, D., Nechifor, C.-S., Oikonomou, G., ... Gavras, A. (2014). *Enabling reliable and secure IoT-based smart city applications.* Paper presented at the 2014 IEEE International Conference on Pervasive Computing and Communication Workshops (PERCOM WORKSHOPS). 10.1109/PerComW.2014.6815175

Wang, X., & Li, Z. (2016). *Traffic and Transportation Smart with Cloud Computing on Big Data.* Academic Press.

Waqas, A., Malik, H. A. M., Karbasi, M., Nawaz, N. A., & Mahessar, A. (2017). CLOUDSIS. *An Application of Cloud Computing for Smart School Management System.* Academic Press.

Wieclaw, L., Pasichnyk, V., Kunanets, N., Duda, O., Matsiuk, O., & Falat, P. (2017). *Cloud computing technologies in "smart city" projects.* Paper presented at the 2017 9th IEEE International Conference on Intelligent Data Acquisition and Advanced Computing Systems: Technology and Applications (IDAACS).

Yang, C., Huang, Q., Li, Z., Liu, K., & Hu, F. (2017). *Big Data and cloud computing: innovation opportunities and challenges.* Academic Press.

Ye, F., Qian, Y., & Hu, R. Q. (2017). *Big data analytics and cloud computing in the smart grid.* Academic Press.

Yin, C., Xiong, Z., Chen, H., Wang, J., Cooper, D., & David, B. (2015). *A literature survey on smart cities.* Academic Press.

Zhang, Y., Huang, T., & Bompard, E. (2018). *Big data analytics in smart grids: a review.* Academic Press.

Zhong, H., Zhu, W., Xu, Y., & Cui, J. (2018). *Multi-authority attribute-based encryption access control scheme with policy hidden for cloud storage.* Academic Press.

Chapter 5
Early Detection and Recovery Measures for Smart Grid Cyber–Resilience

Ismail Butun

iD https://orcid.org/0000-0002-1723-5741

Chalmers University of Technology, Sweden & Konya Food and Agriculture University, Turkey & Royal University of Technology, Sweden

Alparslan Sari

University of Delaware, USA

ABSTRACT

The internet of things (IoT) has recently brought major technological advances in many domains, including the smart grid. Despite the simplicity and efficiency that IoT brings, there are also underlying risks that are slowing down its adoption. These risks are caused by the presence of legacy systems inside existing infrastructures that were built with no security in mind. In this chapter, the authors propose a method for early-stage detection of cyber-security incidents and protection against them through applicable security measures. This chapter introduces security techniques such as anomaly detection, threat investigation through a highly automated decision support system (DSS), as well as incident response and recovery for smart grid systems. The introduced framework can be applied to industrial environments such as cyber-threats targeting the production generator as well as the electricity smart meters, etc. The chapter also illustrates the framework's cyber-resilience against zero-day threats and its ability to distinguish between operational failures as well as cyber-security incidents.

DOI: 10.4018/978-1-7998-7468-3.ch005

INTRODUCTION

Cybersecurity has a very important role in information and computing technology (ICT) systems, such as ensuring the reliability and safety of the provided services. This is a non-trivial task hence cybersecurity of the systems is difficult to maintain and operate when compared to all other services being provided. One of the prominent reasons is that the traditional cyber-security solutions are becoming obsolete as many vulnerabilities are being discovered by hackers every day (such as in the case of Zero-day attacks) on the systems and networks that are being used today.

Apart from the ICT domain, cybersecurity in the power domain is even more important and difficult due to the diverse networking and communication technologies used which exposes the whole energy grid to be vulnerable to cyber-attacks and hacks. Recent history has taught us that cybersecurity in the power domain (including industrial networks) has utmost importance as the resulting failures and enforced accidents (cyber incidence-related disasters such as explosions) might be life-threatening to the people.

For instance, Stuxnet is a malware initially distributed over Microsoft (MS) Windows platforms. It became recognized after it attacked the Iranian nuclear reactor in June 2010. It attacked Siemens programmable logic controllers (PLCs) step-7 software through computers that are running MS Windows. Stuxnet specifically attacked the PLCs that are operating in Iranian nuclear facilities: 1) By gathering industrial systems' information, 2) initiating a sequence to cause centrifuges to enter in a super fast-spinning mode, 3) eventually the catastrophic events ended up by which the centrifuges have torn themselves apart and destroyed their surrounding structures (Karnouskos, 2011).

Smart Grid is also not resistant to cyber-attacks (Butun, dos Santos, 2020). It can be both targeted at the controller side (command capture attacks on electric utility providers) and distributor side (manipulation attacks on the billing). In a modern factory (e.g. that produces paper polishing material from marble dust), one can observe that several automated machinery equipments is armed with IIoT sensors and actuators for an illustration). Some of the equipment is mainly composed of: grinders, mixers, heaters, conveyor bands. These IIoT sensors and actuators facilitate mainly three functions (Forsström, 2018):

1. Digitized on-the-go remote monitoring and control of equipment.
2. Optimization of machines within a production line (monthly or annual) due to collected short/long-term process-related data.
3. Instant alarming and shutting down of the equipment in the case of emergency situations.

In this specific factory example, adversaries can target function #1 and function #3. In this kind of facility, especially heat and pressure sensors are highly critical: Any kind of outside intervention might cause malfunctions which eventually would end up not only with batch and/or property damage but also casualties due to the unpreventable explosions. Hence these systems (sensors and actuators) are mostly IIoT enabled, they are hackable and reachable by adversaries unless special cyber-security precautions are taken.

Timely addressing the challenges and implications mentioned above in securing the Electrical Power and Energy Systems (EPES) sector against cyber-attacks and hackers is of utmost importance. This chapter broadly captures the needs of EPES operators and combines the latest technologies for vulnerability assessment, supervision, and protection to draft an imaginary vision of a defensive toolkit. For instance, in such a tool kit, anomalies that might be caused by the system users can be monitored; which later on would be mapped into the systems vulnerability analysis tool to identify and close the security gaps in the systems that will be used by the EPES vendors.

Anomaly detection is the methodology of detecting unusual, unexpected, or suspicious events/activities based on the collected data or metrics from digital networks and other connected devices. Machine Learning (supervised or unsupervised learning) can be utilized to find anomalies efficiently. In cybersecurity, intrusion detection is the fundamental application of anomaly detection. From a broad perspective, anomaly detection is used for system health monitoring (fault detection) or detecting changes in the digital ecosystem. There are many software packages (Splunk[1], Dynatrace[2], or custom, etc.) deployed to detect anomalies in the digital ecosystem. Risk assessment should be completed based on anomaly detection results and overall system metrics to generate a mitigation plan for the issue.

Risk assessment is the first step of the mitigation process to prepare an efficient response. Risk assessment is a process to identify potential failures and vulnerabilities in the ecosystem and it helps prediction and prevention of risks and failures. Risk assessment is a concern of reliability engineering to focus on availability. Theoretically, a reliable system should be fault-tolerant, error-free, and functional. Reliability is tightly coupled with availability, testability, maintainability, and maintenance. Risk assessment should be completed prior to introducing new changes to the ecosystem. This could be deploying a new project or applying a fix to production.

Figure 1. Risk assessment steps are illustrated.

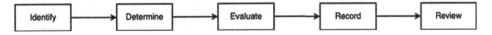

The first step of the risk assessment is identifying the problem (hazard). The second step is to find out about the impact and affected components. What is going to be impacted and how is it going to be affected. The third step is evaluating the risks and decision-making about the response. The fourth step is documenting the findings and implementing a solution. This step describes the mitigation procedure. The final step is reviewing the risk assessment and making changes if necessary.

The response is the process of preparing and applying a solution to mitigate an identified threat. If there is an immediate threat, mitigation steps should be applied quickly to minimize the damage and limit the danger. This could be blocking security breaches, patching the vulnerable software, or improving the network defense. Hardening the overall security is a required response after identifying an issue against future assaults. Even unsuccessful attacks should be considered as an incident and should be investigated thoroughly.

Recovery is the last step of the cybersecurity incident life cycle. Due to the threat or mitigation steps, the system could be in maintenance mode or down. All elements of the threat should be removed from the environment if not completed in incident response. Hypothetically the affected system should be operational after a successful response. The recovery process should be executed in an accurate and fast manner to bring production systems online.

In this chapter, we will explain how cyber-security issues should be addressed in the new generation EPES which is also known as the smart grid. Several available tools from the IT sector will be discussed and introduced as a cyber-defense solution, such as following: intrusion prevention, detection, and mitigation.

The rest of the chapter is as follows: The background section provides the necessary background to the reader on the fields of EPES networks and cybersecurity. The next section describes various components of the EPES networks. This is followed by the methodology section which describes a generic cyber-incident response model for EPES. Tools section presents generic available cyber-security tools on the market today which can be adopted by and adapted to the EPES deployments. Future work presents future trends and expectations within the EPES cybersecurity domain. Finally, the conclusion section wraps up the chapter.

BACKGROUND

In this chapter, the cyber-resilience of the EPES against cyber-attacks is discussed thoroughly. In this regard, we first introduce the cyber-security lifecycle for the generic computer networks and discuss its applicability to EPES keeping the DSS in mind.

The security life-cycle of a computer network has been identified and described in (Butun, 2013)'s work and it is shown in Figure-2. It consists of three major categories (or steps) that are situated and categorized due to the nature of the response to cyber-attacks: *Prevention* deals with attacks before they happen. In other words, this step involves taking actions to fill in the gaps of a wall of defense (for instance Firewall systems) in order to keep attackers outside of the intended system. On the other hand, the *Detection* step is more of the actions on identifying the attackers that can pass the wall of defense and capable of harming the systems (Stallings, 2015). Finally, in the *Mitigation* step, the attackers identified by the detection step are thwarted (or neutralized) from the computer network.

Figure 2. The cyber-security lifecycle of a computer network.

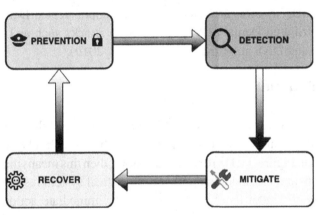

EPES networks can benefit from this defense architecture if every component is tailored to the needs and specifications accordingly. As such, the tailoring of the intrusion prevention, detection, and mitigation systems should be executed in accordance.

Intrusion Prevention

Prevention of intrusions is the first line of defense in the cyber-security of computer networks including EPES. Intrusion Prevention Systems (IPS) constitute an important layer in securing networks and valuable assets. They work on preventing pre-identified threats (intruders, malware, bots, etc.) by blocking them to reach critical system resources such as configuration files. As such, their working principle is signature-based (chronologically, the threat first needs to be identified by an expert in the field; then prevention mechanism is devised and implemented), they are vulnerable to Zero-Day attacks. Examples of IPS are; firewalls (including Next-Generation Firewalls - NGFW, antivirus systems, anti-worm systems, etc.

Intrusion Detection

Detection of intrusions constitutes the second line of defense in the cyber-security of computer networks including EPES. Intrusion Detection Systems (IDS) constitute the 2nd layer of defense in cybersecurity as shown in Figure-1. If an attacker manages to circumvent the IPS system, then should be pacified by the measures taken by the IDS. IDS should be able to react to Zero-Day exploits. As such, they are equipped with Anomaly-based detection mechanisms. The rationale behind this is pinpointing anomalies by detecting variations from a long time recorded normal system behavior called benchmark (variations on either network throughput, the total number of incoming transactions from a single source, Round-Trip delay Time - RTT, etc) (Butun, 2020). IDS systems are effective also on sophisticated Denial of Service (DoS) and Distributed Denial of Service (DDoS) attacks such as UDP flooding, SYN flooding, and DNS amplification (Österberg, 2019).

Intrusion Mitigation

Mitigation of intrusions constitutes the third line (and last) of defense in the cyber-security of computer networks including EPES. If both the 2nd layer of the cyber-security system in Figure-1 (IDS) detects intrusions, then this means that the attackers are in the system and are about to approach the critical system resources (log files, valuable and confidential data, etc.). Henceforth, immediate action needs to be taken. Sometimes, the mitigation systems are also referred to as Intrusion Detection and Prevention Systems (IDPS), not to be confused with single IPS or IDS. IDPS includes detection of intrusions and then mitigating them. For example, an IDPS can work as adjusting the firewall rules on the fly and blocking and/or dropping suspected (malicious) traffic when it is identified/detected.

Cybersecurity Solutions

Cybersecurity of smart grid systems might rely on many solutions. These solutions need to be used in an orchestrated and innovative way:

- **Hardware-Based Solutions:** The importance and benefits of fog computing for IoT networks are escalating nowadays, hence providing the means of hardware security to these devices, including but not limited to Hardware Security Module (HSM), Physically Unclonable Function (PUF), System on a Chip (SoaC), and Tamper Resistant Memory (TRM) are utmost important (Butun, I., Sari, A., & Österberg, P., 2020).

- **Intrusion/Anomaly Detection:** The terms of IDS and ADS (Anomaly Detection System) are sometimes interchangeably used. ADS refers to the detection of suspicious behavior in the system which is deviating from the normal operating point. From the cybersecurity point of view, the ADS installed at EPES networks first needs to learn the system norms under normal operating conditions without any intrusion/anomaly introduced. After this phase, the ADS agents are installed at the junctions of the critical information flow of the EPES to identify the anomalies emanating from the following sub-components but not limited to PLCs, PIDs, Remote Terminal Units (RTUs), Human Machine Interfaces (HMIs), and SCADA systems. Some commonly used IDS algorithms in the industry are Suricata, Snort, Wireshark, Zeek, etc.
- **Firewall:** A traditional firewall is an essential security component in an industrial network to filter the traffic (in/out) based on predefined rules and policies. An application-level firewall (WAF) is also needed in the security ecosystem to filter or block data packages in an application domain to prevent cross-site scripting (XSS) or injection-related attacks (such as JavaScript and SQL injection) etc.
- **SIEM (Security Information and Event Management):** Data aggregation from multiple sources is an important concept in SIEM tools to analyze and detect abnormal events (potentially security issues). SIEM tools should have at least the following functionalities: alerting, forensics, incident response & management, log collection & analysis, monitoring, threat detection, etc. Dynatrace, IBM QRadar, LogRhythm, and Splunk are the widely adopted SIEM tools in the industry. Dynatrace and Splunk are thoroughly introduced in the following sections. SIEM tools also include the Vulnerability Analysis (VA) platform in which the system administrator can observe and analyze the overall system VA reports to take further actions.

EPES Network Architecture

EPES networks can be considered under either the IT (Information Technology) or OT (Operation Technology) domain; or more broadly, under the intersection of both domains. To understand EPES network architecture, one needs to learn more about the components that comprise it (Lekidis, 2020):

- **Remote Terminal Units (RTU)s:** In Supervisory Control And Data Acquisition (SCADA) systems, RTU refers to an electronic device (generally microprocessor-controlled one) that interfaces (provides the electronic bridge) end units/devices in the application floor to the digital world. Sometimes, they are also called Remote Telemetry Unit or Remote Telecontrol Unit.

- **Smart Meters:** These are also affiliated with Advanced Metering Infrastructure (AMI), and provide calibrated (instant or cumulated) electrical power consumption readings to the grid provider for billing and/or maintenance operation purposes.
- **Data Collectors:** These are also referred to as Utility Access Point (UAP) and they are located in between smart meters and the Utility Data Control Center (UDCC)'s. They perform on-site data analytics and also provide useful consumption data to the UDCC for remote decision-making and further action-taking.
- **Utility Data Control Center (UDCC):** All RTUs, SCADA networks, smart meters, and UAPS connect at the UDCC for ensuring centralized and immediate decision making.
- **Data/Signaling Network/Communication Protocols:** There are various networking technologies devised for industrial networks (Fieldbus, 2020):
  - **CAN:** During the 1980s, to solve communication problems between different control systems in cars, the German company Robert Bosch GmbH first developed the Controller Area Network (CAN). The concept of CAN was that every device can be connected by a single set of wires, and every device that is connected can freely exchange data with any other device. CAN soon be migrated into the factory automation marketplace with many others.
  - **INTERBUS:** In 1987 Phoenix Contact developed a serial bus to connect spatially distributed inputs and outputs to a centralized controller. The controller sends one frame over a physical ring, which contains all input and output data. The cable has 5 wires: besides the ground signal two wires for the outgoing frame and two wires for the returning frame. With this cable is it possible to have the whole installation in a tree topology. The INTERBUS was very successful in the manufacturing industry with more than 22,9 million devices installed in the field.
  - **BACnet:** The BACnet is a building automation standard that was initially developed in 1987 and maintained by the American ASHRAE Society since then. BACnet is an ANSI standard, a European standard, a national standard in many countries, and a global ISO standard (ISO-16484) since 2003. In 2017, BACnet had a market share of 60% in the market of building automation.
  - **SCADA:** Supervisory control and data acquisition (SCADA) is a control system architecture consisting of single computers, networking elements, and graphical user interfaces (GUI) that are altogether designed for high-level process supervisory management. Moreover, SCADA also includes various peripheral devices such as Programmable

Logic Controllers (PLC) and Proportional Integral Derivative (PID) controllers that help interfacing with other process plants and devices (equipment such as machines).

○ **DLMS/COSEM:** Device Language Message Specification (DLMS) is a bunch of standards suited by the DLMS User Association (DLMS UA) and has been adopted by the IEC-TC13/WG14 into the IEC-62056 standard series. On the other hand, Companion Specification for Energy Metering (COSEM) includes a set of specifications that defines the application and transport layers of the DLMS protocol.

○ **DNP3:** Distributed Network Protocol 3 (DNP3) is a set of communications protocols that are used by the components of the process automation systems. DNP3 is mainly used in utility providers such as gas, water, and electricity distribution companies. It plays an important role in SCADA systems, as they are widely deployed by the SCADA Master Stations (a.k.a. Control Centers), Remote Terminal Units (RTUs), and Intelligent Electronic Devices (IEDs). It was developed for providing seamless communications in between various types of data acquisition and control equipment.

○ **Fieldbus:** Fieldbus is the name of a family of real-time distributed control protocols that are attributed to the use of industrial networks. Fieldbus provides means of communicating with input sensors (sensors, switches, etc.) and output actuators (valves, drives, indication lamps, etc.) without the need of connecting each sensor/actuator directly to the controller (PLC, SCADA, etc.). Therefore, overall, Fieldbus can reduce costs. Fieldbus protocols are standardized by the International Electrotechnical Commission (IEC) as IEC 61784/61158. Here are some Fieldbus variants:

§ **MODBUS:** Modbus is a serial bus to connect programmable logic controllers (PLCs) via a two-wire cable with EIA 485 (to carry UART signals). The protocol itself is straightforward with a master/slave protocol. The number of data types is limited to those understood by PLCs at the time of invention (1979). Nevertheless, Modbus is with its Modbus-TCP version still one of the most used industrial networks, especially in the building automation networking (BAN) field.

§ **CANopen:** It is a communication protocol and device profile specification for embedded systems used in automation networks. In terms of the Open System Interconnect (OSI) model, CANopen is responsible for implementing the network layer and above OSI layers.

§ **EtherCAT**: It stands for Ethernet for Control Automation Technology protocol and refers to an Ethernet-based Fieldbus system, which was invented by Beckhoff Automation Inc. The EtherCAT protocol is very well described by the IEC 61158 standard and is suited to both soft/hard real-time computing requirements of the automation technology.

§ **PROFIBUS**: A research project with the financial support of the German government defined in 1987 the Fieldbus PROFIBUS based on the Fieldbus Message Specification (FMS). It showed in practical applications, that it was too complicated to handle in the field. In 1994 Siemens proposed a modified application layer with the name Decentralized Periphery (DP) which reached a good acceptance in the manufacturing industry. 2016 the Profibus is one of the most installed Fieldbuses in the world.

§ **Ether Powerlink**: It is an open protocol managed by the Ethernet POWERLINK Standardization Group (EPSG). Ether Powerlink is a real-time protocol for standard Ethernet connection, which was first introduced in 2001 by an Austrian automation company B&R.

- **Digital Twin:** *"The digital twin is the virtual representation of a physical object or system across its life-cycle. It uses real-time data and other sources to enable learning, reasoning, and dynamically recalibrating for improved decision making."* [3] Digital Twin is a software-driven important technological advancement that will impact the industrial environments like production life-cycle management (PLM) etc. It will help to enhance the production monitoring and predictability of unexpected events such as malfunctions and cybersecurity-related availability issues. A digital twin is tightly coupled with Industry 4.0 and IoT since it uses collected data from connected devices during the PLM.

- **Industry 4.0**: The industrial revolution started with the mechanization (water/steam power) of the production pipelines. Steam engines are used in production and transportation. The second transformation has happened once steam power is replaced with electricity. Breakthrough in transistor and electric circuits technology produced computers which triggered the third industrial revolution. Mass device connectivity nudges the fourth industrial revolution which is enhanced with smart devices and advanced artificial intelligence algorithms like machine learning. The main components of Industry 4.0 and IoT are as follows: Cloud, cyber-security, IoT, system integration, simulation, autonomous robots, Big Data, augmented reality, and additive manufacturing. (Sari, 2020) Connectivity will enable advanced intelligent devices to work towards a common goal utilizing available technologies.

Smart devices/sensors can collect, process, or share environmental data if necessary. Connectivity (data collection/sharing between devices) will help business owners to improve efficiency in the manufacturing process and also plan preventative maintenance on machinery. Another benefit would be identifying or predicting errors or faults in the production pipeline as soon as it emerges to reduce the production and maintenance costs.

Figure 3. An example of corporate and industrial network integration.
Source: https://www.processindustryforum.com/article/what-is-fieldbus

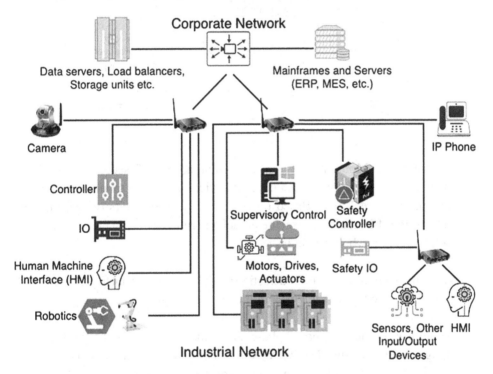

METHODOLOGY

A generic cyber-incident response model is illustrated for EPES infrastructures in Figure 4. There are many tools used in production environments to provide end-to-end security. Securing the network is a continuous process and should be real-time monitored to detect any faults or abnormalities in the industrial networks. An EPES cyber-resilience methodology should have at least the following phases: monitoring, diagnose, restore and recover.

Figure 4. A generic EPES cyber-resilience methodology.

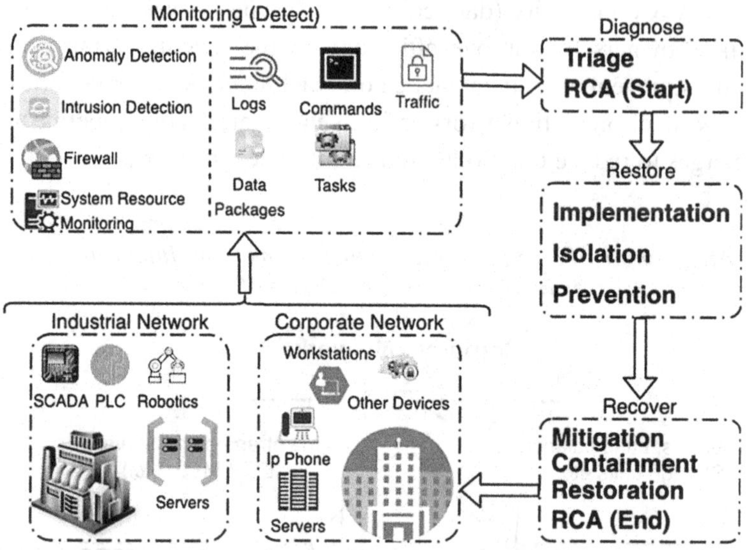

- **Monitoring:** Monitoring is an important aspect of securing the EPES architecture. The network and internal devices should be monitored to detect anomalies in real-time. Based on the real-time parameters or log analysis, advanced SIEM tools can execute predefined rules to inform human operators of physical or cyber-related issues.

Intrusion detection and anomaly detection modules are important to give protection against unauthorized or suspicious activities in the monitored network.

- **Diagnose**: In the "diagnose" phase, an incident management team starts the triage about the issue. The RCA (Root Cause Analysis) process also starts as soon as the initial fault is detected by monitoring alerts or reported by human operators.
- **Restore**: The faulty (or compromised) system is isolated from the production environment and the solution is being implemented here towards mitigation of the issue. Isolation strategy helps the prevention goal. Prevention is the strategy for stopping disturbance in the production environment by faulty systems or cyber threats. RCA continues in this phase as well, all findings and taken actions are being recorded for future analysis.
- **Recover:** System recovery actions are mitigation, containment, and restoration. The impacted EPES system should be working as expected after the issue is mitigated. The malicious payload should be removed from the

source or it should be isolated from the network. If there is any malfunctioning unit identified, it should be replaced with a backup to ensure the EPES system availability is not *degraded*. Restoration steps are focused on the restoration of the full functionality of EPES.

TOOLS

- **Nmap[4]:** Nmap (Network Mapper) is an open-source command-line tool to discover hosts and services in a network. It is used for auditing and penetration testing to do vulnerability analysis and checking port availability. Nmap provides hosts and services info such as OS-related information, network devices-related information, and firewall details, etc.
- **Snort[5] - Network Intrusion Detection & Prevention System:** Snort is an open-source intrusion prevention system that can analyze real-time traffic. It can detect various attack vectors such as buffer overflows, stealth port scans, CGI attacks, SMB probes and OS fingerprinting attempts, etc.
- **Traceroute[6]:** Traceroute is another command-line tool for monitoring the packages across the network. This tool identifies how data flows through connected networks. It is mostly used for information gathering purposes to identify the network's infrastructures and IP ranges. It is useful to identify where specific packages are being caught or stopped (identify firewalls that may be blocking traffic).
- **The Zeek[7] Network Security Monitor:** Zeek is an open-source network security monitoring tool. It is not an active security component. It is embedded in a sensor device (hardware, software, virtual, or cloud platform) and it passively observes the network traffic then collects data further aggregated to another SIEM tool for further review.
- **Wazuh[8] - The Open Source Security Platform:** Wazuh is an open-source SIEM tool for continuous monitoring, threat detection, and incident response. It is categorized as a host-based intrusion detection system (HIDS). Wazuh collects and aggregates data in real-time to detect possible anomalies, intrusions, and threats in the monitored domain. It has the following features; alerting, detection (intrusion, threat, rootkit), log analysis, monitoring (file integrity, windows registry, etc.)
- **Wireshark[9]:** Wireshark is an open-source network protocol analyzer focused on advanced information gathering. It captures the network traffic, analyzes packages, and shows the activities in the network at the micro-level. Usually, it is used by network administrators to troubleshoot problems or detect unusual traffic. Wireshark could be used by hackers to understand the targeted

network and gathering regarding information (vulnerability identification and penetration). It can gather real-time data from Ethernet, IEEE 802.11, PPP/HDLC, ATM, Bluetooth, USB, Token Ring, Frame Relay, FDDI, and many more. It also provides decryption support for various protocols, such as IPsec, ISAKMP, Kerberos, SNMPv3, SSL/TLS, WEP, and WPA/WPA2.

- **Web Application Firewall (WAF):** A web application firewall is a monitoring tool to filter or block data packages in an application domain. Simply, WAF monitors and intercepts the HTTP traffic prior to the application server to protect against denial-of-service (DoS) attacks. WAF also provides enhanced security at the application level to prevent malicious attacks like SQL injection, cross-site scripting (XSS), Cross-Site Request Forgery (CSRF) and cookie poisoning, etc. WAF is also effective against unauthorized access or data transfer from the server. WAF can enforce defined security policies for organizations. A WAF can be implemented as a software or hardware component and also deployable to the cloud easily. The benefit of using a well-configured WAF is to mitigate various threats and provide enhanced security. The major weakness is latency and cost. Based on the WAF selection and configuration it may cause latency to interrupt the user experience. A capable WAF provides input validation & protection, data leakage protection, automated attack prevention, and policy-based vulnerability management.

A traditional firewall (Intrusion detection systems or intrusion prevention systems) protects the traffic between servers, whereas a WAF is configured to protect a specific web application. A WAF can detect application-specific threats and vulnerabilities to mitigate. Nowadays, machine learning embedded WAFs are dominating the market to monitor the application domain to detect anomalies and mitigate them.

Figure 5. Show the web application firewall illustration in the cloud.

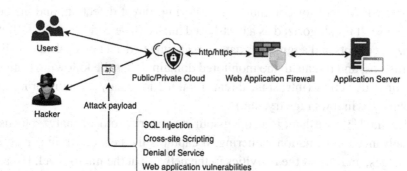

SIEM for Advanced Monitoring of the EPES Systems

There are many advanced SIEM tools available in the market. In this section, we are introducing cutting-edge monitoring and decision support tools for advanced threat analysis.

- **Splunk:** Splunk is an advanced SIEM monitoring program to gather logs from the ecosystem and perform analyzing, searching, and visualizing the machine-generated data in real-time. It can create alerts, graphs, and dashboards. It is really helpful to perform the triage process and root cause analysis. Incident search capability enables investigating specific issues. Analyzed data is indexed and metrics built to make informed decisions. Based on collected log files from various sources valuable information is being extracted and can be funneled to its machine learning engine to detect anomalies. Briefly, Splunk optimizes the security operations, provides well-established end-to-end monitoring coverage, has enhanced investigation capabilities, and supports making informed decisions. One major benefit is the infrastructure of Splunk. The data is being collected from the edge of the network and forwarded to a cloud location for data storage, indexing, and analysis. IoT-based devices do not have much hardware specification so just lightweight log forwarded is needed for Splunk to be operational in Fog/IoT networks. The major issue of Splunk is the application cost which can be an expensive tool for many organizations.

Universal Forwarder (UF) is a lightweight component that collects data from installed machines and forwards data into Splunk for indexing and consolidation. The main responsibility is just forwarding the log data. Load Balancer (LB) is helping to distribute log collection to work to available HFs. Heavy Forwarder (HF) component performs parsing data tasks before forwarding data and based on the rules such as source or type of events data can be routed to a specific indexer. In simple terms, HF is enabling data to be filtered. Majority of the time UF is the best way to forward data. Indexer helps to store and index collected data to improve search performance. Data is being indexed based on predefined or custom criteria such as host, source, date & time, and event type (error, success), etc. In summary, forwarders collect data from installed machines which are usually located on the edge of the network and forward data to the indexer in real-time. Indexers process the collected data and store & indexes them in real-time. Figure 6 is the illustration of the overall process.

Figure 6. Illustrates Splunk system architecture. How logs are forwarded and indexed/ analyzed on the cloud. Anomaly or threat detection is completed on the cloud.

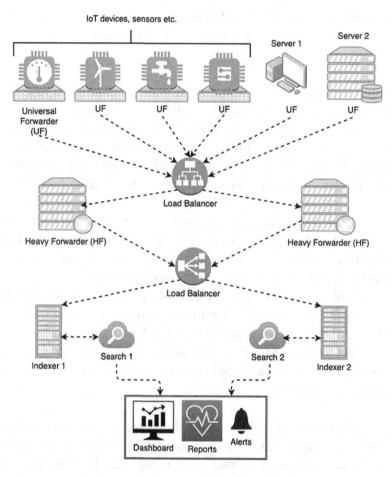

Splunk uses its "Search Processing Language" to retrieve stored data and perform analysis based on the constructed Splunk query (Figure below). It converts logs to human-readable form (summarizing them or generating other metrics etc.) Briefly, it consumes massive amounts of structured or unstructured data collected from applications, sensors, IoT devices, servers, networks to perform data analysis and visualizations.

- **Dynatrace:** Dynatrace is another type of SIEM, which is a software intelligence platform to monitor and optimize the application performance (APM - application performance monitoring) and IT infrastructure. Application monitoring is a focus of application availability and performance. Dynatrace gets all metrics in real-time and auto-detects application dependencies to track end-to-end transactions across the network. Dynatrace also supports anomaly detection for dynamic environments. Dynatrace and Splunk have similar features such as log monitoring, dashboards and alerting, etc. Splunk is like a data repository and performs analysis based on collected data whereas Dynatrace is generating the APM data from its agents from the host system. In this sense, we can say that Dynatrace is better suited for end-to-end application monitoring and end-user monitoring, etc. Dynatrace provides real user monitoring, synthetic transactions, environment/topology mapping & discovery, APM, database monitoring, automatic problem identification & root cause determination, and finally, packet-level network monitoring.

Figure 7. Shows a sample Splunk query and its syntax.

```
1   index="*IoT*" host=*.foobar.com source=*security.log* type="usage" earliest=-30d@d
2     | bin _time span=15m
3     | stats sum(b) AS byte_sum by idx, _time
4     | stats avg(byte_sum) as average, stdev(byte_sum) as std by idx
5     | outputlookup blacklist.csv
```

FUTURE RESEARCH DIRECTIONS

The future of the EPES cybersecurity systems will involve the development of agile systems that are able to produce rapid-response in order to prevent monetary losses as well as protection of critical infrastructure and human lives. This can be achieved by the deployment of the on-site agents to acquire real-time data from the OT and IT side of the smart grid systems including the generation, distribution, and consumption side of the EPES infrastructure.

It is predicted that future generation cybersecurity tool kits will propose a wholesome approach by employing various components such as follows but not limited to; SIEM, vulnerability analysis, firewall, DoS detection/mitigation, IPDS, etc.

CONCLUSION

In this chapter, the authors aim at providing the rationale behind the benefits of detecting cyber-security incidents in a timely manner. One of these beneficiaries of this service is the Decision Supports Systems running at the backhaul of the EPES providers.

To enhance the overall security of- and trust to- smart grid systems, the cyber-security of the smart meters and actuators should be solidified. This can be achieved by the usage of specific solutions, for instance, especially by using hardware-based security components such as HSM, PUF, SoaC, and TRM.

ACKNOWLEDGMENT

This work was funded in parts by the Swedish Foundation for International Cooperation in Research and Higher Education (STINT) Initiation Grants program under Grant No. IB2019-8185 and the European Union's H2020 research and innovation programme under the Grant Agreement No. 832907.

REFERENCES

Butun, I. (2013). *Prevention and detection of intrusions in wireless sensor networks* (Ph.D. Thesis). University of South Florida.

Butun, I., dos Santos, D., Lekidis, A., & Papatriantafilou, M. (2020). *Deliverable 3.4 Adaptive and Continuous Intrusion and Anomaly Detection for Smart Grid Systems*. United Grid, H2020 Project deliverable.

Butun, I., Lekidis, A., & dos Santos, D. R. (2020). Security and Privacy in Smart Grids: Challenges, Current Solutions, and Future Opportunities. In ICISSP (pp. 733-741). Academic Press.

Butun, I., Morgera, S. D., & Sankar, R. (2014). A survey of intrusion detection systems in wireless sensor networks. *IEEE Communications Surveys and Tutorials, 16*(1), 266–282. doi:10.1109/SURV.2013.050113.00191

Butun, I., & Österberg, P. (2019). Detecting intrusions in cyber-physical systems of smart cities: Challenges and directions. In *Secure Cyber-Physical Systems for Smart Cities* (pp. 74–102). IGI Global. doi:10.4018/978-1-5225-7189-6.ch004

Butun, I., Sari, A., & Österberg, P. (2019, January). Security implications of fog computing on the internet of things. In *2019 IEEE International Conference on Consumer Electronics (ICCE)* (pp. 1-6). IEEE. 10.1109/ICCE.2019.8661909

Butun, I., Sari, A., & Österberg, P. (2020). Hardware Security of Fog End-Devices for the Internet of Things. *Sensors (Basel), 20*(20), 5729. doi:10.339020205729 PMID:33050165

Fieldbus. (2021). *Process Industry Forum, acquired: 13/2/2021, "What is Fieldbus?"* https://www.processindustryforum.com/article/what-is-fieldbus

Forsström, S., Butun, I., Eldefrawy, M., Jennehag, U., & Gidlund, M. (2018, April). Challenges of securing the industrial internet of things value chain. In *2018 Workshop on Metrology for Industry 4.0 and IoT* (pp. 218-223). IEEE. 10.1109/METROI4.2018.8428344

Karnouskos, S. (2011, November). Stuxnet worm impact on industrial cyber-physical system security. In *IECON 2011-37th Annual Conference of the IEEE Industrial Electronics Society* (pp. 4490-4494). IEEE.

Sari, A., Lekidis, A., & Butun, I. (2020). Industrial Networks and IIoT: Now and Future Trends. In *Industrial IoT* (pp. 3–55). Springer. doi:10.1007/978-3-030-42500-5_1

Stallings, W., & Brown, L. (2015). *Computer security: principles and practice* (4th ed.). Pearson Education.

KEY TERMS AND DEFINITIONS

Agent: It is part of a software (most generally a SIEM tool) and consists of a program installed at the host machine to execute the following tasks: Event filtering, event aggregation, normalization of aggregated events, sending the results to the central management software (the SIEM tool) for further inspection.

Anomaly: A deviation from the normal behavior (also called abnormal) of the system or user.

Denial-of-Service (DoS): Represents a class of attack in which the targeted network or system disconnects and halts the intended mode of operation.

Event: An expected or unexpected happening related to systems that are in operation. Events are especially useful for monitoring tools such as the SIEM.

Firewall: A software or hardware that is designed to block and prevent unwanted or unauthorized network traffic between computer networks or hosts.

Intrusion: An event that an unauthorized user gathers a piece of information or an access right that he/she is not allowed to. Mostly represented by the events in IDSs.

Log File: It is a file that keeps records of events, which happen, in an operating system or other software runs. Logging is the function of keeping a log in a specific place. Log files are especially useful for SIEM tools.

Security Risk Assessment: Identifying the vulnerabilities of a system along with the possible worst-case scenarios as well as the evaluation of total property losses in case of such events. This is also referred to as "vulnerability analysis" in the literature.

Sensors: These are responsible for collecting evidence regarding events. Especially, if the agents mentioned earlier are in the form of hardware, they are referred to as "sensors."

ENDNOTES

[1] https://www.splunk.com/
[2] https://www.dynatrace.com/
[3] https://www.ibm.com/blogs/internet-of-things/iot-cheat-sheet-digital-twin/
[4] https://nmap.org/
[5] https://www.snort.org/
[6] https://www.sciencedirect.com/topics/computer-science/traceroute-command
[7] https://zeek.org/
[8] https://wazuh.com/
[9] https://www.wireshark.org/

Chapter 6
A Case Study of Decision Support System and Warehouse Management System Integration

Alparslan Sari
University of Delaware, USA

Ismail Butun
iD https://orcid.org/0000-0002-1723-5741
*Chalmers University of Technology, Sweden & Konya Food and Agriculture
University, Turkey & Royal University of Technology, Sweden*

ABSTRACT

A warehouse is an indispensable part of the logistics. A warehouse management system (WMS) is designed to improve efficiency in warehouses to increase their throughput and potential. The rise of IoT and its commercialization enabled 'smart things' to be widely adopted by hobbyists and companies. Cheap sensors and smart devices triggered better automation opportunities. Many devices and sensors that are being deployed in the industry and warehousing are affected by this trend. A well-designed WMS is needed to connect devices and humans in a heterogenous warehouse environment. This chapter introduces a prototype of a WMS powered by a decision support system (DSS) based on real-life requirements. In order to have fast, reliable, and efficient decision making in warehousing, the importance of employing DSS in the WMS is emphasized. Warehouse-related IoT technology is briefly introduced, and its security considerations are discussed thoroughly. The main contribution of this chapter is to show how warehouse operations can be modeled in business process model notation and executed in a DSS.

DOI: 10.4018/978-1-7998-7468-3.ch006

INTRODUCTION

Logistic is one of the major powerhouses to advance human civilization from the old times to the modern age. Many civilizations collapsed due to famine and lack of resources in the past. However, the improvement in logistics enabled resource sharing between nations in a cost-efficient manner and the industrial revolution enabled large-scale production with low cost. The Internet was a game-changer for traditional commerce where customers needed to go to stores for shopping. Rapid development in e-commerce triggered storage problems for produced products as well as for raw materials. Therefore, industrialization and logistics contributed to human welfare to help fight against famine and prevent the collapse of civilizations in the modern age. Industrial mass production helped to reduce the purchase cost and bring improvement in logistics - distribution of these products made them available in the global market at a fair price. A **warehouse** is an integral piece in the supply chain concept to store and forward goods. Many warehouses are being used for storing goods or processing the products in a custom manner like repackaging and bundling/knitting etc. The performance of the warehouse operations affects the overall productivity and cost for all stakeholders. The whole supply chain is tightly coupled with warehouse operations. In warehouse operations, repacking/preparing an order can be considered a labor-intensive and high-cost operation. In order to overcome this tedious manual-intensive labor, Amazon Inc. built semi-autonomous warehouses, which utilize almost 200,000 robots in operation within its warehouses in the US[1]. Amazon Inc. also cut jobs to replace manual work with automation and robot workers to optimize warehouse operations[2]. Amazon Inc. tries to increase the efficiency and throughput in warehouses with the power of automation. Any performance issues or complications in warehouse operations may result in congestion and delays in logistics, which causes financial loss, reputation loss, and reducing customer satisfaction, and affect the overall standing of an enterprise and other unwanted conditions.

The fundamental of warehousing is to provide essential services such as receiving shipments (inbound), storing, pick & pack process and sending (outbound) shipments. The pick and pack process is usually considered the most manual-intensive process in warehouse operations and it gets complex based on many different parameters such as working with many customers, managing a mix of large inventory (please see Figure 1). Major issues are inbound shipment scheduling, item processing in the warehouse (cleaning, repackaging, bundling, etc.), outbound shipment scheduling, optimizing financial cost, reconciliation process between customers.

The end-to-end warehouse process starts with a third-party logistics company transporting the delivery with a truck that docks the warehouse. Warehouse operators need to empty the truck at a given time. Based on the warehouse capacity, there are a limited number of docks available. If there is any slowness, all docks can be occupied with trucks and new truck arrivals cause congestion. Once the trucks are being emptied, operators need to store these products in a temporary space. If there is no sorting automation available that will fasten the overall process, operators manually sort the goods based on the customer then store them in a designated zone for these products which are assigned by WMS. These will prevent possible fragmentation of customer goods in the warehouse and will speed up the overall process. Also, the order picking process can be considered a highly time-consuming activity and a bottleneck in warehouse operations. To improve the operational efficiency and optimize the order picking process efficient location management is needed. Location management should be tightly coupled with inventory management (product location and storage location). Most of the time, products need to be processed per customer request then shipped to the final destination. The final destination could be another warehouse or an individual. These warehousing workflows briefly show us the need for efficient warehouse management systems with a decision support capability.

A warehouse management system (WMS) is used to track the inventory life cycle in a warehouse or between warehouses and/or distribution centers (or an individual). Optimization is a key objective to reduce operation costs and maximize the processing output in industrial logistics. A WMS helps to improve warehouse operations like receiving a shipment, storing the product, preparing a product, or shipping away a product accurately and efficiently. Decision Support Systems (DSS) is a kind of advanced software to help decision-making on critical determinations and judgments in an organization, based on analysis of collected data from various sources in a flexible manner. It is also an integral part of a WMS to contribute to the overall optimization process. A DSS can operate autonomously, supervised by humans, or both. The goal is to make informed decisions in a fast and accurate manner to do the planning, event management, and other decision-making-related tasks. A DSS collects data from various components (IoT devices, sensors, or third-party sources), business flow (time-series data in a specific business, transactions, etc.), documents, or personnel knowledge.

WMS-DSS covers many predefined business workflows and what-if cases. Based on scenario rules and collected data, DSS optimizes the business process, adjusts scheduling, etc. Personnel staffing (headcount) for each day is advised by DSS based on collected data such as expected inbound shipment, items needed to process in the warehouse, service level agreement (SLA) promised to clients, and other factors like time of the year (Holiday season, Black Friday, Cyber Monday, etc.). A well-designed WMS-DSS standardizes the data quality by setting up business rules about data collection, data generation, and data store procedures. Without a WMS-DSS all decisions need to be made by human decision-makers based on human experience and beliefs but this increases the complexity of the warehouse operations. On a busy season like Black Friday or Christmas, multiple teams work in parallel while sharing resources. There could be bias based on human emotions. Therefore, it is essential to use automation as much as possible to reduce manual effort and a WMS-DSS can eliminate many manual challenging tasks like scheduling and other decision required efforts.

Figure 1. The abstract view of warehouse operations and interactions.

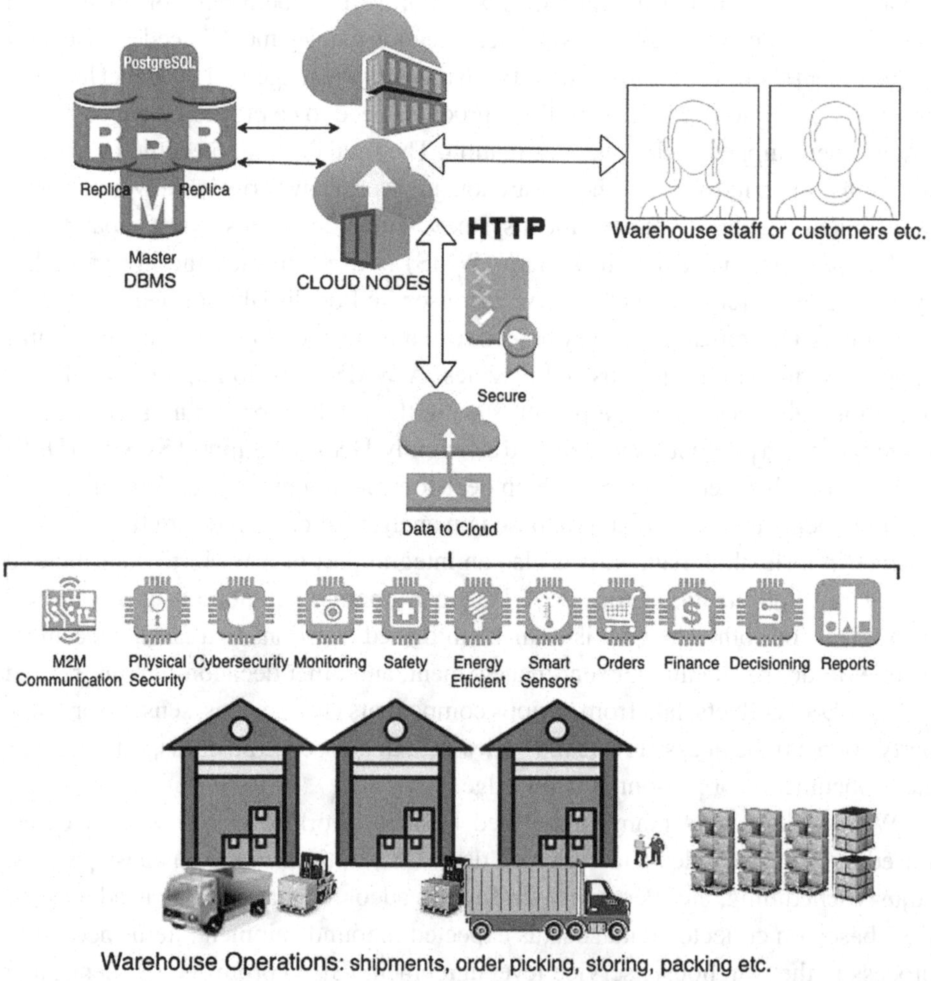

In industry, one can find many WMS systems based on needs and complexity. It is possible to find an enterprise resource planning (ERP) that may address the customer needs but it is hard to find a generic WMS-DSS system. However, many logistic companies and warehouse owners have different business requirements so one software for all is not a good choice. Many logistic companies require customized WMS and because of different business models and warehouse operation requirements, it is hard to do standardization for a WMS. Most of the time it is hard to customize the available open-source projects.

It is not possible to cover every aspect of warehousing technologies in one chapter but we will briefly introduce WMS-DSS integration and its security concerns as a showcase with this chapter. We also will not focus on distributed warehouse management and DSS modules. We introduced the ideas and implementations primarily for a single warehouse. However, our design is quite scalable and this WMS-DSS integration can be extended for distributed warehouse management systems seamlessly. In our design, customers are interacting with a warehouse and WMS-DSS collects information in every step of the business flow. The first step is when a customer places the shipment orders to the warehouse, WMS needs to collect the required information for the warehouse to process expected inbound shipments. Based on shipment volume, a DSS can detect the current load of the warehouse (Is it at full capacity?) and advise managers how many employees needed for a specific date to handle incoming shipments or advise customers to send their shipments to another warehouse that has a better bandwidth to support customer needs. A DSS can also inform customers about their product cost/profit analysis to show which product is profitable on their end. Improving warehouse productivity is a challenging task but a warehouse can increase its throughput dramatically with optimization and standardization techniques supported by the software. Increasing warehouse productivity means increasing profit in business and lowering the cost for customers as well.

In this chapter, we will explain how the DSS concept can be integrated with IoT devices and WMS. The traditional warehouse management operation without DSS and/or IoT is the major bottleneck for a successful company. There are many examples in the industry that a modern WMS makes a higher profit than the old-school version. A modern WMS uses IoT technologies to collect data or improve features like sorting incoming shipments or adopting wearable RFID devices in the warehouse to operate faster. The purpose of this chapter is to give an example of how a WMS system can be integrated with DSS to optimize warehouse operations for possible stakeholders. Technical details about IoT hardware specifications and communication technologies are omitted in this work since the primary focus is WMS-DSS integration and their security concerns.

Main considerations of designing a new WMS-DSS in this chapter:

1. Cost: Reducing cost in warehouse operations, (detecting material consumption and enabling bulk ordering with cheaper price), optimizing staffing, optimizing

warehouse operations to increase warehouse processing capacity. 1M revenue to 20M revenue increase is possible with the same warehouse.

2.   Information availability between stakeholders to complete reconciliation processes and to make informed decisions. Inbound/outbound shipments etc.
3.   Long-term benefits: branding, profit, etc.

In conclusion, we will show a real-world example of how a DSS integrates with an IIoT oriented WMS system to assist customers and business management to analyze structured or unstructured data to solve problems (scheduling conflicts, etc) and propose efficient decisions in different situations. Most of the DSS-WMS projects are designed to operate in a single warehouse. However, our design supports multi-warehouses and we use the conceptual design of a Camunda based DSS integration with a highly scalable warehouse management system.

The remainder of the chapter is organized as follows: The Background section introduces the history of the WMS and DSS systems. Whereas, the WSM and DSS sections present important points related to each of these technologies. In the Use-Case Scenario section, real implementation of a WMS-DSS architecture is introduced via a bottom-up approach. The Future Research Directions section identifies possible extensions of this work for the authors and other researchers. Finally, the Conclusion section concludes this study.

BACKGROUND

An early research study introduced a decision support system for vendor management inventory two decades ago (Achabal, D. et al, 2000). The system is implemented by a manufacturer and over 30 of its retail partners. It described market forecasting and inventory management (Vendor Managed Inventory) components of a decision support system to improve customer service level agreements and increase inventory turnover targets. However, our system is designed for multiple warehouses, many retailers, and individuals in a highly scalable manner. Our design complexity is higher than Achabal et al. and many others. Our target audience is all individuals who do e-commerce business and more.

The historical IIoT evolution, its current state of the art, and future trends are well explained in a recent book chapter (Sari, A. et al, 2020). There is a lot of research for DSS in warehousing. For instance, an example case of a warehousing decision support system is illustrated (Min, 2009). Warehouse operations and logistics are well-established topics in the research community. A DSS is proposed to improve order planning and customer order fulfillment in the warehouse to enhance the overall supply chain performance (Lam, C.H.Y. et al, 2011). The DSS is mostly focused on order picking and planning but in our research, we consider a scalable system focused on end-to-end warehousing problems. Another research (Lao, S.I. et al, 2011) has developed a real-time inbound DSS for food-related warehouses using RFID (Radio-Frequency IDentification), case-based reasoning (CBR), and fuzzy reasoning (FR). A decision support system for public logistics information service management is proposed and it focuses on optimization to reduce logistic cost (Hu, Z.H. et al, 2014). Another DSS is proposed to design better management and control of warehousing systems which enables development and configure different scenarios (Accorsi, R. et al, 2014). It has a simulation option to simulate different warehouse scenarios to choose routing and order batching strategies. An IoT-based WMS is proposed based on collected data from a case company (Lee, C.K.M. et al, 2017). Operational risk management in the supply chain with 3PL providers is studied in the DSS concept as well (Gómez, J. C. O. et al, 2017). A group decision-making system for selecting logistic providers using quality function deployment and fuzzy linguistic terms is designed (Yazdani, M. et al, 2017). A DSS incorporating an agent-based simulation and dynamic routing procedures to investigate e-grocery inventory and delivery operations is developed (Fikar, C. (2018)). An illustration of how a decision-support tool (DST) that aids 3PL managers to decide on the proper warehouse management system (WMS) customization is proposed (Baruffaldi, G. et al, 2019). The tool addresses the cost of the information sharing, the scarce visibility of the client's data, and the uncertainty of quantifying the return from investing into a WMS feature. A different DSS is designed to propose simultaneous collaboration and sustainability functionalities (Allaoui, H. et al, 2019). Another study reviewed IoT-based smart warehouse monitoring systems. They presented a model IoT system that points out the shortcomings of existing solutions focusing on warehouse monitoring and control systems based on IoT (Čolaković, A. et al, 2020). Finally, a showcase of an intelligent drug management system based on RFID (designing an intelligent monitoring cabinet) for drug-specific warehouses is presented (Li, S. et al, 2020).

METHODOLOGY

We designed and implemented a basic WMS based on the business requirements and warehouse properties. It is deployed to Amazon Web Services (AWS) as a cloud node in 2018. The project itself is implemented with the following technology stack: PHP, JavaScript, and SQLite. Graphical user interface (GUI) is designed in HTML, Bootstrap, Jquery, and JavaScript. The backend server is coded in PHP. SQLite is used as a lightweight database. The prototype WMS is used in a 6000sq feet warehouse for order fulfillment and repackaging service, and it handled more than

500,000 transactions in the past year. However, we redesigned the initial prototype to integrate with a decision support system for this case study. The new technology stack is Angular/React/Vue (one of them can be used for designing frontend GUI), Camunda BPM (a decision support tool based on business process modeling), Java Spring Boot (Backend), and PostgreSQL (database). The final project can be deployed either public cloud services like Azure, AWS, Google-Cloud, etc., or a private cloud. The GUI and backend design will be omitted in this chapter since the primary focus of this chapter is integrating the WMS and DSS and its security considerations.

Data collection is important for detecting bottlenecks and finding optimization opportunities. Therefore, we will collect meaningful data in each step of warehouse operations (from multiple resources: IoT devices, human operators, inventory life cycle track based on SKU or FNSKU, the dimension of a product, number of items received, timestamp collection for each operation, receiving location, shipment info, etc.). Moreover, for better planning and decision purposes, we require data from other stakeholders such as customers (shipment info, orders, etc.), logistic company (tracking info, ETA), etc. Collecting data in each step provides transparency in operations and improves the reconciliation process. Reconciliation is an important factor between stakeholders to establish trust. Hence data aggregation is needed to build a meaningful DSS. Finally, the aim in this chapter is to remove ambiguity in WMS and implement a simple robust modular system design.

WAREHOUSE MANAGEMENT SYSTEM

Warehouse operations are getting complex each day due to the high demand for online shopping and increased complexity in logistics. Customer orders are getting complex as well, a good and improved fulfillment strategy needs to be adopted. Frequent order changes, customer returns, or availability of a product in a single warehouse are some of the major contributing factors in the complexity. By its nature, a classical WMS system just works as a bookkeeping software whose main functionality is displaying real-time information without any decision-making capabilities. However, a well-designed DSS supports complex problem-solving and decision-making capabilities to optimize the overall process. WMS helps to optimize the warehouse operations to achieve cost reduction and improve the speed of preparing/processing items. The reconciliation process would be easier with customers. Moreover, WMS can build advanced auditing options to trace every operation in the warehouse business process to make it transparent. A well-designed WMS also supports real-time information sharing with all stakeholders. A change request from a customer can immediately be updated in the WMS.

Traditionally, warehouse operations were handled with generic Enterprise resource planning (ERP) modules. However, with the recent increase of e-commerce and demand in online shopping globally, customized WMS is needed to handle and optimize warehouse operations better. Each business has unique warehousing problems but the success parameters in warehousing are efficient inventory management, packaging, and shipment processing in general. Automation and computerization are major contributing factors to achieve high processing metrics in warehouse environments. Large-scale warehouse operations tend to expose uncertain conditions such as the dependency of weather, inbound shipment delay, and third-party vendor dependency, etc. Inefficient or inaccurate product fulfillment increases the overall cost, such as extra shipment cost, return cost, time loss, operation cost, and reputation loss, etc. Vice versa an efficient fulfillment operation lowers the cost (material, wage, shipment, etc.) and improves the profit with increasing throughput in the warehouse. Other affected costs are the cost of unloading and loading (money, time, etc.), processing cost (picking, packing, etc).

Industry 4.0 revolution enabled advanced technological features such as automation and robotics which helps warehouses to handle more bandwidth to process more items. Industrial IoTs are used in automation and robotics to perform tasks or handle monitoring. Smart technologies like sensors and actuators are an integral part of Industry 4.0. These features are designed and implemented to improve safety, speed, and cost reduction. Industry 4.0 and the Industrial IoT concept is well explained (Sari, 2020). RFID/NFC and WSANs (Wireless Sensors and Actuator Networks) are key communication technologies in warehouse operations. RFID technology is used to identify and track the products in the warehouse life cycle.

Monitoring temperature fluctuations and humidity changes may be critical in a warehouse. Therefore, using IoT-based devices will help us to monitor changes such as safety, efficiency, and QoS (quality of service). A devastating event happened in Beirut in 2020 (207 deaths, 7,500 injuries, 15US$ billion estimated damage, and an estimated 300,000 people became homeless), the explosion caused by a large amount of ammonium nitrate[3]. A dangerous material seems to be stored in a warehouse without proper safety procedures in place for almost six years. Certain products require specific safe storage conditions such as temperature, humidity, pressure, and static electric-free environments. These parameters need to be monitored all the time for safety requirements. Hazardous materials should be handled according to safety regulations and policies. Smoke detectors, gas detectors, etc. should be active all the time to monitor environmental parameters along with warehouse security sensors, security cameras against theft and hazardous situations. Motion detection sensors can be used. A simple 2D barcode can be used as a product identifier and location tracker. Sensors and RFID tags can be the next level for inventory management to track the actual position of the product inside/outside of the warehouse with GPS technology. This will enable the smart inventory plan and control the current inventory.

Barcode and RFID tags should be an essential part of the automation process to handle large volumes of items in an efficient manner. WMS can capture information via barcode or RFID to update necessary information in DB without any human involvement which will improve the overall operation speed significantly. The main goal is to eliminate the toil (repeated tasks and manual work) as much as possible to improve the overall operation stability, scalability, and efficiency. Therefore, we used 2D barcode-based location management for all products due to the cost. RFID is implemented for certain strategic products to store and retrieve.

Machine to Machine (M2M) communication is another important aspect in WMS to eliminate human involvement in operations. A conveyor belt carries shipments; a barcode reader can read the packages and mark them as received items from DB without human involvement. The M2M concept is another important topic in automation and digitization in WMS which speeds up the overall process with minimum errors.

We will use a hybrid approach of FOG and cloud concepts. IoT generated data would be processed on edge, however, the raw data and results will be stored in the cloud for future analysis. All other human-related generated data will be collected in the cloud and retrieved from the cloud once needed. Data collection is an important part of the critical decision process. DSS needs data to provide accurate optimization solutions. Data collection enables us to design and implement advanced analytical capabilities which will be funneled to feed DSS and other critical systems.

DECISION SUPPORT SYSTEMS

DSS study is around for almost half a century (Power:2008) and used in many different areas such as in agriculture, business, healthcare, industry, logistic, real estate, military, and etc. There are many variations of it such as communication-driven (to collaborate with many on a task), data-driven (to focus analyzing data from internal and external sources), document-driven (to process unstructured information from many resources like cloud storage, shared drives, or third party APIs), knowledge-driven (to delivering informed decision based on scenarios) and model-driven (to analyze based on statistical models).

A DSS is computer software that helps human operators to make decisions in the business workflow. A DSS analyzes the gathered data from various sources to make informed decisions or performs automated calculations based on predefined rules. There are ERP/standalone, and SaaS (Software as a Service) options are available. Any constraints on any business model or workflow complicate the overall problem. In most cases, a human authority needs to make decisions based on the circumstances, or trade-off between options. Scheduling or arithmetic data is used to make this kind of decision. DSS enables resource scheduling, making decisions quickly and accurately. These features should have a positive contribution to warehouse throughput.

The benefits of using DSS are improving speed and efficiency in decision-making-related activities. Communication and collaboration between stakeholders are established. Enforces business rules to collect data to automate analysis and managerial duties. Finally, it applies to use-case scenarios on given data sets and generates accurate projections based on data analysis and learned business rules. On the other hand, the disadvantages of DSS are the cost related issues (implementation, integration, maintenance cost, and etc.), feature creep (adding too many parameters in decision-making pipeline would miss simplest and efficient solutions), and negative effect on non-managerial employees (not realistic goals or heavy tasks are assigned from DSS) Core components are a modeling system (to collect and analyze data, decision-making), a database management system (DBMS store data), and support tools (user interface, reporting tools, and etc.)

In our design, the DSS is part of the data collection process from various sources (collect and organize) and analyzing the data (Figure 2). DSS will help warehouses to manage the customer inventory, project revenue, inbound and outbound shipments, etc. Our DSS implementation is fully automated without human involvement in the process. We adopted BPM (Business Process Modeling) to handle business process management. We will use Camunda for BPM and decision-making automation. There are some alternatives like Bonita, Bizagi, IBM BPM, Pega BPM, Appian, etc. The main reason for our selection is based on Camunda being an open-source software and has a free licensing option.

Camunda BPM is an open-source process automation software based on BPMN 2.0 (Business Process Model and Notation). A business process is defined by three key elements: a collection of interrelated activities (human or machine), a response to an independent trigger (customer complaints, etc.), and a specific result (a well-defined end state). BPMN enables the design of business processes graphically with provided tools using visual representations of events, tasks, gateways, etc. Camunda creates and executes the business workflow. It is powered by a workflow and decision engine. It is implemented in Java and it provides a REST API to connect its work engine.

Figure 2. Representation of abstract data pipeline (data ® business rules ® solution) and its interactions

Structured or Unstructured Data

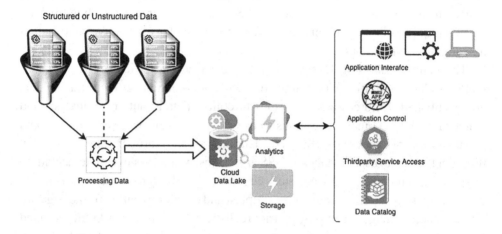

USE-CASE SCENARIO

Preliminary Risk Analysis

Risk Management involves assessing and mitigating financial or reputation loss. Risk management has non-technical and technical considerations and the following is a sample subset of possible warehousing-related risks. Non-technical issues are accidents in the warehouse, inaccurate information about the shipments, documental problems, human errors, supply chain-related issues: shipment delays, lost/damaged items in shipment or warehouse inventory, physical security, etc. Technical issues are database replication, multiple cloud node availability, cybersecurity, technical faults - all digital or analog machinery faults, etc… Risk analysis and prevention are important in operational aspects: to prevent lost goods, reconciliation between sender and customer. End-to-end validation is important to mitigate the possible loss for both warehouse and customers, starting from front-end to server, all data is validated in each step.

To mitigate monetary loss, a well-defined and balanced business should be enforced. For instance, a shipment package that has high monetary value should be handled in a special way. Package opening will be recorded to video as proof that all items are presented as promised or any missing item there. This evidence collection would slow down the overall operation speed or put extra cost (storage, time to video extract, etc.) so based on available data (shipment value, previous incidents) the DSS should suggest a threshold value to perform the special instructions.

Sample DSS Rule:

If *Acceptable loss threshold > amounts based on a certain value*
then *packages with over acceptable loss value will be handled in a special manner.*

DSS Risk Management Steps:

- Risk Identification: the value of inbound goods, shipment delays, lost/ damaged items.
- Risk Prioritization: the value of goods, cost of shipment delay, cost of lost/ damaged items.
- Risk Quantification: grouping risks (technical defects, shipment, monetary loss, etc.).
- Risk Management: eliminate or mitigate the risk.

System Architecture

WMS is the backbone for seamless operations in a warehouse and it provides service for both clients and warehouse operators. The WMS-DSS architecture is shown in Fig 1, which has a heterogeneous environment consisting of mobile terminal stations, printing nodes, barcode readers, and their cloud integration. In this section, we briefly explain the WMS-DSS design principles and introduce the core modules for the WMS. How modules are interacting with each other and human operators are shown. Warehouse policies regarding its operation, safety, and security are discussed. Labor-intensive, not automated warehouses usually boost their throughput and profit with advanced machinery and automation. Well-defined business process policies should be also compatible with automation implementations such as security (physical or cyber), shipment, preparation, safety, storage or problem management policies, etc.

A warehouse should be operating based on the business needs with different modes such as first-in-first-out (FIFO), the last-in-first-out (LIFO), first-expiring-first-out (FEFO), last-expiring-first-out (LEFO). Service level agreements (SLA) should be defined clearly. For instance, after receiving the shipment, the products should be prepared for the next destination and shipped out in 72 hours, etc. The warehouse should be operated based on well-defined SLAs and KPIs and the DSS should manage the warehouse schedule and decision based on these metrics. A decision-making process related to resource scheduling in warehouse operations (work prioritization, staffing, etc.) is also affected by defined metrics.

Time is a good KPI metric to evaluate warehouse operations. Processed item count, lost items in the warehouse, sent shipment volume could be considered as KPIs. Following KPIs could be collected for optimization and performance measurement metrics: receiving KPIs (time), preparation KPIs (time, % success and wasted material, cost attached), packaging KPIs (time, % of success), picking KPIs, shipment KPIs (% of wrong order). Cost analysis per SKU for both warehouse and customers and cost analysis regarding storage usage vs rent could be other financial KPIs.

The core modules of the WMS are order management, location management, inbound shipment management, outbound shipment management, finance management, problem management, customer management. Customer management will be omitted since it is nothing special and common for many ERP systems providing standard services like login/register, password assistance, and building user profiles.

Information Availability

Our system collects information in every step of the warehouse product life cycle. Data collection starts when the inbound shipments are received and the following information is collected: timestamp, tracking number, package condition, and receiver info. Product dimensions are also collected during the item receive process and will be mapped to a unique identifier such as an SKU, FNSKU, and ASIN. The next step is the product location in the warehouse that is actively kept track: on a conveyor belt or in a bin, shelf, rack position, etc. Item preparation time, outbound shipment process time, used items, and staff information are being recorded as well. Based on collected metrics, managerial teams clearly define the key performance metrics (KPI) for the warehouse and compare KPIs monthly, quarterly or yearly to monitor the organizational success. Information availability provides transparency in the warehousing operations and establishes a seamless audit process. Customers can also perform analysis to explore their business in detail based on information availability.

Stakeholders and Key Process Decisions

The main stakeholders are clients who want to send shipments to a warehouse to get some kinds of service (store, forward, repackage, send items to other individuals), warehouse staff (managers, supervisors, operators), and other third party logistic entities. Key decisions are made by all stakeholders. A customer can make a decision on inbound shipments or store forward, return requests. Warehouse management can make decisions on a shift schedule, work prioritization, etc. These decisions should be manageable in an easy manner.

Task Assignment

Task assignment is an important component for non-automated and semi-automated warehouses which relies heavily on the human workforce. There could still be a need for an assignment module for fully automated warehouses as well. All task assignments should be easily done via UI and work progress can be trackable. The assignments should be suggested by the DSS (Figure 3) based on the parameters (staff scheduling, warehouse load, work needs to be done, the priority of the work, SLAs, KPIs, etc.) as of the task assignment time.

Figure 3. Shows the BPMN representation of the task assignment

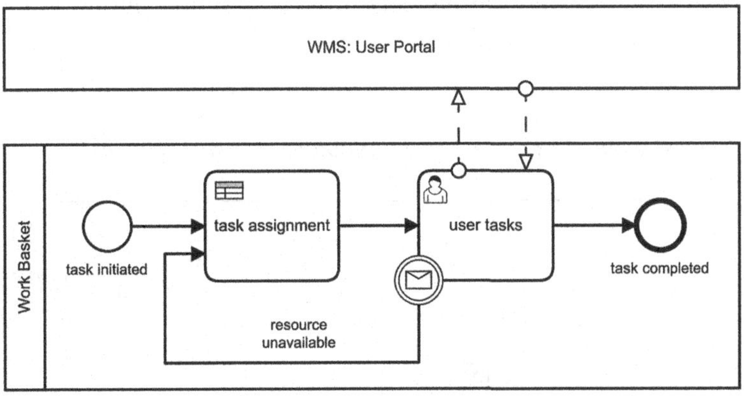

Inbound Process

Inbound shipment process can be considered as the initial stage of warehouse operations. The first step of inbound shipment is data collection from the customer about the inbound shipment. In order to get informed decisions (Figure 4) data collection related to inbound shipment from customers is a must. The following information can be considered as critical for this stage: estimated delivery date, expected products, quantity, SKU or FNSKU, tracking number, product monetary value, etc.

The next step is receiving the shipments from the delivery company (unloading a truck and checking product conditions for any damage). Receiving operations is tightly coupled with product sorting based on customer ids on shipment labels and location management to store the products. Shipment sorting can be done while unloading from the truck via customized package sorter machinery.

Receiving items may require tedious manual work to open packages and check if there is any damaged, missing product. If so, open a problem case to resolve the issue to inform the customer to advise to contact the delivery or insurance company to get recompensed. If the item quantity is less or more than expected, again inform the customer to contact the sender about the mistake. The warehouse system should provide evidence of the box opening, to document there is no theft happening in the warehouse and this is a genuine issue from the sender side. Hence the warehouse should not be accountable for the missing product. These examples should be part of the well-defined warehouse operation policies.

In summary, the inbound process has the following business flow: data collection from a customer, unloading a truck, receiving packages, quality and quantity control, sorting (automatic or manual), read the tracking # to reconcile with a logistics company to acknowledge the received packets to find if any were lost during shipment and be accountable of the received packages.

Figure 4. Shows camunda BPMN for the inbound shipment process.

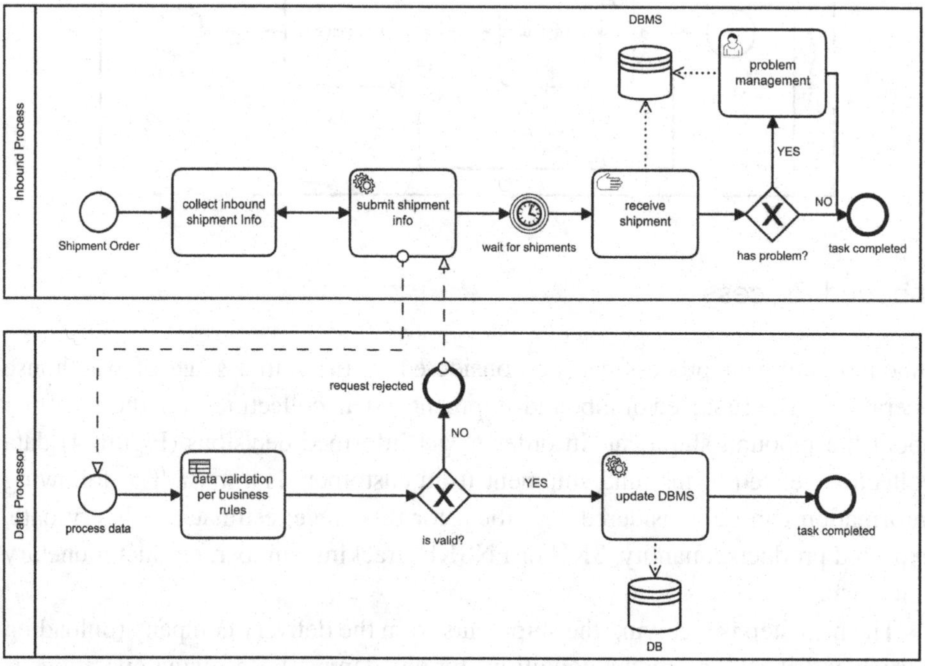

Inventory Management

The inventory management process is important as it is connected to inbound, outbound shipments, and location management. A customer inventory constantly changes, and it needs to be tracked accurately and efficiently (Figure 5). Tracking inventory life cycles in warehouses is a vital process. Integrating inventory and location management is important to prevent misplaced items or lost items in the warehouse. Finding or making corrections in the inventory is a time-consuming task if not a monetary loss.

Figure 5. Shows the BPMN representation of the inventory management

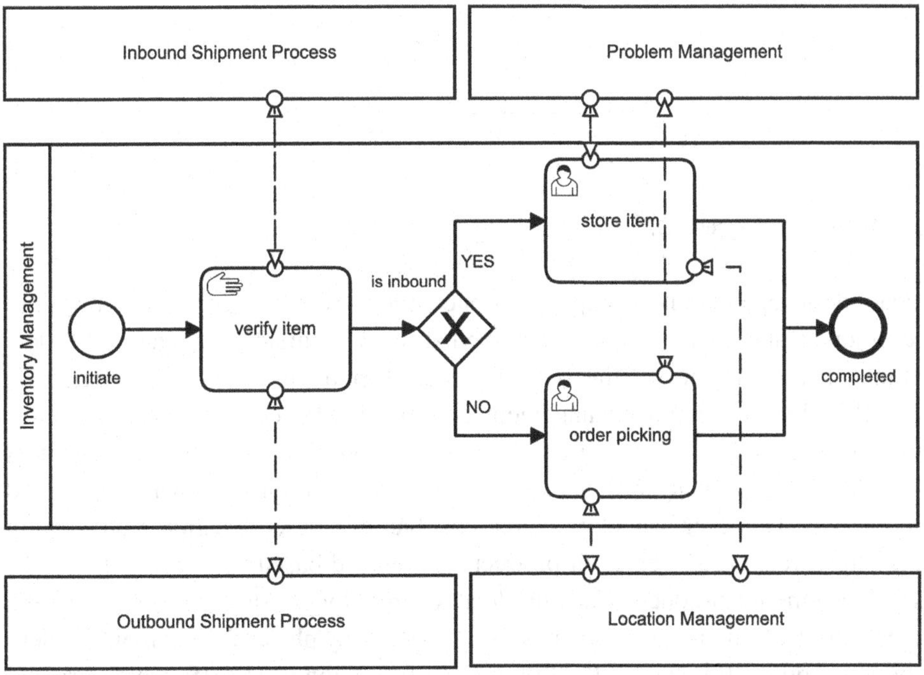

Order Fulfillment

It is an important challenge in logistics and order picking is considered one of the most time-consuming operations in warehousing. Once a customer buys a product it should be prepared by the warehouse and sent to the customer in an error-free and timely manner. Therefore, information sharing between customers and WMS is required. Real-time information accessing is important for all stakeholders to track the order status and other important business process information. This may help to improve the overall auditing process (defining and enforcing SLAs) regarding order fulfillment. A well-defined policy should be implemented about order picking: Should it be an individual pick, batch pick, or sequential pick? The policy should be generated on the fly by DSS (Figure 6) based on the given order and item location.

Figure 6. Shows the BPMN representation of the order fulfillment.

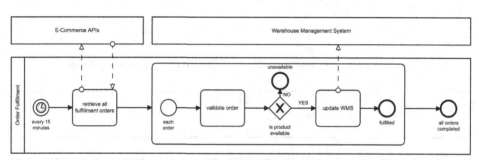

Location Management

Location management is an important concept for a warehouse to efficiently store the products and retrieve them when needed in an accurate, efficient, and timely manner. It also minimizes the risk of the product being lost in the warehouse. The RFID-based location management concept is adapted in many warehouses with the rise of IoT technologies. Therefore RFID-based location management is implemented in many warehouses and expected to improve order picking and productivity. However, we adopted low-cost barcode-based location management in this research. Once a batch of products is received based on availability, WMS assigns a zone for products. Each product is sorted by customer id and assigned a barcode for tracking its location in the warehouse. Any physical movement of these products requires tracking of the following information in DBMS; which product is being moved, origin and destination. Location management enables the picking and storing process seamlessly in a time-saving manner. The major limitation of the location management is the required physical space of the warehouse to assign dedicated space for each customer and fragmented inventory (inefficient space usage).

Space availability in the warehouse to accept new shipments or storing products in warehouses based on safety policies is determined in this module (Figure 7).

Figure 7. Shows the BPMN representation of location management.

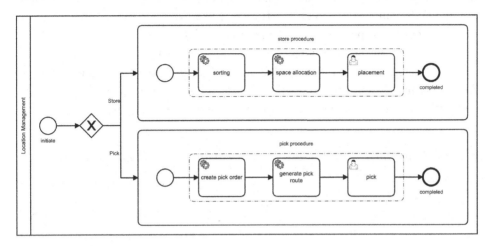

Outbound Process

Outbound is the last stage for an item in the warehouse product life cycle. The outbound process takes care of the item shipment (single or bulk) and updates regarding database tables. Outbound process tightly coupled with inventory management and finance module. If needed WMS makes connections with problem management and location management modules (Figure 8).

Figure 8. Shows the BPMN representation of the outbound process.

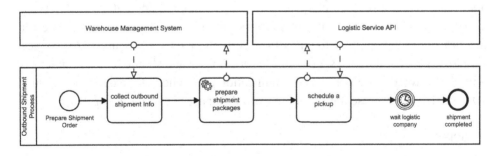

Problem Management

Problem management is an integral and critical operation in warehousing. Any inconsistency in the data should be investigated and corrected. A customer or warehouse staff can report errors or request reconciliation. DSS should be utilized to mitigate the problems in the process (Figure 9). For instance, based on the aggregated data, the DSS could advise to be careful while working with high monetary value items or packages to process to minimize financial loss. The DSS policy could be defined as if the product contains high monetary value items: check if the sender provided expected quantity otherwise document the evidence about missing items (the system should capture the moment of box opening to prove that the responsibility stays with the sender) so the warehouse should not be accountable.

Figure 9. Shows the BPMN representation of the problem management.

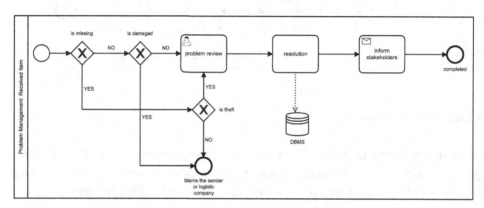

Finance Module

The finance module is another critical piece of the WMS. It should be secure, stable, and error-free. All service charges should be calculated accurately, and service charges should be validated prior to processing payment. Increase of a user error this process should support modification, correction, or reconciliation. An invoice should be generated with a service charge breakdown and should be communicated with the customer based on the communication preference of the customer. Figure 10 is the BPMN representation of the overall finance transaction workflow.

Policies

Warehouse operations should be designed based on policies to guarantee the quality of service to customers. Policies should clearly define SLAs and KPIs based on the industry standards and the warehouse service offered. Every operation and workflow are executed based on policies. Problem management and reconciliation processes are also tightly coupled with policies. Briefly, a well-implemented WMS should cover end-to-end warehouse policies such as accepting inbound shipments then receiving and storing or processing them should be based on policies defined by decision-makers. In this project, we define and enforce policies based on the Camunda tool and WMS interface.

Figure 10. Shows the BPMN representation of the finance process.

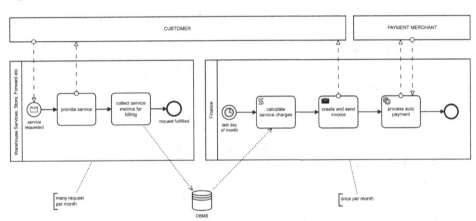

Security Concerns

Physical and cybersecurity are both important and legit concerns in warehousing. Both physical and cybersecurity concerns may result in monetary loss and reputation loss. In order to enhance physical security a camera-based surveillance system should be used and an industrial safety and security system should be subscribed to work with law enforcement to mitigate physical security concerns. Possible physical threat vectors are theft and arson.

Cybersecurity principles should be followed such as access controls, using secure software packages, etc. Cybersecurity-related issues could result in data leaks or data loss. Unsecure software systems can be compromised and susceptible to various attacks such as computer viruses, malware, and ransomware attacks.

A warehouse has physical and cybersecurity standards and protocols. A DSS can help to implement such protocols based on the business need. For instance, based on the product type, location management can be influenced by DSS where to store goods in the warehouse. Ex. flammable material should not stay with reacting material etc.

CYBER-SECURITY CONSIDERATIONS FOR THE WMSS

WMSs include many IoT end-devices especially during the asset racking phase of the operation. Traditionally, these devices are managed by the command center; however, with the recent developments in the field of fog/edge computing, they are being controlled and commanded at the edge of the network (at the factory floor). This introduces many advantages such as fast processing and decision-making. On the other hand, it brings cyber-security implications due to the added abstract layer in the management process (Butun, I., Sari, A., Österberg, P., 2019). There are ways of improving the cyber-security of fog computing such as hardware-based security of IoT fog end-devices (Butun, I., Sari, A., & Österberg, P., 2020), which is an important concept to be considered regarding WMS security.

As Cyber-Physical Systems (CPSs) are one of the main soft components of the WMS, they might also constitute a single point of failure where attackers can benefit. Intrusions can always happen in computer systems and CPS is not safe either. Therefore, instance intrusion detection (Butun, I. et al, 2015) is identified as the main pillar of cyber defense for Cyber Security systems. As such, intrusion detection systems (IDS) play an important role in defending CPSs (Butun, I., & Österberg, P., 2019) and can be employed by WMS security systems. For instance, anomaly-based IDSs (operated on the anomalies, which indicates an identifiable deviation from the nominal operation condition) can be employed at the WMS, to detect and identify zero-day attacks, which is one of the most dangerous and threatening amongst all other cyber-attacks (Butun, I., Österberg, P., & Song, H., 2019).

Another kind of advanced attack called Denial-of-Service (DoS) can target the web interface of the WMS system. These cyber-attacks can be crucial, as they can take down the e-services offered via web servers and harm the provided service availability. As mitigation, cloud-supported load-balancing services can be engaged.

In e-commerce and marketing, tracking emails are practiced by the majority of companies. The privacy and security risk assessment of email tracking is explained in a recent study (Xu, H. et al, 2018). In this study, we used a standard email tracking system to determine the opening rate for the emails sent by us.

FUTURE RESEARCH DIRECTIONS

A follow-up study can be performed to measure the efficiency of the implemented WMS-DSS system to analyze the improvement or bottlenecks in warehousing. This can be achieved by identifying KPIs and measuring these before and after deployment scenarios.

Moreover, cyber-security-related implications of WMS-DSS systems can also be analyzed. Effects of advanced cyber-attacks (such as DoS attacks, etc.) against these systems can be identified and countermeasures can be taken accordingly.

CONCLUSION

A warehouse has a heterogeneous and volatile environment considering that both humans and machines are part of the operation life cycle. The digital ecosystem is also very diverse since many actuators, sensors, electronic or automation devices (conveyer belt, a barcode reader to smart devices) are deployed in warehouses and they are connected via a hardwire or wireless network. We designed and implemented a highly scalable WMS-DSS system based on the warehouse ecosystem and business requirements. Finally, we discussed the possible cybersecurity-related issues in the digital warehouse plane.

REFERENCES

Accorsi, R., Manzini, R., & Maranesi, F. (2014). A decision-support system for the design and management of warehousing systems. *Computers in Industry*, *65*(1), 175–186.

Achabal, D. D., McIntyre, S. H., Smith, S. A., & Kalyanam, K. (2000). A decision support system for vendor managed inventory. *Journal of Retailing*, *76*(4), 430–454.

Allaoui, H., Guo, Y., & Sarkis, J. (2019). Decision support for collaboration planning in sustainable supply chains. *Journal of Cleaner Production*, *229*, 761–774.

Baruffaldi, G., Accorsi, R., & Manzini, R. (2019). Warehouse management system customization and information availability in 3pl companies. *Industrial Management & Data Systems*.

Butun, I., Morgera, S. D., & Sankar, R. (2014). A survey of intrusion detection systems in wireless sensor networks. *IEEE Communications Surveys and Tutorials*, *16*(1), 266–282. doi:10.1109/SURV.2013.050113.00191

Butun, I., & Österberg, P. (2019). Detecting intrusions in cyber-physical systems of smart cities: Challenges and directions. In *Secure Cyber-Physical Systems for Smart Cities* (pp. 74–102). IGI Global. doi:10.4018/978-1-5225-7189-6.ch004

Butun, I., Österberg, P., & Song, H. (2019). Security of the Internet of Things: Vulnerabilities, attacks, and countermeasures. *IEEE Communications Surveys and Tutorials*, *22*(1), 616–644. doi:10.1109/COMST.2019.2953364

Butun, I., Ra, I. H., & Sankar, R. (2015). An intrusion detection system based on multi-level clustering for hierarchical wireless sensor networks. *Sensors (Basel)*, *15*(11), 28960–28978. doi:10.3390151128960 PMID:26593915

Butun, I., Sari, A., & Österberg, P. (2019, January). Security implications of fog computing on the internet of things. In *2019 IEEE International Conference on Consumer Electronics (ICCE)* (pp. 1-6). IEEE. 10.1109/ICCE.2019.8661909

Butun, I., Sari, A., & Österberg, P. (2020). Hardware Security of Fog End-Devices for the Internet of Things. *Sensors (Basel)*, *20*(20), 5729. doi:10.339020205729 PMID:33050165

Čolaković, A., Čaušević, S., Kosovac, A., & Muharemović, E. (2020, June). A Review of Enabling Technologies and Solutions for IoT Based Smart Warehouse Monitoring System. In *International Conference "New Technologies, Development and Applications"* (pp. 630-637). Springer.

Fikar, C. (2018). A decision support system to investigate food losses in e-grocery deliveries. *Computers & Industrial Engineering*, *117*, 282–290.

Gómez, J. C. O., Duque, D. F. M., Rivera, L., & García-Alcaraz, J. L. (2017). Decision support system for operational risk management in supply chain with 3PL providers. In *Current trends on knowledge-based systems* (pp. 205–222). Springer. doi:10.1007/978-3-319-51905-0_10

Hu, Z. H., & Sheng, Z. H. (2014). A decision support system for public logistics information service management and optimization. *Decision Support Systems*, *59*, 219–229.

Lam, C. H., Choy, K. L., & Chung, S. H. (2011). A decision support system to facilitate warehouse order fulfillment in cross-border supply chain. *Journal of Manufacturing Technology Management*, *22*(8), 972–983. doi:10.1108/17410381111177430

Lao, S. I., Choy, K. L., Ho, G. T. S., Tsim, Y. C., & Lee, C. K. H. (2011). Real-time inbound decision support system for enhancing the performance of a food warehouse. *Journal of Manufacturing Technology Management*, *22*(8), 1014–1031. doi:10.1108/17410381111177467

Lee, C. K. M., Lv, Y., Ng, K. K. H., Ho, W., & Choy, K. L. (2018). Design and application of Internet of things-based warehouse management system for smart logistics. *International Journal of Production Research*, 56(8), 2753–2768. doi:10.1080/00207543.2017.1394592

Li, S., You, X., & Sun, Z. (2020). Drug Management System Based on RFID. In *Data Processing Techniques and Applications for Cyber-Physical Systems (DPTA 2019)* (pp. 1955–1958). Springer.

Min, H. (2009). Application of a decision support system to strategic warehousing decisions. *International Journal of Physical Distribution & Logistics Management*, 39(4), 270–281. doi:10.1108/09600030910962230

Power, D. J. (2008). Decision support systems: a historical overview. In *Handbook on decision support systems 1* (pp. 121–140). Springer.

Sari, A., Lekidis, A., & Butun, I. (2020). Industrial Networks and IIoT: Now and Future Trends. In *Industrial IoT* (pp. 3–55). Springer. doi:10.1007/978-3-030-42500-5_1

Stallings, W., & Brown, L. (2015). *Computer security: principles and practice* (4th ed.). Pearson Education.

Xu, H., Hao, S., Sari, A., & Wang, H. (2018, April). Privacy risk assessment on email tracking. In *IEEE INFOCOM 2018-IEEE Conference on Computer Communications* (pp. 2519-2527). IEEE. 10.1109/INFOCOM.2018.8486432

Yazdani, M., Zarate, P., Coulibaly, A., & Zavadskas, E. K. (2017). A group decision making support system in logistics and supply chain management. *Expert Systems with Applications*, 88, 376–392.

ADDITIONAL READING

Butun, I. (2017, January). Privacy and trust relations in internet of things from the user point of view. In 2017 IEEE 7th annual computing and communication workshop and conference (CCWC) (pp. 1-5). IEEE. 10.1109/CCWC.2017.7868419

Butun, I., Almgren, M., Gulisano, V., & Papatriantafilou, M. (2020). Intrusion Detection in Industrial Networks via Data Streaming. In *Industrial IoT* (pp. 213–238). Springer. doi:10.1007/978-3-030-42500-5_6

Butun, I., Morgera, S. D., & Sankar, R. (2014). A survey of intrusion detection systems in wireless sensor networks. *IEEE Communications Surveys and Tutorials*, 16(1), 266–282. doi:10.1109/SURV.2013.050113.00191

Choudhary, K., Gaba, G. S., Butun, I., & Kumar, P. (2020). MAKE-IT—A Lightweight Mutual Authentication and Key Exchange Protocol for Industrial Internet of Things. *Sensors (Basel)*, 20(18), 5166. doi:10.339020185166 PMID:32927788

KEY TERMS AND DEFINITIONS

Anomaly: An abnormal behavior of the system or user.

Denial-of-Service (DoS): A class of attack in which the targeted network or system disconnects and seizures the intended mode of operation.

DSS: A decision support system is software responsible for making decisions based on collected data and environmental inputs to support human operators. It could be fully automated or semi-automated (human input required to make decisions).

ERP: Enterprise resource planning is a software package used for business process management. It helps in collecting, analyzing, and storing data as well as assisting business activities.

Event: An expected or unexpected happening related to systems that are in operation.

Intrusion: An event in which an unauthorized user gathers a piece of information or an access right that he/she is not allowed to.

NFC: Near-Field Communication is a low-speed and close range (less than 4cm) wireless communication protocol. It is used for contactless operations such as payment and identification, etc.

RFID: Radio-frequency identification uses electromagnetic fields to communicate between a radio transmitter and receiver. The data transmitted is used for identification and mostly used for inventory management and item tracking.

Security Risk Assessment: Identifying the vulnerabilities of a system along with the possible worst-case scenarios as well as the evaluation of total property losses in case of such events.

Sensors: These are responsible for collecting evidence regarding events.

WMS: A warehouse management system is a software package that is used to track the inventory life cycle in a warehouse or between warehouses and/or distribution centers (or an individual). It helps improve the warehouse operations like receiving a shipment, storing the product, preparing a product, or shipping away a product accurately and efficiently. It optimizes the warehouse operations and increases throughput.

ENDNOTES

[1]   https://roboticsandautomationnews.com/2020/01/21/amazon-now-has-200000-robots-working-in-its-warehouses/28840/

[2]   https://www.reuters.com/article/us-amazon-com-automation-exclusive/exclusive-amazon-ro lls-out-machines-that-pack-orders-and-replace-jobs-idUSKCN1SJ0X1

[3]   https://en.wikipedia.org/wiki/2020_Beirut_explosion

APPENDIX: ABBREVIATIONS

BPM: Business Process Modeling
BPMN: Business Process Model Notation
DBMS: DataBase Management System
DSS: Decision Support System
DoS: Denial-of-Service
ERP: Enterprise Resource Planning
IoT: Internet of Things
IIoT: Industrial Internet of Things
KPI: Key Performance Indicator
M2M: Machine-to-Machine
NFC: Near-Field Communication
RFID: Radio-frequency identification
SLA: Service Level Agreement
WMS: Warehouse Management System

Section 3
DSS for Vehicular Networks

Chapter 7
Services in Connected Vehicles:
Security Risks and Countermeasures

Marcus Bertilsson
Chalmers University of Technology, Sweden

Michel Folkemark
Chalmers University of Technology, Sweden

Qingyun Gu
Chalmers University of Technology, Sweden

Viktor Rydberg
Chalmers University of Technology, Sweden

Abdullah Yazar
Marmara University, Turkey

ABSTRACT

Smart vehicles have introduced many services which can be categorized by their functionality (infotainment, comfort, ADAS, OEM services). Introducing new services increases the risk of compromising security. A mobile app used by drivers to connect the vehicle could be infected with malware and spread to the vehicle. Forging remote starting signals enables an attacker to start the vehicle without a key. Security implications of these services should be investigated and addressed thoroughly. This chapter investigates such problems and provides an overview of vulnerabilities, attacks, and mitigations related to these services along with findings including software bugs and insecure protocols. The mitigations for these attacks

DOI: 10.4018/978-1-7998-7468-3.ch007

include strengthening the security protocol of the vehicle CAN bus and incorporating security protocols such as TLS and IPsec. It is hard to say that all connected vehicles are secured. In conclusion, security cannot be neglected, and best practices like sufficient logging (e.g., IDS), reviewing, security testing, and updating of software and hardware should be used.

INTRODUCTION

Nowadays, vehicles are deeply rooted in our daily lives integrating with social and economic factors. Vehicles were invented as a purely mechanical machine, but it is now becoming more and more complex as computers and electronics are embedded into every component of newly designed vehicles. Today, connected vehicles not just provide basic transportation service but also can provide services like information, entertainment, communication, etc. Basically, a vehicle is a set of networks and electrical control units (ECUs) that are connected to the Internet, with the purpose of providing different functions and services that fits the users' needs (Stoltzfus, 2020). Some of these functions are relatively simple such as controlling lights or seats, others are more advanced e.g. collision detection and automatic parking. Figure 1 illustrates the use of radar and collision detection systems in action. A smart vehicle is usually connected to an external network in order to provide information services, get updates or diagnostics to the vehicle which exposes the internal systems to external threats. There is also an increase in security problems with the increasing complexity of smart vehicles and their software needs. In 2019, the number of reported cyber-attacks on connected vehicles was seven times higher compared to 2016 (Upstream, 2020). According to Ponemon Institute's (2018) survey in the automotive industry, 84% of the respondents believed that security practices taken Today are not keeping up with the evolution of technology. This indicates that the security implications of smart vehicles are highly concerned by the consumers and should be addressed accordingly.

This chapter aims to investigate the security of connected smart vehicles with respect to services provided. A comprehensive overview of previous attacks, weaknesses that were exploited to achieve a successful attack, and possible countermeasures against identified attack vectors are provided. Although a broad perspective of the overview of smart connected vehicles is provided, this chapter does not deep dive into technical details.

Figure 1. Illustration of smart vehicles traveling on a highway with radar and collision detection mechanism enabled.
(Courtesy of Getty Images)[2]

In vehicular systems, Decision Support System (DSS) can help to make decisions based on internal (vehicle's sensor data) and external conditions such as road infrastructure, traffic intensity, weather (rain, snow, ice, wind, and visibility) to control embedded devices like rain intensity sensing wipers, adaptive cruise control, stability control, and driver-assist systems more efficiently. Based on the condition, DSS can provide crucial warnings and recommendations to the driver to avoid potentially dangerous situations. If the vehicle is in autonomous mode, the decisions should be executed promptly by the DSS in an error-free manner to avoid crashes and possibly fatalities. Security of a DSS system is critical since any wrong input to a DSS may result in fatal and unrecoverable situations. In this sense, the cybersecurity consideration of smart vehicles is an important issue.

The chapter starts with the Introduction section by providing essential background on the information security that is related to vehicular networks. This is followed by the Related-work section which introduces the relevant literature. The Methodology section introduces the methodology followed for this study. The chapter continues by discussing different categories of services such as what types of services they include as well as known attacks, exploited weaknesses, and countermeasures in the Services section. In the Discussion section, the current state of security practices in today's vehicles is discussed. Finally, the Conclusion section provides insight into the areas on which vehicle manufacturers and researchers should focus on.

BACKGROUND

Smart vehicles have computer systems of high complexity, with unique features and constraints. There are several different components, entities, and unique bus architectures (CAN, LIN, MOST) in vehicles. One can view it as a system where most of the ECUs (nodes) are linked together through a bus system (CAN). This section provides related background information and discusses the categorization of services. In the in-vehicle network, communication between the ECUs is done through a bus system, allowing interconnection between the components. There are numerous communication protocols (or types of buses) for a vehicle bus, each with its own strengths and weaknesses. The most common automotive buses are the Controller Area Network (CAN), FlexRay, Local Interconnect Network (LIN), and Media Oriented Systems Transport (MOST). They each serve different purposes, e.g., in regard to cost and data rate/speed. For example, CAN is a low-cost, low-speed serial bus while MOST is a high-speed multimedia interface [1,2].

Vehicle Components

There are many different components in a smart vehicle (Figure 2), this section presents some of them with the focus of the core components regarding vehicle communication.

Telematic Control Unit (TCU)

A Telematic Control Unit (TCU[4a]) is an on-boarded embedded system, which controls wireless tracking, diagnostics, and communication in the vehicle[3]. Furthermore, the TCU has an external interface for mobile communications, so that it can receive traffic based on GSM, GPRS, Wi-Fi, WiMax, or LTE. It also contains a GPS unit for keeping track of the vehicle in terms of its latitude and longitude coordinates. Finally, the TCU is a vital component of a vehicle and an important part of its purpose is to handle many different communication protocols. It is also essential to note that the operating system of the TCU usually is Linux based[4b].

Vehicle Gateway

The vehicle gateway (the Central Gateway, CGW) is the gateway for the in-vehicle network. It is an important communication security component of the vehicle as it functions as the central communication node in the network[5]. It functions as a router for in-vehicle communication, allowing secure data exchange between different domains (the different ECU networks) and to external interfaces. The vehicle gateway provides physical isolation of the components as well as some security functions, e.g., firewall, Hardware Security Module (HMS), and Intrusion Detection System (IDS) to protect the in-vehicle network.

Figure 2. Illustration of self-driving cars and their interaction with possible provided services.
(Courtesy of Getty Images)²

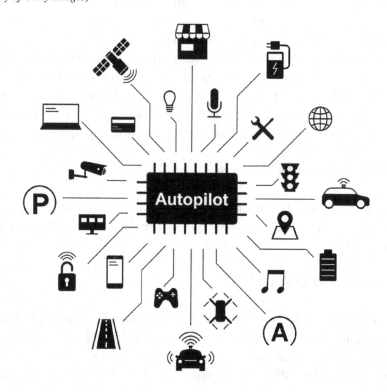

Security Mechanisms

As mentioned in (Butun and Song, 2019) and (Sari, 2020); the cyber-security of any complex system should follow a bottom-up approach by considering each and every part in the system as a vulnerable component, and relevant countermeasures should be taken at each level. As such, in order to protect a vehicle and its communication, there are many security mechanisms that can be utilized, both in the vehicle itself and in the external systems. This section presents some of the most common security mechanisms to be considered in protecting vehicular systems against cybersecurity threats:

Transport Layer Security (TLS)

Transport Layer Security (TLS) is a cryptographic protocol designed to provide communication security over a computer network. It is an IETF standard for Internet security, operating in the application layer of the OSI model. TLS provides confidentiality and data integrity between two or more applications. TLS itself consists of several smaller protocols and one of them is the handshake protocol. In this handshake, the client and the server will exchange certificates to perform authorization and agree on security parameters such as cipher suite. They will also share a secret key for data encryption[6].

Internet Protocol Security (IPsec)

IPsec is an IETF standard for Internet security, on the Internet layer. This protocol authenticates and encrypts the packets of data, in order to provide secure communication. To give a short overview of the protocol there are two operating modes, Tunnel mode, and Transport Mode. There are two sub-protocols, Authentication Header (AH) and Encapsulating Security Payload (ESP). Lastly, there is one key exchange protocol, Internet Key Exchange protocol (IKE)[7].

Firewall

A firewall is a common security component of any system looking to enhance its security. A firewall monitors the incoming and outgoing traffic at a certain point in a network of systems and while monitoring the traffic, the traffic gets analyzed by the firewall, and the packages are either dropped or allowed based on its configuration and set of rules (Stallings, 2017). In the context of vehicles, a firewall could protect the internal systems of the vehicle from all external network traffic not originating from the manufacturer and its infrastructure.

Intrusion Detection System (IDS)

An Intrusion Detection System (IDS) is similar to a firewall in the sense, it also monitors the incoming and outgoing traffic at a certain point in a network. Its purpose however is to detect unauthorized access or attacks against the network based on detecting unusual activity or anomalies (Aydogan, 2019). This is either done by being a signature-based IDS where the signatures of known attacks are added to its configuration or being an anomaly-based IDS where the IDS is able to detect anomalies in the network traffic after being trained on normal network traffic (Butun, 2014, 2015, 2019). When using an IDS there is always a trade-off between detection rate (ability to detect intrusions) and false alarms which puts greater emphasis on customization to fit the system in question (Stallings, 2017).

Other than generic security solutions mentioned above, customized solutions, such as hardware-assisted security modules (HSM) can be used onboard a vehicle to mitigate possible security implications (Butun, Sari, 2020). Apart from onboard security solutions, fog computing-related cyber-security solutions can help the RTUs (Remote Terminal Units) and RSUs (Road-Side Units) of a vehicular network (Butun, Sari, 2019).

RELATED WORK

As a basis for defining the service categories presented in this chapter, some existing categorizations of services are examined. Gong (2019) lists a large number of services provided by various connected vehicles in the market Today and groups them into 5 categories: infotainment, comfort, Original Equipment Manufacturer (OEM), emergence, and Advanced Driver-Assistance Systems (ADAS) services (Gong, 2019). Infotainment includes services such as vehicle app integration and geolocation. Comfort encompasses services allowing remote control of certain aspects of the vehicle, such as starting the car engine and the AC system. OEM services include the ability to diagnose and collect vehicle data. Emergence services assist during the case of an accident by e.g. contacting police. Finally, ADAS consists of services aiding the driver while the vehicle is in motion, including collision warning and driver behavior monitoring.

A report on the connected car market does a similar categorization (Everis, 2015). In the Everis report, the services are divided into the following categories: traffic safety, connected infotainment, traffic efficiency, cost-efficiency, convenience, and interaction. The same type of services as those listed in (Gong, 2019) are recurrent but occasionally fall under different categories. Other publications (Araniti et al, 2013), (Rosenstatter, 2017), (Jasek, 2015) have also made similar categorizations, mostly differing in how broad the categories are as well as under which category certain services fall under.

METHOD

To provide an overview of the topic, the approach in this chapter is to collect information about services and functions from scientific papers and from company product information secondarily. The previous research was reviewed in the area as well as articles from security blogs and other venues. The gathered information will be a sample or a snapshot of which will be categorized by functionality. For each classified category, the following will be considered: discussing issues, vulnerabilities, attacks, and countermeasures to provide a security overview of each specific category. This is finally used to analyze the security of the vehicle and its systems as a whole.

Categorization of Services

A connected car provides a vast amount of services of different types. A categorization of these services will be performed, in order to provide a clear organization and delimitation of them. An assortment of publications from different fields has already put in the effort of creating such categorizations, most with respect to the functionality a service provides. The aim is to use these existing categorizations as a basis for defining the categories mentioned in this chapter. An audit of existing categorizations is given in the related work section.

SERVICES

This section provides a categorization of the various services which a connected car can offer, including the reasoning for why the specific categories were chosen. After that, each category is investigated further. For each category, first, a brief overview is given to services contained in that category. It is followed by a description of vulnerabilities that these services have along with the attacks that can be performed against them and countermeasures against these attacks.

Service Categories

The categories chosen to be used for services in this section are: Advanced Driver-Assistance Systems (ADAS), comfort, infotainment, and OEM. These categories were chosen for a few reasons. First, the chosen categories were recurrent in most of the publications examined in the related work section, albeit with different names and varying in how broadly they encompassed services. Second, these categories also seem the most interesting ones and they would provide a lot of material base for the research. Lastly, the categories are clear and concise enough to guide the research into the different services.

Advanced Driver-Assistance Systems (ADAS)

Advanced Driver-Assistance Systems (ADAS) are designed to assist the driver in handling different driving situations to avoid accidents occurring. The assistance they provide varies by several aspects. The simplest one is to present information from other systems, such as infotainment systems. More advanced assistance may include smartphone connectivity, adaptive cruise control, pedestrian detection, collision warning, blind-spot detection and to incorporate GPS and traffic warnings, etc. In critical situations, the ADAS is able to take over the driving tasks (automate braking, etc.). ADAS may also provide features like recognizing the driver's command by haptic, voice, or gestures, improving the communication efficiency between the driver and the vehicle (Uhlemann, 2015).

Briefly, the mechanism of ADAS is to gather the data from other supported systems and generate recommended driving behaviors accordingly. The information ADAS receive can be from vision/camera systems, sensor technology, vehicle data networks, vehicle-to-vehicle (V2V) or vehicle-to-infrastructure (V2I) communications systems (Uhlemann, 2015). As a consequence, attacks on ADAS can be taken by fooling other cooperative systems. With the misleading information, ADAS may lose functionality or make wrong decisions. Among those potential consequences, some are trivial as activating wipers when not needed, but some have severe consequences as to mislead the car to the wrong lane or even worse, to control the car. Examples are shown below:

The Keen Security Lab (Tencent Keen Security Lab, 2019a) has conducted experiments on Tesla's Autopilot feature and published the security research report in 2019, illustrating the vulnerabilities they found. Autopilot is an Advanced Driver-Assistance System feature offered by Tesla that provides sophisticated autonomous driving to some degree to provide decision-making capabilities. Subsets of the features it supports were mainly mentioned in the report: adaptive cruise control (ACC) as well as the ability to automatically change lanes with driver's confirmation. The report demonstrated a vulnerability that enables gaining root privileges of APE (ver 18.6.1) remotely, and thereby control of the car. APE ("Autopilot ECU" module), the core unit of Tesla's ADAS, is designed to control the steering system and electronic speed of the car in the assisted driving and automatic parking mode. These features rely on high-level vision and automotive Bus (Ethernet, CAN, LIN, FlexRay) systems (Tencent Keen Security Lab, 2019b), which was compromised in the experiment to gain root privileges of APE.

After reverse engineering on services (canrx, cantx, etc.) associated with the CAN bus in APE, researchers first figured out the CAN bus communication between APE, LP, and other ECUs (EPAS, EPB) related to steering system control. In the network architecture of APE's CAN bus system, LP is connected to a private CAN bus for redundant mechanism, and EPAS is a unit that cooperates with APE to control the steering system. The cantx service transforms the intermediary signals from the vision system to the vehicle control commands. These commands will then be encapsulated and forwarded via the LB unit. Moreover, researchers discovered an essential CAN message DasSteeringControlMessage (DSCM), which is designed for steering system control when the car is in ACC (Adaptive Cruise Control) and APC (Automatic Parking Control) modes. As one of the keys to CAN message, DSCM is protected with a message timestamp and counter, as well as a redundancy CAN (Tencent Keen Security Lab, 2019b).

In order to have full access to the APE's system, one can inject malicious DSCM from APE to LB and break the barriers of security mechanisms for the APE's CAN bus system, as mentioned before, message timestamp and counter and redundancy CAN, in ahead. An effective solution can be simplified as: dynamically inject malicious code into the cantx service and hook the function of the cantx service that finalizes DSCM to reuse the DSCM's timestamp and counter to manipulate the DSCM with any value of steering angle. By executing that, the CAN bus in APE was compromised, researchers were able to control the vehicle's steering system with a gamepad. Furthermore, they managed to take control of the car with or without limitations under 4 situations: parked, being switched from Reverse mode to Drive mode by the shifting handle, in the ACC mode with a high speed, and not in ACC mode.

The Keen Security Lab (2019) report also presented an attack that confused the vision systems to direct the vehicle in Autosteer mode to the reverse lane. During the test, two kinds of attacks were deployed. One of them was the eliminate lane attack, which aimed to disable APE's lane recognition function with interference markings on the road. Considering the fact that the lane recognition module will not work when the vehicle camera has been disturbed or the lane was covered up, neither of these approaches was taken. Instead, they first added some patches around the left lane line in the physical world and then increased noise to lane detection output using black-box optimization algorithms. As shown in the results, the left lane seems to have disappeared from the Autopilot system and the vehicle was misguided. The other attack was the fake lane attack. In this attack, researchers conducted a test on a road that has an intersection in the middle of the right lane, with a continuous left lane opposite the intersection. Three small stickers were pasted on the ground from the right to the center of the lane, so that wrong information was delivered to the Autopilot system. When the vehicle traveled to the middle of the intersection, it took those interference patches and the real left lane as the continuation of its right lane and drove into the reverse lane.

Similarly, confusing images generated by their algorithm were displayed to the car to test the weather recognition function. These pictures had the same effect as sprinkling water to the windshield. As a result, the Autopilot system interfered successfully and then turned on the wipers.

Comfort

Comfort services are made to facilitate the customer's use of the vehicle, providing a better driving experience or emergency services. Some services which belong to the comfort category would be the remote heat control to make sure the vehicle is heated before the trip starts in winter, automatic seat adjustments, driver profiles with settings & preferences for each driver, medical/emergency assistance, and fatigue detection to detect when the driver is tired and should take a break.

Vehicle emergency notification systems aim to reduce the time between a crash or medical emergency and medical assistance is provided. These systems are also useful for giving the emergency assistance personnel further life-saving information about the life-threatening issue in order to prepare better treatments. Volvo and Autoliv together were one of the first car manufacturers to introduce such a system (Autoliv, 2000). Their system could detect a crash by registering the deployment of the vehicle's airbags and then call emergency services through the vehicle's integrated telephone. If no passengers could respond, an ambulance would be sent to the vehicle's location provided by its GPS. A Finnish study estimated that such a system could reduce the number of deaths on the road by 4-8% and the number of deaths on the road involving motor vehicles by 5-10% (Virtanen et al, 2006). An attack against such a system could be life-threatening since it could lead to the system being disabled or providing wrong information like location and causing emergency responders to fail to provide assistance in case of an emergency.

Security researcher Troy Hunt (2016) discovered a vulnerability in the API used by the companion app for the Nissan LEAF. The companion app lets customers control the vehicle's air conditioning, check the battery level, and view driving logs. Using only the Vehicle Identification Number (VIN), Hunt discovered that it was possible to perform the API requests outside of the app. He exploited the fact that there was no real authorization present in the API calls other than the VIN, which is not a secret number at all. He was able to remotely control the vehicle's air conditioning, heated seating, heated steering wheel and get access to the vehicle's driving logs. Although the security implications of this vulnerability are not on the level of attacks like the one Charlie Miller and Chris Valasek (2015) performed on the Jeep Cherokee, where the vehicle's steering could be remotely controlled, being able to remotely control the vehicle's air conditioning and similar services could drain its battery, making it unable to start when needed. Being able to receive access to driving logs also raises concerns about the privacy of customer data. Fortunately, the countermeasure to this attack is relatively straightforward. It would be enough to include an authorization token in the calls to the API as performing the attack using an invalid authorization token would deny access to the API. The authorization token would be requested by the application before any other API calls and is used to verify the requests in terms of audience and permissions (Hardt, 2012).

Another common feature in connected vehicles is some type of keyless entry or keyless ignition system. A keyless entry system enables opening the vehicle using a button on a key fob or by being in near proximity of the vehicle. A keyless ignition system enables starting the vehicle just by keeping the key fob in near proximity followed by pressing a start/stop button inside the vehicle. Keyless systems were found to be the most common attack vector in connected vehicles, representing 30% of all attacks between 2010 and 2019 (Upstream, 2020). Furthermore, German General Automobile Club (ADAC) tested 237 vehicles with keyless systems and found that only 3 models were considered secure and unable to be unlocked or started without access to the real key (ADAC, 2019). One way of attacking the keyless system is to perform a relay attack. A relay attack in this context is the process of picking up the wireless signal from a key fob and relaying it to a device held near the vehicle. When the relayed signal reaches the keyless system of the vehicle, the system thinks the signal is valid and thus unlocks and/or starts the vehicle. Unlocking and starting the vehicle enables thieves to easily steal the vehicle, a likely cause for why attacks on keyless systems are common.

In terms of countermeasures against the relay attacks on keyless systems, there are several approaches taken by the industry. Some manufacturers including Volkswagen, Audi, and BMW have released motion sensor keys where the key has an internal timer keeping track of its movements. If the key has been stationary for a set amount of time, it stops transmitting the wireless signals making it impossible to relay (Thatcham Research, 2020) (Thomas, 2019). Although motion sensor keys provide some protection against relay attacks, they do not offer any additional protection when the key is moving e.g. when the key is a pocket or bag of a moving customer. Another approach has been taken by Jaguar Land Rover who released keys to some of its models using alternative wireless technologies like Ultra Wide Band (UWB) (Mistry, 2019). These types of keys transmit signals over a wide range of channels making the signals difficult to lock into and relay (Mistry, 2019). The models from Jaguar Land Rover using this technology were the only ones being considered to be secure in the study by ADAC (2019).

Another possible way to attack the keyless system is by spoofing the cryptographic keys used in the communication between the key fob and the vehicle, essentially cloning the key. In 2018 researchers at KU Leuven university were able to clone the key fob of a Tesla Model S, stealing the vehicle in a couple of seconds (Wouters et al, 2018). The researchers exploited the outdated and insecure cipher where the key could be exhaustively searched. They also exploited the lack of mutual authentication in the challenge-response protocol, allowing anyone to send challenges to and receive responses from the key fob. A challenge-response protocol consists of a challenge presented by one party to which another party must provide a valid response. The purpose of this protocol is to authenticate the party responding to the challenge. Without going into further details about how the attack was performed, as it is out of the scope of this paper, countermeasures to the attack would be to upgrade the cipher to an updated and secure alternative where the keys are not able to be exhaustively searched. The second part of the countermeasures would be to modify the challenge-response protocol to authenticate both parties, preventing an attacker from sending a challenge and receiving a response from the key fob.

Infotainment

Infotainment service provides entertainment and information to the driver. Examples of these services are vehicle app integration, phone connectivity via Bluetooth, multimedia streaming, Wi-Fi capability as well as geolocation, traffic, and weather condition reporting. Checkoway (2011) illustrated how full control of a specific vehicle could be achieved by exploiting various vulnerabilities in infotainment services. Multiple vulnerabilities were found in the car's media player such as a CD containing a file with a specific filename would be recognized as a firmware update by the media player, which would automatically update its firmware with the contents of the file. Therefore, an attacker could create such a CD with a malicious payload and, through e.g. social engineering, manipulate the vehicle owner to insert the CD into the media player, allowing the attacker to compromise the security of the vehicle. Another media player vulnerability could be exploited when audio files were played from a CD if an audio file contains a malicious payload targeting a buffer overflow vulnerability in the media player firmware. The CD would appear to play music normally, but in the background, malicious packets are being injected into the car's internal network.

Another infotainment service examined in Checkoway et al, (2011) was the functionality for pairing a cell phone to the vehicle via Bluetooth. The authors found that the car's Bluetooth software contained code susceptible to buffer overflows. The vulnerability could be exploited by e.g., installing a trojan horse application on a cell phone already paired with the vehicle. This application is then able to covertly send malicious packets to the vehicle, thus compromising its security. The authors suggested several countermeasures for these attacks, including basic buffer overflow protection mechanisms such as ASLR and stack cookies (canaries). They conclude that even though the proposed countermeasures are efficient and simple to implement but for some reason, it has been overlooked by manufacturers. This could be due to the fact that car manufacturers tend to outsource the programming of software for vehicle components to external suppliers. This leads to car manufacturers not having a complete understanding of the software and thus not efficiently being able to evaluate security vulnerabilities when integrating components into the vehicle.

Similar to Checkoway et al, (2011), Woo et al. (2015) describe an attack involving the injection of malicious data into the CAN bus via a fraudulent application on the vehicle owner's smartphone. In this case, the app is disguised as a self-diagnostic app for use with a vehicle scan tool. The authors note that the potential for the attack arises from the CAN bus lacking in basic security properties such as encryption and data frame authentication. As a solution, they propose a security protocol designed by the authors that adds security to the CAN bus.

Mazloom et al. (2016) describe another attack involving a malicious smartphone app. As in Checkoway et al. (2011), the vulnerability roots from the vehicle software code being susceptible to buffer overflows. Similar to Checkoway et al. (2011), the authors suggest these problems are a product of vehicle manufacturers outsourcing programming of components to external suppliers. Since suppliers don't usually fully disclose software code for components, car manufacturers thus may have difficulty performing thorough security audits of component firmware. A proposed solution is for suppliers to move towards writing software using higher-level languages, which are not susceptible to the same vulnerabilities.

Legitimate connected car apps also could be exploited via potential attack vectors on a vehicle as described by Mandal et al. (2018) who performed a comprehensive security audit of all Android Auto (popular connected car app platform) apps available in the Google Play Store. It turned out that 80% of apps had some type of vulnerability, which could leave the security of a vehicle at serious risk.

Finally, Zhang et al. (2014) describe how malware can infect the internal system of a connected car via infotainment services such as vehicle-incorporated web browsers and media ports. The authors mention that one factor limiting a car's defense against malware is the lack of security in the CAN bus, which does not provide basic security properties such as device authentication and message confidentiality. Another factor is electronic devices on a vehicle having limited resources due to the cost constraints and thus not being capable to deal with malware. The authors propose a cloud-based malware defense mechanism, which can handle the work of defending against malware.

Original Equipment Manufacturer (OEM) Service

Original Equipment Manufacturer (OEM) services are performed for fulfilling the purposes of the OEM. These services revolve around data, which the OEM uses to improve such as the user experience and vehicle performance, but also for repair purposes. Some key characteristics of these services are that the vehicle receives (or could be theoretically scheduled) some requests for diagnostic data and when these requests are done executing, the data is sent to the OEM servers, for further analysis in order to draw conclusions.

Privacy is an important aspect of OEM services since the resulting data might contain private information or personally identifiable information. To get an idea of what data is being collected, one could take a look at a car manufacturer's privacy notice[8,9]. Some examples of data that Toyota may collect are; location data, remote access data (real-time), vehicle health information (e.g., Diagnostic Trouble Code (DTCs)), and more. In its privacy notice, Toyota also provides a short overview of its security measures. However, they do not completely ensure or warrant the security of any data.

Two services belonging to the OEM category are "Remote diagnostics for repair purposes" and Remote Vehicle Data Collection (RVDC). They are rather similar communication-wise, which means that they are also similar security-wise. In terms of analyzing their security, it is sufficient to analyze just one of them. This will provide a necessary understanding of the security risks and countermeasures for this category.

Remote Vehicle Data Collection (RVDC) remotely collects diagnostic data from vehicles and this data is usually saved in a cloud (for example OEM servers) for further analysis. Mayankutty and Sereti (2017) conducted a comparative case study where one of the cases is related to RVDC regarding security modeling in the automotive industry. The authors present high-level information on the implementation of RVDC, which they have studied. In the studied implementation the vehicle receives a freshly sent request from the OEM, a so-called measurement assignment. This new measurement assignment is then executed by the vehicle whenever some specific conditions are satisfied (e.g., user consent needs to exist). The vehicle finally proceeds with sending the result to the OEM server when possible.

In more technical details, RVDC revolves around the communication between the external server, the vehicle, and its in-vehicle ECUs. The requests are sent by the server to the TCU, which then forwards the requests to the in-vehicle network through the vehicle gateway (CGW). ECUs respond to the requests with the requested data back through the gateway and the TCU.

There are apparently few old well-known attacks directly targeting OEM services. It could be the case that they are unknown, or that the attacks are not published. However, there are some papers and articles which identify threats for RVDC. Gong identifies threats and proposes countermeasures for RVDC (Gong, 2019). Threats identified by Gong (2019) for RVDC are presented in the list below:

- Communication between the TCU and OEM servers: An attacker could potentially sniff ("unauthorized access") messages, manipulate messages, or even perform IP address spoofing attacks on the TCU. Since the attacker could potentially use the OEM servers' IP addresses as their false source IP address. However, the attacker needs to first identify the OEM servers' IP addresses. One can note that the TCU has already stored the OEM servers' IP addresses.

- Communication between the TCU and the gateway: Attackers could potentially also here sniff messages, and manipulate messages. Furthermore, according to Gong most of the messages are control messages, and an attacker may perform replay attacks (most of the RVDC messages are similar, i.e., predictable).
- In-vehicle network: In the in-vehicle network, a scenario identified is that an attacker may control some ECUs, and then keep sending high-priority messages to perform a DoS attack. Spoofing could be done in the in-vehicle network, either impersonating the TCU or some ECUs.

Countermeasures proposed by Gong:

- Communication between the TCU and OEM servers: A countermeasure for spoofing is authentication. For example, exchanging certificates between TCU and OEM servers. This will ensure the TCU showing that the messages are from a trusted source. The connection should be based on TLS, which is suitable for this server-client communication model and provides high-level security. Furthermore, a firewall for the TCU could be added, which should add the OEM servers' IP addresses to its whitelist (allow).
- Communication between the TCU and the gateway: Gong (2019) presents two different countermeasures for replay attacks. The first is to use a Time-Based One-Time Password Algorithm. This will lead to the key used in the replayed message and the key used in a fresh message are different, making a replay attack unsuccessful. The second is to add a fresh index in the message payload. Furthermore, IPsec can be deployed to ensure confidentiality, authenticity, and integrity of messages. It could also be used with one of the methods explained above, in order to provide freshness. Lastly, the TCU should also use a firewall, to protect, for example, the in-vehicle network from possible malicious messages.
- In-vehicle network: As stated earlier in the paper, ECUs are mostly connected with each other through the CAN bus. However, the CAN bus fails to provide any security, at least in the original version. There exist some versions which add for example encryption, but this is not optimal from a security perspective. Lastly, an IDS for the gateway is suggested. An IDS would mitigate the threat of malicious communication in the in-vehicle network.

DISCUSSION

There are many services present in the modern connected vehicle and all service categories have their own weaknesses and challenges in terms of security. When it comes to ADAS, several vulnerabilities can be exploited and some of them could have fatal implications, as Keen Lab proved. Technically, by enhancing the security measures of the CAN bus and improving the neural networks used in recognition functions, the vulnerabilities mentioned can be fixed or made more difficult to exploit. However, not all of them are worth being considered from a business perspective. According to Tesla's response to the findings, they fixed the vulnerability of the "Control Steering System with a Gamepad" through a robust security update in 2017, followed by a comprehensive security update in 2018. Both updates were released before Tesla was notified about the research findings (Tencent Keen Security Lab, 2019a). The two attacks against Autowiper and Lane Recognition were regarded as having no real-world concerns, given that a driver can easily override Autopilot at any time and stop improper behaviors.

When examining the comfort services provided in connected vehicles, we saw that even in the most basic services like controlling the air conditioning, there is a potential for attackers to do harm. In the case of Nissan LEAF, the countermeasures needed to prevent the attack were relatively simple, and despite being simple to implement they were still neglected, causing unnecessary problems. In the case of keyless systems, the most common attack vector is possible to attack considered to be secure protocols and services if the underlying technology is not suitable for the use case.

The CAN bus is extensively used in the systems of connected vehicles and we have discussed some attacks and vulnerabilities regarding the use of CAN. As stated by Woo et al. (2015) and Zhang et al. (2014) as previously mentioned, the security provided by the CAN bus is very limited, with basic security properties either being lacking or non-existent. This suggests a modification or replacement of the CAN protocol could aid in securing vehicles against attacks in the future. However, due to the CAN bus being such a widespread standard, a replacement could require an exhaustive and expensive effort. Another solution would be to add a security protocol to aid in securing the CAN bus as proposed by Woo et al. (2015).

When it comes to security, an important point is that some vehicle vulnerabilities stem from software bugs, suggesting a need for software design of vehicle components to be more secure. As stated by Checkoway et al, (2011) and Mazloom et al. (2016), these problems arise partly from a lack of synchronization between vehicle manufacturers and external suppliers of components. A tighter coupling between these parties would help to mitigate the possible problems in vehicle software related to the design, implementation, and testing of the security components.

In terms of the OEM services, several threats exist but also several possible countermeasures are available, as presented by Gong (2019). Toyota is a manufacturer that deploys several of these countermeasures, such as multiple layers of security, firewalls, IDS, encryption, and dedicated private networks between OEM servers and the TCU[8,9]. In addition to these security practices, Toyota also uses code and design reviews, as well as regular security testing. It is important to understand that even if a vehicle manufacturer puts lots of effort into software and hardware security, there are still attack vectors and weaknesses that can be found by others to exploit. The security mostly depends on the strength and use of the security mechanisms, such as TLS, IPsec, cipher suites, key lengths, and firewalls, etc. Furthermore, attacks can be made possible due to security bugs and security vulnerabilities in the implementations of these practices, both in the manufacturer's own implementations and in standards such as TLS[10].

CONCLUSION

In this paper, an overview of the security of services in connected vehicles is provided. The importance of security issues of a smart car and its effects on DSS is introduced. A DSS should not be compromised by any other external factors to function in a safe manner without violating its integrity. Different types of services through a categorization of their functionality are discussed along with the weaknesses exploited in previous attacks as well as countermeasures against them. The observations related to attacks are sometimes simple to perform and there are also countermeasures available against them. Some of the attacks may not cause enough concern to be considered in future work, which gives less incentive to develop fully secure systems. However, It is important for a vehicle manufacturer to thoroughly plan and design the systems as even the basic security measures like authorization in API calls can be neglected. It is clear that security cannot be an afterthought and that security needs to be an iterative process. Sufficient logging (e.g., IDS), reviewing, security testing, and updating of software and hardware is necessary to prevent attacks and minimize potential vulnerabilities. As new technologies are constantly developed, manufacturers need to closely collaborate with third parties and other stakeholders to fully understand how new technologies should be designed and integrated with smart vehicles, in order to prevent future security problems.

REFERENCES

Araniti, G., Campolo, C., Condoluci, M., Iera, A., & Molinaro, A. (2013). LTE for vehicular networking: A survey. *IEEE Communications Magazine, 51*(5), 148–157. doi:10.1109/MCOM.2013.6515060

Autoliv. (2000). *Autoliv and Volvo Launch New Safety System*. Press Release.

Aydogan, E., Yilmaz, S., Sen, S., Butun, I., Forsström, S., & Gidlund, M. (2019, May). A central intrusion detection system for RPL-based Industrial Internet of Things. In *2019 15th IEEE International Workshop on Factory Communication Systems (WFCS)* (pp. 1-5). IEEE.

Butun, I., Morgera, S. D., & Sankar, R. (2014). A survey of intrusion detection systems in wireless sensor networks. *IEEE Communications Surveys and Tutorials, 16*(1), 266–282. doi:10.1109/SURV.2013.050113.00191

Butun, I., & Österberg, P. (2019). Detecting intrusions in cyber-physical systems of smart cities: Challenges and directions. In *Secure Cyber-Physical Systems for Smart Cities* (pp. 74–102). IGI Global. doi:10.4018/978-1-5225-7189-6.ch004

Butun, I., Österberg, P., & Song, H. (2019). Security of the Internet of Things: Vulnerabilities, attacks, and countermeasures. *IEEE Communications Surveys and Tutorials, 22*(1), 616–644. doi:10.1109/COMST.2019.2953364

Butun, I., Ra, I. H., & Sankar, R. (2015). An intrusion detection system based on multi-level clustering for hierarchical wireless sensor networks. *Sensors (Basel), 15*(11), 28960–28978. doi:10.3390151128960 PMID:26593915

Butun, I., Sari, A., & Österberg, P. (2019, January). Security implications of fog computing on the internet of things. In *2019 IEEE International Conference on Consumer Electronics (ICCE)* (pp. 1-6). IEEE. 10.1109/ICCE.2019.8661909

Butun, I., Sari, A., & Österberg, P. (2020). Hardware Security of Fog End-Devices for the Internet of Things. *Sensors (Basel), 20*(20), 5729. doi:10.339020205729 PMID:33050165

Checkoway, S., McCoy, D., Kantor, B., Anderson, D., Shacham, H., Savage, S., Koscher, K., Czeskis, A., Roesner, F., & Kohno, T. (2011). *Comprehensive experimental analyses of automotive attack surfaces*. Academic Press.

Everis. (2015). *Everis connected car report*. Author.

Gong, X. (2019). *Security threats and countermeasures for connected vehicles*. Academic Press.

Hardt, D. (2012). *The OAuth 2.0 authorization framework.* https://tools.ietf.org/html/rfc6749#section-1.4

Hunt, T. (2016). *Controlling vehicle features of Nissan LEAFs across the globe via vulnerable APIs.* https://www.troyhunt.com/controlling-vehicle-features-of-nissan/

Jasek, S. (2015). *Connected car security threat analysis and recommendations.* Securing. https://www.securing.pl/wp-content/uploads/2015/10/SecuRing-Connected-Car-Security-Threat-Analysis-and-Recommendations.pdf

Mandal, Cortesi, Ferrara, Panarotto, & Spoto. (2018). *Vulnerability analysis of android auto infotainment apps.* Academic Press.

Mayankutty, S. C., & Sereti, A. (2017). *Security modelling in automotive industry.* https://odr.chalmers.se/handle/20.500.12380/250232

Mazloom, S., Rezaeirad, M., Hunter, A., & McCoy, D. (2016). *A security analysis of an in vehicle infotainment and app platform.* Academic Press.

Miller, C. (2015). *Remote exploitation of an unaltered passenger vehicle.* http://illmatics.com/Remote%20Car%20Hacking.pdf

Mistry, H. (2019). *Jaguar Land Rover models are the only cars immune to keyless entry attacks.* Academic Press.

Ponemon Institute. (2018). *Securing the modern Vehicle:A study of automotive industry cybersecurity practices.* https://www.synopsys.com/content/dam/synopsys/sig-assets/reports/securing-the-modern-vehicle.pdf

Rosenstatter, T. (2017). *A state-of-the-art report on vehicular security.* Academic Press.

Sari, A., Lekidis, A., & Butun, I. (2020). Industrial Networks and IIoT: Now and Future Trends. In *Industrial IoT* (pp. 3–55). Springer. doi:10.1007/978-3-030-42500-5_1

Stallings, W. (2017). *Cryptography and network security: Principles and practice.* Pearson Education.

Stoltzfus, J. (2020). *Your car, your computer: ECUs and the controller area network.* https://www.techopedia.com/your-car-your-computer-ecus-and-the-controller-area-network/2/32218

Tencent Keen Security Lab. (2019a). *Experimental security research of tesla autopilot.* https://keenlab.tencent.com/en/whitepapers/ExperimentalSecurityResearchofTeslaAutopilot.pdf

Tencent Keen Security Lab. (2019b). *Tencent keen security lab: Experimental security research of tesla autopilot.* https://keenlab.tencent.com/en/2019/03/29/Tencent-Keen-Security-Lab-Experimental-Security-Research-of-Tesla-Autopilot/

Thatcham Research. (2020). *Thatcham research consumer security rating.* https://www.thatcham.org/what-we-do/security/consumer-rating/

Thomas, P. (2019). *Thatcham releases the latest results of motion sensors in key fobs that block relay attacks.* Academic Press.

Uhlemann, E. (2015). Introducing connected vehicles. *IEEE Vehicular Technology Magazine, 10,* 23–31.

Upstream. (2020). *Upstream security's global automotive cybersecurity report.* https://www.upstream.auto/upstream-security-global-automotive-cybersecurity-report-2020

ADAC Vehicle Technology. (2019). *Motorcycles and cars tested by German automobile club.* ADAC.

Virtanen, N., Schirokoff, A., & Kulmala, R. (2006). *Impacts of an automatic emergency call system on accident consequences.* Academic Press.

Woo, Jo, & Lee. (2015). A practical wireless attack on the connected car and security protocol for in-vehicle CAN. *IEEE Transactions on Intelligent Transportation Systems, 16,* 993–1006.

Wouters, L., Marin, E., Ashur, T., Gierlichs, B., & Preneel, B. (2018). *Fast, furious and insecure: Passive keyless entry and start systems in modern supercars.* Academic Press.

Zhang, T., Antunes, H., & Aggarwal, S. (2014). Defending connected vehicles against malware: Challenges and a solution framework. *IEEE Internet of Things Journal, 1*(1), 10–21. doi:10.1109/JIOT.2014.2302386

ENDNOTES

1   Davis, L. (2015). Automotive buses. http://www.interfacebus.com/DesignConnectorAutomotive.html

2   The Clemson University Vehicular Electronics Laboratory. (n.d.). Automotive data communication buses. https://cecas.clemson.edu/cvel/auto/autobuses01.html

[3] Infineon Technologies. (2020b). Telematics control unit. https://www.infineon. com/cms/en/applications/automotive/automotive-security/telematics-control-unit/

[4a] Texas Instruments. (2020). Telematics control unit. https://www.ti.com/ solution/automotive-telematics-control-unit#technicaldocuments

[4b] Alissa Valentina Knight. (2018). The hitchhiker's guide to hacking connected cars: The devil in the details of TCU init scripts in android. https://www. linkedin.com/pulse/hitchhik ers-guide-hacking-connected-cars-devil-tcu-valentina-knight

[5] Infineon Technologies. (2020a). Gateway. https://www.infineon.com/cms/en/ applications/automotive/body-electronics-and-lighting/gateway/

[6] IETF contributors. (2018). The transport layer security (TLS) protocol version 1.3. https://tools.ietf.org/html/rfc8446

[7] IETF contributors. (2005). Security architecture for the internet protocol. https://tools.ietf.org/html/rfc4301

[8] Toyota. (2020a). Connected vehicle services privacy and protection notice. https://www.toyota.com/privacyvts/images/doc/privacy-portal.pdf

[9] Toyota. (2020b). Privacy and protection. https://www.toyota.com/privacyvts/

[10] Common Vulnerabilities and Exposures and contributors. (2013). CVE-2014-0160. https://cve.mitre.org/cgi-bin/cvename.cgi?name=cve-2014-0160

[1] https://www.gettyimages.com/detail/illustration/collision-detection-radar-illustration-royalty-free-illustration/481496943

[2] https://www.gettyimages.com/detail/illustration/self-driving-car-icons-vector-illustration-royalty-free-illustration/1178874789

Chapter 8
Security of In–Vehicle Communication Systems:
A Survey of Possible Vulnerabilities

Dennis Dubrefjord
Chalmers University of Technology, Sweden

Myeong-jin Jang
Chalmers University of Technology, Sweden

Oscar Carlsson
Chalmers University of Technology, Sweden

Hayder Hadi
Chalmers University of Technology, Sweden

Tomas Olovsson ·
iD https://orcid.org/0000-0001-9548-819X
Chalmers University of Technology, Sweden

ABSTRACT

The automotive industry has seen remarkable growth in the use of network and communication technology. These technologies can be vulnerable to attacks. Several examples of confirmed attacks have been documented in academic studies, and many vehicular communications systems have been designed without security aspects in mind. Furthermore, all the security implications mentioned here would affect the functionality of decision support systems (DSS) of IoT and vehicular networks. This chapter focuses on in-vehicle security and aims to categorize some attacks in this field according to the exploited vulnerability by showing common patterns. The conclusion suggests that an ethernet-based architecture could be a good architecture for future vehicular systems; it enables them to meet future security needs while still allowing network communication with outside systems.

DOI: 10.4018/978-1-7998-7468-3.ch008

INTRODUCTION

Vehicles become smarter and more complicated every day due to the development in automotive electronics, which consists of various subsystems including engine electronics, transmission electronics, chassis electronics, and entertainment systems. The percentage of the electronic systems' cost in an automobile has gradually increased from approximately 1 percent in 1950 to about 30 percent in 2010 (Wagner, 2020). However, along with the rapid growth, security concerns regarding the communication systems in vehicles have not been considered. Therefore, vehicles are no longer in an acceptable state in terms of information security. This can lead to negative consequences for the passengers in the vehicle, but also other road users since a malfunction in one vehicle can cause accidents that harm both passengers and others. Furthermore, the stakes are quickly rising as the evolution towards smart cities means that the vehicles become more connected to other systems, such as decision support systems. In other words, vehicles are becoming more and more like Internet of Things (IoT) devices. An attacker who is able to compromise a vehicle can send arbitrary data to other, connected systems, affecting their ability to function as intended.

One example that shows how vulnerable vehicular networks are was presented at the Black Hat USA 2015 security conference by the researchers Charlie Miller and Chris Valasek (Drozhzhin, 2019). The researchers showed that a vehicle that was produced by a major car corporation could easily be hacked. The demonstration started by showing the ease of taking control of a Jeep vehicle's multimedia system by finding out its password. How to access it remotely over a cellular network was also presented. Furthermore, the researchers were able to control every component of the car through the Controller Area Network (CAN) bus, which is extremely vulnerable from a cybersecurity perspective. The demonstration delivered a clear message showing how insecure vehicular communication systems currently are and the severity of attacks where a remote attacker can be in full control of all functions in a moving vehicle.

Therefore, understanding automotive security vulnerabilities in vehicular communications are very important, not only to experts in the field but also to people in related fields of research. Thus, this chapter aims to provide readers with a comprehensive understanding of automotive security vulnerabilities, specifically inside the in-vehicle communication systems.

The methodology behind this chapter is a study of recent research related to the topic which is categorized and summarized. The scope is restricted to in-vehicle communication, meaning it excludes communication between the vehicle and its surroundings. Within in-vehicle communication, the authors focus on currently existing technologies such as the CAN bus and Local Interconnect Network (LIN) bus,

FlexRay, and automotive Ethernet. To provide a broad and overarching perspective, this chapter provides an analysis of attacks in different communication technologies in a sequence: categorized automotive security attacks; explanations about major attacks' implementations; technical limitations in major vehicle communications; expected or reported negative consequences; and solutions.

The remaining part of the chapter is organized as follows: Background describes general aspects of vehicular communications, then the major communications technologies CAN, LIN, FlexRay and automotive Ethernet are discussed in order, followed by Future Research Directions where the found attacks and the core issues of the system are discussed.

BACKGROUND

Connected vehicles are essentially IoT devices. Thus, to understand automotive security more broadly, IoT security must be considered. The security implications of IoT were introduced in Butun et. al (2019). Most of the research conducted in the area is focused on software-related security principles but Butun et al. (2020) showed the importance of hardware-assisted security. These points apply equally to automotive security as well.

Vehicle communications can be categorized into two parts, which are inter-vehicle communications and in-vehicle communications. Inter-vehicle communications transfer information between vehicles and other objects including pedestrians and infrastructure, while in-vehicle communications provide communication channels inside of a vehicle.

Vehicles in the past did not provide customers with dedicated automotive electronics like today. For instance, the electronic systems' cost of an automobile was approximately only 1 percent in 1950 (Wagner, 2020) and consequently earlier in-vehicle communication techniques were not designed to provide sophisticated security measures. In Cybersecurity Challenges in Vehicular Communications (El-Rewini et al., 2020, p. 100214), three reasons for the security vulnerabilities in in-vehicle communications have been identified:

- **Limited Connectivity:** Compared to IT devices that can update their security protections periodically through the Internet, vehicles are limited in that perspective. Thus, vehicle communications tend to be more vulnerable to attacks.
- **Technical Limitations of In-Vehicle Communications:** Simple communications cost less, and still provides benefits. Communications such as CAN and LIN are relatively old protocols and have been used

by automotive manufactures for a long time. However, when attacks in automotive security become more advanced, the drawbacks of these simple communication protocols become apparent. Most in-vehicle communications are not flexible enough to be able to support important security functions providing confidentiality and authentication.

- **Threats are Hard to Predict:** Even today's vehicles that are far from autonomous, are still using systems consisting of many complex subsystems that have hundreds of Electric Control Units (ECU), connected over different internal networks and that interact with each other in complicated ways, where each interaction may contain a vulnerability that can be exploited by attackers. Thus, automotive manufacturers have difficulties predicting which part of their systems can be exploited and how it can be done.

In this chapter, LIN, CAN, FlexRay, and Automotive Ethernet are discussed, with each communications' characteristics and vulnerabilities. The reason behind the separation is that they are built on fundamentally different communication techniques with different features and limitations, thereby exposing different security vulnerabilities.

CAN

The Controller Area Network (CAN) is currently the most common network type in a car as it is reliable and does not require a lot of communication wires. Many of the internal networks in a modern vehicle are based on CAN, and when CAN was introduced in vehicles around 1990, security was not an issue. Important security features such as confidentiality and authentication were not implemented, which today opens up several attack vectors (Woo et al., 2014, p. 10).

Gaining access to a CAN network may be done through different means depending on the complexity of the vehicle. In a more complex vehicle, there might be wireless networks that are connected to CAN networks which can be used to gain remote access to essential ECUs. Another simpler way is to use an On-Board Diagnostic II (OBD2) port, which is a standardized physical connection to the vehicle that is normally used to connect to the vehicle's self-diagnostics systems (Kelarestaghi et al., 2019, p. 1).

One example of an attack is to use a diagnostics tool that connects to the OBD2 port. Attacking a vehicle in this way is typically not plausible, as it requires constant physical access. However, Kelarestaghi et al. (2019, p. 1) suggest another way to attack the ECUs through the OBD2 port. Their suggestion requires that the vehicle owner uses a wireless diagnostics unit that is connected to their smartphone and operated using an app. The attack starts by eavesdropping on a diagnostics unit to extract CAN frames that can later be used to gain control of the ECU that the attacker wants to target. Then, assuming that the target installs the malicious app created by the attacker, the attack can begin. With the target having its wireless diagnostics unit connected to its vehicle, the attacker can listen to all the data transmitted to the diagnostics unit through the app over the internet. The attacker can now at any point transmit its malicious CAN frame to the vehicle through their malicious app. CAN's inability to check for authentication is what makes it possible to execute this replay attack (Kelarestaghi et al., 2019, p. 1).

The vulnerabilities in the CAN network can lead to serious consequences for the target vehicle. With the CAN network connected to many important features in the vehicle, it is possible to seriously harm or even kill the people in the vehicle. In the article by Greenberg (2018), Miller and Valasek, two security researchers, took control over the CAN network in a Jeep Cherokee while a test person was driving the vehicle on a highway. Since Miller and Valasek did not want to induce any harm to the driver, they limited their attacks to increasing the volume of the radio, activating the windshield wiper fluids, controlling the air conditioning, and killing the engine. When the test was finished, the driver described the event as a traumatic experience. Miller and Valasek also showed some other more serious attacks in a parking lot. They were able to control the steering of the vehicle as long as it was at a low speed and the vehicle was driving in reverse. They were also able to lock the doors of the vehicle, change the speedometer and disable the breaks.

There are several different protocols that researchers have implemented on top of CAN in an effort to compensate for its lack of security. The greatest issues to tackle are the low bandwidth of the CAN network (typically 1 Mbps), its maximum packet size of 8 bytes, and the low performance of most ECUs which is a cost issue. This makes it challenging to implement advanced protocols on top of CAN while preserving the existing architecture. Woo et al., (2014, p. 11) propose a security protocol that they compare with a protocol by Groza and Murvay (2013, p. 2035) and a protocol by Lin and Sangiovanni-Vincentelli (2012, p. 2). Their conclusion of the comparison is that only their own protocol is viable to be deployed in a vehicle. Their protocol implements authentication and confidentiality while keeping the bus load below 50%. See Table 1 for an overview of the comparisons done.

LIN

LIN is a simple broadcast serial network protocol that was developed to provide inexpensive communication in automotive networks. For example, the protocol is much cheaper to implement than CAN. It provides a communication channel to smaller subnets of automotive electronics, typically for simple sensors and engine control. The LIN protocol uses master and slave architecture. Often, the master node is connected to CAN, and up to 16 nodes work as slaves. The master's role is to regulate communications between slaves using scheduling to prevent collisions. The node that is designated to transmit information is a publisher and nodes that are supposed to receive that information are subscribers. This scheduling of communication is implemented by sending headers to the subscribers and publishers. A LIN frame consists of break, sync, ID, data, and checksum as shown in figure 1.

Table 1. Comparison of the different CAN protocols, done by Woo et al. (2014, p. 3)

	(Woo et al., 2014, p. 3)	(Groza & Murvay, 2013, p. 2038)	(Lin & Sangiovanni-Vincentelli, 2012, p. 4)
Data Confidentiality	O	X	X
Data Authentication & Integrity	O	O	O
Connectivity with External Device	O	X	X
Increased BUS load	X	O	O
Resistance to Replay-attack	O	X	O

Figure 1. The LIN frame structure

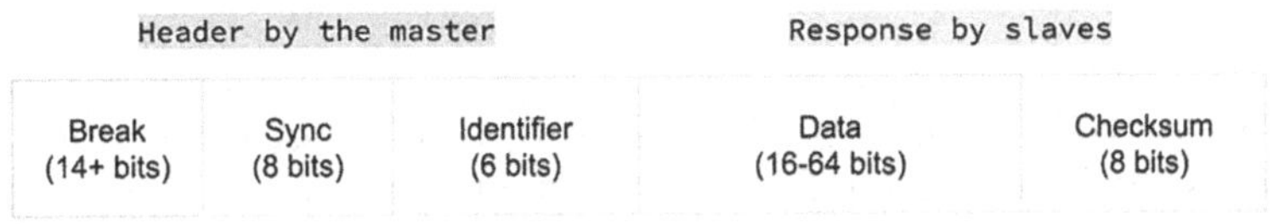

Header by the master			Response by slaves	
Break (14+ bits)	Sync (8 bits)	Identifier (6 bits)	Data (16-64 bits)	Checksum (8 bits)

Headers that consist of break, sync, ID are transmitted by the master, and data and checksum are completed by slaves, i.e., the specific node that has its ID in the ID field. The break-field indicates the start of a new frame and the Sync field allows baud rate detection. Especially, understanding the Identifier field is important to find vulnerabilities in the LIN bus. The total number of provided IDs in LIN is 64 and they can be separated into three groups. The first group (0-59) is used for signal carrying, 60, and 61 are used for diagnostic, and the remaining 62, and 63 are reserved slots. Particularly, ID 60 executes a critical function called 'Sleep and Wake-up'. As the name implies, it is used to force all slave nodes to go sleep mode for longer than four seconds. This characteristic of LIN can be exploited by attackers (El-Rewini et al., 2020, p. 100214). If an attacker can access a LIN bus and transmit a message that maliciously contains ID 60, which indicates sleep mode, it is possible to forcibly shut down all slave nodes on the network which could be dangerous. To execute the attack, the attacker sends a false header which prompts slaves 1 and

2 to change their modes to sleep. This means the attacker can shut down all slave nodes, even when the vehicle is moving. Slave nodes can handle various functions including door locks, window wipers, and cooling fan motors. For example, the window wipers could be stopped suddenly by an attacker when the car is driving on the highway on a rainy day, which at best could distract the driver and at worst could make it impossible for the driver to see the road ahead. It is easy to imagine that an attack like this could result in an accident with fatal outcomes. This attack is shown in Figure 2.

Figure 2. LIN attack 1 – message spoofing attacks

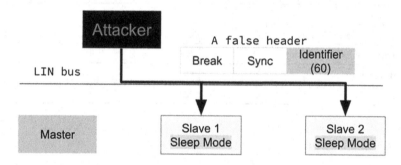

This type of attack is an example of a message spoofing attack. Since only the master sends the header in the LIN bus, if an attacker sends a header containing inappropriate information, the slave nodes must listen to the false message and have no way of knowing whether the request is authentic or not due to slave nodes having no methods to figure out whether the message came from the master or others. Fundamentally, spoofing attacks can be prevented by authentication, but LIN does not provide it.

Also, the collision handling in the LIN bus can be exploited by attackers since if any node, including the master, detects a collision during their transmission they must stop and wait until they receive a new header from the master. This means that the time slot between a collision and a new header arriving can be used by malicious nodes to deliver false information or to control slave nodes. This type of attack is called response collision attacks. The process of Response Collision Attacks, with its four steps, is described in Figure 3.

Step 1, the master transmits a header to designate a subscriber and a publisher. In figure 3, slave 1 is a publisher that will respond in the next time slot. At that time, the attacker purposely transmits signals to provoke a collision (step 2). Then, the publisher detects a collision and stops its transmission (step 3). In step 4, the attacker now can send a false response with a correct checksum to the subscriber. A checksum is an uncomplicated way to detect errors in received messages so that if a checksum is correct then any messages will be accepted. Unfortunately, since a checksum in LIN is just the sum of data and Identifier, it is trivial to calculate and send a correct one.

Figure 3. LIN attack 2 – response collision attacks

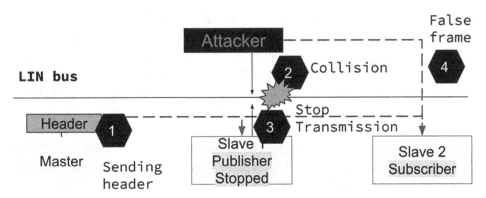

Furthermore, attackers can halt the master's transmissions too. This type of attack is called header collision attacks (El-Rewini et al., 2020, p. 100214) and is explained in figure 4.

Figure 4. LIN attack 3 – header collision attacks

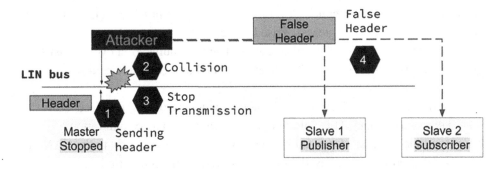

The attack is very similar to the response collision attack, except for the fact that the target this time is the master node. Thus, when the master sends a header the attacker simultaneously sends signals to create collisions.

Currently, there are no technical measures to prevent these attacks. One suggestion by El-Rewini et al., (2020, p. 100214) is to locate important data at the beginning of a transmission so even if a collision occurs which is created by an attacker, there is a chance that the important data will be delivered. Fundamentally, this is not a solution since it cannot prevent collisions or block malicious messages.

FLEXRAY

Due to the need for a protocol with more capabilities and characteristics to adapt to the increasing number of systems and controllers used in modern automobiles, the FlexRay bus was created and developed by the FlexRay industry consortium. It is a high-speed, deterministic, and fault-tolerant communication protocol, based on hard real-time usage, and can handle data transmission rates up to 10Mbps. FlexRay is featured with a bus guardian technique that offers both safety and some security functionality. It protects the network against possible faulty actions, such as preventing flooding or monopolizing the bus by other devices (Smith et al., 2016). It was designed for safety-critical applications where message transmissions must follow a precise timing schedule (El-Rewini et al., 2020, p. 100214). Therefore, it is used for time-sensitive real-time communication and safety-critical systems such as High-Performance Powertrain and X-by-wire (Driving, steering, braking, adaptive cruise control, etc. all done by wire).

All communication between FlexRay nodes is based on a communication schedule, and each node includes a couple of communication channels to enable redundancy. Both channels can be used in parallel to increase the data rate to 20M bit/s if redundancy is not required.

In a FlexRay network, all ECUs must be synchronized to a global time, where the maximum time unit is called a cycle. The FlexRay communication cycle acts as the main element of media-access. Based on network design, each cycle has a fixed duration, typically around 1-5 milliseconds. The communication cycle consists of four main parts (Murvay et al., 2018), as described in figure 5, they are:

1. Static segment (Mandatory segment) which includes reserved slots for deterministic data. This data requires arrival within a fixed duration.
2. Dynamic segment (Optional segment) which works similarly to the CAN bus and is used for event-based data with no determinism required.
3. Symbol window (Optional segment) used for network maintenance.
4. Network idle time (Mandatory time segment) which is responsible for synchronization between node clocks.

A fundamental feature of FlexRay is that it combines time-triggered and event-triggered communication. Time-triggered events will be associated with the static segment which guarantees that messages will have a reserved time slot and always can be delivered with real-time guarantees. The dynamic segments will be responsible for the event-triggered events, using event-driven communication where messages are delivered when the bus becomes available (El-Rewini et al., 2020, p. 100214).

Figure 5. FlexRay communication cycle

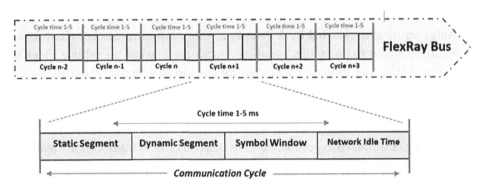

Like the other in-vehicle network buses, FlexRay lacks sufficient protection and is vulnerable to different security threats that target the ECUs on the FlexRay network. Attacks can be life-threatening especially since ECUs connected by FlexRay buses are often providing high capabilities of control and maneuverability in the vehicle. One of the attacks is message spoofing which occurs when the attacker, despite the inability to break the cryptographic primitives, records, and replays messages, then uses it illegitimately to inject forged traffic to the FlexRay bus, thus controlling or altering functionality in targeted ECUs.

It is essential to look at the FlexRay frame structure to understand the weaknesses discussed later. The frame is composed of three segments (Header, Payload, and Trailer). The static segment which is divided into predefined slots can transmit one static frame per slot each cycle. But the case is different for dynamic segments. The dynamic frames are transmitted arbitrarily as there are no guarantees that enough slots are available in each round to transmit a message.

Figure 6. FlexRay attack - spoofing attack on star topology

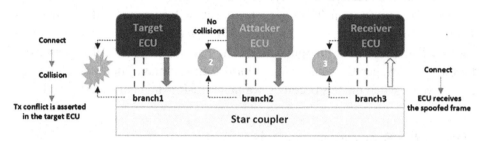

An experiment conducted by a Panasonic Corporation researcher (Kishikawa et al., 2019) aimed to prove that spoofing attacks are feasible on vehicle FlexRay networks. Active star topology was used for the target network where ECUs are connected via a star coupler, as described in Figure 6. The coupler had multiple branches, each one connected to FlexRay's bus (transceivers). The network was designed in this flexible way to allow access to any branch. After analyzing the frames using customized experimental tools, several critical frames were identified as targets. These target frames were exploited by injecting spoofed frames instead which enabled unplanned control of some of the vehicle's essential functions such as steering, braking, and acceleration. They found that the most critical messages were transmitted through the static frames. However, static frames were also the most exploitable. The scenario of the spoofing attack targeting the steering system occurred as follows:

The steering ECU (receiver ECU) controls steering, based on park assist frames received from the park assist ECU (target ECU whose messages will be spoofed). The attacker ECU needs to have access to any branch other than the branch to which the target ECU is connected in order to inject spoofed frames. When an ECU sends messages, they will be forwarded to the other branches by the star coupler. However, if the attacker ECU transmits a spoofed frame from its branch just microseconds before the legitimate frame should be forwarded, the star coupler will also forward this spoofed message and drop the legitimate message to prevent a collision. As a result, the steering ECU will receive only the spoofed park assist frames. Knowing that the exact timing is known in the static segment, it is possible to exploit the critical frames assigned to the static frames. Furthermore, this attack is applicable to the other x-by-wire systems connected by FlexRay. In fact, although this protocol has more capabilities than CAN, such as an error-handling mechanism, it could not detect or prevent the spoofed frames. In this example, the success of the attack depends on the topology of the design, see Table 2 Possibilities of a spoofing attack. In other words, if the same experiment were to be applied to a Bus topology, it will be so difficult for the attacker to inject spoofed static frames into the receiver ECU since a collision would be visible to both the transmitter and the receiver.

In general, it is still not easy to find real FlexRay attacks on real vehicles as no such study of FlexRay vulnerabilities or known attacks exists. Most studies are theoretical and focus on simulation experiments and the spoofing attack was the closest one to reality. The basic countermeasure on the horizon is providing message authentication codes (MACs) but that involves key distribution which can be difficult. Another important feature of FlexRay with respect to security is the network design which effectively reduces the possibilities of spoofing attacks when using a Bus topology.

Table 2. Spoofing attack possibility

Topology	Static Frame	Dynamic Frame
Bus	No	Yes
Star	Yes	Yes

(Kishikawa et al., 2019)

AUTOMOTIVE ETHERNET

Ethernet is widely used in networking and has begun to enter the automotive field as well. It connects different units using switches that route the packets to the correct receiver. This routing is something that makes Ethernet special in the automotive sphere (Dibaei et al., 2020, p. 400). Ethernet is also very fast. Speeds from 100 Mbps up to 10 Gbps are available today and Rodriguez-Perez et al. (2020, p. 2) state that 25 Gbps is on the horizon. The speeds make Ethernet an attractive networking solution in the automotive sphere since it is expected that higher speeds will be necessary as vehicles become more and more autonomous and thus relies heavily on big amounts of sensor data being sent to processing devices on the network. Additionally, there exist several implementations of automotive Ethernet, like Time-Triggered Ethernet and Time-Sensitive Networking which provide Ethernet with timing guarantees. These timing guarantees make Ethernet, much like FlexRay, a powerful technology for real-time applications as well. However, a drawback of Ethernet according to Dibaei et al. (2020, p. 400) is that it is currently more expensive to implement than CAN, LIN, and FlexRay.

As is known from other network security fields, ethernet has some vulnerabilities. El-Rewini et al. (2020, p. 100214) state that if an attacker can access a switch, by default it is possible to gain access to the network by simply plugging a device into one of the unconnected ports. Once inside the network, the attacker can map out the network architecture. Further, they explain that since ethernet lacks any measures of authentication, it is also possible for the attacker to send packets with a spoofed source address, with the purpose of fooling the receiving system. In the same manner, an attacker could replay old messages in the network. For instance, the attacker might be able to replay the packet for triggering the airbag or turning off the engine.

When Ethernet is deployed in a vehicle, it is also reasonable to assume that other Internet protocols like IP, TCP, and UDP will be used. Since all these protocols lack any kind of authentication, an attacker is also able to affect the routing of packets inside the system by utilizing Address Resolution Protocol (ARP) and Dynamic Host Configuration Protocol (DHCP) poisoning attacks (El-Rewini et al., 2020, p. 100214). Affecting the routing could open the door to man-in-the-middle attacks, whereby the attacker can edit the packets sent from one node to another. Finally, it is also possible to perform Denial-of-Service attacks by flooding some part of the network with traffic, making it unresponsive to legitimate users. The consequences of such an attack could be dire, as it might, for example, mean that the packets sent from the brake pedal cannot reach the breaks. It might also mean that the packets being sent to trigger the airbag will not reach the airbags.

Although automotive Ethernet is a new technology, some countermeasures have been suggested to mitigate the vulnerabilities present in the Ethernet technology. These suggestions are similar to the protections utilized in other Ethernet-based networks and have likely drawn inspiration from other systems. However, because the ECUs in the Ethernet network can be severely limited resource-wise in the automotive Ethernet case, Corbett et al. (2016) state that the security solution can not be identical to those found in other Ethernet-based systems. For example, encrypting all the data that is being sent is a good practice in most Ethernet-based systems. However, in the automotive case, encryption algorithms can be too resource-demanding, thus creating a bottleneck that increases the latency of the system. Since speed and timing guarantees are paramount in a vehicle, this is not ideal. Instead, Corbett et al. (2016) suggest that Message Authentication Codes (MAC) could be used to guarantee integrity and provide authentication in a less resource-intensive way.

A feature of Ethernet is that it is easily extensible and supports a very dynamic topology. However, according to Corbett et al. (2016) this should be limited in vehicles to make sure that no malicious units get access to the network. They suggest that this limitation can be done through the usage of firewalls, packet filters, network segmentation, or Virtual Local Area Networks (VLAN). This not only makes the network harder to access, but also has the added perk of making the automotive Ethernet network topology very rigid. Furthermore, since the passengers and users are only meant to interact with the vehicle through the Human Machine Interface (HMI), the traffic generated can also be more regular than traffic generated in other Ethernet networks. This regularity in the automotive Ethernet network makes it relatively easy to detect malicious or faulty traffic from an ECU, which makes anomalous behavior detection systems, or other Intrusion Detection Systems (IDS), an effective solution in the environment.

FUTURE RESEARCH DIRECTIONS

There are many security weaknesses in all protocols described. In fact, there is a disturbing lack of security features in every technology presented. A common flaw in all the systems is the lack of authentication, which makes it possible to send faked and replayed packets. These packets can influence the systems in the car, with possibly lethal outcomes. A challenge in solving this issue is the concurrent usage of multiple technologies in a vehicle since each technology increases the attack surface and require their own specialized solutions to deal with security issues.

Thus, mitigating security risks in the current architecture is hard. At the same time, expecting automotive manufacturers to replace the architecture is not a realistic short-term solution. In the current system, the first step of conducting an attack is to get access to the vehicle's networks, thus, preventing unwanted connections from the outside could be a way to mitigate security risks. However, connections to outside nodes provide the driver with a lot of features, such as diagnostics tools and infotainment. Limiting access to the vehicular networks from the outside while still keeping the useful features of said access is certainly a challenge.

The bandwidth required in vehicles is likely to increase in the future, as the vehicles collect and transmit and process more and more sensor data. Thus, it is reasonable to expect that at least some parts of the internal network of vehicles will be replaced by Ethernet since it is the technology with the highest band capabilities when it comes to speed. A future solution to the issue of having multiple network technologies might be to allow automotive Ethernet to replace FlexRay and CAN completely since it has the technical capability to do so. This comes with the added benefit of making the vehicle system more homogenous, shrinking the attack surface, and also more similar to other Ethernet-based systems, to which plenty of security solutions already exist. For example, there are solutions for authentication in other Ethernet systems that could be adjusted to fit automotive Ethernet as well. Another benefit is the increased speeds of the Ethernet network compared to other technologies.

However, since automotive Ethernet currently seems to be more expensive than FlexRay and CAN, it is not clear whether the benefits currently outweigh the costs from an economic perspective. An economic analysis of the costs and gains of automotive Ethernet is a great opportunity for future research. If automotive Ethernet is currently too expensive, it might be a feasible solution in the future if the cost of automotive Ethernet is brought down by technological advancements and higher adoption rates by the industry.

Another trend that also to some extent solves network problems is to consolidate functionality into fewer and more powerful ECUs reducing the need for node-to-node communication. Advanced low-power processors are now available at competitive prices and processing power is constantly increasing. This makes it possible to create more robust architectures and use techniques like memory protection, virtualization, containers, secure boot, and have firewall functionality built-in to almost all functions in a vehicle.

Regardless of whether it is possible to decrease the attack surface by using more similar technologies, in-vehicle security is a field that could benefit greatly from more research. Especially considering that the evolution towards smart cities means that the security of the vehicle protects not only the vehicle, along with its passengers and road users surrounding it but also connected systems whose malfunction can have severe consequences. The security of vehicles must be well designed, considering both software and hardware security solutions to mitigate possible threats. Currently, neither of these are at a satisfactory level.

CONCLUSION

The analysis of the in-vehicle communication protocols CAN, LIN, FlexRay, and automotive Ethernet has shown that all protocols are developed with hardly any thought of security in mind. Some countermeasures or fixes have been listed for the different protocols, but the simplicity of the protocols often makes it impractical or impossible to apply the fixes. The four above-mentioned protocols all miss security features for authentication, which makes it possible to, for example, perform replay-attacks and spoof messages. This lack of security has broader implications since vehicles are now becoming connected to the Internet. A vulnerability may be remotely exploited allowing an attacker to take control over the subsystems of the vehicle. The authors believe that a transition to an Ethernet-based internal network is a crucial step forward for securing future connected vehicles. Ethernet is a well-researched area when it comes to security and it makes it possible to transfer well-known protocols and security technologies to vehicular networks, with some adjustments. The cost of Ethernet is what currently makes it unattractive, but the authors believe prices will go down when it becomes a more mature and commonly used technology in our vehicles.

ACKNOWLEDGMENT

First and foremost, we would like to express our gratitude to Ismail Butun for giving us the incredible opportunity to contribute to this exciting book which we are certain is going to be a valuable addition to the fields of DSS and IoT industry. We would also like to thank Tomas Olovsson for his mentorship, supervision, and guidance in writing this chapter. Finally, we would like to thank Linus Elwing Malmfelt for providing iterative feedback, increasing the quality of the chapter.

REFERENCES

Butun, I., Sari, A., & Österberg, P. (2019, January). Security implications of fog computing on the internet of things. In *2019 IEEE International Conference on Consumer Electronics (ICCE)* (pp. 1-6). IEEE. 10.1109/ICCE.2019.8661909

Butun, I., Sari, A., & Österberg, P. (2020). Hardware Security of Fog End-Devices for the Internet of Things. *Sensors (Basel)*, 20(20), 5729. doi:10.339020205729 PMID:33050165

Corbett, C., Schoch, E., Kargl, F., & Preussner, F. (2016). Automotive Ethernet: security opportunity or challenge? In Sicherheit 2016 - Sicherheit, Schutz und Zuverlässigkeit. Bonn: Gesellschaft für Informatik e.V.

Dibaei, M., Zheng, X., Jiang, K., Abbas, R., Liu, S., Zhang, Y., Xiang, Y., & Yu, S. (2020). Attacks and defences on intelligent connected vehicles: A survey. *Digital Communications and Networks*, 6(4), 399–421. doi:10.1016/j.dcan.2020.04.007

Drozhzhin, A. (2019, November 15). *Black Hat USA 2015: The full story of how that Jeep was hacked.* Kaspersky Official Blog. https://www.kaspersky.com/blog/blackhat-jeep-cherokee-hack-explained/9493/

El-Rewini, Z., Sadatsharan, K., Selvaraj, D. F., Plathottam, S. J., & Ranganathan, P. (2020). Cybersecurity challenges in vehicular communications. *Vehicular Communications*, 23, 100214. doi:10.1016/j.vehcom.2019.100214

Greenberg, A. (2015, July 21). Hackers Remotely Kill a Jeep on the Highway—With Me in It. *Wired.* https://www.wired.com/2015/07/hackers-remotely-kill-jeep-highway/

Groza, B., & Murvay, S. (2013). Efficient Protocols for Secure Broadcast in Controller Area Networks. *IEEE Transactions on Industrial Informatics*, 9(4), 2034–2042. doi:10.1109/TII.2013.2239301

Kelarestaghi, K. B., Foruhandeh, M., Heaslip, K., & Gerdes, R. (2019). Intelligent Transportation System Security: Impact-Oriented Risk Assessment of In-Vehicle Networks. *IEEE Intelligent Transportation Systems Magazine, 1.* Advance online publication. doi:10.1109/MITS.2018.2889714

Lin, C.-W., & Sangiovanni-Vincentelli, A. (2012). Cyber-Security for the Controller Area Network (CAN) Communication Protocol. *2012 International Conference on Cyber Security,* 1–7. 10.1109/CyberSecurity.2012.7

Murvay, P. S., & Groza, B. (2018, October). Practical Security Exploits of the FlexRay In-Vehicle Communication Protocol. In *International Conference on Risks and Security of Internet and Systems* (pp. 172-187). Springer.

Rodriguez-Perez, A., de Aranda, R. P., Prefasi, E., Pablo, J. S., Dumont, S., Rosado, J., Enrique, I., Pinzon, P., & Ortiz, D. (2020). Towards the Multi-Gigabit Ethernet for the Automotive Industry. *2020 IEEE International Symposium on Circuits and Systems (ISCAS),* 1–5. 10.1109/ISCAS45731.2020.9180481

Smith, C. (2016). *The car hacker's handbook: a guide for the penetration tester.* No Starch Press.

Wagner, I. (2020, October 8). *Car costs - automotive electronics costs worldwide2030.* https://www.statista.com/statistics/277931/automotive-electronics-cost-as-a-share-of-total-car-cost-worldwide/

Woo, S., Jo, H. J., & Lee, D. H. (2014). A Practical Wireless Attack on the Connected Car and Security Protocol for In-Vehicle CAN. *IEEE Transactions on Intelligent Transportation Systems,* 1–14. .2351612 doi:10.1109/tits.2014

KEY TERMS AND DEFINITIONS

Automotive Ethernet: Ethernet technology used in a vehicle that has the functionality necessary to replace other in-vehicle networking technologies.

Automotive Security: The IT security of an automotive vehicle system.

Controller Area Network (CAN): A networking technology used for in-vehicle communication. It is currently the most common bus used in the network of a vehicle. Messages being sent on the CAN bus are referred to as CAN frames.

Decision Support System (DSS): A subsystem responsible for aiding decision-making by compiling and presenting data to the decision-maker.

Electronic Control Unit (ECU): An embedded system used to control the electric subsystems in vehicles.

FlexRay: A networking technology used for in-vehicle communication. Compared to CAN, it is faster and more reliable. However, it's also more expensive.

In-Vehicle Communication: The communication used internally within the vehicle, between different sub-systems. For example, the signals that release the airbag are an example of in-vehicle communication.

Internet of Things (IoT): Small electronic systems connected to the internet, usually with limited computational resources.

Intrusion Detection System (IDS): A system that detects intrusions in a network by inspecting the traffic, trying to identify malicious packets.

IT Security: The security of an IT system, meaning its resilience of cyber-attacks targeting assets. It maintains the confidentiality and integrity of sensitive information and guarantees that the system is not made unavailable because of a cyber-attack.

Local Interconnect Network (LIN): A networking technology used for in-vehicle communication. Compared to other technologies, LIN is relatively cheap and is mostly used in less time-crucial parts in the network of a vehicle.

On-Board Diagnostics 2 (OBD2): A diagnostics system used in vehicles to monitor the other systems of the vehicle. The system is connected to the CAN bus.

X-by-Wire: A term used to describe that the automotive functionality X (which might be steering, braking, etc.) is achieved through an electrical system, instead of a mechanical one. The signals necessary for the functionality thus travel by wire.

Section 4
DSS Applications From Various IoT Domains

Chapter 9
Body Motion Capture and Applications

Çağlar Akman
Havelsan, Turkey

Tolga Sönmez
Havelsan, Turkey

ABSTRACT

The motion capture (MoCap) is a highly popular subject with wide applications in different areas such as animations, situational awareness, and healthcare. An overview of MoCap utilizing different sensors and technologies is presented, and the prominent MoCap methods using inertial measurement units and optics are discussed in terms of their advantages and disadvantages. MoCap with wearable inertial measurement units is analyzed and presented specifically with the background information and methods. The chapter puts an emphasis on the mathematical model and artificial intelligence algorithms developed for the MoCap. Both the products from the important technology developers and the proof-of-concept applications conducted by Havelsan are presented within this chapter to involve an industrial perspective. MoCap system will act as a decision support system in either application by providing automatic calculation of metrics or classification, which are the basic tools for decision making.

DOI: 10.4018/978-1-7998-7468-3.ch009

INTRODUCTION

As digitalization rises with the widespread use of available high-tech computers and autonomous systems, people from various sectors extensively apply intelligent solutions and smart human-machine interfaces to expedite their business. Motion capture (MoCap) is another inevitable digitalization technology, which captures and models the human motion varying from a single gesture to the full-body motion, to generate a digital twin of the subject for a predefined purpose. The MoCap technology is rigorously used in ample applications. The technology has been mostly used to generate animations and characters in the entertainment sectors like computer games and movies. Besides, the MoCap systems play a role in assisting decision support and monitoring system in the healthcare applications such as physiotherapy, rehabilitation, ergonomics, and tracing the treatment of posture-related anomalies. Similarly, it is also applicable in sports to monitor and measure the performance and metrics of a trainee in an exercise. MoCap systems have also miscellaneous application sectors like robotics in which emulations of human gestures and motions are used to interact remotely with the robots and smart autonomous systems.

The pioneer sector improving the MoCap technology is the entertainment sector as Max Fleischer invented the device called *rotoscope* in 1915. The device was projecting the image of a real human onto a light-table frame by frame so that the cartoons can be drawn more realistically by tracing the required edges (Kitagawa & Windsor, 2020). However, it was time-consuming, expensive, and limited to 2D. This technology has been further improved to the exoskeletons, inertial, and optical MoCap systems to model human motions in 3D (Menache, 2000). Currently, the optical MoCap is used in animations and character generation. It is not hard to predict that the entertainment sector (i.e., animations, video games, movies) will continue demanding more robust and accurate MoCap in the future.

The clinical applications use MoCap for monitoring the treatment of neuromuscular and musculoskeletal anomalies in physiotherapy and rehabilitation. The analysis of human locomotion is the fundamental of biomechanical and biomedicine concepts in the treatment (Dariush, 2003). As the analysis of lower limbs has been performed to make gait analysis (Wang, Ning, Tan, & Hu, 2004; Tao, Liu, Zheng, & Feng, 2012) for a very long time, there are established kinematics and biomechanics. On the other hand, the kinematics and biomechanics of the upper extremes are more complex due to the free movement of the arms; nevertheless, the transfer of profound knowledge and well-defined measurement techniques from lower limbs to upper limbs is difficult. The studies (van Andel, Wolterbeek, Doorenbosch, Veeger, & Harlaar, 2008; Rau, Disselhorst-Klug, & Schmidt, 2000) establish the methods for the biomechanics of the upper limbs. Furthermore, the full-body MoCap is significantly important to extract and analyze information and biomechanics for full-body motion disorders like Parkinson's disease.

Advances in genetics and medicine lead to a new paradigm in clinical diagnosis and treatments. It has been clear that each patient requires personalized medicine due to unique genetic characteristics (Liao & & Tsai, 2013). Hence, the physicians and the physiotherapists also need qualified tools to analyze the disease's progress and propose individualized treatment. For example, MoCap provides tremendous benefits by individual analysis of the Parkinson's disease tremor to assess the tremor severity and adjust the medication accordingly (Delrobaei, et al., 2018). Das et al. (2011) claim that a trained physician can assess the tremor severity by analyzing MoCap data of tremor action, gait, leg agility, and postural stability.

Knippenberg et al. (2017) state that MoCap should involve the client-centered task-oriented approach for the rehabilitation of neurological diseases such as multiple sclerosis (MS), stroke, and spinal cord injury (SCI) affecting the motor and sensory functions of upper and lower limbs. This study indicates the requirement for long-term motion capture by highly sensitive sensors to obtain appropriate accuracy. Subsequently, the long-term motion storage for activity monitoring requires sensor portability so that neither the movements of the patient are hindered, nor the patient is limited to a laboratory. Although there are plenty of optical-based MoCap solutions in the literature, the wearable sensor-based MoCap system can meet the requirement for portability.

The activity monitoring of a person can also be used in the situational awareness of operational teams like first responders or construction workers. The construction workers work for long durations in severe conditions and the workers can develop work-related musculoskeletal anomalies and, even worse, undesired accidents can occur. Yu et al. (2019) propose a non-invasive optical-based MoCap to monitor and assess the fatigue level of the workers and compared the results with the ground truth data collected by the fifteen wearable inertial measurement units (IMU) on the subject. Additionally, Hernandez et al. (2020) applied time-series machine learning models like recurrent neural networks (RNN) to assess the workers' fatigue level. It also suggests using IMU-based MoCap for real-time monitoring of the workers since such systems provide flexibility for collecting and recording data compared to the optical-based MoCap.

Similar systems can also be used for the first responders working under severe conditions such as natural disasters, fires, earthquakes, etc. Endsley and Jones (2016) define one of the drawbacks of situational awareness on an individual level as stressors such as anxiety, excessive workload, and fatigue. Under such circumstances, the first responders can lose their concentration and cannot make the correct decision, in turn, severe accidents might occur. MoCap systems can be used as activity monitoring to assess the fatigue level of the first responders for sake of operational efficiency and success. For example, the SAFESENSE project establishes a situational awareness system for the first responders to monitor the firefighter status by recognizing predefined activities (i.e., crawling, walking, jumping, falling, sitting, standing, etc.) (Scheurer, Tedesco, Brown, & O'Flynn, 2017). In this study, the classification is conducted on the motion data collected from wearable wireless IMUs.

The organization of the chapter involves detailed background information for different MoCap solutions with a comparison of each solution. Specifically, the inertial-based MoCap system is explained in terms of mathematical modeling and artificial intelligence algorithms. This section is succeeded with industrial inertial MoCap products to involve an industrial perspective. The chapter concludes with the use-cases such as health monitoring and situational awareness systems.

BACKGROUND

There are different techniques and methods used in the implementation of the MoCap system. The sensory system and corresponding measurement methods vary with respect to the problem definition and system requirements. The sensory used in MoCap systems can be categorized under three main topics, namely optical, inertial, others (i.e., mechanical, magnetic, hybrid, etc.). This categorization can be further detailed according to the measurement techniques associated with the sensory system. Furthermore, a MoCap system may involve a single sensor type as well as a combination of different types of sensors to increase system performance. A graphical representation of the MoCap system classification is shown in Figure 1.

Figure 1. Categorization of MoCap systems according to involved sensory technologies

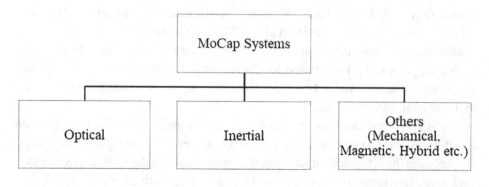

There are several categorization studies for MoCap systems in the literature. Zhou & Hu (2008) provides a categorization under the concept of rehabilitation: the systems firstly are divided into non-visual, visual, and robotic aided systems, then divided into subcategories concerning the sensor technologies used within the system. There is also another study of categorization depending on the sensory system and data acquisition methods (Rahul, 2018). Field et al. (2009) approach the same problem and imply the advantages and disadvantages in the robotic field. Nogueria (2011) states motion capture categorization and comparative analysis in real-world applications.

According to the studies in the literature, the MoCap systems are expected to perform accurate motion recognition and tracking in real-time or near real-time. Furthermore, the use-cases determine the restrictions and functional requirements of the MoCap systems. For example, while a recording room involving the setup of infrared and video cameras is required in animation generation, it is not feasible for a motion tracking of a first responder nor health monitoring of a patient in daily activities. Therefore, functional properties like size, weight, and setup should also be considered while analyzing the MoCap systems. This section involves categorized MoCap systems illustrated in Figure 1 in terms of the sensory system, data acquisition method, data processing methods, functional properties, and setup.

Optical MoCap

Advances in computer vision technologies and the availability of a wide variety of electro-optical sensors make this technology fundamental for data collection and processing systems. Optical sensors, indeed, are used to detect and track the position of the object in the captured image. There are marker-based and no-marker optical MoCap systems. While the marker-based systems use passive markers like reflectors or active markers like LEDs on the subject to be located, the no-marker systems detect and locate the contours and edges of the subject. In the marker-based optical MoCap systems, the high-resolution cameras are populated around a recording room where the subject wears detectable markers. The optical MoCap system generates the 3D position of the markers on the subject by processing the 2D position data gathered from each camera. Then, advanced vision techniques are used to cover this motion model with an appropriate texture according to the visualization details. The marker-based optical MoCap system diagram and is illustrated in Figure 2.

Figure 2. Basic diagram for an optical motion capture system

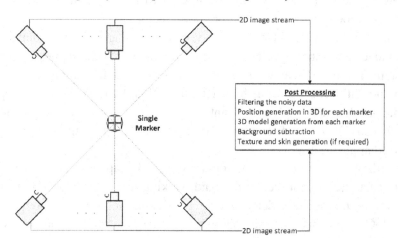

Guerra-Filho (2005) proposes a theory and the implementation process of the optical MoCap. This study involves required resources for such a MoCap system as well as each step as marker detection, positioning, tracking, and post-processing (further visual techniques, filtering, etc.). A body-worn marker suit and volumetric reconstruction of a body posture presented in this study are illustrated as further visualization of marker-based optical MoCap in Figure 3.

The state-of-the-art of marker-based optical MoCap has reached a maturity level such that there are many available commercial systems (VICON, n.d.; OPTITRACK, n.d.; PHASESPACE, n.d.; QUALISYS, n.d.). The positioning of available commercial systems is highly accurate. For example, the system positioning accuracy of VICON is around 1mm (Merriaux, Dupuis, Boutteau, Vasseur, & Savatier, 2017).

Although the marker-based optical MoCap provides highly accurate position information, the system cannot handle the local orientation of the joints axes nor occluded body parts due to the obstacles or overlapped body parts. There is an enhancement study for predicting the missing markers by filtering the collected data under the assumption of a constant rotation of occluded limbs in a limited time (Aristidou & Lasenby, 2013). Nevertheless, the performance of the optical motion capture reduces significantly, as the hindered markers increase or the number of cameras capturing the markers on the subject decreases.

There is another drawback of the optical MoCap systems depending on the use-case of the system setup. If the target subjects are people in their daily activities or operational activities, the optical MoCap becomes unfeasible due to its limitation of the measurement range. The MoCap systems are restricted to a capturing room or a laboratory. Hence, optical MoCap is not suitable for long time duration activity monitoring.

Figure 3. (a) Bodysuit of markers from different angles of camera views (b) Volumetric postural view of kneeling action (both of them as reprinted in Guerra-Filho, 2005). From "Optical Motion Capture: Theory and Implementation", by Guerro-Filho, 2005, RITA, 12(2), 61-90. Copyright 2005 by RITA.

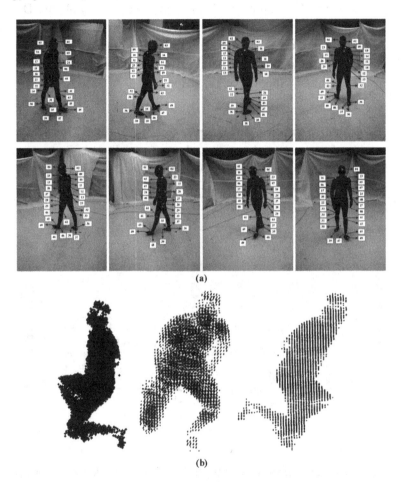

(a)

(b)

The no-marker-based optical MoCap has been improved and the researchers still work on this area with motivation due to the main drawbacks of the marker-based optical MoCap. In detail, the vibration and motion of markers due to soft tissue can generate noise; markers can be misaligned; markers generate noisy data due to their own inertia during the motion (Zhou & Hu, 2008). The marker-free-based MoCap, indeed, transfer the complexity to the processing units since filtering and post-processing requirements increase.

There have been several studies in the field of marker-free MoCap systems in recent decades. For example, Davison et al. (2001) proposed a method using particle filter-based method for marker-free MoCap to generate 3D animation with complex full-body movements. Shotton et al. (2011) published a study about 3D positions of body joints and 3D poses of the marker-free subject from a single depth image used in Kinect. In this study, the average joint prediction from inferred body parts is 0.731, while the average joint prediction from ground-truth body parts is 0.914 as illustrated in Figure 4 (Shotton, et al., 2011).

Figure 4. Joint prediction accuracy of marker-free MoCap with Kinect. Comparison of the actual performance of the proposed system (red) with the best achievable results (blue) given the ground truth body part labels
(as reprinted in Shotton, et al., 2011).
From "Real-time human pose recognition in parts from single depth images ", by Shotton, et al., 2011, CVPR 2011, pp. 1297-1304. Copyright 2011 by CVPR.

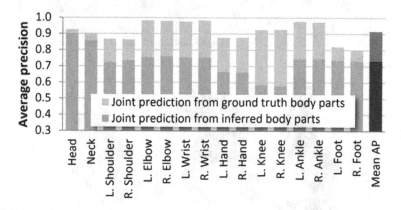

There have been several studies for the assessment of markerless MoCap systems in clinical applications. Ceseracciu et al. (2014) compared the marker-based and no-marker MoCap to assess the applicability of them in clinical gait analysis. They stated that the precision of motion capture is critical in clinical applications and the no-marker-based system has low accuracy in the transverse plane dividing the body up and down, while it has appropriate accuracy in the sagittal plane, dividing the body into left and right (Ceseracciu, Sawacha, & Cobelli, 2014). In addition, Ma et al. (2019) studied the reliability and validity of Kinect-based gait analysis on a limited patient group (people of 10). In this research, they concluded that the system has poor validity, but a potential to be improved. Similarly, Latorre et al. (2019) studied the validity of Kinect-based gait analysis and fall-risk assessment on a patient group (people of 82). In this study, the researchers concluded that the system has limited sensitivity to kinematic parameters, but it is still be used for gait assessment and fall-risk identification.

Optical MoCap systems are widely used in many sectors. The availability of electro-optical sensors and advances in computer vision result in high-capable electro-optical systems. The marker-based systems propose very accurate positioning. Although marker-free systems are used in commercial products, they are still improving. Optical MoCap has the aforementioned superiority and flaws depending on the system requirements. Thus, the MoCap systems should be tuned according to the system requirements.

Inertial MoCap

Inertial MoCap uses IMUs (accelerometer, gyroscope, and magnetometer) to model the body kinematics and associated motion. While optic-based systems rely on the position of the joints in collected images, inertial MoCap relies on the rotational and acceleration information. This information is processed to detect and track the position, orientation, and rotation of a joint with respect to a reference frame of the subject. The overview of the inertial MoCap system diagram is shown in Figure 5.

Figure 5. Basic diagram for an inertial motion capture system

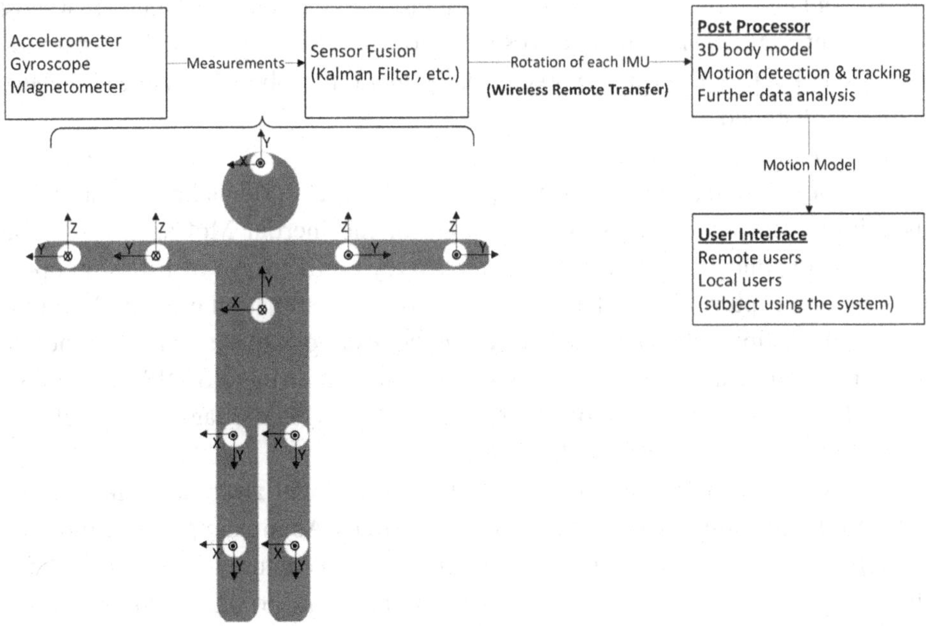

The inertial MoCap concept can be considered as a body sensor network. In detail, the subject puts on the wearable wireless IMUs on the joints appropriately. IMUs continuously measure the acceleration and rotation of the joints and sensor fusion algorithms are used to obtain the orientation of each limb and joint. In detail, the rotational rate is fused with acceleration and magnetometer for more accurate heading to obtain a resultant orientation of each body part. An example of sensor fusion algorithms that are used in IMU is Kalman-based Madgwick filters (Madgwick S., 2010). The fused data generated in a reference frame is also converted to a global frame so that a compact body model can be generated with respect to the same global frame. As the data generated by IMU is low, even a low-power wireless communication protocol like Bluetooth 4.0 (Decuir, 2010) can be used for data transmission. The transmitted data is processed to model a 3D motion model so that one can further process and analyze the data. Finally, the generated 3D body model and associated motion detection and tracking can be visualized via a user interface.

The recent advances, miniaturization, and availability of low-cost MEMS IMUs boost the use of wearables. Furthermore, the sensitive measurement capability of IMUs makes inertial MoCap suitable for numerous applications. A recent validation study of commercial IMU (APDM) by Taylor et al. (2017) shows that the accuracy within 0.6° with a precision of 0.1° for static and 4.4°/sec with a precision of 0.2°/sec for dynamic measurement are achievable. Additionally, Robert-Lachaine et al. (2017) compared a commercial IMU (XSENS) with an eight-camera Optotrak system (Northern Digital Inc.) under long-duration tasks. The researchers stated that most of the joint angle measurement errors are below 5° RMS during the long-duration tasks, specifically, the track worker's daily motion (Robert-Lachaine, Mecheri, Larue, & Plamondon, 2017).

Due to its cost-effective solution and other benefits (i.e., portability, size and weights of the units, and ease of use), inertial MoCap systems have been widely used in clinical applications. The accuracy of the inertial MoCap is sufficient for clinical applications. For instance, the survey on the usage of IMUs on upper limb motion capture shows that an average position estimation error of 35 mm is achievable (Filippeschi, et al., 2017). As another example, the validation of inertial MoCap for clinical movement analysis shows that the IMU (XSENS) used in the research has similarities with optical MoCap (VICON) in the sagittal, frontal, and transverse planes (Al-Amri, et al., 2018).

The inertial MoCap can also be used for situational awareness and activity detection by attaching the IMUs to the necessary limbs. As an example of partial body motion capture, Yan et al. (2017) used inertial motion capture for musculoskeletal disorder prevention by attaching IMUs to the head and trunk. In this study, the workers can be aware of their postural situation as illustrated in Figure 6 (Yan, Li, Li, & Zhang, 2017).

Figure 6. (a). Laboratory experiment-imitated rebar tying, (b). Laboratory experiment-imitated brick lifting
(*as reprinted in Yan, et al., 2017*).
From "Wearable IMU-based real-time motion warning system for construction workers' musculoskeletal disorders prevention", by Yan, et al., 2017, Automation in Construction, 74, 2-11. Copyright 2017 by Automation in Construction.

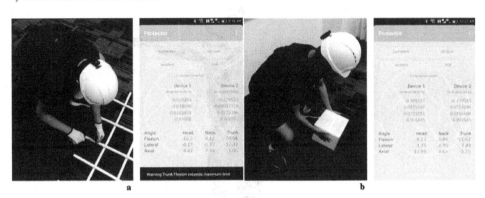

a   b

The subjects need to wear an IMU suit or wear IMUs on the limbs, torso, and head to cover all of the body movements. There are several studies of full-body MoCap with commercially available IMUs. For example, Roetenberg et al. used the full body sensor suit with 6-DOF IMU (XSENS) to collect data to model animating actors, skiers, basketball players, baseball players, volleyball players, skydivers, even a horse. The sensor suit used by Roetenberg et al. (2009) in the full-body human MoCap is illustrated in Figure 7. Some of the activities modeled with inertial MoCap are depicted in Figure 8.

The IMU modules can also be attached to the body segments separately. Each IMUs can be connected either wired or wireless; no matter how they are connected; the collected data can be transmitted wireless to a remote terminal. The advanced full-body suits with XSENS IMU, which provide flexibility and mobility to the user, are depicted in Figure 9. The validation results of the inertial MoCap for long duration (90 min) activities such as walking and running show that the error of the joint angles with less than 5° RMS is achievable (Schepers, Giuberti, & Bellusci, 2018).

The main drawbacks of inertial MoCap systems are namely drifts due to integration of accelerations and rotational velocities in the position estimation and magnetic distortion due to ferromagnetic in the environment. There are several reduction methods for the drift error and magnetic distortion in the literature such as magnetic distortion compensation (Madgwick, Harrison, & Vaidyanathan, 2011); applying a magnetic distortion model (Roetenberg, Baten, & Veltink, 2007) adding resting condition for magnetometer-based drift correction during body motion (Wittmann, Lambercy, & Gassert, 2019).

Figure 7. Xsens MVN Suit for the convenient placement of 17 IMU modules around the human body.
(as reprinted in Roetenberg, et al., 2009).
From "Xsens MVN: Full 6DOF human motion tracking using miniature inertial sensors", by Roetenberg, et al., 2009, Xsens Technologies BV, Tech. Rep. Copyright 2009 by Xsens Technologies BV.

Figure 8. (a) Skier with MVN Suit (b) Volleyball player with MVN Suit
(both of them as reprinted in Roetenberg, et al., 2009).
From "Xsens MVN: Full 6DOF human motion tracking using miniature inertial sensors", by Roetenberg, et al., 2009, Xsens Technologies BV, Tech. Rep. Copyright 2009 by Xsens Technologies BV.

(a)   (b)

Figure 9. Wireless MVN Awinda and Wired MVN Link
(as reprinted in Schepers, et al., 2018).
From "Xsens MVN: Consistent Tracking of Human ", by Schepers, et al., 2018, Xsens Technologies
BV, Tech. Rep. Copyright 2018 by Xsens Technologies BV.

Another drawback of the inertial MoCap systems is that there is no reference position in the system. There is a need for an external positioning system to obtain the global position of the subject. A global navigational satellite system (GNSS) system can be used outdoor. As GNSS cannot work indoors, various types of indoor localization systems (ILS) can be integrated into the system to obtain reference positioning. For example, BLE beacons (Zhuang, Yang, Li, Qi, & El-Sheimy, 2016) or ultra-wide-band (UWB) tags (Ridolfi, Van de Velde, Steendam, & De Poorter, 2018) can be used as ILS solutions.

Other Types of MoCap Systems

While most MoCap systems use inertial and optical solutions, other systems deploy various sensors and methods such as mechanical, magnetic, acoustic, etc. O'Brien et al. (1999) showed that the full-body motion capture and associated joint parameter estimation with wearable magnetic motion capture data. In recent studies, magnetic sensors are mostly used with inertial sensors as the sensors reduce in size and cost. The MoCap also utilizes ultrasonic sensors and microphones to measure acoustic signals to track motion (Wang & Gollakota, 2019). However, this kind of solution suffers from self-occlusion due to body parts hindering the measurements and the system is limited to the measurement range.

The mechanical MoCap systems use exoskeletons, which continuously measure the angles between the limbs and joints to determine the position and orientation of the body parts. In detail, this system mimics the motions of the body parts since they are directly attached to the body parts. Therefore, the motion on the exoskeleton can be converted to digital signals so that it can be further processed in computers to model the kinematics and visualize the motion. There are recent studies in this field used in virtual reality applications (Gu, et al., 2016) or task-specific motion modeling (Hansen, Gosselin, Mansour, Devos, & Marin, 2018).

Each solution has its own drawbacks and superiors and the recent studies focused on optical and inertial MoCap systems due to the sufficient performance results and ease of implementation. Furthermore, combinatorial usage of systems is also considered to mitigate the flaws of individual systems such as drifts in inertial MoCap and limb orientation errors in optical MoCap. In the inertial-optical hybrid solution, while IMUs are used to obtain accurate limb orientation, video data is used to obtain drift-free position data (Pons-Moll, Baak, Müller, Seidel, & Rosenhahn, 2010). However, the cost and complexity of these systems increase as the number of components and complexity of the technology increase.

Comparison of MoCap Systems

The advantages and disadvantages of the aforementioned MoCap systems are listed in Table 1.

CASE STUDY: BODY MOTION ANALYSIS SYSTEM (HAVELSAN)

This section involves a case study of proof-of-concept (POC) development of an inertial MoCap called "*Body Motion Analysis System – BMAS*" (HAVELSAN). The aiming objectives of the POC are clinical and situational awareness applications. The MoCap is designed as inertial instead of optical as inertial MoCap provides scalability and flexibility for complex indoor and outdoor actions as well as clinical measurements (Solberg & Jensenius, 2016; Bergmann, Mayagoitia, & Smith, 2009). In addition, there is a survey (Cornacchia, Ozcan, Zheng, & Velipasalar, 2016) showing that wearables are rigorously used for full-body motion capture and global activity detection, which is the core of situational awareness systems.

This section involves the system architecture of BMAS, associated data collection methods, system calibration methods, and data processing with neural network-based activity detection methods. The section also involves the performance and test results of the system.

Table 1. Comparison of MoCap systems

	Optical		Inertial	Others		
	Marker-based	Marker-free		Magnetic	Ultrasonic	Mechanic
Position Accuracy	High (<1 mm)	Medium (High noise)	Medium (No reference position)			
Precision Accuracy	Low (Only position)		High (<1 mm)	Medium	Medium	Medium
Range Limit	Low		High	Low	Low	High
Data Bandwidth	High		Low	Low	Low	Low
Real-time	Low		Medium	Medium	Medium	Medium
Outdoor Usage	Low		High	Low	Low	High
Ease of setup (calibration)	Medium		High	High	High	Medium
Flexibility of movement	High		High	High	High	Low (restricted motion)
Noise sources	Occlusion Light		Drift & Magnetic disturbance	Magnetic disturbance	Ambient noise	Intrinsic noises

BMAS System Architecture

BMAS contains a set of wearable sensors consisting of ten edge units, one wearable gateway, one server, and multiple client terminals. Edge units continuously collect angular orientation data of the limb to which they are attached. The data is continuously transmitted from the gateway to the server on the cloud or a local network. The gathered data is processed by biostatistics, bioanalysis, anomaly detection, and data analysis algorithms. The results of data analytics are transmitted through a server to remote or local clients. BMAS conceptual system block diagram is shown in Figure 10.

BMAS Edge Units

3 degrees of freedom (DOF) gyroscope and 3-DOF accelerometer are used as BMAS edge units to measure the orientation of the joint and limbs. The gyroscope is used to measure angular rotation while the accelerometer is used to detect the gravity so that the rotations can be measured on a local coordinate frame. However, this angular

measurement drifts and the precision fails after some time. A 3-DOF magnetometer is additionally used to resolve this drift. The magnetometer measures the magnetic field of the earth to detect the north and fix the drift in the frame.

Figure 10. BMAS conceptual system architecture design

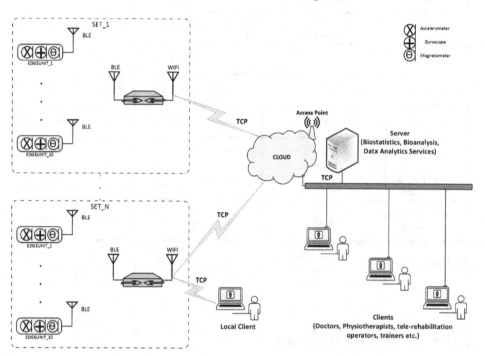

When the axis of gravity is set to "down" and the axis measured north by magnetometer is set to "north", the whole coordinate system is set on a non-drifting local frame on earth. Thus, any measurement on this frame can be converted directly to a motion on earth. For example, if the subject wearing this system turns left with a definite angle, then this movement can be mapped to the same angle but transformed to the earth coordinate system. However, this system needs to be calibrated to work properly and it is explained in detail in the calibration section.

BMAS edge units are placed at 10 limbs of the body such as head (1 module), trunk (1 module), arms (left and right, 4 modules), and legs (left and right, 4 modules) which is illustrated in Figure 5. The maximum frequency of human body motion is about 10 Hz (Zeng & Zhao, 2011). Therefore, the sampling rate should be at least 20Hz due to Nyquist sampling rate. The ideal sampling frequency for maximizing accuracy without losing data is determined as 25-50 Hz as a result of empirical laboratory tests. The position and orientation information gathered from the edge units are filtered and converted to the quaternion format by the Madgwick filter (Madgwick S., 2010) and transmitted to the gateway. The mobility of the subject is provided by wireless communicated edge units, which are also powered by a battery. For low energy consumption, Bluetooth 4.0 (BLE) is used as a wireless communication protocol (Decuir, 2010).

Figure 11. Sensor placement on the body model

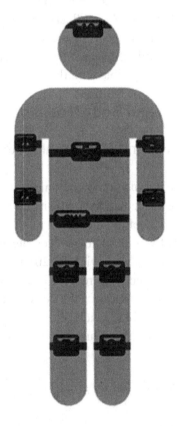

Gateway

In each BMAS edge unit set, there is also one corresponding gateway. The gateway can be mounted to a stationary place or used as a wearable unit to provide mobility in a larger area if needed. BMAS gateway merges quaternion data obtained from the edge units via BLE. Then, it attaches a timestamp and transmits data to the local or remote terminal via TCP for further data processing.

Local User Terminal/ Cloud Integration

BMAS is able to work as a standalone system such that the gateway directly communicates with a local client terminal via TCP. Body motions are modeled in 3D modeling programs running on the terminal, biostatistics, and bioanalysis operations are applied on the same terminal. This type of terminal is needed in applications of sports and rehabilitation where subjects need to capture and observe their own movements.

Cloud integration is essential when data transmission is needed for remote users or to access data from everywhere. The data collected from multiple users are processed on the cloud to represent the movements of the subject on a body model. Remote user (i.e., medical doctor, rehabilitation operator, a trainer, an operation leader, etc.) can access to user interface compatible with the client's needs.

BMAS Data Collection and Body Modelling Software

Edge Unit Sensor Fusion and Filtering Algorithm

The accelerometer uses gravity, and the magnetometer uses the magnetic field of the earth to generate a reference and reduce axis shifting in the gyroscope measurements in the BMAS edge system. Therefore, the fusion of gyroscope, accelerometer, and magnetometer is significantly important for accurate measurement. In fact, the Kalman-based Madgwick filter (Madgwick S., 2010) is applied for this purpose. The measurement data is filtered with respect to the previous measurements to obtain higher accuracy and smoothness of the body motions. The quaternion data (Kuipers, 1999) obtained by the Madgwick filter and the corresponding data flow from the sensors to the BLE radio are illustrated in Figure 12.

Figure 12. BMAS edge unit data flow diagram

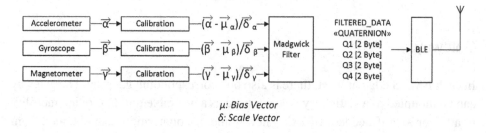

198

The actual measurement of each sensor is calibrated to obtain a corresponding bias for the shift in the measurements and a scale factor for normalization so that the measurements are converted to a zero-mean normalized distribution. The calibration procedure and the corresponding steps are explained in detail with a flow diagram in the system calibration section.

The calibrated form of the actual data of the accelerometer ($\vec{\alpha}$), gyroscope ($\vec{\beta}$), and magnetometer ($\vec{\gamma}$) is input to the Madgwick filter. The Madgwick filter is used to process inertial measurements to estimate actual data. In detail, the filter collects the calibrated sensor measurements and obtains orientation increment due to accelerometer, gyroscope, and magnetometer in a period. Then, all of the incremental measurements are fused to obtain an estimated measurement. This procedure repeats every time instant.

Data Merging on Gateway

The quaternion data gathered from each edge unit has a size of 8 Bytes. The data sampled around 25-50Hz is merged and attached with a timestamp in the gateway. The data format of the edge unit and gateway is depicted in Figure 13.

Figure 13. BMAS (for a single set of 10 IMUs) gateway data output.

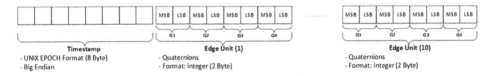

Data size (1) and bandwidth (2) obtained from merging edge unit data with a 25Hz sampling rate for a complete set consisting of 10 units are presented, respectively.

Data size = quaternion size * # of edge unit + timestamp size = 8Bytes * 10 + 8Bytes = 88Bytes (1)

Bandwidth = data size * transmission frequency = 8 * 88bit * 25Hz = 17.6Kbps (2)

Body Motion Modelling and Quaternion Filtering Algorithm

The coordinate system of each limb is determined by considering the right-hand rule in the body model in which a limb can move according to the connected limb. The position of edge units and the axis of the limbs of the body model used in BMAS is represented in Figure 14.

Figure 14. (a) Local coordinates of IMUs on the body and (b) local coordinates of body model

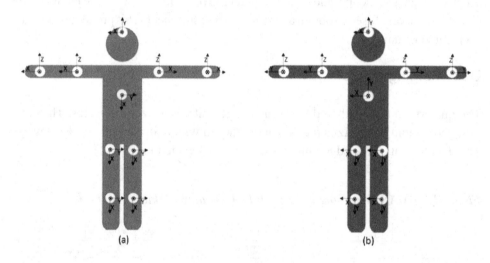

Quaternion data processed in the gateway is transmitted to modeling software working on the client. Moving Average Filter (3) of a period of 500ms is applied to data to reduce noise and prevent glitches in the 3D model. The duration of the average filter is selected so that the movements are smoothed and the high-frequency noise on the measurements is filtered out.

$$y[n] = \frac{1}{N}\sum_{i=0}^{N-1} x[n-i], \ N = 0.5\,sec \times f_{measurement}, \ N \in Z \tag{3}$$

The orientation of each limb is measured with IMU units; however, that orientation cannot be directly used in calculations without correcting with respect to the body bone model and the position of the IMU unit on the body. There is a need for a mathematical model and related quaternion relations to make measurements reliable. The orientation of the limb is calculated as (4).

$$q_B = q_R q_A q_R^* = \left(q_0 + q_1 i + q_2 j + q_3 k\right)\left(xi + yj + zk\right)\left(q_0 - q_1 i - q_2 j - q_3 k\right)$$

$$(4)$$

The term q_A represents actual quaternion of limbs and the term q_B represents corrected quaternion of limbs with respect to rotation. The term q_R represents the rotation quaternion, which is calculated differently for each modeling environment. In detail, it is the rotation vector depending on the rotation from the initial position of the IMU unit to the position of that unit on the body, and the rotation from the body to the position of the defined bone model as shown in (5). In other words, this vector is required to exactly matching the initial position and orientation of the IMU units at rest with the initial position and orientation of the bone model on which the subject's movement is simulated. When the rotation quaternion is obtained, then it is used to convert actual measurements to the corrected quaternions according to the body bone model.

$$q_R = Q_{InitialBox}^{BoxOnBody} * \left(Q_{Bones}^{BoxOnBody}\right)^{-1}$$

$$(5)$$

As an example, head and chest q_R quaternion calculations which are the same due to position and orientation on the body, are further analyzed and defined in (6). The modules for chest and head are notated with 5 and 10, respectively as illustrated in Figure 11.

$$Q_{InitialBox(Chest\&Head)}^{BoxOnBody(Chest\&Head)} = \begin{bmatrix} 1 & 1 & 0 & 0 \end{bmatrix}$$
$$Q_{(Chest\&Head)Bones}^{BoxOnBody(Chest\&Head)} = \begin{bmatrix} 0 & -1 & 1 & 0 \end{bmatrix}$$

$$(6)$$

It is assumed that modules are in (0, 0, 0) state, while the x-axis of the modules are directed to the North and the z-axis of the modules are directed to the up. These directions are due to the sensor placement in the modules. North-East-Down (NED) and module coordinate systems are shown in Figure 15 (a).

When the modules (5: chest and 10: head) are attached to the body as illustrated in Figure 11, the coordinate system of the edge unit is converted to a new coordinate frame as depicted in Figure 15 (b). Finally, the coordinate systems are adapted according to the used 3-D model under the assumption that the model is in T-pose as shown in Figure 14. The new state of the coordinate system is shown below in Figure 15 (c). The term q_R (5) is calculated according to all the conversions from state (a) to state (c).

Figure 15. Coordinate systems concerning observer (a) The coordinate system of the edge unit (left) and global NED coordinate systems on (0,0,0) state (right) (b) The coordinate system for the edge unit (head and chest) placed on the body (c) The coordinated system of the 3-D model (head and chest).

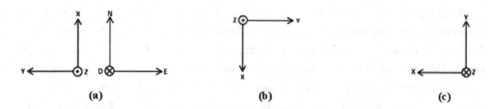

(a)   (b)   (c)

This conversion is applied to the rest of the IMUs on the body parts (legs and arms). According to the local frames of sensors on the body and local frames of the body model illustrated in Figure 14, q_R calculations for legs and arms are calculated as (7).

$$
\begin{aligned}
Q^{BoxOnBody(Legs)}_{InitialBox(Legs)} &= \begin{bmatrix} 1 & 1 & 0 & 0 \end{bmatrix} \\
Q^{BoxOnBody(Legs)}_{(Legs)Bones} &= \begin{bmatrix} 1 & 0 & 0 & -1 \end{bmatrix} \\
Q^{BoxOnBody(Right\ Arms)}_{InitialBox(Right\ Arms)} &= \begin{bmatrix} 1 & 0 & 0 & 1 \end{bmatrix} \\
Q^{BoxOnBody(Right\ Arms)}_{(Right\ Arms)Bones} &= \begin{bmatrix} 1 & 0 & 0 & -1 \end{bmatrix} \\
Q^{BoxOnBody(Left\ Arms)}_{InitialBox(LeftArms)} &= \begin{bmatrix} 1 & 0 & 0 & -1 \end{bmatrix} \\
Q^{BoxOnBody(LeftArms)}_{(LeftArms)Bones} &= \begin{bmatrix} 1 & 0 & 0 & -1 \end{bmatrix}
\end{aligned}
\qquad (7)
$$

The quaternion calculation for upper and lower arm is explained to understand the mathematical model of the BMAS. The upper and lower arm diagram with related coordinate frames is depicted in Figure 16.

The corresponding forward kinematic equations and position estimation of this example are shown in equations (8)-(9). The elbow is defined as a hinge joint because of its one-directional movement capability; therefore, in the figure and calculations, the rotation of the elbow is stated as 2-axis (1 plane). Similarly, the movement of the shoulder is stated as 3-axis (Al-Faiz, Ali, & Miry, 2011).

$$T_5^0 = A_1 \ldots A_5 = \begin{bmatrix} r_{11} & r_{12} & r_{13} & d_x \\ r_{21} & r_{22} & r_{23} & d_y \\ r_{31} & r_{32} & r_{33} & d_z \\ 0 & 0 & 0 & 1 \end{bmatrix} \tag{8}$$

$$c_n = \cos\theta_n \text{ and } s_n = \sin\theta_n \tag{9}$$

Figure 16. Rotation kinematics for arm (example)

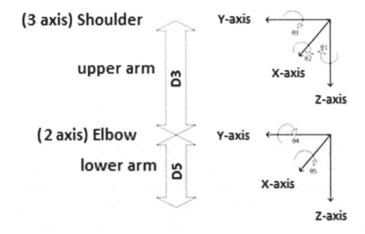

BMAS Calibration Method

There are two types of calibration in BMAS. One of them corresponds to the calibration of the IMU sensors used as the core of the inertial MoCap. The other one is the full-body model calibration. While the former is used to calibrate the intrinsic parameters of the system, the latter is used to calibrate the model fit with the actual motion.

Edge Unit Calibration

The mathematical model for calibration of accelerometer and gyroscope depending on the error characteristics are shown in equation (10) and (11), respectively. The term $\vec{\mu}$ represents bias and $\vec{\delta}$ represents the scaling vectors. Actual and calibrated data of the accelerometer $\left(\vec{\alpha}_{K'}, \vec{\alpha}_K\right)$ and the gyroscope $\left(\vec{\beta}_{K'}, \vec{\beta}_K\right)$ and are represented accordingly.

$$\begin{bmatrix} \vec{\alpha}_X \\ \vec{\alpha}_Y \\ \vec{\alpha}_Z \end{bmatrix} = \begin{bmatrix} \dfrac{\vec{\alpha}_{X'} - \vec{\mu}_X}{\vec{\delta}_X} \\ \dfrac{\vec{\alpha}_{Y'} - \vec{\mu}_Y}{\vec{\delta}_Y} \\ \dfrac{\vec{\alpha}_{Z'} - \vec{\mu}_Z}{\vec{\delta}_Z} \end{bmatrix} \qquad (10)$$

$$\begin{bmatrix} \vec{\beta}_X \\ \vec{\beta}_Y \\ \vec{\beta}_Z \end{bmatrix} = \begin{bmatrix} \dfrac{\vec{\beta}_{X'} - \vec{\mu}_X}{\vec{\delta}_X} \\ \dfrac{\vec{\beta}_{Y'} - \vec{\mu}_Y}{\vec{\delta}_Y} \\ \dfrac{\vec{\beta}_{Z'} - \vec{\mu}_Z}{\vec{\delta}_Z} \end{bmatrix} \qquad (11)$$

The 6-DOF gyroscope and accelerometer bias and scale values are measured in the laboratory (TUBITAK-SAGE) as shown in Figure 17. In detail, a rotation table with two-axis and adjustable constant acceleration and angular velocity is used in tests. The edge units are rotated in all axes with 10-100-200 °/sec angular velocity to obtain the calibration parameters in dynamic tests. Furthermore, the intrinsic parameters for the accelerometer calibration values are calculated by applying ±1g in every axis of edge units.

Figure 17. Dynamic test setup (TUBITAK-SAGE)

The calibration of the magnetic sensor is applied by rotating the magnetic sensor in each axis to measure the required parameters for the calibration equations (12)-(16)

$$\vec{\gamma}_{K'\_min} = \min\left(\vec{\gamma}_{K'\_min}, \vec{\gamma}_{K'}\right) \tag{12}$$

$$\vec{\gamma}_{K'\_max} = \max\left(\vec{\gamma}_{K'\_max}, \vec{\gamma}_{K'}\right) \tag{13}$$

$$\vec{S} = \frac{\vec{\gamma}_{max} - \vec{\gamma}_{min}}{2} \tag{14}$$

$$\vec{\beta} = \frac{\vec{\gamma}_{max} + \vec{\gamma}_{min}}{2} \tag{15}$$

$$\begin{bmatrix} \vec{m}_X \\ \vec{m}_Y \\ \vec{m}_Z \end{bmatrix} = \begin{bmatrix} \dfrac{\vec{m}_{X'} - \vec{\beta}_X}{\vec{S}_X} \\ \dfrac{\vec{m}_{Y'} - \vec{\beta}_Y}{\vec{S}_Y} \\ \dfrac{\vec{m}_{Z'} - \vec{\beta}_Z}{\vec{S}_Z} \end{bmatrix} \tag{16}$$

The magnetic field of an ideal magnetometer can be modeled in a spherical form centered at the origin; however, the magnetic field model of a non-calibrated magnetometer would resemble an elliptic form, which has a center shifted from the origin. The magnetometer can be calibrated by rotating it on every axis and an elliptic formed realistic magnetometer model can be converted to spherical form; this process is shown in Figure 18.

Model Calibration

The model calibration is important in that it avoids modeling distortions caused by BMAS edge units' placement in different directions and orientations. The calibration procedure is conducted with respect to a reference posture (N-pose: arms in two sides, standing up, upright posture).

Figure 18. Calibrated and non-calibrated magnetometer data. Black dots represent calibrated data while red, green, and blue dots represent the non-calibrated data for a view of (a) X-Y, (b) Y-Z, and (c) X-Z.

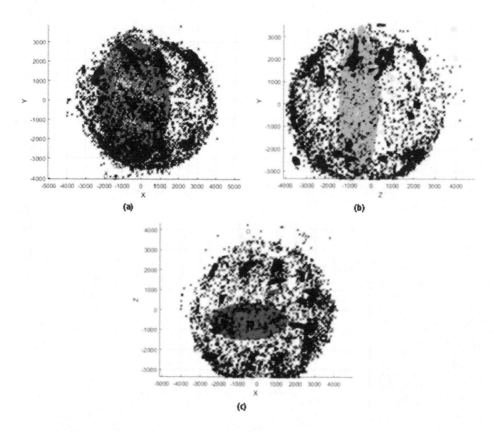

Calculation of transformation from distorted posture rotation matrix $\left(Q_{init}^{3x3}\right)$ to reference posture $\left(S_R^{3x3}\right)$, results with calibration matrix (C^{3x3}) (17). Actual rotation data (Q^{3x3}) collected from edge units are transformed to calibrated rotation data (Q_e^{3x3}) by using C^{3x3} (18).

$$C^{3x3} = (Q_{init}^{3x3})^{-1} * S_R^{3x3} \tag{17}$$

$$Q_e^{3x3} = (Q^{3x3}) * C^{3x3} \tag{18}$$

BMAS Data Processing Method

When the motion data is captured and the body model is obtained, further processes can be achieved according to the specific requirements. BMAS prototype involves situational awareness and clinical applications as use-cases. In terms of clinical applications, angular measurements are the basic needs. In addition, activity detection is significantly important for both situational awareness and clinical applications. In this concept, BMAS applies a neural network-based activity detection method called BMAS-Net to detect predefined activities such as sitting, standing, T-pose, walking, running, etc.

BMAS-Net utilizes BMAS as a data supplier for the deep neural network application and it captures motion data by BMAS. BMAS-Net can be used as an assistive diagnostic tool, for diseases restricting a patient's motion capability like Parkinson's disease or illnesses depending on body posture anomalies like multiple sclerosis. The use of BMAS-Net as a diagnostic examination method requires a serious amount of patient movement data from all phases of that disease, to make a comparison between sick and healthy people's movements.

There are two neural network modules for BMAS-Net, the first one is used to train collected data and add new motions to the feature list, its output is a model for body motion; the second one is used to classify online motion data. BMAS-Net system architecture diagram can be seen in Figure 19. BMAS-Net deployed windowed-convolutional neural network (WCNN) and long short-term memory (LSTM) based neural network to detect activities.

Windowed Convolutional Neural Network (WCNN)

A convolutional neural network is constructed for the implementation of the BMAS-Net algorithm, which extracts and models features from a spatial input space. In this application, CNN is used for interpreting the movement features inside a time-varying image-like IMU data. Panwar et al., (2019) proposed a CNN topology called Rehab-Net in which IMUs are used for temporal input features. BMAS-Net also uses CNN topology for activity detection. In detail, the method of WCNN in BMAS-Net uses all the quaternion values (9 quaternion difference values, between the torso IMU and others, 36 features per temporal slice). Furthermore, BMAS-Net considers spatial dimensionality rather than the temporal dimensionality of the input data. The input data is windowed with 50% overlapping to cope with temporal changes within time-dependent data.

Figure 19. BMAS-Net system architecture diagram

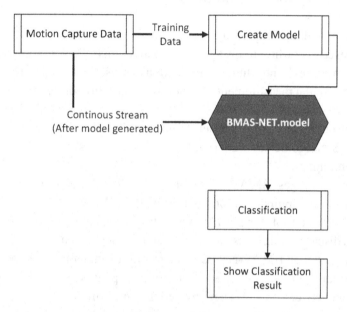

The input data for the neural network is indicated in Figure 20. The frame size can be adapted but it is ideally chosen as 50. The data sampling period is 2ms; therefore, 100ms duration data is fed to the neural network for classification. Each frame consists of nine quaternion data, which represent the angle difference between the sensor attached to the torso and other sensors attached to the rest of the body.

Figure 20. BMAS-Net input data shape (Size: 50 x 36)

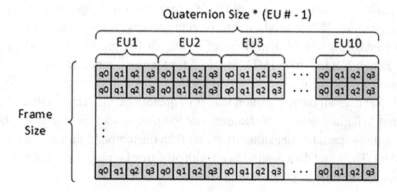

Four random samples are plotted in Figure 21 to visualize the corresponding motion data. The yellow shades indicate quaternion values closer to 1 and darker blue shades indicate values that are closer to -1. The first three samples (horizontal parallel lines) indicate stationary motion types. The last sample indicates the dynamic motion of "Walking". Even though horizontal lines dominate in the walking sample, quaternion values vary for each frame so there are also vertical patterns available for dynamic motion type.

Figure 21. Quaternion data samples indicated with respect to the frame

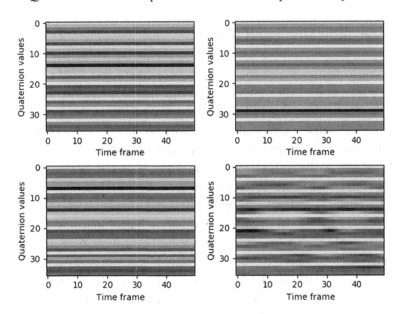

The aforementioned frames of size 50 are used as channels in Keras since one-dimensional convolution and max-pooling are performed. One-dimensional operations are used since the relations between the different quaternion values also matter in this application. Furthermore, the two dimensions of the input data should be separately checked since they should be independent of each other. The number of filters in each convolutional layer is selected as 40, an indication of the data having around 40 features to be extracted. The kernel size of convolutional layers was selected as 4 for seeking possible relations inside one quaternion and multiple quaternions. The pooling size was selected as 2 for seeking dominant features of quaternion data. The 2-layer topology of the network is used for reducing the high dimensionality of the input data to dominant features. The WCNN BMAS-Net topology is represented in Figure 22.

Figure 22. BMAS-Net WCNN topology.

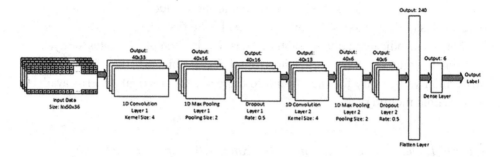

Long Short-Term Memory (LSTM)

BMAS-Net also deploys a recursive neural network that is an LSTM model based on data properties and the PEEK architecture (Drummond, Marques, Vasconcelos, & Clua, 2018). The architecture PEEK is a proposed LSTM model for implementing a body motion classifier, which takes data from two IMUs placed on both arms of the user (Drummond, Marques, Vasconcelos, & Clua, 2018). BMAS-Net relies on IMUs placed around the body (10 IMUs), and it only takes the quaternion variables as input. In fact, it takes the difference between the quaternion value of the torso and all other quaternions from remaining IMUs (for robustness to body direction of the user), causing this model to get 9 quaternions as input (36 features per window). Furthermore, BMAS- Net has more employability for more body motion classes (even though 6 movements are to be tested) since it relies on data from IMUs placed all over the body. As this model has a chance of expanding the motion classes, a more complex LSTM model than PEEK is proposed since this model has more input features and seemingly less distinguishable motion classes (i.e., crouching and kneeling). BMAS-Net LSTM Topology is illustrated in Figure 23.

Figure 23. BMAS-Net LSTM topology

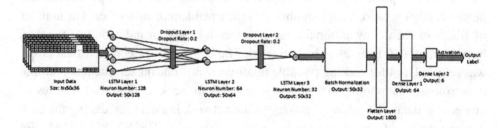

Performance of WCNN and LSTM in BMAS-Net

The benchmark between WCNN and LSTM is conducted to extract the performances of both algorithms. The activities like crouching, kneeling, sitting, standing, T-pose, and walking are used as sample activities to be detected and classified by the proposed methods. In detail, crouching and kneeling are similar activities. Furthermore, standing and walking are confusable if the activities are not considered temporally. The performance results of LSTM and WCNN algorithms are illustrated in Figure 24 and Figure 25, respectively. This test is performed offline on collected data after training the corresponding models with a separate set. There is confusion between standing and walking WCNN. The performance of LSTM is better in offline processing.

Figure 24. LSTM confusion matrix for last epoch

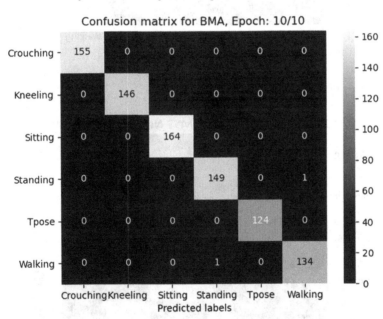

The performance of the activity classification during only motion capture is depicted in Figure 26 and Figure 27, respectively. Probability matrices constructed by using the same online data sets indicate that the WCNN algorithm is more successful in classifying both static and dynamic postures. Thus, the WCNN algorithm is chosen as the BMAS-Net algorithm.

Figure 25. WCNN confusion matrix for last epoch

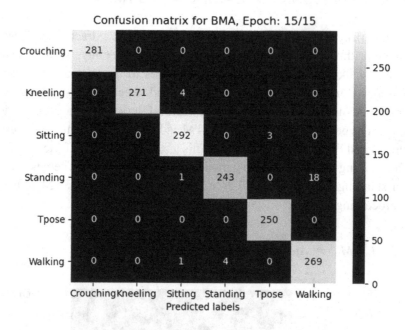

Figure 26. LSTM confusion matrix for last epoch

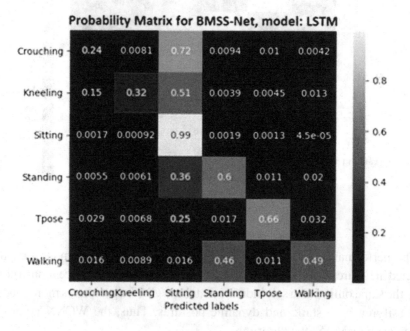

Figure 27. WCNN confusion matrix for last epoch

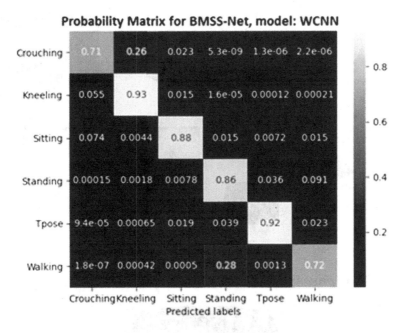

BMAS Data Processing Method

BMAS edge units contain, miniaturized module (TINYTILE) which contains 6 DOF IMU and BLE communication interfaces, a magnetometer (LIS3MDL), and a lithium-polymer (Li-Po) battery for power. The gateway (Raspberry-Pi-Zero-W) is used to collect IMU data via BLE and transmit it to the remote server. The user interface (BLENDER) is used as a 3D modeling program to show quaternion data collected from the subject on a body model. User interfaces can also be accessed from both 3D modeling programs and AR interfaces (glasses, tablets). Application fields for BMAS are determined as a digital twin in health and sports and situational awareness as activity detection. The prototype of BMAS is illustrated in Figure 28. The single wireless IMU module is also illustrated in Figure 29 and the specifications are listed in Table 2.

Figure 28. BMAS prototype system

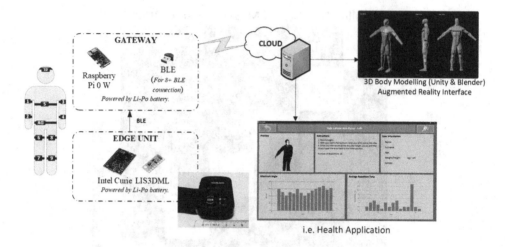

Figure 29. BMAS prototype system

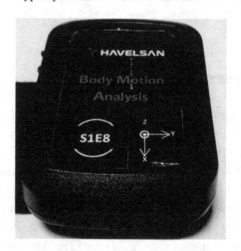

Table 2. BMAS performance values.

Angular Measurement Accuracy (Roll/Pitch)	< 0.5 ° RMS (static) < 1 ° RMS (dynamic)
Angular Measurement Accuracy (Heading)	< 0.5 ° RMS (static) < 1 ° RMS (dynamic)
Latency	< 40ms
Battery Consumption	12 hr. (continuous use)
Dimensions	65 x 50 x 20 mm
Weight	40 gr

Applications

Healthcare Applications

BMAS can be used in clinical applications as an assistive diagnosis tool. BMAS can be used as a full-body MoCap as well as a partial MoCap to monitor specific parts of the body. For instance, a person with a motion capability loss of an upper limb can only wear the BMAS modules on arm. Full body MoCap is required mostly to detect diseases like Hemiplegia disease, Parkinson's disease, seizures in case of epilepsy, and postural anomalies. Furthermore, BMAS can also be integrated with other wearable sensors (i.e., heartbeat monitoring sensor) to enhance clinical analysis.

As BMAS can connect to a cloud or a network, it provides remote monitoring capability. Therefore, it can be used for telerehabilitation by physicians. For example, the patient can perform the rehabilitation exercises at home while BMAS record the body motions. During the exercises, the patient can monitor the exercises via the local user interface. BMAS has also the capability of alerting the patient whether the exercises are done correctly. In a defined period, the physician can check the results from the remote interface to assess the progress of the body's motion capabilities. An example set of exercises for telerehabilitation is illustrated in Figure 30.

Figure 30. BMAS – Remote monitoring of rehabilitation exercises.

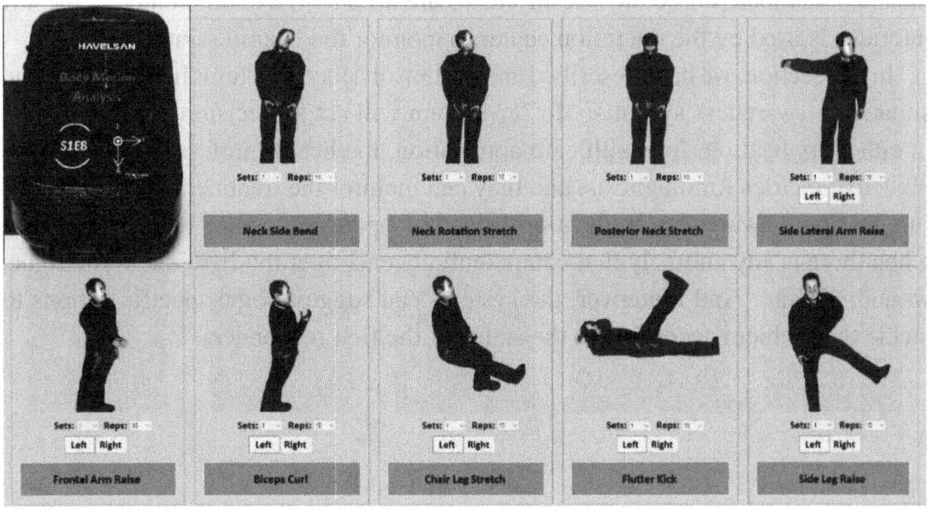

Situational Awareness Applications

BMAS can be used for situational awareness applications as it has the capability of full-body motion monitoring as well as activity detection. It can be used in first-responder operations to provide situational awareness to the members during the save and rescue. It is significantly important to monitor and know the status of the members in such circumstances. BMAS can provide fatigue analysis, postural information about the first responders lying, sitting, running, walking, holding a hose, abnormal body postures (alerts), etc.

In the scope of situational awareness, BMAS is integrated with indoor/outdoor localization systems and wearables such as smart health monitoring modules, cameras, augmented reality (AR) devices, and virtual reality (VR) devices as illustrated in Figure 31. This system provides continuous monitoring and tracking of the activity, health, and location of each team member. Wearable cameras are also used for scene sharing between team members.

Each member wears AR glasses so that they can see the status of the other members while they can see the operation scene at the same time. In other words, each team member will be aware of what the other members are doing so that they can plan the safe and rescue operation efficiently. Furthermore, they will be able to respond to urgent cases. For example, the team member will be able to see a member lying on the floor or a stuck member under a load with the locations via AR glasses. Hence, the team will be able to respond to this urgent case to rescue the team member. While the AR interfaces are used by the team members, the VR interface is used by the operation center to monitor the overall scene.

In this section, we have described application of Mocap systems in healthcare and situational awareness systems. MoCap system will act as decision support system in either application. In health care application, the health professionals can have objective metrics for diagnosis, and they can monitor the treatment even remotely. In situational awareness applications, head of operation center will be informed when there is any anomaly that can potentially endanger the lives such as fatigue, wound, or faint. And moreover, the systems can suggest some specific actions to tackle the problem according to the status of the first responders.

Figure 31. BMAS – Situational awareness application

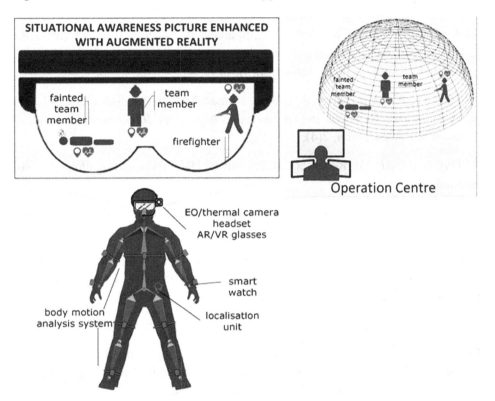

CONCLUSION

Today, transferring real-world motion data to the digital world is crucial for biometrics, visualization, and remote monitoring. All these functionalities are part of a decision support system in different applications. The MoCap systems can be used for medical analysis such as to make early diagnosis and treatment planning as well as a part of the decision support system in situational awareness. In this chapter, we focused on MoCap methodologies, namely optical-based and inertial-based. This chapter involves a benchmark analysis and describes the pros and cons of each method. The alternative methods are also studied to compare with these basic methodologies. These methodologies have some solid use-cases in different applications. It is expected that applications of inertial MoCap emerge in the future with reductions in cost and size of low power inertial sensors. Furthermore, there will be a rising trend for wearable MoCap systems embedded into clothes with energy harvesting methods. This chapter also presents a thorough case study in terms of inertial MoCap developed by Havelsan with two concrete applications.

217

REFERENCES

Al-Amri, M., Nicholas, K., Button, K., Sparkes, V., Sheeran, L., & Davies, J. L. (2018). Inertial measurement units for clinical movement analysis: Reliability and concurrent validity. *Sensors (Basel), 18*(3), 719.

Al-Faiz, M., Ali, A., & Miry, A. (2011). Human Arm Inverse Kinematic Solution Based Geometric Relations and Optimization Algorithm. *International Journal of Robotics and Automation, 2*(4), 245–255.

APDM. (n.d.). *APDM*. Retrieved 2021, from APDM Products: https://apdm.com/wearable-sensors/

Aristidou, A., & Lasenby, J. (2013). Real-time marker prediction and CoR estimation in optical motion capture. *The Visual Computer, 29*(1), 7–26.

Bergmann, J. H., Mayagoitia, R. E., & Smith, I. C. (2009). A portable system for collecting anatomical joint angles during stair ascent: A comparison with an optical tracking device. *Dynamic Medicine, 8*(1), 3.

BLENDER. (n.d.). *Blender*. Retrieved 2021, from https://www.blender.org/

Ceseracciu, E., Sawacha, Z., & Cobelli, C. (2014). Comparison of markerless and marker-based motion capture technologies through simultaneous data collection during gait: Proof of concept. *PLoS One, 9*(3), e87640.

Cornacchia, M., Ozcan, K., Zheng, Y., & Velipasalar, S. (2016). A survey on activity detection and classification using wearable sensors. *IEEE Sensors Journal, 17*(2), 386–403.

Dariush, B. (2003). Human motion analysis for biomechanics and biomedicine. *Machine Vision and Applications, 14*(4), 202–205. doi:10.100700138-002-0108-8

Das, S., Trutoiu, L., Murai, A., Alcindor, D., Oh, M., De la Torre, F., & Hodgins, J. (2011, August). Quantitative measurement of motor symptoms in Parkinson's disease: A study with full-body motion capture data. *2011 Annual International Conference of the IEEE Engineering in Medicine and Biology Society*, 6789-6792. 10.1109/IEMBS.2011.6091674

Davison, A. J., Deutscher, J., & Reid, I. D. (2001). Markerless motion capture of complex full-body movement for character animation. Computer Animation and Simulation 2001, 3-14.

Decuir, J. (2010). Bluetooth 4.0: low energy. Cambridge, UK: Cambridge Silicon Radio SR plc.

Delrobaei, M., Memar, S., Pieterman, M., Stratton, T. W., McIsaac, K., & Jog, M. (2018). Towards remote monitoring of Parkinson's disease tremor using wearable motion capture systems. *Journal of the Neurological Sciences, 384*, 38–45. doi:10.1016/j.jns.2017.11.004 PMID:29249375

Drummond, R. R., Marques, B. A., Vasconcelos, C. N., & Clua, E. (2018). International Conference on Computer Graphics Theory and Applications. *PEEK: An LSTM Recurrent Network for Motion Classiðcation from Sparse Data*, 215-222.

Endsley, M. R., & Jones, D. G. (2016). *Designing for situation awareness: An approach to user-centered design*. CRC Press.

Field, M., Stirling, D., Naghdy, F., & Pan, Z. (2009, December). Motion capture in robotics review. *2009 IEEE International Conference on Control and Automation*, 1697-1702.

Filippeschi, A., Schmitz, N., Miezal, M., Bleser, G., Ruffaldi, E., & Stricker, D. (2017). Survey of motion tracking methods based on inertial sensors: A focus on upper limb human motion. *Sensors (Basel), 17*(6), 1257.

Gu, X., Zhang, Y., Sun, W., Bian, Y., Zhou, D., & Kristensson, P. O. (2016, May). Dexmo: An inexpensive and lightweight mechanical exoskeleton for motion capture and force feedback in VR. *Proceedings of the 2016 CHI Conference on Human Factors in Computing Systems*, 1991-1995.

Guerra-Filho, G. (2005). Optical Motion Capture: Theory and Implementation. *Research Initiative, Treatment Action, 12*(2), 61–90.

Hansen, C., Gosselin, F., Mansour, K. B., Devos, P., & Marin, F. (2018). Design-validation of a hand exoskeleton using musculoskeletal modeling. *Applied Ergonomics, 68*, 283–288.

HAVELSAN. (n.d.). *HAVELSAN*. Retrieved 2021, from HAVELSAN Products: https://www.havelsan.com.tr/en

Hernandez, G., Valles, D., Wierschem, D. C., Koldenhoven, R. M., Koutitas, G., Mendez, F. A., . . . Jimenez, J. (2020, January). Machine Learning Techniques for Motion Analysis of Fatigue from Manual Material Handling Operations Using 3D Motion Capture Data. *2020 10th Annual Computing and Communication Workshop and Conference*, 300-305.

Kitagawa, M., & Windsor, B. (2020). *MoCap for artists: workflow and techniques for motion capture*. CRC Press.

Knippenberg, E., Verbrugghe, J., Lamers, I., Palmaers, S., Timmermans, A., & Spooren, A. (2017). Markerless motion capture systems as training device in neurological rehabilitation: A systematic review of their use, application, target population and efficacy. *Journal of Neuroengineering and Rehabilitation, 14*(1), 1–11. doi:10.118612984-017-0270-x PMID:28646914

Kuipers, J. B. (1999). *Quaternions and rotation sequences* (Vol. 66). Princeton university press.

Latorre, J., Colomer, C., Alcañiz, M., & Llorens, R. (2019). Gait analysis with the Kinect v2: Normative study with healthy individuals and comprehensive study of its sensitivity, validity, and reliability in individuals with stroke. *Journal of Neuroengineering and Rehabilitation, 16*(1), 1–11.

LIS3MDL. (n.d.). *LIS3MDL*. Retrieved 2021, from https://www.st.com/en/mems-and-sensors/lis3mdl.html

Liao, W. L., & Tsai, F. J. (2013). Personalized medicine: A paradigm shift in healthcare. *Biomedicine (Taipei), 3*(2), 66–72. doi:10.1016/j.biomed.2012.12.005

Ma, Y., Mithraratne, K., Wilson, N. C., Wang, X., Ma, Y., & Zhang, Y. (2019). The validity and reliability of a kinect v2-based gait analysis system for children with cerebral palsy. *Sensors (Basel), 19*(7), 1660.

Madgwick, S. (2010). *An efficient orientation filter for inertial and inertial/magnetic sensor arrays*. Academic Press.

Madgwick, S. O., Harrison, A. J., & Vaidyanathan, R. (2011, June). Estimation of IMU and MARG orientation using a gradient descent algorithm. *2011. IEEE International Conference on Rehabilitation Robotics*, 1–7.

Menache, A. (2000). *Understanding motion capture for computer animation and video games*. Morgan Kaufmann.

Merriaux, P., Dupuis, Y., Boutteau, R., Vasseur, P., & Savatier, X. (2017). A study of vicon system positioning performance. *Sensors (Basel), 17*(7), 1591.

NDI. (n.d.). *Northern Digital Inc*. Retrieved 2021, from NDI Products: https://www.ndigital.com/products/legacy-products/

Nogueria, P. (2011). Motion capture fundamentals. *Doctoral Symposium in Informatics Engineering*, 303-314.

O'Brien, J. F., Bodenheimer, R. E. Jr, Brostow, G. J., & Hodgins, J. K. (1999). *Automatic joint parameter estimation from magnetic motion capture data.* Georgia Institute of Technology.

OPTITRACK. (n.d.). *OPTITRACK.* Retrieved 2021, from OPTITRACK Products: https://optitrack.com/

Panwar, M., Biswas, D., Bajaj, H., Jöbges, M., Turk, R., Maharatna, K., & Acharyya, A. (2019, February 18). Rehab-Net: Deep Learning framework for Arm Movement Classification using Wearable Sensors for Stroke Rehabilitation. *IEEE Transactions on Biomedical Engineering, 66*(11), 3026–3037. doi:10.1109/TBME.2019.2899927

PHASESPACE. (n.d.). *PHASESPACE.* Retrieved 2021, from PHASESPACE Products: https://www.phasespace.com/

Pons-Moll, G., Baak, A. H., Müller, M., Seidel, H. P., & Rosenhahn, B. (2010, June). Multisensor-fusion for 3d full-body human motion capture. *2010 IEEE Computer Society Conference on Computer Vision and Pattern Recognition,* 663-670.

QUALISYS. (n.d.). *QUALISYS.* Retrieved 2021, from QUALISYS Products: https://www.qualisys.com/

Rahul, M. (2018). Review on motion capture technology. *Global Journal of Computer Science and Technology, 18,* 23–26.

Raspberry-Pi-Zero-W. (n.d.). *Raspberry Pi Zero W.* Retrieved 2021, from https://www.raspberrypi.org/products/raspberry-pi-zero-w/

Rau, G., Disselhorst-Klug, C., & Schmidt, R. (2000). Movement biomechanics goes upwards: From the leg to the arm. *Journal of Biomechanics, 33*(10), 1207–1216. doi:10.1016/S0021-9290(00)00062-2 PMID:10899329

Ridolfi, M., Van de Velde, S., Steendam, H., & De Poorter, E. (2018). Analysis of the scalability of UWB indoor localization solutions for high user densities. *Sensors (Basel), 18*(6), 1875.

Robert-Lachaine, X., Mecheri, H., Larue, C., & Plamondon, A. (2017). Validation of inertial measurement units with an optoelectronic system for whole-body motion analysis. *Medical & Biological Engineering & Computing, 55*(4), 609–619.

Roetenberg, D., Baten, C. T., & Veltink, P. H. (2007). Estimating body segment orientation by applying inertial and magnetic sensing near ferromagnetic materials. *IEEE Transactions on Neural Systems and Rehabilitation Engineering, 15*(3), 469–471.

Roetenberg, D., Luinge, H., & Slycke, P. (2009). *Xsens MVN: Full 6DOF human motion tracking using miniature inertial sensors.* Xsens Technologies BV, Tech. Rep.

Schepers, M., Giuberti, M., & Bellusci, G. (2018). *Xsens MVN: Consistent Tracking of Human.* Xsens Technologies BV, Tech. Rep, 1-8.

Scheurer, S., Tedesco, S., Brown, K. N., & O'Flynn, B. (2017, May). Human activity recognition for emergency first responders via body-worn inertial sensors. *2017 IEEE 14th International Conference on Wearable and Implantable Body Sensor Networks (BSN),* 5-8.

Shotton, J., Fitzgibbon, A., Cook, M., Sharp, T. F., Moore, R., Kipman, A., & Blake, A. (2011, June). Real-time human pose recognition in parts from single depth images. *CVPR, 2011,* 1297–1304.

Solberg, R. T., & Jensenius, A. R. (2016). *Optical or Inertial? Evaluation of two motion capture systems for studies of dancing to electronic dance music.* Sound and Music Computing.

Tao, W., Liu, T., Zheng, R., & Feng, H. (2012). Gait analysis using wearable sensors. *Sensors (Basel), 12*(2), 2255–2283. doi:10.3390120202255 PMID:22438763

Taylor, L., Miller, E., & Kaufman, K. R. (2017). Static and dynamic validation of inertial measurement units. *Gait & Posture, 57,* 80–84.

TINYTILE. (n.d.). *tinyTile.* Retrieved 2021, from https://www.element14.com/community/docs/DOC-82913/l/tinytile-intel-curie-based-miniaturised-adaptation-of-the-arduinogenuino-101-board

TUBITAK-SAGE. (n.d.). *TUBITAK SAGE.* Retrieved 2021, from https://www.sage.tubitak.gov.tr/

Unity. (n.d.). Retrieved 2019, from https://unity.com/

van Andel, C. J., Wolterbeek, N., Doorenbosch, C. A., Veeger, D. H., & Harlaar, J. (2008). Complete 3D kinematics of upper extremity functional tasks. *Gait & Posture, 27*(1), 120–127. doi:10.1016/j.gaitpost.2007.03.002 PMID:17459709

VICON. (n.d.). *VICON.* Retrieved 2021, from VICON Products: https://www.vicon.com/

Wang, A., & Gollakota, S. (2019, May). Millisonic: Pushing the limits of acoustic motion tracking. *Proceedings of the 2019 CHI Conference on Human Factors in Computing Systems,* 1-11.

Wang, L., Ning, H., Tan, T., & Hu, W. (2004). Fusion of static and dynamic body biometrics for gait recognition. *IEEE Transactions on Circuits and Systems for Video Technology*, *14*(2), 149–158. doi:10.1109/TCSVT.2003.821972

Wittmann, F., Lambercy, O., & Gassert, R. (2019). Magnetometer-based drift correction during rest in IMU arm motion tracking. *Sensors (Basel)*, *19*(6), 1312.

XSENS. (n.d.). *XSENS*. Retrieved 2021, from XSENS Products: https://www.xsens.com/products

Yan, X., Li, H., Li, A. R., & Zhang, H. (2017). Wearable IMU-based real-time motion warning system for construction workers' musculoskeletal disorders prevention. *Automation in Construction*, *74*, 2–11.

Yu, Y., Li, H., Yang, X., Kong, L., Luo, X., & Wong, A. Y. (2019). An automatic and non-invasive physical fatigue assessment method for construction workers. *Automation in Construction*, *103*, 1–12. doi:10.1016/j.autcon.2019.02.020

Zeng, H., & Zhao, Y. (2011). Sensing movement: Microsensors for body motion measurement. *Sensors (Basel)*, *11*(1), 638–660.

Zhou, H., & Hu, H. (2008). Human motion tracking for rehabilitation—A survey. *Biomedical Signal Processing and Control*, *3*(1), 1–18.

Zhuang, Y., Yang, J., Li, Y., Qi, L., & El-Sheimy, N. (2016). Smartphone-based indoor localization with bluetooth low energy beacons. *Sensors (Basel)*, *16*(5), 596.

Chapter 10

Decision Making in IoT Systems Based on Guided Self-Organization and Autonomic Computing in the Context of the I4.0 Era

Luis Eduardo Villela Zavala
Cinvestav Unidad Guadalajara, Mexico

Mario Siller
Cinvestav Unidad Guadalajara, Mexico

ABSTRACT

Internet of things (IoT) systems are taking an important role in daily life. Each year the number of connected devices increases considerably, and it is important to keep systems working appropriately. There are some options related to decision support systems to perform IoT systems tasks such as deployment, maintenance, and its operation on environments full of different connected devices and IoT systems interacting among them. For the decision-making process, the authors consider the complexity nature observed in IoT systems and their operational context and environments. In this sense, rather than using grain and fixed control rules/laws for the system design, the use of general principles, goals, and objectives are defined to guide the system adaptation. This has been referred to as guided self-organization (GSO) in the literature. The GSO design approach is based in evaluating the system entropy to reduce the emergence and enable self-organization. Also, in this chapter, a series of study cases from different IoT application domains are presented.

DOI: 10.4018/978-1-7998-7468-3.ch010

INTRODUCTION

Today the Internet of Things (IoT) systems have acquired considerable relevance in people's daily lives, from the basic automation of primary processes in our homes, through ubiquitous computer systems with which we interact without even giving us account, until its widespread use in the manufacturing industry and activities such as food production. Even during 2020 and early 2021, the use of IoT devices increased significantly due to the Coronavirus COVID-19 pandemic, especially in the health area to perform medical processes and in open public spaces to perform medical procedures safely, monitoring the people's temperature and being able to apply sanity measures to prevent the spread of the virus in public spaces.

Although there have been significant advances in IoT and decision-making processes in recent years, there are still opportunities for improvement and some questions remain unanswered: Is the current decision-making process in IoT systems sufficient to satisfy current needs? How to carry out the decision-making process in IoT systems with a high level of uncertainty? Is there a way to measure chaos in IoT systems?

This chapter presents a study of how IoT challenges such as high device volume, heterogeneity, diversity, and security can be addressed in overall design, considering how current non-functional properties (Self-Adaptation, Self-Configuration, and Interoperability) can be extended using the Self-Star* autonomic computing properties proposed by Kephart from IBM. For this, the incorporation of knowledge and objective bases based on the Autonomic Control Loop (ACL) MAPE-K (Modeling - Analysis - Planning - Execution - Knowledge) is introduced. Four properties were considered in the proposed architectural designs: Self-Configuration, Self-Optimization, Self-Healing, and Self-Protection. These designs are intended to reduce human intervention and dependency during the life cycle of IoT systems after implementation. Furthermore, this work considers Industry 4.0 design guidelines in terms of vertical and horizontal integration in the end-to-end value chains related to the application domain.

For the decision-making process, it is important to consider the complexity observed in IoT systems and their context and operating environments, using different principles, goals, and objectives it is possible to design the adaptation of the system (Guided Self-Organization (GSO)). The GSO design approach proposed is based on evaluating the entropy of the system to reduce chaos and allow self-organization. In this context, an algorithm calculates the entropy value and uses it for the decision-making process, taking as a reference the knowledge previously obtained from the information processing.

The objectives that will be discussed in this chapter are to provide an overview of decision making in IoT systems when they are under uncertainty, propose an architectural model for autonomic IoT systems with uncertainty management through entropy, analyze entropy in IoT application scenarios such as urban agronomy, within the domain of Smart Cities and open a panorama of decision-making under uncertainty in systems within the domain of Industry 4.0. The content of this chapter is presented as follows: The Background section shows an overview of the topics to be discussed, how other authors treat them, and what has been done; In the section of Decision Making Under Uncertainty in IoT Systems, the work development process, analysis carried out and a proposal is presented; The Solutions and Recommendations section briefly analyzes the relevant aspects to consider about the emerging behaviors of the agents; the Future Research Directions section mentions the course that the research should take and some of the future work to be done and finally, the Conclusion summarizes the findings of the previous sections.

The main contribution of this Chapter is to show the research work that has been carried out for some years related to the autonomic architecture of IoT and a part of the tests that have been carried out as part of obtaining preliminary results of the oriented entropy analysis to IoT systems, finally, the relationship of autonomic IoT systems, decision-making systems under uncertainty and the multiple application domains on which tests can be applied is established.

BACKGROUND

Decision-making occurs continuously in all scenarios of daily life; from the moment humans get up to start a new day until they go to rest; everything humans do in their daily lives is full of decision-making. Deciding what to eat, the route to follow to get to work, what tasks to carry out, the priority of each one, what clothes to wear, among others, are decisions that are made throughout the day.

It is not only people who make decisions. Decisions are also made in the field of complex systems, in which the Internet of Things (IoT) is cataloged. IoT sensors and actuators interact with each other to keep a certain system working correctly, in addition to collecting data in real-time that allows the acquisition of information and knowledge, which will be used later for the operation of the system. Industry 4.0 is considered as the "Fourth Industrial Revolution" by many researchers, Hoffmann mentions that reliability supports strategic decisions in the context of Industry 4.0 and the development of the decision-making process in this area (Souza et. Al, 2020). Industry 4.0 refers to the merging of the digital, virtual, and physical worlds, providing opportunities to increase productivity and restore the competitive landscape with new service models, smart products that lead to the next generation of operational excellence, intelligent automation, and connectivity (Von Scheel, 2020).

Related to the Industry 4.0 area, there is a concept used within the IoT, which works in conjunction with cloud computing, known as "Fog Computing"; which was introduced by Cisco (Cisco, 2015) as a way to enable IoT devices to work from the edge of the network; later Bonomi mentions that Fog Computing is an extension of Cloud Computing with smart devices (Bonomi, Milito, Zhu, Addepalli, 2012), among the benefits it brings are obtaining a quick and agile response to requests made within the system; something indispensable in areas such as the "Industrial Internet of Things (IIoT)"; at the same time, it allows solving problems of heterogeneity and scalability in the network, adding protection to data and providing support for context-aware computing. (Butun, Sari and Österberg, 2020)

Taking into account the series of benefits that "Fog Computing" offers, it must be taken into account when designing a new IoT architecture, which works as a middleware between the local-part and the cloud computing part; and it is here where the data processing should be carried out, by guiding it and applying it to the Industry 4.0 area, the automation process would be considerably improved; and if it is carried out in conjunction with the incorporation of autonomic computing, an IoT system oriented to Industry 4.0 would be obtained practically independent and robust with multiple long-term benefits, such as cost reduction and production delays; agile and fast responses and a considerable increase in security. (Butun, Sari and Österberg, 2019)

There is a close relationship between IIoT and Industry 4.0; To achieve this, the 7 Tom Bradicich's IIoT principles must be considered: (1) Large amount of analog data, (2) Perpetual connectivity, (3) Real-time data streaming, (4) Data insights, (5) Trade-off between time and depth of knowledge, (6) Big Data visibility and (7) Edge computing. These, in turn, can be combined with Artificial Intelligence (AI) techniques such as Natural Language Processing (NLP), multi-agent systems, computer vision, neurosciences, decision making under uncertainty, among others. To solve, algorithms must be developed that meet these objectives and are oriented to the final system, in this way it constitutes the main pillar in the integration of IIoT with Industry 4.0 since IIoT is a network of physical objects, systems, and applications that contain integrated technologies to communicate and share intelligence between them, the environment and external users of the system; increase the productivity and competitiveness of the systems, which favors industrial economic development. (Sari, Lekidis and Butun, 2020).

The many decisions that are made daily are fraught with uncertainty. Uncertainty corresponds to the unknown, it arises when deciding because it is not known with certainty what the consequences of deciding will be. Air traffic control, accident and disaster prevention, and active vehicle safety are scenarios in which decision-making under uncertainty is common and systems have been implemented to automate this process. Decision-making can be studied from the point of view of multi-agent systems driven by observations of their environment made by agents, which can be physical or non-physical entities (Kochenderfer, 2015).

In the IoT, physical agents can be humans (people who interact directly or indirectly with a system), sensors, or actuators. As for non-physical entities, it could be, for example, a decision support system fully implemented in software. Multi-agent systems can be used to model, simulate, and design complex systems. A complex system is a network composed of several elements that interact with each other, which can evolve based on Self-organization and the emergent behaviors that may arise. (Sayama, 2015).

To study complex systems we use computational, mathematical, and conceptual tools. Complex systems have different behaviors and interactions between their components, these are known as Emerging Behaviors and are characterized by their unpredictability. An example of emergent behavior is the movement that a person makes while walking, it is difficult to determine which is the direction that the person is going to follow or follows a route and changes course unexpectedly. Emergence occurs on a macroscopic scale and is derived from the microscopic properties of a system. The process of forming macroscopic structures or order is known as self-organization. A system has the capacity for Self-Organization when its agents adapt their behavior to achieve a specific objective. Some cyber-physical systems (CPS) can be considered complex systems. These systems belong to a new generation of digital systems in which the "cybernetic" part (data processing algorithms, analysis, results collection, etc.) is integrated with the "physical" part (sensors, actuators, an environment, infrastructure, etc.), generating a system that solves a particular problem. In 2010 Rajkumar defined CPS as physical engineering systems that encompass operations such as monitoring, coordination, control, and integration through communication and computer processing, which manifests itself from a microscopic level to a macroscopic level. (Rajkumar, 2010)

Bahati and Gill in 2011 defined CPS as a new generation of systems with integrated physical and computing capabilities capable of interacting with humans through new modalities, which in turn will be key to the future development of new technologies. (Bahati and Gill, 2011).

Humans can interact with a cyber-physical system directly or indirectly. In direct interaction, there is physical contact between the user and the system, and the user is aware that he is using the system for a purpose. In indirect interaction, the user never has contact with the system, in many cases, he does not even know that he is using it, which means that he is ubiquitously interacting with the system. Examples of cyber-physical systems are the Internet of Things (IoT) systems, which comprise elements with unique identities and are connected to a network within which the components interact with each other. The main objective of the IoT is to provide elements that would not normally be connected to the network, control, and configuration capabilities.

ISO / IEC establishes that the IoT is an infrastructure of objects, people, systems, and information resources that are interconnected and have intelligence services that allow the processing of information from both the physical world and the virtual world (ISO, 2018). It is important to mention that things in IoT have some characteristics such as their own identity, they have monitoring capacity and/or actuators, they exchange data with other devices and applications that are in the same network or another network to be able to carry out the treatment of the data obtained. IoT is a dynamic global network infrastructure that enables the integration of physical and virtual elements. An IoT system has the properties shown in Table 1.

Table 1. IoT features

Feature	Description
Data correlation and information retrieval	• Use of data collected to generate a statistical report on the general status of the IoT system and to be able to analyze when this system is not working properly.
Security and Privacy	• It is essential to provide IoT systems with the capacity to contribute to the security of the system due to the high interaction of devices that present this type of systems.
Dynamic and Self-Adaptive	• IoT devices must have the ability to dynamically adapt to changes and prevent problems that may arise as a result.
Self-Configuration	• IoT devices must change their configuration by themselves using the infrastructure available in the system.
Heterogeneity	• IoT devices must be able to interoperate with multiple communication protocols given that the nature of IoT systems involves devices interacting completely different.
Unique identity	• Each IoT device has an identifier to be used within the IoT system in order to be identified by other nodes in the system.
Integrated in an information network	• Allow data to be communicated and exchanged between them, either within the same IoT network or in another remote IoT network.

Source: (ISO, 2018) (Bahga and Madisetti, 2014)

IoT systems are present in multiple application domains, these application domains can contain subdomains, so several IoT systems can work independently or interact with systems from other domains or subdomains. One of the most important application domains is Smart Cities, from which subdomains arise such as urban mobility, transport logistics, Smart Health, Urban Agronomy, energy systems, communications, among others. Each subdomain has a different purpose and has its own IoT systems in charge of solving one or more needs in a city; either by themselves or in conjunction with other systems with which they are interacting.

In this work, two subdomains in the Smart Cities area are emphasized: Urban Agronomy, which focuses mainly on food production in controlled environments located in confined spaces, and Industry 4.0, important for the industrial needs of the city.

The data collection process within an IoT system is crucial to meet the objectives of the system, through the sensors the data is collected in real-time of execution. Said data can be processed either in the physical part, in case of having a server dedicated to this task, or the most common and practical way of doing it, within a server located in the cloud using Cloud Computing, the data is sent to the cloud where it is processed to obtain information and finally to be able to infer knowledge that will be useful for the system to meet a series of well-defined specific objectives. These in turn are associated with the application domain corresponding to the IoT system and complement the knowledge base to be used in subsequent processes.

Knowledge is essential for autonomic computing systems, as Kephart researched, autonomic computing encompasses computing systems with the ability to manage themselves using high-level goals defined by system administrators, and an IoT system can become an autonomic system. The term "Autonomic Computing" comprises a hierarchy of Self-Governing Systems, which have various objectives and interests and can achieve them with the help of independent and autonomous components using the knowledge acquired in real-time and a set of goals that are stored in an objectives base and are provided by the administrator before the system runs. (Kephart, 2003). An autonomic system can maintain or change its configuration parameters depending on multiple internal or external factors. This is achieved since the essence of autonomic computing is reflected in the Self-Management property, which comprises four main properties: Self-Configuration, Self-Optimization, Self-Healing, and Self-Protection. Table 2 shows a brief explanation of each of them.

Table 2. Autonomic computing properties

Property	Description
Self-Configuration	• The autonomic systems will configure themselves according to the application policies, business level objectives and current execution of the scenario.
Self-Optimization	• Autonomic systems will continually look for ways to improve their operations such as changing settings and using knowledge.
Self-Healing	• Detect, diagnose and repair problems caused by software errors or hardware failures.
Self-Protection	• Autonomic systems will defend the system as a whole and anticipate problems based on reports generated by the system's sensor networks.

Source: (Kephart, 2003)

In Autonomic Computing the decision-making process is important since it uses the objectives provided by the system administrator and the knowledge previously generated or in real-time of execution to make the best decision considering various factors depending on the system and the domain application on the one, they are working on. An Autonomic Control Loop (ACL) is required to achieve the objectives, it contains a set of tasks that the system must execute to achieve Self-Management using an autonomous administrator, these tasks range from monitoring the managed components, interacting with other regional administrators, the analysis and processing of the data and the planning process and definition of the subsequent tasks that the system must carry out. There are multiple reference frameworks to define ACLs, one of the most used is MAPE-K (Monitor, Analyze, Plan, Execute - Knowledge), proposed by IBM (IBM, 2006).

MAPE-K is a reference model for an ACL, whose main function is to provide an overview of the basic components of an autonomic administrator, architecturally represents each of the elements that compose it and shows how they communicate with each other (IBM, 2006) (Movahedi, Avari, Langar and Pujolle, 2011). The model consists of a high-level objective and a knowledge base that together make up the knowledge component; a monitor to observe the environment in which the system operates; an analysis and planning component of utmost importance in MAPE-K, this is where the knowledge processing is executed and all the intelligence of the system is carried out such as the prediction of events, determining if optimization is required or if it is possible to predict a specific event to define the tasks that must be carried out in the future by the autonomic system and, therefore, carry out decision-making. Finally, there is a running component, which has two main tasks: initializing the system configuration when it starts up and reconfiguring it based on the decisions previously made by the planning and analysis component.

Now, for decision-making under uncertainty, it is necessary to consider the properties of autonomic computing, so that the system can decide without the need for an administrator who is making decisions using the collected knowledge and the objectives set at the beginning of the system. Figure 1 presents an initial outline of the basic elements of decision making and the four main autonomic properties (Self-* Properties) (Table 2) (Kephart, 2003). With the autonomic properties enabled, it is possible to manage the decision-making process autonomically, but autonomic computer systems require a series of objectives stored in a database (Objectives Base), the objectives are given by the system administrator at the beginning of execution time, then when the system is running it generates knowledge, this is stored in a knowledge base and together with the objectives base it can be used to reduce the uncertainty of the system and allow the taking of decisions to be carried out.

It is possible to guide the adaptation of an autonomic system through Guided Self-Organization (GSO). Although there is no single definition of GSO, there are some authors who have carried out studies on the subject, one of them is Claudius Gros, who studies GSO as natural behaviors of systems using functionals based on probability distributions for dynamic systems, and information theory. (Gros, 2014). GSO can be seen as a combination of Self-Organization with the design of strategies by systems. Adaptability, robustness, anti-fragility, the use of mediators, a "slower is faster" effect, and natural heterogeneity on the part of the system are the properties of systems using GSO.

A system that constantly generates information through the data collected is a system that requires that such information be taken into consideration when making decisions under uncertainty, for this, it is essential to have a robust decision-making system that considers all the possible sources of uncertainty to make decisions and even predict future events. Kochenderfer explains that it is important to compare the plausibility of the different events that are likely to occur within the problems related to uncertainty, this procedure allows obtaining a series of conditional probabilities and degrees of belief that will be useful to solve the problem. He also mentions that the Bayes Rule will be of great importance within the process since the conditional probabilities can be represented compactly with a Bayesian network that will allow visualizing the possible causes and effects within the system in question and forming a table of conditional probabilities. (Kochenderfer, 2015). Once you have the probabilities, you must apply some technique that helps you make a rational decision under uncertainty, at this stage utility theory enters. The use of utility theory for decision making under uncertainty will help to select the best decision based on the data produced by the system, for this, it considers the utility functions, which consider the system restrictions, probabilistic measures, and parameters of the system preferences, all this helps to generate a measure of real utility. The utility values associated with different probabilistic values can be stored within a lottery, which is a set of probabilities associated with another set of outputs, which are already previously calculated and verified by the system and allows to save processing time later in systems that usually keep similar parameters.

Within decision-making under uncertainty, there is another concept that has become popular in recent years, known as Entropy, which is thought to have control of the information available within a certain system and to know the level of chaos and uncertainty of the same considering the probabilities of the present events. One of the pioneers in the study of entropy is Shannon, he presents a series of theorems and mathematical formalisms to propose a formal definition of entropy. (Shannon, 1948).

Figure 1. Basic elements of a decision-making process under uncertainty

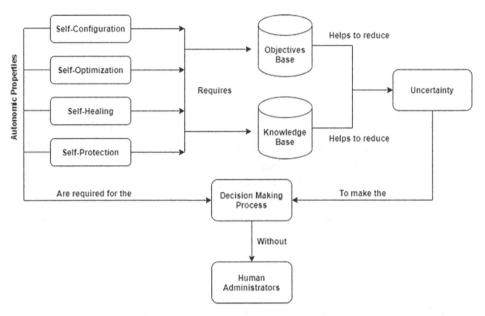

Entropy is the expected value (Average) of the content of the information contained in each message of the system, that is, it takes the measure of the chaos and disorder of the system, it can also be a measure of the lack of knowledge that one has about the operation of the system or irreversible changes within him. The information content of Shannon is a natural measure of the information content of a given event, in a simplified way it is known as "Information Content" and its unit of measurement is the bits; The entropy is the average of the Shannon information content for output, to be processed multiple values of the Shannon information content are required and thus perform the calculation. Entropy is also known as uncertainty. (MacKay, 2010).

As shown in Figure 2, there is a relationship between utility theory and Shannon entropy, both are essential for decision making under uncertainty and it is important to be considered in a decision making under uncertainty oriented IoT architecture proposal to be applied in autonomic IoT systems.

For some of the systems that perform entropy analysis, algorithms have been developed that facilitate the calculation and processing of information to obtain an entropy value, but within the area of IoT systems, there is very little information available on the state of the art, that is, precisely on this subject that we are going to work on in the following sections.

DECISION MAKING UNDER UNCERTAINTY ON IOT SYSTEMS PROCESS

IoT systems perform numerous operations of which a significant amount, depending on the type of system, is performed under a certain degree of uncertainty. IoT systems exposed to uncertain conditions require additional processing to be able to execute operations. Most of the processes that are carried out in IoT systems that present uncertainty is related to decision-making within the system, these decisions can range from processing in the cloud, activating or deactivating actuators to sending data to other IoT systems that are found on the network.

To develop decision-making systems, it is important to have a framework that enables the capacities to carry out this process. Although today there are some proposals for IoT architectures, many of these do not contemplate decision-making natively but are widely used in IoT systems with previously defined decision-making processes.

Figure 2. Comparison between utility theory and Shannon entropy

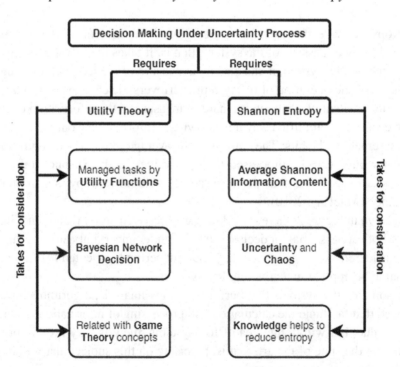

Decision Making on Internet of Things Systems

As part of the decision-making process within the IoT systems, each IoT architecture must have one or more blocks that enable the decision-making process. There are multiple IoT architectures, each one oriented to a specific purpose, and with certain functionalities added between one and the other, within which decision-making is considered to a certain degree. Bahga and Madisetti defined a set of 6 multilevel IoT architectural patterns (Bahga & Madisetti, 2014). Level 1 is the one with the least functionality and Level 6 is the one with the most.

Starting from a multilevel IoT architecture offers several possibilities because these architectures can increase their functionality if they are extended through additional functional blocks and data sources to be used within the IoT system. Part of what can be done with the architecture is to provide it with autonomic properties to obtain an IoT architecture in which autonomic computing IoT systems can operate. It is important to consider that IoT architectures must be at least semi-autonomic so that decision-making can be enabled and used by the same system without the need for a human administrator to intervene during the process.

Autonomic IoT Systems and Guided Self-Organization

As part of the design and construction process of an autonomic IoT architecture, the authors start from a multilevel IoT architecture because it is versatile, and it is easy to add or modify functionality through the representation of blocks. The authors have been working with semi-autonomic IoT architectures for some years, in 2018 they presented a proposal for a semi-autonomic IoT architecture that enables the autonomic property of Self-Configuration and was tested within an urban agronomy scenario, which in turn is a subdomain of the area of Smart Cities (Villela, 2018). This proposed architecture is based on the MAPE-K ACL presented by Kephart (Kephart, 2003) and some new blocks were created and some that already existed within level 5 of Bahga and Madisetti were modified to enable the autonomic property of Self-Configuration; With the implementation of the completely autonomous architecture remaining as future work, this is achieved by adding the rest of the autonomous properties (Self-Optimization, Self-Healing, Self-Protection).

One of the advantages that the Bahga and Madisetti multilevel IoT architectures provide is the scalability that allows them to increase their functionality and in case a centralized controller is needed between the local-part and the part located in the cloud, it can be easily migrated to level 6; another advantage is that these architectures are designed for use within applications that are based on the cloud, in such a way that they can carry out their processes, saving processing within the local-part and also, taking into account that an autonomic IoT system must have connectivity to the cloud to access its knowledge base and the objective base, necessary to provide autonomic properties to IoT systems.

Now, about Guided Self-Organization (GSO), it should be considered that when the system decides what to do, strategies previously designed based on the knowledge acquired are taken into account. Based on the objectives that were provided by the administrator when the system was run for the first time, a strategy that can be proposed is to consider the behaviors that occur within the system and the knowledge generated with those behaviors and interactions. One of the challenges of applying GSO to IoT systems is that many of the behaviors that occur are emergent, that is, spontaneous or instinctive behaviors due to the interaction of physical components and the environment in which they develop, therefore, should be considered during the development of decision-making process for IoT systems.

Figure 3. Overview of the architecture proposal

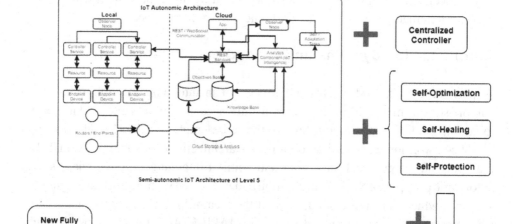

To address the problem, the authors are working on an architecture proposal, it is currently in process and the general scheme, which can be seen in Figure 3, is based on the previous architecture (Villela, 2018) and the final architecture can be considered it as an evolution. The new architecture requires to be migrated from

Level 5 to Level 6 of the multilevel architectural patterns proposed by Bahga and Madisetti (Bahga, 2014), to carry out the migration a Centralized Controller for the architecture is necessary, this controller can be seen as a middleware between the local section and the cloud to carry out the exchange of data between local and cloud and vice versa. Also, the architecture must be autonomic, for this, the missing autonomic properties (Self-Optimization, Self-Healing, Self-Protection) will be added, continuing with a decision network to manage decision-making under the uncertainty process in the system (Possibly a Bayesian Network) and chaos management techniques (Entropy).

Emergent Behaviors on IoT Systems

IoT systems perform multiple interactions, either between their components or with elements belonging to other IoT systems, generally each of these interactions has a set of rules that govern them. But having multiple interactions constantly gives rise to emergent behaviors between the elements of the IoT system with their environment, this type of behavior is quite common in Ultra-Large-Scale Systems; these types of systems are generally made up of multiple IoT systems that work together and belong to different application domains. The Smart Cities domain is an example, here each subdomain has its systems working together with other subdomain systems to achieve common goals, in this case, the proper functioning of a city. Said IoT architecture bases its decision-making process on the behaviors and interactions that occur between IoT devices and the environment in which they operate (Roca, Nemirovsky, Nemirovsly, Milito & Valero, 2016).

It is important to consider emerging behaviors that occur within IoT systems because they are crucial to achieving the goals of the system. Consider the example of an autonomous vehicle, which in addition to the elements that make up the conventional mechanics of the car, what differentiates it from a conventional vehicle is its ability to be driven with a minimum of human intervention, and to achieve this, it incorporates a sophisticated set sensors of multiple types, these sensors are constantly generating data making the system know various characteristics and behaviors that occur with the other elements of its environment (road conditions, most used or less crowded routes, the behavior of other vehicles, among others). In a scenario such as that of a car traveling from point A to point B, many emergent behaviors can occur, from the appearance of a pothole in the street that the car is not aware of reckless behaviors on the part of other elements (Traffic cut, pedestrians crossing streets in prohibited areas, presence of an emergency vehicle, among others). All the actions carried out by the car due to these events are emergent because the moment in which they will occur is unknown, and in many cases, the system does not know how to react, so it must have the ability to process the knowledge acquired to decide.

In addition to the communication of the IoT components within the system and with the environment, other factors affect the decision-making process. Examples of these factors are ignorance or lack of information about the process and the interactions carried out by the system, as well as the increase in chaos within it.

Information Theory and Entropy

The information generated as a result of the data collected by an IoT system has rarely been the object of study in decision-making, although it is important to consider it when wanting to provide the IoT system with autonomic capabilities. If a system has insufficient information about the environment in which it is located, it will not know what to do, so it will generate behaviors that may not be appropriate depending on the situation. This phenomenon is known as uncertainty, which, as mentioned above, is the lack of information necessary to act within the system, which generates chaos between the components of the system, so that conventional decision-making processes will no longer be useful, now they will have to. be handled as a decision-making process under uncertainty.

In the state of the art of IoT systems at this time there is no knowledge of previously available proposals that address decision making under uncertainty. It is essential to open an overview of decision making under uncertainty processes to apply them to most IoT systems.

By using the collected data in conjunction with goals and knowledge bases, an IoT system can perform analysis to make decisions under conditions of uncertainty. To carry out the process, it is important to calculate the content of the information in the data; the system requires prior knowledge of the possible data that may appear within the system. A probability value is assigned to the data and represents the frequency with which the data appears. In some static systems, this value will never change, but in dynamic and complex systems, such as autonomic IoT systems, these values will constantly change during system execution.

If the IoT system does not have previously acquired knowledge, then the system must run for a period to obtain it. As census and processed data are obtained, probability values will be assigned, as in dynamic systems. A compelling example of this scenario is a system that allows us to perform an analysis of body temperature to determine if you have an infectious disease, such as influenza, the COVID-19 coronavirus, the common flu, among others.

The formula to obtain the information content of an event denoted by x was defined by Shannon and is represented as: (Shannon, 1948)

$$h\left(x\right) = \log_2 \frac{1}{P\left(x\right)}$$

It is important to mention that all data, probabilities, and information content can be stored in a lottery in the same way that it is done when working with utility theory to make traditional decisions. A lottery saves processing time once the system is up and running and is quite useful in systems where some events have a high probability of occurring. For example, since the sensors will continuously record the same data, allowing Shannon's information content to be calculated only once; From the second record, the system will be able to take the value directly, unless the system presents new behaviors where it is necessary to modify the probability values, but it would no longer be performed at the time of reading, once a different value is obtained you get an update for all data.

Shannon's information content yields a value in bits that represents the information content of an event given a probability value denoted by $P(x)$, said probability varies according to the system in which one is working. Now, if what you want to obtain is the average information of the system, then you need to calculate the Shannon Entropy, which is represented by the following formula:

$$H\left(X\right) = \sum_{x \in A_x} P\left(x\right) \log \frac{1}{P\left(x\right)}$$

Algorithm 1: Entropy Calculus

```
Input: A data vector S, a counter c
Output: Entropy value H for S
H ¬ 0
ArrayProbabilities ¬ []
for i in S do:
        ArrayProbabilities.append(i[-1]/c)
end for
for i = 0 to length (ArrayProbabilities) do:
        if (i != 0) then
                Logarithm = Math.log2(1/ArrayProbabilities[i])
        else
                Logarithm = 0
        end if
        H = H + (ArrayProbabilities[i] * Logarithm)
```

```
end for
return H
```

Algorithm 2: Get Entropy from DataFile

```
Input: Data from IoT system
Output: Entropy vector H
Counter ¬ 0
H ¬ []
Lottery = []
UtilityObject = []
for row in DataFile do:
        Counter = Counter + 1
        UtilityObject.append(row)
        UtilityObject.append(getUtility(row))
        UtilityObject.append(1)
        if (Lottery != [] ) then:
                Aux ¬ 0
                for i in Lottery:
                        if (UtilityObject[0] == i[0]) then:
                                i[1] = i[1] + 1
                                Aux ¬ 1
                                break
                        end if
                end for
                if (Aux == 0) then:
                        Lottery.append(UtilityObject)
                end if
        else:
                Lottery.append(UtilityObject)
        end if
        UtilityObject = []
        H.append(EntropyCalculus(Lottery, Counter)
end for
return H
```

As part of the proposal, it is important to develop an algorithm to express the entropy calculation taking as a starting point the data received from an IoT system, for which the authors are currently working on the algorithmic proposal. It consists of two algorithms, Algorithm 1 consists of obtaining the entropy calculation of a utility lottery, for this the algorithm receives a lottery expressed as an array, takes the lottery to obtain the probabilities of each contained data, remember that a lottery can store some value and the frequency of occurrence, to obtain the probability of each lottery value it is necessary to receive the iteration counter, the iteration counter is the number of times that Algorithm 2 receives data from the system, once the probabilities have been calculated, Algorithm 1 calculates the Shannon entropy for that lottery and returns the value to Algorithm 2.

Algorithm 2 is responsible for receiving the data from the system. The data can be received in a CSV file or in real-time, once the data is available, the algorithm separates it into different arrays, one for each factor or parameter to be analyzed, and stores each value in a UtilityObject array. It is important to mention that a UtilityObject is required for each factor or system parameter. Once the algorithm has separated the data, the next step is to calculate the utility values for each object. Utility formulas are required, but they are not expressed in the Algorithms because each utility formula is different depending on the parameter, the utility formulas can be taken from specialized bibliography related to the scenario in which the algorithms are to be executed. Once the utilities are calculated, the given value, the utility value, and a counter initialized to 1 are stored in the UtilityObject; remember that this step needs to be repeated for each factor or parameter.

Moving on, a lottery validation is required, if the lottery corresponding to a parameter is empty, just store the UtilityObject in it, otherwise, validate if the value in the UtilityObject is already in the Lottery, if it is in the lottery, then increases its counter by 1; otherwise store UtilityObject in Lottery, repeat for each UtilityObject. Finally, calculate the entropy for each lottery using the general data counter, simply calling Algorithm 1, and sending the lottery and the counter as parameters, once received the entropy stores it in H, this will generate a record of historical entropy for future processes.

To provide decision making under uncertain conditions to IoT systems, it is important to consider the following points:

- The IoT architecture used must be autonomic or at least semi-autonomic, that is, it must be based on an ACL to provide the architecture with each of the autonomic properties.
- The objective base is fundamental to be able to apply the principles of the GSO within the system.
- The architecture must contain blocks that are responsible for the analysis of information and entropy.
- Remember that the greater the entropy, the greater the level of chaos in the system. The entropy value should always be kept as low as possible.

- Once the information and entropy analysis has been carried out, the system can now decide what to do, all based on the data received by its sensors.

Figure 4. Design schema of the hydroponic/aeronomic test bed

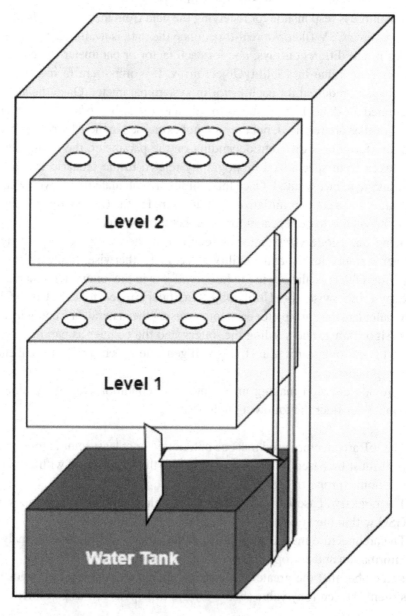

Application Domains: Smart Cities and Industry 4.0

All of the above can be applied in multiple application domains where IoT is present. The authors have been working intensively within the domain of Smart Cities, mainly in the sub-domain of urban agronomy, starting from the problem of the availability and distribution of organic food (specifically fruits and vegetables) to areas of difficult access or in cities where there is not enough for everyone. The proposal that the authors handle is the design of an intelligent hydroponic / aeroponic bed using IoT, autonomic computing and GSO to achieve this objective. Broadly speaking, the IoT system is responsible for managing almost entirely the operation of the system, from irrigation to controlling the lighting of the bed. The authors in a previous work approached the decision making of the testbed processes from the point of view of the utility theory, which indicated the moment in which some action should be executed, mainly activating or deactivating actuators or modify the configuration of these, as well as carry out the continuous census of the data of the sensor networks. This project was carried out using a semi-autonomic IoT architecture focused on Self-Configuration, obtaining satisfactory results.

Part of the authors' ongoing work is the construction of the hydroponic / aeroponic test bed geared towards urban agriculture. At this time, the authors have a small prototype, which consists of two levels interconnected between PVC pipes and electronic components such as sensors and actuators. Each level has temperature sensors, a lighting system (as it is an interior system, it is important to simulate natural lighting using high intensity LED lamps), a ventilation system and access to a water tank with liquid nutrients supplied to the crops. through a water pump and distributed to each level in a hydroponic (level tank water filling) or aeroponic (sprinkler system) mode.

Each sensor in the system will collect data from the test bed, at this time the authors collected temperature and nutrient values and used them to calculate the entropy of each. Figure 4 shows a model of the hydroponic / aeroponic test bed and in Figure 5 some images of the progress of the test bed.

As can be seen in Table 3, there is a small conjunction of data obtained through a random number generator because at this time there is no access to the test bed due to the COVID-19 pandemic, taking as reference the ideal temperature values (Maximum, minimum and optimum) and nutrient requirements for baby corn crops. The data will be used with Algorithm 1 and Algorithm 2, the objective of the work is to calculate the utility values for temperature, lighting and nutrients, then proceed to calculate the entropy for each one to see a perspective of the entropy behavior of the system when new data is received and processed at each step along with the previous analyzed data.

Figure 5. Some pictures of the construction progress of the hydroponic/aeroponic test bed

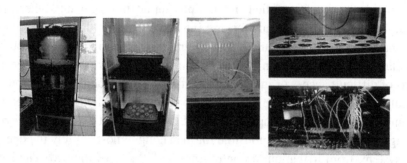

Table 3. Values of temperature, illumination and nutrients (nytrogen, phosforus, potassium, calcium, magnessium and sulfur) from the hydroponic/aeroponic test bed

Tem	Illu	N	P	K	Ca	Mg	S	Tem	Illu	N	P	K	Ca	Mg	S
20	1	9.7	3.4	18.8	4.2	4.2	2	24	1	8.5	5.5	1.1	1.9	5.4	2.9
19	1	11.6	3.4	15.8	2.6	5	1.4	25	1	7.6	4.1	5.7	3.7	4	3.7
21	1	9.4	2.8	19.1	4.1	4.3	1.9	23	1	10.1	5	8.7	2.4	3.6	4.6
21	1	9	2.6	17.4	5.9	4	1.1	25	1	8.8	5.5	6	2.9	4.6	5.5
23	1	10.4	2	21	7.6	4.7	0.1	24	1	10.7	4.8	1.4	2.7	5.3	5
21	1	8.9	2.2	24.1	7.7	3.7	1	24	1	13.2	3.4	4.7	3.2	6.5	4
19	1	7.7	3.4	23.9	7.3	3.3	0.8	25	1	13.8	2.3	1.8	1.5	7.5	4.9
19	1	7.7	4.9	27.8	5.9	2.3	0.2	26	1	12.5	0.9	6.3	2.3	6.5	4.4
19	1	10.3	5.4	26.1	5.4	3	1	28	1	11	0.9	3.8	1.5	7.8	3.5
17	1	12.8	6.6	27.2	3.9	2.9	1.1	29	1	11	1	6.2	1.7	7.9	4.1
17	1	15	5.2	22.9	3.8	1.7	0.3	31	1	12.5	2.3	1.3	2.5	7.1	4.8
18	1	14	6.2	22.2	5.1	0.9	1	30	1	14.6	3.5	1	4.1	7.5	4.1
19	1	16.5	5.5	21.3	4.8	2.1	0.5	28	1	12.3	2.5	5.8	3.5	6.5	4.3
20	1	15	4.4	16.8	3.7	2.3	1.4	30	1	14.2	2.2	9.1	1.6	5.1	5.1
18	1	16.4	5.2	21.7	3.9	0.9	2.2	30	1	12.4	1.3	4.3	3.1	5.6	4.3
16	1	13.5	6.2	18.1	4	1.8	2.6	28	1	10.7	1.3	0.3	2.3	5.1	4.9
17	1	12.8	5.5	14.7	5.3	2	3.4	28	1	10.2	1.1	1	4.3	5.7	5.8
15	1	13.8	4.9	10.5	4	1.1	2.8	29	1	10	0.9	1	3.8	6.3	5.6
16	1	13.5	3.7	12.6	5.6	0.3	3.2	30	1	9.2	1.6	1.6	3.9	7.6	4.8
15	1	13	3.5	14.9	6.7	1	3.4	28	1	7.4	2.3	0.8	5.2	6.5	4.7
17	1	11.1	4.1	16.8	8.5	1	3.1	27	1	9.7	1.3	1	3.2	6	4.4
17	1	13.3	5.5	17.9	7.3	2.1	2.5	29	1	11.1	1.2	4.3	4.5	4.8	4

continues on following page

Table 3. Continued

Tem	Illu	N	P	K	Ca	Mg	S	Tem	Illu	N	P	K	Ca	Mg	S
17	1	11.3	6.6	15.8	8.8	1.7	3.4	27	1	12.5	1	8.6	5.9	3.3	3.4
15	1	11.4	5.5	19	7.7	0.7	3.9	28	1	12.8	0.2	7.8	4.4	3.8	3.9
17	1	11.6	4.8	20.3	7.6	1.8	3.2	27	1	10.2	0.9	3.3	4.1	3.2	4.2
16	1	11.3	3.9	18.5	8.7	1.6	2.3	27	1	7.5	0.6	5.5	4.9	4.5	3.3
15	1	14	4.8	15.7	7.6	1.6	2.6	28	1	10.4	0.8	1.1	5.3	3.2	3
13	1	12.8	5.5	12.4	7.5	0.2	3.5	27	1	11.9	0.2	5.4	6.1	1.9	3.5
13	1	13.9	4.1	9.9	8.1	0.9	2.8	27	1	12	1	1	6.2	0.6	3.6
13	1	16.6	3.4	8.6	6.1	0	2.7	25	1	10.6	2.2	1	6	1.5	2.7
14	1	16.5	2.3	9.5	4.8	1	2.4	25	1	8.1	1	1	6.2	1.7	2.9
16	1	14.3	3.5	8.6	5.3	2.3	2.5	23	1	10	2	3.5	5.3	2.2	3.1
15	1	15.4	3.6	12	4.7	2.1	1.8	23	1	10.3	1.4	1	5.4	1.3	3.4
17	1	17.8	3.3	8.1	4	2.1	2.1	23	1	12.7	1.9	1	4.1	0.8	3.3
17	1	16.6	2.5	6.9	4.5	0.9	1.7	23	1	11	3.2	1	5.2	1.6	3.5
19	1	16.5	3.1	2.3	3.7	1.9	2	25	1	9.5	4.1	3.6	3.2	2.6	3.7
18	1	16.5	2.3	5	1.8	1.7	2.3	23	1	12.4	4.4	1	3.8	3.1	4
17	1	15.4	2.1	0.9	2.3	1.3	1.8	23	1	9.5	5.6	1	4	3	3.7
19	1	16.5	1.4	1	1.9	2.6	2.2	25	1	9.2	5.7	3.6	3.2	3.8	4.3
21	1	16.5	1.9	3.9	0.1	1.8	1.6	25	1	10.2	6.1	6.4	4.6	4.9	4
19	1	14.8	3	6.3	1	1.6	0.9	25	1	12.2	5.5	6.1	5.8	4	3.4
19	1	17.4	3.6	5.2	1	2.1	0.4	26	1	12.8	4.1	8.5	4	3.4	4.3
20	1	16.5	3.1	6	2	3.2	0.7	26	1	14.6	5.1	12.6	2.2	2.9	5
22	1	16.6	1.7	6.3	2.7	4.7	1.1	24	1	12.2	6	14.5	2.9	3.6	5.6
23	1	16.7	2.5	4.3	1.1	4.5	1.9	24	1	11	5.7	17.7	1	3.9	5.9
25	1	16.5	3	1	2.6	3.5	2.4	23	1	8.2	6.4	20.3	0.6	5.1	4.5
24	1	14.8	3.9	0.6	1.3	4.2	1.5	21	1	5.8	5.5	16.2	1.8	5.2	3.8
26	1	13	4.7	1	1.6	4.8	2	21	1	5.1	4.8	19.4	1.1	4.9	3.8
24	1	10.2	5.6	3.6	1.1	4.9	2.4	22	1	5.7	5.1	21.2	1	4.9	3
25	1	7.6	7	5.5	1.3	5	3.4	20	1	3.3	4.8	20.6	0.1	4.7	3.6

Once the algorithms have been executed using Python, the entropy values obtained can be seen in Table 4. In the case of Nutrient Entropy, the entropy value constantly increases due to the fact that most of the nutrient data were different, which means that the uncertainty increased as a greater number of data obtained was produced, leading the system to a high entropy value. For lighting entropy currently, there is no utility formula to use, but the authors decided to use 1 as the lighting utility value for each step, this generates a lighting entropy value equal to zero because the probability of getting the same utility value for lighting is the maximum (probability equal to 1), which means there is no uncertainty for lighting. Finally, the temperature entropy varies markedly, but it does not compare to the nutrient entropy because there are many repeated temperature values during the test scenario. Part of the results expressed in Table 4 are represented in Figure 6.

Table 4. Results of algorithms execution: entropy values for the hydroponic/aeroponic test bed factors

Iteration	H(Nutr)	H(Temp)	H(Ilum)	Iteration	H(Nutr)	H(Temp)	H(Ilum)
1	0	0	0	51	4.231	3.469	0
2	1	1	0	52	4.287	3.486	0
3	1.585	1.585	0	53	4.341	3.504	0
4	2	1.5	0	54	4.394	3.512	0
5	2.322	1.922	0	55	4.445	3.52	0
6	2.585	1.792	0	56	4.495	3.522	0
7	2.807	1.842	0	57	4.508	3.524	0
8	2.75	1.811	0	58	4.522	3.555	0
9	2.948	1.753	0	59	4.476	3.618	0
10	3.122	2.046	0	60	4.47	3.68	0
11	3.278	2.118	0	61	4.472	3.741	0
12	3.418	2.355	0	62	4.519	3.799	0
13	3.547	2.288	0	63	4.533	3.825	0
14	3.664	2.353	0	64	4.547	3.85	0
15	3.774	2.416	0	65	4.592	3.863	0
16	3.875	2.602	0	66	4.551	3.876	0
17	3.97	2.61	0	67	4.511	3.882	0
18	4.059	2.774	0	68	4.471	3.906	0
19	4.037	2.821	0	69	4.468	3.911	0
20	4.122	2.866	0	70	4.466	3.912	0
21	4.202	2.851	0	71	4.428	3.964	0
22	4.278	2.824	0	72	4.444	3.976	0
23	4.35	2.79	0	73	4.488	3.999	0
24	4.418	2.809	0	74	4.451	3.995	0
25	4.484	2.773	0	75	4.446	4.007	0
26	4.547	2.796	0	76	4.437	4.013	0

continues on following page

Table 3. Continued

Iteration	H(Nutr)	H(Temp)	H(Ilum)	Iteration	H(Nutr)	H(Temp)	H(Ilum)
27	4.607	2.8	0	77	4.402	4.007	0
28	4.566	2.923	0	78	4.368	4.008	0
29	4.625	2.969	0	79	4.334	4.006	0
30	4.574	2.989	0	80	4.3	4.004	0
31	4.543	3.099	0	81	4.267	4	0
32	4.601	3.101	0	82	4.26	4.006	0
33	4.658	3.093	0	83	4.227	4.009	0
34	4.712	3.066	0	84	4.195	4.008	0
35	4.765	3.036	0	85	4.164	4.004	0
36	4.715	3.027	0	86	4.175	3.998	0
37	4.662	3.05	0	87	4.168	3.993	0
38	4.606	3.022	0	88	4.158	3.986	0
39	4.548	3.01	0	89	4.201	3.979	0
40	4.49	3.022	0	90	4.242	3.971	0
41	4.431	3.008	0	91	4.283	3.961	0
42	4.373	2.991	0	92	4.323	3.975	0
43	4.315	3.016	0	93	4.362	3.983	0
44	4.328	3.104	0	94	4.4	3.984	0
45	4.325	3.145	0	95	4.438	3.983	0
46	4.271	3.227	0	96	4.455	3.976	0
47	4.218	3.307	0	97	4.492	3.981	0
48	4.166	3.384	0	98	4.508	3.982	0
49	4.225	3.418	0	99	4.544	4.003	0
50	4.282	3.451	0	100	4.515	4.012	0

As a conclusion to the exercise, the authors mention some important observations:

- At the beginning of the run, if the system receives a completely different data reading from the sensors, the entropy will increase considerably.
- If all the probability data calculated from the data collected from the system are different, then the system will obtain the maximum possible entropy for the given data because each event is equiprobable and tends to a uniform distribution.
- An indicator to determine if the system is maintaining its ideal values within its parameters is to verify the entropy, it is important to maintain a lower

entropy as close to zero. In this exercise, there is no near zero for nutrients and temperature. To solve this, it is necessary to design a strategy based on decision networks based on utility theory to determine when it is necessary to enable or disable actuators in the system to regulate the temperature or the level of nutrients.

- Because there is a large data set, the entropy could be considerably lower because the probability distribution is unknown.

Figure 6. Entropy plot from Algorithm 2

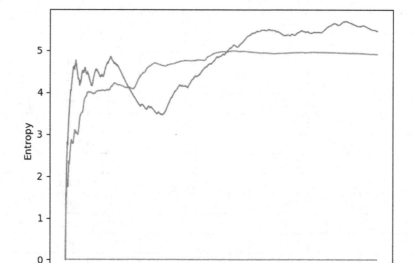

Another domain that has become very important in recent years within IoT systems is Industry 4.0, which includes the incorporation of cyber-physical systems within industrial processes, ranging from production lines, the use of autonomous robots, digital manufacturing, among others. Within Industry 4.0 it is necessary to have a robust data analysis system, oriented to Big Data and data analytics; Within which different techniques are covered, including the one known as Machine Learning (ML), which refers to the analysis of large volumes of data-oriented to learning using sophisticated algorithms for this.

Zheng et. Al mentions that Industry 4.0 is a concept that is used in the manufacturing sector and encompasses a series of applications that range from product design to product logistics and propose a framework oriented to Industry 4.0 where some of the areas that they include, among which stand out decision-making driven by Big Data, analysis and data collection; and implementation of sensors and actuators to monitor and control systems (Smart Design, Smart Monitoring, Smart Matching, Smart Control, and Smart Scheduling). (Zheng et. Al, 2018), all this in practice is represented by data analysis (Big Data and Machine Learning), autonomous machines, simulations, horizontal and vertical integration of systems; IoT, cybersecurity, cloud computing, among others (Sari, Güles and Yiğitol, 2020).

Industry 4.0 also has several specific functionalities and technologies, such as Radio Frequency Identification Devices (RFID), integration of critical components such as sensors and actuators; cameras, and data collection and analysis devices. All this is incorporated into the Smart Machining framework, which shows the integration of all these components with communication systems and monitoring systems, which are essential to modern industrial processes (Zheng et. Al, 2018).

SOLUTIONS AND RECOMMENDATIONS

One of the most important challenges when working with IoT systems and providing them with autonomic properties is the management of the blocks within the architecture. It is difficult to design an architecture capable of adopting autonomic properties. To address this challenge, it is useful to take as a reference previously existing architectural models and some ACLs that allow opening an overview of how the processes involved in the use of each of the autonomic properties will be handled. Another crucial point is the decision-making process under uncertainty, although most IoT systems present a decision-making process, the emergent behaviors of the agents or objects that interact within the system are generally not considered. It is important to use some information and entropy analysis mechanism to be able to determine what action should be taken within the system, using the objective base and the knowledge base applying autonomic computing and the principles of the GSO.

FUTURE RESEARCH DIRECTIONS

Autonomic IoT systems capable of making decisions under conditions of uncertainty are on the rise. Systems are being developed every day in multiple application domains and gradually incorporate these capabilities into their daily processes, mainly within Industry 4.0, an area in which there is already a considerable increase in the use of this type of systems, mainly in lines production, where many of these do not require human intervention for multiple tasks and processes, although there are still many IoT systems that are not autonomic and incapable of making decisions under uncertainty that have been perfected and are already used in the industry.

Within the scope of the research, as part of future work, it is considered to improve the previously developed architecture in such a way that it becomes completely autonomic, incorporating an entropy analysis process to avoid chaos within systems when occurring emergent behaviors and a decision network based on utility theory, it is also expected to improve the developed algorithm and perform tests both on the hydroponic/aeroponic test-bed directly (Post-pandemic) and in other application domains, such as Industry 4.0, which is being incorporated gradually to research, or in another subdomain of the Smart Cities area such as the health area, which is an area that in 2020 acquired considerable importance due to the COVID-19 Coronavirus pandemic, or within the urban mobility area, which ranges from efficient route design, mass intelligent transport systems, road modernization (data census at traffic lights, speed controls, etc.) to autonomous vehicle driving.

CONCLUSION

This chapter presented an overview on the use of GSO-based decision-making processes under uncertainty within IoT systems oriented to application domains such as Smart Cities or Industry 4.0. Points of view from different authors, backgrounds, and previously performed work are covered, and the topics are linked to each other to reach the foundations of a proposal that is currently being prepared to obtain fully autonomic IoT systems that can make decisions considering uncertainty of the system.

We believe that this proposal will radically change the course of IoT systems since it will not only allow decisions to be made within the system when they present emerging behaviors but will also use the objectives and the knowledge processed to properly guide the system, to meet its objectives thanks to GSO. Finally, we point out that the proposed systems open new opportunities to incorporate IoT in new fields.

REFERENCES

Bahati, R., & Gill, H. (2011). Cyber-physical Systems. *The Impact of Control Technology.*, *12*, 161–166.

Bahga, A., & Madisetti, V. (2014). *Internet of Things: A hands-on approach*. VPT.

Bonomi, F., Milito, R., Zhu, J., & Addepalli, S. (2012, August). Fog computing and its role in the internet of things. In *Proceedings of the first edition of the MCC workshop on Mobile cloud computing* (pp. 13-16). 10.1145/2342509.2342513

Butun, I., Sari, A., & Österberg, P. (2019, January). Security implications of fog computing on the internet of things. In *2019 IEEE International Conference on Consumer Electronics (ICCE)* (pp. 1-6). IEEE. 10.1109/ICCE.2019.8661909

Butun, I., Sari, A., & Österberg, P. (2020). Hardware Security of Fog End-Devices for the Internet of Things. *Sensors (Basel), 20*(20), 5729. doi:10.339020205729 PMID:33050165

Chen, H. (2017). Applications of Cyber-Physical System: A Literature Review. *Journal of Industrial Integration and Management, 2*(03), 1750012. doi:10.1142/S2424862217500129

Cisco, C. (2015). *Fog Computing and the Internet of Things: Extend the Cloud to Where the Things Are.* Available online: https://www.cisco.com/c/dam/en_us/solutions/trends/iot/docs/computing-overview.pdf

Comfort, L. K. (1994). Self-organization in complex systems. *Journal of Public Administration Research and Theory: J-PART, 4*(3), 393–410.

Computing, A. (2006). An architectural blueprint for autonomic computing. *IBM White Paper, 31*(2006), 1-6.

Gros, C. (2014). Generating functionals for guided self-organization. In *Guided self-organization: inception* (pp. 53–66). Springer. doi:10.1007/978-3-642-53734-9_3

Haken, H., & Portugali, J. (2017). Information and Self-Organization. *Entropy Journal. MDPI, 19*, 18.

ISO. (2018). *ISO/IEC 30141:2018 Internet of Things (IoT) – Reference Architecture.* https://www.iso.org/standard/65695.html

Kephart, J. O., & Chess, D. M. (2003). The vision of autonomic computing. *Computer, 36*(1), 41–50. doi:10.1109/MC.2003.1160055

Kocnehderfer, M. J. (2015). *Decision Making Under Uncertainty: Theory and Application.* MIT Lincoln Laboratory Press. doi:10.7551/mitpress/10187.001.0001

MacKay, D. (2010). *Information Theory, Inference, and Learning Algorithms.* Cambridge University Press.

Mitchell, M. (2009). *Complexity: A Guided Tour.* Oxford University Press.

Movahedi, Z., Ayari, M., Langar, R., & Pujolle, G. (2011). A survey of autonomic network architectures and evaluation criteria. *IEEE Communications Surveys and Tutorials, 14*(2), 464–490. doi:10.1109/SURV.2011.042711.00078

Nadkarni, M. G. (2010). *Basics of Shannon Entropy*. Mathematics Newsletter. Special Issue

Rajhans, A., Cheng, S. W., Schmerl, B., Garlan, D., Krogh, B. H., Agbi, C., & Bhave, A. (2009). An architectural approach to the design and analysis of cyber-physical systems. *Electronic Communications of the EASST*, 21.

Rajkumar, R. R., Lee, I., Sha, L., & Stankovic, J. (2010, June). Cyber-physical systems: The next computing revolution. In *Proc. 47th Design Automation Conf.* (pp. 731–736). IEEE.

Roca, D; Nemirovsky, D; Nemirovsly, M; Milito, R & Valero, M. (2016). Emergent Behaviors in the Internet of Things: The Ultimate Ultra-Large-Scale System. *IEEE Micro Journal, 36*(6).

Sari, A., Lekidis, A., & Butun, I. (2020). Industrial Networks and IIoT: Now and Future Trends. In *Industrial IoT* (pp. 3–55). Springer. doi:10.1007/978-3-030-42500-5_1

Sari, T., Güles, H. K., & Yiğitol, B. (2020). Awareness and Readiness of Industry 4.0: The case of Turkish Manufacturing Industry. *Advances in Production Engineering & Management (APEM) Journal, 15*, 57–68.

Sayama, H. (2015). *Introduction to the Modeling and Analysis of Complex Systems*. Open SUNY Textbooks.

Shannon, C. E. (1948). A Mathematical Theory of Communication. *The Bell System Technical Journal, 27*(3), 379–423, 623–656. doi:10.1002/j.1538-7305.1948.tb01338.x

Souza, M. L. H., da Costa, C., de Oliveira, G., & da Rosa, R. (2020). A Survey on Decision-Making Based on System Reliability in the Context of Industry 4.0. *Journal of Manufacturing Systems, 56*, 133–156. doi:10.1016/j.jmsy.2020.05.016

Villela, L. (2018). *Arquitectura y Algoritmo de Gestión para Redes IoT Autonómicas* [Lexical Characteristics of Spanish Language] [Master Thesis]. Centro de Investigación y de Estudios Avanzados del Instituto Politécnico Nacional (CINVESTAV) Unidad Guadalajara, Guadalajara, México.

Von Scheel, H. (2020). *Henrik von Scheel – Industry 4.0 originator*. http://von-scheel.com/industry40/

Yukalov, V & Sornette, D. (2014). Self-Organization in Complex Systems as Decision Making. *Advances in Complex Systems Journal, 17*(3), 1450016.

Zavala, L. E. V., García, A. O., & Siller, M. (2019, July). Architecture and Algorithm for IoT Autonomic Network Management. In *2019 International Conference on Internet of Things (iThings) and IEEE Green Computing and Communications (GreenCom) and IEEE Cyber, Physical and Social Computing (CPSCom) and IEEE Smart Data (SmartData)* (pp. 861-867). IEEE. 10.1109/iThings/GreenCom/CPSCom/SmartData.2019.00155

Zheng, P., Sang, Z., Zhong, R. Y., Liu, Y., Liu, C., Mubarok, K., ... Xu, X. (2018). Smart manufacturing systems for Industry 4.0: Conceptual framework, scenarios, and future perspectives. *Frontiers of Mechanical Engineering*, *13*(2), 137–150. doi:10.100711465-018-0499-5

KEY TERMS AND DEFINITIONS

Autonomic Computing: Includes self-sufficient computer systems, that is, capable of managing themselves using a set of objectives and the knowledge generated in real time of execution to know what to do in each situation.

Cyber-Physical Systems (CPS): Systems those integrate the physical part with the computational part and expand the capabilities of the physical environment in which they interact with the support of a network of sensors and actuators.

Emergent Behaviors: Series of behaviors that arise constantly in a complex system, many of these changes occur unexpectedly.

Entropy: It is a unit of measurement of the chaos and the content of the information available in a given system.

Guided Self-Organization (GSO): Enable Self-Organization taking into consideration the level of chaos of the system and its given goals.

Information: Product obtained from data processing, in which a meaning and purpose is given to each data.

Internet of Things (IoT): It is an infrastructure composed of one or multiple networks interconnected and composed of a set of elements with different properties that interact by collecting data and by means of actuators to achieve a set of previously specified goals.

Knowledge: Product obtained from information processing; it is used for future processing into the IoT system.

Objectives: Set of guidelines assigned by the administrator that the system must follow to fulfill the tasks it must do.

Self-Organization: Dynamic process belonging to complex systems in which the system changes behaviors to perform one or more tasks.

Uncertainty: Level of ignorance that users have about the processes that a system performs.

Utility Theory: Allows to analyze the possibilities that a system has to carry out a process and to know the level of benefit or prejudice that said change will bring with it when taking one or another action.

Compilation of References

AboBakr, A., & Azer, M.A. (2017). Iot ethics challenges and legal issues. *2017 12th International Conference on Computer Engineering and Systems (ICCES),* 233–237.

Accorsi, R., Manzini, R., & Maranesi, F. (2014). A decision-support system for the design and management of warehousing systems. *Computers in Industry, 65*(1), 175–186.

Achabal, D. D., McIntyre, S. H., Smith, S. A., & Kalyanam, K. (2000). A decision support system for vendor managed inventory. *Journal of Retailing, 76*(4), 430–454.

ADAC Vehicle Technology. (2019). *Motorcycles and cars tested by German automobile club.* ADAC.

Adebomehin, A. A., & Walker, S. D. (2016). Enhanced ultrawideband methods for 5g los sufficient positioning and mitigation. *2016 IEEE 17th International Symposium on A World of Wireless, Mobile and Multimedia Networks (WoWMoM),* 1–4.

Ahmed, N., Michelin, R. A., Xue, W., Ruj, S., Malaney, R., Kanhere, S. S., Seneviratne, A., Hu, W., Janicke, H., & Jha, S. K. (2020). A survey of covid-19 contact tracing apps. *IEEE Access: Practical Innovations, Open Solutions, 8,* 134577–134601. doi:10.1109/ACCESS.2020.3010226

Al Nuaimi, E., Al Neyadi, H., Mohamed, N., & Al-Jaroodi, J. (2015). *Applications of big data to smart cities.* Academic Press.

Al-Amri, M., Nicholas, K., Button, K., Sparkes, V., Sheeran, L., & Davies, J. L. (2018). Inertial measurement units for clinical movement analysis: Reliability and concurrent validity. *Sensors (Basel), 18*(3), 719.

Al-Faiz, M., Ali, A., & Miry, A. (2011). Human Arm Inverse Kinematic Solution Based Geometric Relations and Optimization Algorithm. *International Journal of Robotics and Automation, 2*(4), 245–255.

Aljumah, A., Kaur, A., Bhatia, M., & & Ahanger, T. (2020). *Internet of things-fog computing-based framework for smart disaster management.* Academic Press.

Allaoui, H., Guo, Y., & Sarkis, J. (2019). Decision support for collaboration planning in sustainable supply chains. *Journal of Cleaner Production, 229,* 761–774.

APDM. (n.d.). *APDM*. Retrieved 2021, from APDM Products: https://apdm.com/wearable-sensors/

Araniti, G., Campolo, C., Condoluci, M., Iera, A., & Molinaro, A. (2013). LTE for vehicular networking: A survey. *IEEE Communications Magazine*, *51*(5), 148–157. doi:10.1109/MCOM.2013.6515060

Aras, E., Ramachandran, G. S., Lawrence, P., & Hughes, D. (2017, June). Exploring the security vulnerabilities of LoRa. In *2017 3rd IEEE International Conference on Cybernetics (CYBCONF)* (pp. 1-6). IEEE. 10.1109/CYBConf.2017.7985777

Aras, E., Small, N., Ramachandran, G. S., Delbruel, S., Joosen, W., & Hughes, D. (2017, November). Selective jamming of LoRaWAN using commodity hardware. In *Proceedings of the 14th EAI International Conference on Mobile and Ubiquitous Systems: Computing, Networking and Services* (pp. 363-372). 10.1145/3144457.3144478

Arasteh, H., Hosseinnezhad, V., Loia, V., Tommasetti, A., Troisi, O., Shafie-khah, M., & Siano, P. (2016). *Iot-based smart cities: A survey.* Paper presented at the 2016 IEEE 16th International Conference on Environment and Electrical Engineering (EEEIC). 10.1109/EEEIC.2016.7555867

Aristidou, A., & Lasenby, J. (2013). Real-time marker prediction and CoR estimation in optical motion capture. *The Visual Computer*, *29*(1), 7–26.

Autoliv. (2000). *Autoliv and Volvo Launch New Safety System*. Press Release.

Aydogan, E., Yilmaz, S., Sen, S., Butun, I., Forsström, S., & Gidlund, M. (2019, May). A central intrusion detection system for RPL-based Industrial Internet of Things. In *2019 15th IEEE International Workshop on Factory Communication Systems (WFCS)* (pp. 1-5). IEEE.

Bahati, R., & Gill, H. (2011). Cyber-physical Systems. *The Impact of Control Technology.*, *12*, 161–166.

Bahga, A., & Madisetti, V. (2014). *Internet of Things: A hands-on approach*. VPT.

Baruffaldi, G., Accorsi, R., & Manzini, R. (2019). Warehouse management system customization and information availability in 3pl companies. *Industrial Management & Data Systems*.

Bergmann, J. H., Mayagoitia, R. E., & Smith, I. C. (2009). A portable system for collecting anatomical joint angles during stair ascent: A comparison with an optical tracking device. *Dynamic Medicine*, *8*(1), 3.

Biswas, K., & Muthukkumarasamy, V. (2016). *Securing smart cities using blockchain technology.* Paper presented at the 2016 IEEE 18th international conference on high performance computing and communications; IEEE 14th international conference on smart city; IEEE 2nd international conference on data science and systems (HPCC/SmartCity/DSS). 10.1109/HPCC-SmartCity-DSS.2016.0198

BLENDER. (n.d.). *Blender*. Retrieved 2021, from https://www.blender.org/

Bonomi, F., Milito, R., Zhu, J., & Addepalli, S. (2012, August). Fog computing and its role in the internet of things. In *Proceedings of the first edition of the MCC workshop on Mobile cloud computing* (pp. 13-16). 10.1145/2342509.2342513

Brent. (n.d.). *By 2030, each person will own 15 connected devices — here's what that means for your business and content.* https://www.martechadvisor.com/articles/iot/by-2030-each-person-will-own-15-connected\-devices-heres-what-that-means-for-your\-business-and-content

Brous, P., Janssen, M., & Herder, P. (2020). The dual effects of the internet of things (iot): A systematic review of the benefits and risks of iot adoption by organizations. *International Journal of Information Management, 51*, 101952. doi:10.1016/j.ijinfomgt.2019.05.008

Butun, I. (2013). *Prevention and detection of intrusions in wireless sensor networks* (Ph.D. Thesis). University of South Florida.

Butun, I., dos Santos, D., Lekidis, A., & Papatriantafilou, M. (2020). *Deliverable 3.4 Adaptive and Continuous Intrusion and Anomaly Detection for Smart Grid Systems.* United Grid, H2020 Project deliverable.

Butun, I., Lekidis, A., & dos Santos, D. R. (2020). Security and Privacy in Smart Grids: Challenges, Current Solutions and Future Opportunities. In ICISSP (pp. 733-741). Academic Press.

Butun, I., Lekidis, A., & dos Santos, D. R. (2020). *Security and Privacy in Smart Grids: Challenges, Current Solutions and Future Opportunities.* Paper presented at the ICISSP. 10.5220/0009187307330741

Butun, I., Lekidis, A., & dos Santos, D. R. (2020). Security and Privacy in Smart Grids: Challenges, Current Solutions, and Future Opportunities. In ICISSP (pp. 733-741). Academic Press.

Butun, I., Sari, A., & Österberg, P. (2019). *Security implications of fog computing on the internet of things.* Paper presented at the 2019 IEEE International Conference on Consumer Electronics (ICCE). 10.1109/ICCE.2019.8661909

Butun, I., Sari, A., & Österberg, P. (2019, January). *Security implications of fog computing on the internet of things.* Academic Press.

Butun, I., Almgren, M., Gulisano, V., & Papatriantafilou, M. (2020). Intrusion Detection in Industrial Networks via Data Streaming. In *Industrial IoT* (pp. 213–238). Springer. doi:10.1007/978-3-030-42500-5_6

Butun, I., Morgera, S. D., & Sankar, R. (2014). A survey of intrusion detection systems in wireless sensor networks. *IEEE Communications Surveys and Tutorials, 16*(1), 266–282. doi:10.1109/SURV.2013.050113.00191

Butun, I., & Österberg, P. (2019). Detecting intrusions in cyber-physical systems of smart cities: Challenges and directions. In *Secure Cyber-Physical Systems for Smart Cities* (pp. 74–102). IGI Global. doi:10.4018/978-1-5225-7189-6.ch004

Butun, I., & Österberg, P. (2020). A Review of Distributed Access Control for Blockchain Systems towards Securing the Internet of Things. *IEEE Access: Practical Innovations, Open Solutions.*

Butun, I., Österberg, P., & Song, H. (2019). Security of the Internet of Things: Vulnerabilities, attacks, and countermeasures. *IEEE Communications Surveys and Tutorials, 22*(1), 616–644. doi:10.1109/COMST.2019.2953364

Butun, I., Pereira, N., & Gidlund, M. (2018). Analysis of lorawan v1.1 security. *Proceedings of the 4th ACM Mobi Hoc Workshop on Experiences with the Design and Implementation of Smart Objects*, 1–6.

Butun, I., Pereira, N., & Gidlund, M. (2019). Security risk analysis of lorawan and future directions. *Future Internet, 11*(1), 3. doi:10.3390/fi11010003

Butun, I., Ra, I. H., & Sankar, R. (2015). An intrusion detection system based on multi-level clustering for hierarchical wireless sensor networks. *Sensors (Basel), 15*(11), 28960–28978. doi:10.3390151128960 PMID:26593915

Butun, I., Sari, A., & Österberg, P. (2020). *Hardware Security of Fog End-Devices for the Internet of Things*. Academic Press.

Butun, I., Sari, A., & Österberg, P. (2020). Hardware Security of Fog End-Devices for the Internet of Things. *Sensors (Basel), 20*(20), 5729. doi:10.339020205729 PMID:33050165

Carron, X., Bosua, R., Maynard, S., & Ahmad, A. (2016). The internet of things and its impact on individual privacy: An australian privacy principle perspective. *Computer Law & Security Review, 21*(1), 4–15. doi:10.1016/j.clsr.2015.12.001

Carter, E., Adam, P., Tsakis, D., Shaw, S., Watson, R., & Ryan, P. (2020). *Enhancing pedestrian mobility in smart cities using big data*. Academic Press.

Catherwood, P. A., Rafferty, J., McComb, S., & McLaughlin, J. (2018). Lpwan wearable intelligent healthcare monitoring for heart failure prevention. *Proceedings of the 32nd International BCS Human Computer Interaction Conference 32*, 1–4. 10.14236/ewic/HCI2018.126

Ceseracciu, E., Sawacha, Z., & Cobelli, C. (2014). Comparison of markerless and marker-based motion capture technologies through simultaneous data collection during gait: Proof of concept. *PLoS One, 9*(3), e87640.

Chaudhari, B. S., Zennaro, M., & Borkar, S. (2020). LPWAN technologies: Emerging application characteristics, requirements, and design considerations. *Future Internet, 12*(3), 46. doi:10.3390/fi12030046

Check Point. (n.d.). *What is a cyber attack?* https://www.checkpoint.com/cyber-hub/cyber-security/what-is-cyber-attack/

Checkoway, S., McCoy, D., Kantor, B., Anderson, D., Shacham, H., Savage, S., Koscher, K., Czeskis, A., Roesner, F., & Kohno, T. (2011). *Comprehensive experimental analyses of automotive attack surfaces*. Academic Press.

Chen, Y., & Han, D. (2018). *Water quality monitoring in smart city: A pilot project.* Academic Press.

Chen, H. (2017). Applications of Cyber-Physical System: A Literature Review. *Journal of Industrial Integration and Management, 2*(03), 1750012. doi:10.1142/S2424862217500129

Chi-Chun, L., & Yu-Jen, C. (1999). Secure communication mechanisms for gsm networks. *IEEE Transactions on Consumer Electronics, 45*(4), 1074–1080. doi:10.1109/30.809184

Cisco, C. (2015). *Fog Computing and the Internet of Things: Extend the Cloud to Where the Things Are.* Available online: https://www.cisco.com/c/dam/en_us/solutions/trends/iot/docs/computing-overview.pdf

Clohessy, T., Acton, T., & Morgan, L. (2014). *Smart city as a service (SCaaS): A future roadmap for e-government smart city cloud computing initiatives.* Paper presented at the 2014 IEEE/ACM 7th International Conference on Utility and Cloud Computing. 10.1109/UCC.2014.136

Čolaković, A., Čaušević, S., Kosovac, A., & Muharemović, E. (2020, June). A Review of Enabling Technologies and Solutions for IoT Based Smart Warehouse Monitoring System. In *International Conference "New Technologies, Development and Applications"* (pp. 630-637). Springer.

Coman, F. L., Malarski, K. M., Petersen, M. N., & Ruepp, S. (2019, June). Security issues in internet of things: Vulnerability analysis of LoRaWAN, sigfox and NB-IoT. In *2019 Global IoT Summit (GIoTS)* (pp. 1-6). IEEE.

Comfort, L. K. (1994). Self-organization in complex systems. *Journal of Public Administration Research and Theory: J-PART, 4*(3), 393–410.

Computing, A. (2006). An architectural blueprint for autonomic computing. *IBM White Paper, 31*(2006), 1-6.

Corbett, C., Schoch, E., Kargl, F., & Preussner, F. (2016). Automotive Ethernet: security opportunity or challenge? In Sicherheit 2016 - Sicherheit, Schutz und Zuverlässigkeit. Bonn: Gesellschaft für Informatik e.V.

Cornacchia, M., Ozcan, K., Zheng, Y., & Velipasalar, S. (2016). A survey on activity detection and classification using wearable sensors. *IEEE Sensors Journal, 17*(2), 386–403.

Cui, Y., Liu, H., Zhang, M., Stankovski, S., Feng, J., & Zhang, X. (2018). Improving Intelligence and Efficiency of Salt Lake Production by Applying a Decision Support System Based on IOT for Brine Pump Management. *Electronics (Basel), 7*(8), 147. doi:10.3390/electronics7080147

Danish, S. M., Nasir, A., Qureshi, H. K., Ashfaq, A. B., Mumtaz, S., & Rodriguez, J. (2018, May). Network intrusion detection system for jamming attack in lorawan join procedure. In *2018 IEEE International Conference on Communications (ICC)* (pp. 1-6). IEEE. 10.1109/ICC.2018.8422721

Dariush, B. (2003). Human motion analysis for biomechanics and biomedicine. *Machine Vision and Applications, 14*(4), 202–205. doi:10.100700138-002-0108-8

Das, S., Trutoiu, L., Murai, A., Alcindor, D., Oh, M., De la Torre, F., & Hodgins, J. (2011, August). Quantitative measurement of motor symptoms in Parkinson's disease: A study with full-body motion capture data. *2011 Annual International Conference of the IEEE Engineering in Medicine and Biology Society*, 6789-6792. 10.1109/IEMBS.2011.6091674

Davis, G. (2018). 2020: Life with 50 billion connected devices. *2018 IEEE International Conference on Consumer Electronics (ICCE)*, 1–1. 10.1109/ICCE.2018.8326056

Davison, A. J., Deutscher, J., & Reid, I. D. (2001). Markerless motion capture of complex full-body movement for character animation. Computer Animation and Simulation 2001, 3-14.

De Los Santos, H., Sturm, C., & Pontes, P. (2015). Introduction to Radio Systems. Springer. doi:10.1007/978-3-319-07326-2_1

Decawave. (2019). *Our Technology*. https://www.decawave.com/technology1/

Decuir, J. (2010). Bluetooth 4.0: low energy. Cambridge, UK: Cambridge Silicon Radio SR plc.

del Peral-Rosado, A. J., Raulefs, R., Lopez-Salcedo, J., & Seco-Granados, G. (2017). Survey of cellular mobile radio localization methods: From 1g to 5g. IEEE Communications Surveys & Tutorials, 20(2), 1124–1148.

Delrobaei, M., Memar, S., Pieterman, M., Stratton, T. W., McIsaac, K., & Jog, M. (2018). Towards remote monitoring of Parkinson's disease tremor using wearable motion capture systems. *Journal of the Neurological Sciences*, *384*, 38–45. doi:10.1016/j.jns.2017.11.004 PMID:29249375

Dibaei, M., Zheng, X., Jiang, K., Abbas, R., Liu, S., Zhang, Y., Xiang, Y., & Yu, S. (2020). Attacks and defences on intelligent connected vehicles: A survey. *Digital Communications and Networks*, *6*(4), 399–421. doi:10.1016/j.dcan.2020.04.007

Drozhzhin, A. (2019, November 15). *Black Hat USA 2015: The full story of how that Jeep was hacked*. Kaspersky Official Blog. https://www.kaspersky.com/blog/blackhat-jeep-cherokee-hack-explained/9493/

Drummond, R. R., Marques, B. A., Vasconcelos, C. N., & Clua, E. (2018). International Conference on Computer Graphics Theory and Applications. *PEEK: An LSTM Recurrent Network for Motion Classiðcation from Sparse Data*, 215-222.

Eldefrawy, M., Butun, I., Pereira, N., & Gidlund, M. (2019). Formal security analysis of lorawan. *Computer Networks*, *148*, 328–339. doi:10.1016/j.comnet.2018.11.017

El-Rewini, Z., Sadatsharan, K., Selvaraj, D. F., Plathottam, S. J., & Ranganathan, P. (2020). Cybersecurity challenges in vehicular communications. *Vehicular Communications*, *23*, 100214. doi:10.1016/j.vehcom.2019.100214

Endsley, M. R., & Jones, D. G. (2016). *Designing for situation awareness: An approach to user-centered design*. CRC Press.

Compilation of References

European Commission. (2020). *Smartcities.* https://ec.europa.eu/info/eu-regional-and-urban-development/topics/cities-and-urban-development/city-initiatives/smart-cities_en

Everis. (2015). *Everis connected car report.* Author.

Fieldbus. (2021). *Process Industry Forum, acquired: 13/2/2021, "What is Fieldbus?"* https://www.processindustryforum.com/article/what-is-fieldbus

Field, M., Stirling, D., Naghdy, F., & Pan, Z. (2009, December). Motion capture in robotics review. *2009 IEEE International Conference on Control and Automation*, 1697-1702.

Fikar, C. (2018). A decision support system to investigate food losses in e-grocery deliveries. *Computers & Industrial Engineering, 117,* 282–290.

Filippeschi, A., Schmitz, N., Miezal, M., Bleser, G., Ruffaldi, E., & Stricker, D. (2017). Survey of motion tracking methods based on inertial sensors: A focus on upper limb human motion. *Sensors (Basel), 17*(6), 1257.

Formisano, C., Pavia, D., Gurgen, L., Yonezawa, T., Galache, J. A., Doguchi, K., & Matranga, I. (2015). *The advantages of IoT and cloud applied to smart cities.* Paper presented at the 2015 3rd International Conference on Future Internet of Things and Cloud. 10.1109/FiCloud.2015.85

Forsström, S., Butun, I., Eldefrawy, M., Jennehag, U., & Gidlund, M. (2018, April). Challenges of securing the industrial internet of things value chain. In *2018 Workshop on Metrology for Industry 4.0 and IoT* (pp. 218-223). IEEE. 10.1109/METROI4.2018.8428344

Frost, S. (n.d.). *Growing industry applications of lpwan technologies.* https://rfdesignuk.com/uploads/9/4/6/0/94609530/murata_lpwan_study.pdf

Gaur, A., Scotney, B., Parr, G., & McClean, S. (2015). *Smart city architecture and its applications based on IoT.* Academic Press.

Gill, S. S., Arya, R. C., Wander, G. S., & Buyya, R. (2018). *Fog-based smart healthcare as a big data and cloud service for heart patients using IoT.* Paper presented at the International Conference on Intelligent Data Communication Technologies and Internet of Things.

Gómez, J. C. O., Duque, D. F. M., Rivera, L., & García-Alcaraz, J. L. (2017). Decision support system for operational risk management in supply chain with 3PL providers. In *Current trends on knowledge-based systems* (pp. 205–222). Springer. doi:10.1007/978-3-319-51905-0_10

Gong, X. (2019). *Security threats and countermeasures for connected vehicles.* Academic Press.

Gopinath, M., Tamizharasi, G., Kavisankar, L., Sathyaraj, R., Karthi, S., & Aarthy, S. (2019). *A secure cloud-based solution for real-time monitoring and management of Internet of underwater things (IOUT).* Academic Press.

Greenberg, A. (2015, July 21). Hackers Remotely Kill a Jeep on the Highway—With Me in It. *Wired.* https://www.wired.com/2015/07/hackers-remotely-kill-jeep-highway/

Gresak, E., & Voznak, M. (2018, September). Protecting gateway from abp replay attack on lorawan. In *International Conference on Advanced Engineering Theory and Applications* (pp. 400-408). Springer.

Gros, C. (2014). Generating functionals for guided self-organization. In *Guided self-organization: inception* (pp. 53–66). Springer. doi:10.1007/978-3-642-53734-9_3

Groza, B., & Murvay, S. (2013). Efficient Protocols for Secure Broadcast in Controller Area Networks. *IEEE Transactions on Industrial Informatics*, *9*(4), 2034–2042. doi:10.1109/TII.2013.2239301

GSM Alliance. (2020). *Mobile IoT Deployment Map.* https://www.gsma.com/iot/deployment-map/#deployments

GSM Association. (2018). *Mobile iot in the 5g future – nb-iot and lte-m in the context of 5g.* https://www.gsma.com/iot/resources/mobile-iot-5g-future/

Güemes, C., Janeczko, J., Caminel, T., & Roberts, M. (2013). *Data analytics as a service: unleashing the power of cloud and big data.* White paper.

Guerra-Filho, G. (2005). Optical Motion Capture: Theory and Implementation. *Research Initiative, Treatment Action*, *12*(2), 61–90.

Gu, X., Zhang, Y., Sun, W., Bian, Y., Zhou, D., & Kristensson, P. O. (2016, May). Dexmo: An inexpensive and lightweight mechanical exoskeleton for motion capture and force feedback in VR. *Proceedings of the 2016 CHI Conference on Human Factors in Computing Systems*, 1991-1995.

Haken, H., & Portugali, J. (2017). Information and Self-Organization. *Entropy Journal. MDPI, 19*, 18.

Hammi, B., Khatoun, R., Zeadally, S., Fayad, A., & Khoukhi, L. (2017). *IoT technologies for smart cities.* Academic Press.

Hansen, C., Gosselin, F., Mansour, K. B., Devos, P., & Marin, F. (2018). Design-validation of a hand exoskeleton using musculoskeletal modeling. *Applied Ergonomics*, *68*, 283–288.

Hardt, D. (2012). *The OAuth 2.0 authorization framework.* https://tools.ietf.org/html/rfc6749#section-1.4

Harshadeep, N. R., & Young, W. (2020). *Disruptive Technologies for Improving Water Security in Large River Basins.* Academic Press.

Hashem, I. A. T., Chang, V., Anuar, N. B., Adewole, K., Yaqoob, I., Gani, A., . . . Chiroma, H. (2016). *The role of big data in smart city.* Academic Press.

HAVELSAN. (n.d.). *HAVELSAN.* Retrieved 2021, from HAVELSAN Products: https://www.havelsan.com.tr/en

Hernandez, G., Valles, D., Wierschem, D. C., Koldenhoven, R. M., Koutitas, G., Mendez, F. A., . . . Jimenez, J. (2020, January). Machine Learning Techniques for Motion Analysis of Fatigue from Manual Material Handling Operations Using 3D Motion Capture Data. *2020 10th Annual Computing and Communication Workshop and Conference*, 300-305.

Hossain, M. M., Fotouhi, M., & Hasan, R. (2015). Towards an analysis of security issues, challenges, and open problems in the internet of things. *2015 IEEE World Congress on Services*, 21–28. 10.1109/SERVICES.2015.12

Hunt, T. (2016). *Controlling vehicle features of Nissan LEAFs across the globe via vulnerable APIs*. https://www.troyhunt.com/controlling-vehicle-features-of-nissan/

Hu, Z. H., & Sheng, Z. H. (2014). A decision support system for public logistics information service management and optimization. *Decision Support Systems*, *59*, 219–229.

Ingham, M., Marchang, J., & Bhowmik, D. (2020). IoT security vulnerabilities and predictive signal jamming attack analysis in LoRaWAN. *IET Information Security*, *14*(4), 368–379. doi:10.1049/iet-ifs.2019.0447

Islam, S. M. R., Kwak, D., Kabir, M. H., Hossain, M., & Kwak, K. (2015). The internet of things for health care: A comprehensive survey. *IEEE Access: Practical Innovations, Open Solutions*, *3*, 678–708. doi:10.1109/ACCESS.2015.2437951

ISO. (2018). *ISO/IEC 30141:2018 Internet of Things (IoT) – Reference Architecture*. https://www.iso.org/standard/65695.html

Jasek, S. (2015). *Connected car security threat analysis and recommendations*. Securing. https://www.securing.pl/wp-content/uploads/2015/10/SecuRing-Connected-Car-Security-Threat-Analysis-and-Recommendations.pdf

Jeong, J.-S., Kim, M., & Yoo, K. (2013). *A content oriented smart education system based on cloud computing*. Academic Press.

Ji, Z., Ganchev, I., O'Droma, M., & Zhang, X. (2014). *A cloud-based intelligent car parking services for smart cities*. Paper presented at the 2014 XXXIth URSI General Assembly and Scientific Symposium (URSI GASS). 10.1109/URSIGASS.2014.6929280

Jiang, J., Tang, S., Han, D., Fu, G., Solomatine, D., & Zheng, Y. (2020). *A comprehensive review on the design and optimization of surface water quality monitoring networks*. Academic Press.

Karnouskos, S. (2011, November). Stuxnet worm impact on industrial cyber-physical system security. In *IECON 2011-37th Annual Conference of the IEEE Industrial Electronics Society* (pp. 4490-4494). IEEE.

Kelarestaghi, K. B., Foruhandeh, M., Heaslip, K., & Gerdes, R. (2019). Intelligent Transportation System Security: Impact-Oriented Risk Assessment of In-Vehicle Networks. *IEEE Intelligent Transportation Systems Magazine*, *1*. Advance online publication. doi:10.1109/MITS.2018.2889714

Kephart, J. O., & Chess, D. M. (2003). The vision of autonomic computing. *Computer*, *36*(1), 41–50. doi:10.1109/MC.2003.1160055

Khalajmehrabadi, A., Gatsis, N., & Akopian, D. (2017). Modern wlan fingerprinting indoor positioning methods and deployment challenges. *IEEE Communications Surveys and Tutorials*, *19*(3), 1974–2002. doi:10.1109/COMST.2017.2671454

Khalel, M. H. A. (2010). Position location techniques in wireless communication systems. Blekinge Institute of Technology Karlskrona, Sweden.

Khan, Z., & Kiani, S. L. (2012). *A cloud-based architecture for citizen services in smart cities.* Paper presented at the 2012 IEEE Fifth International Conference on Utility and Cloud Computing. 10.1109/UCC.2012.43

Khan, M. A., & Salah, K. (2018). Iot security: Review, blockchain solutions, and open challenges. *Future Generation Computer Systems*, *82*, 395–411. doi:10.1016/j.future.2017.11.022

Kilgallin, J., & Vasko, R. (2019, December). Factoring RSA Keys in the IoT Era. In *2019 First IEEE International Conference on Trust, Privacy and Security in Intelligent Systems and Applications (TPS-ISA)* (pp. 184-189). IEEE. 10.1109/TPS-ISA48467.2019.00030

Kirk, J. (n.d.). *Study: IoT Devices Have Alarmingly Weak RSA Keys.* Technical report, bankinfosecurity.

Kitagawa, M., & Windsor, B. (2020). *MoCap for artists: workflow and techniques for motion capture.* CRC Press.

Kitchin, R. (2016). The ethics of smart cities and urban science. *Philosophical Transactions - Royal Society. Mathematical, Physical, and Engineering Sciences*, *374*(2083), 20160115. doi:10.1098/rsta.2016.0115 PMID:28336794

Knippenberg, E., Verbrugghe, J., Lamers, I., Palmaers, S., Timmermans, A., & Spooren, A. (2017). Markerless motion capture systems as training device in neurological rehabilitation: A systematic review of their use, application, target population and efficacy. *Journal of Neuroengineering and Rehabilitation*, *14*(1), 1–11. doi:10.118612984-017-0270-x PMID:28646914

Kocnehderfer, M. J. (2015). *Decision Making Under Uncertainty: Theory and Application.* MIT Lincoln Laboratory Press. doi:10.7551/mitpress/10187.001.0001

Koivisto, M., Hakkarainen, A., Costa, M., Kela, P., Leppanen, K., & Valkama, M. (2017). High-efficiency device positioning and location-aware communications in dense 5g networks. *IEEE Communications Magazine*, *55*(8), 188–195. doi:10.1109/MCOM.2017.1600655

Krejčí, R., Hujňák, O., & Švepeš, M. (2017, November). Security survey of the IoT wireless protocols. In *2017 25th Telecommunication Forum (TELFOR)* (pp. 1-4). IEEE. 10.1109/TELFOR.2017.8249286

Kuipers, J. B. (1999). *Quaternions and rotation sequences* (Vol. 66). Princeton university press.

Kumar, D. S., Askarunisa, A., & Kumar, R. (2020). *Embedded processor based automated assessment of quality of the water in an IoT background.* Academic Press.

Lambrinos, L. (2019). Internet of Things in Agriculture: A Decision Support System for Precision Farming. In 2019 IEEE Intl Conf on Dependable, Autonomic and Secure Computing, Intl Conf on Pervasive Intelligence and Computing, Intl Conf on Cloud and Big Data Computing, Intl Conf on Cyber Science and Technology Congress (DASC/PiCom/CBDCom/CyberSciTech) (pp. 889-892). IEEE. doi:10.1109/DASC/PiCom/CBDCom/CyberSciTech.2019.00163

Lam, C. H., Choy, K. L., & Chung, S. H. (2011). A decision support system to facilitate warehouse order fulfillment in cross-border supply chain. *Journal of Manufacturing Technology Management, 22*(8), 972–983. doi:10.1108/17410381111177430

Lao, S. I., Choy, K. L., Ho, G. T. S., Tsim, Y. C., & Lee, C. K. H. (2011). Real-time inbound decision support system for enhancing the performance of a food warehouse. *Journal of Manufacturing Technology Management, 22*(8), 1014–1031. doi:10.1108/17410381111177467

Latorre, J., Colomer, C., Alcañiz, M., & Llorens, R. (2019). Gait analysis with the Kinect v2: Normative study with healthy individuals and comprehensive study of its sensitivity, validity, and reliability in individuals with stroke. *Journal of Neuroengineering and Rehabilitation, 16*(1), 1–11.

Latre, S., Leroux, P., Coenen, T., Braem, B., Ballon, P., & Demeester, P. (2016). City of things: An integrated and multi-technology testbed for iot smart city experiments. *2016 IEEE International Smart Cities Conference (ISC2),* 1–8.

Leccese, F., Cagnetti, M., Giarnetti, S., Petritoli, E., Luisetto, I., Tuti, S., . . . Bursić, V. (2018). *A simple takagi-sugeno fuzzy modelling case study for an underwater glider control system.* Paper presented at the 2018 IEEE International Workshop on Metrology for the Sea; Learning to Measure Sea Health Parameters (MetroSea). 10.1109/MetroSea.2018.8657877

Lee, C. K. M., Lv, Y., Ng, K. K. H., Ho, W., & Choy, K. L. (2018). Design and application of Internet of things-based warehouse management system for smart logistics. *International Journal of Production Research, 56*(8), 2753–2768. doi:10.1080/00207543.2017.1394592

Liao, W. L., & Tsai, F. J. (2013). Personalized medicine: A paradigm shift in healthcare. *Biomedicine (Taipei), 3*(2), 66–72. doi:10.1016/j.biomed.2012.12.005

Lin, C.-W., & Sangiovanni-Vincentelli, A. (2012). Cyber-Security for the Controller Area Network (CAN) Communication Protocol. *2012 International Conference on Cyber Security,* 1–7. 10.1109/CyberSecurity.2012.7

Li, S., You, X., & Sun, Z. (2020). Drug Management System Based on RFID. In *Data Processing Techniques and Applications for Cyber-Physical Systems (DPTA 2019)* (pp. 1955–1958). Springer.

LIS3MDL. (n.d.). *LIS3MDL.* Retrieved 2021, from https://www.st.com/en/mems-and-sensors/lis3mdl.html

Liu, H., Darabi, H., Banerjee, P., & Liu, J. (2007). Survey of wireless indoor positioning techniques and systems. *IEEE Transactions on Systems, Man and Cybernetics. Part C, Applications and Reviews, 37*(6), 1067–1080. doi:10.1109/TSMCC.2007.905750

Lora Alliance. (2015). *LoRaWAN 1.0 Specification*. Author.

Lora Alliance. (2017). *LoRaWAN 1.1 Specification*. LoRa Alliance Technical Committee.

Lora Alliance. (2017). *LorawanTM1.1 specification*. https://lora-alliance.org/resource-hub/lorawanr-specification-v11

LoRa Alliance. (2020). *Smartcities*. https://lora-alliance.org/lorawan-vertical-markets/cities

MacKay, D. (2010). *Information Theory, Inference, and Learning Algorithms*. Cambridge University Press.

Madgwick, S. (2010). *An efficient orientation filter for inertial and inertial/magnetic sensor arrays*. Academic Press.

Madgwick, S. O., Harrison, A. J., & Vaidyanathan, R. (2011, June). Estimation of IMU and MARG orientation using a gradient descent algorithm. *2011. IEEE International Conference on Rehabilitation Robotics*, 1–7.

Mandal, Cortesi, Ferrara, Panarotto, & Spoto. (2018). *Vulnerability analysis of android auto infotainment apps*. Academic Press.

Mårlind, F., & Butun, I. (2020, October). Activation of LoRaWAN end devices by using Public Key Cryptography. In *2020 4th Cyber Security in Networking Conference (CSNet)* (pp. 1-8). IEEE.

Martín, A. C., Alario-Hoyos, C., & Kloos, C. D. (2019). *Smart education: a review and future research directions*. Paper presented at the Multidisciplinary Digital Publishing Institute Proceedings. 10.3390/proceedings2019031057

Massobrio, R., Nesmachnow, S., Tchernykh, A., Avetisyan, A., & Radchenko, G. (2018). *Towards a cloud computing paradigm for big data analysis in smart cities*. Academic Press.

Ma, Y., Mithraratne, K., Wilson, N. C., Wang, X., Ma, Y., & Zhang, Y. (2019). The validity and reliability of a kinect v2-based gait analysis system for children with cerebral palsy. *Sensors (Basel), 19*(7), 1660.

Mayankutty, S. C., & Sereti, A. (2017). *Security modelling in automotive industry*. https://odr.chalmers.se/handle/20.500.12380/250232

Mazloom, S., Rezaeirad, M., Hunter, A., & McCoy, D. (2016). *A security analysis of an in vehicle infotainment and app platform*. Academic Press.

Mekki, K., Bajic, E., Chaxel, F., & Meyer, F. (2019). A comparative study of lpwan technologies for large scale iot deployment. *ICT Express, 5*(1), 1–7.

Menache, A. (2000). *Understanding motion capture for computer animation and video games.* Morgan Kaufmann.

Merriaux, P., Dupuis, Y., Boutteau, R., Vasseur, P., & Savatier, X. (2017). A study of vicon system positioning performance. *Sensors (Basel)*, *17*(7), 1591.

Miller, C. (2015). *Remote exploitation of an unaltered passenger vehicle.* http://illmatics.com/Remote%20Car%20Hacking.pdf

Min, H. (2009). Application of a decision support system to strategic warehousing decisions. *International Journal of Physical Distribution & Logistics Management*, *39*(4), 270–281. doi:10.1108/09600030910962230

Mistry, H. (2019). *Jaguar Land Rover models are the only cars immune to keyless entry attacks.* Academic Press.

Mitchell, M. (2009). *Complexity: A Guided Tour.* Oxford University Press.

Mitton, N., Papavassiliou, S., Puliafito, A., & Trivedi, K. S. (2012). *Combining Cloud and sensors in a smart city environment.* SpringerOpen. doi:10.1186/1687-1499-2012-247

Mohammadi, M., & Al-Fuqaha, A. (2018). *Enabling cognitive smart cities using big data and machine learning: Approaches and challenges.* Academic Press.

Movahedi, Z., Ayari, M., Langar, R., & Pujolle, G. (2011). A survey of autonomic network architectures and evaluation criteria. *IEEE Communications Surveys and Tutorials*, *14*(2), 464–490. doi:10.1109/SURV.2011.042711.00078

Munoz, D., Bouchereau Lara, F., Vargas, C., & Enriquez-Caldera, R. (2009). *Position location techniques and applications.* Academic Press.

Murvay, P. S., & Groza, B. (2018, October). Practical Security Exploits of the FlexRay In-Vehicle Communication Protocol. In *International Conference on Risks and Security of Internet and Systems* (pp. 172-187). Springer.

Nadkarni, M. G. (2010). *Basics of Shannon Entropy.* Mathematics Newsletter. Special Issue

Navani, D., Jain, S., & Nehra, M. S. (2017). The internet of things (iot): A study of architectural elements. *2017 13th International Conference on Signal-Image Technology Internet-Based Systems (SITIS)*, 473–478.

NDI. (n.d.). *Northern Digital Inc.* Retrieved 2021, from NDI Products: https://www.ndigital.com/products/legacy-products/

Nikolov, R., Shoikova, E., Krumova, M., Kovatcheva, E., Dimitrov, V., & Shikalanov, A. (2016). *Learning in a smart city environment.* Academic Press.

Nogueria, P. (2011). Motion capture fundamentals. *Doctoral Symposium in Informatics Engineering*, 303-314.

O'Brien, J. F., Bodenheimer, R. E. Jr, Brostow, G. J., & Hodgins, J. K. (1999). *Automatic joint parameter estimation from magnetic motion capture data*. Georgia Institute of Technology.

OPTITRACK. (n.d.). *OPTITRACK*. Retrieved 2021, from OPTITRACK Products: https://optitrack.com/

Osman, A. (2019). *A novel big data analytics framework for smart cities*. Academic Press.

Osman, A. M. S., Elragal, A., & Bergvall-Kåreborn, B. (2017). *Big Data Analytics and Smart Cities: A Loose or Tight Couple?* Paper presented at the 10th International Conference on Connected Smart Cities 2017 (CSC 2017), Lisbon, Portugal.

Panwar, M., Biswas, D., Bajaj, H., Jöbges, M., Turk, R., Maharatna, K., & Acharyya, A. (2019, February 18). Rehab-Net: Deep Learning framework for Arm Movement Classification using Wearable Sensors for Stroke Rehabilitation. *IEEE Transactions on Biomedical Engineering*, *66*(11), 3026–3037. doi:10.1109/TBME.2019.2899927

Perlroth, N., & Krauss, C. (n.d.). A cyberattack in saudi arabia had a deadly goal, experts fear another try. *The New York Times*.

PHASESPACE. (n.d.). *PHASESPACE*. Retrieved 2021, from PHASESPACE Products: https://www.phasespace.com/

Ponemon Institute. (2018). *Securing the modern Vehicle:A study of automotive industry cybersecurity practices.* https://www.synopsys.com/content/dam/synopsys/sig-assets/reports/securing-the-modern-vehicle.pdf

Pons-Moll, G., Baak, A. H., Müller, M., Seidel, H. P., & Rosenhahn, B. (2010, June). Multisensor-fusion for 3d full-body human motion capture. *2010 IEEE Computer Society Conference on Computer Vision and Pattern Recognition*, 663-670.

Porretta, M., Nepa, P., Manara, G., & Giannetti, F. (2008). Location, location, location. *IEEE Vehicular Technology Magazine*, *3*(2), 20–29. doi:10.1109/MVT.2008.923969

Power, D. J. (2008). Decision support systems: a historical overview. In *Handbook on decision support systems 1* (pp. 121–140). Springer.

QUALISYS. (n.d.). *QUALISYS*. Retrieved 2021, from QUALISYS Products: https://www.qualisys.com/

Quwaider, M., & Jararweh, Y. (2015). *Cloudlet-based efficient data collection in wireless body area networks*. Academic Press.

Quwaider, M., Al-Alyyoub, M., & Jararweh, Y. (2016). *Cloud support data management infrastructure for upcoming smart cities*. Academic Press.

Rahul, M. (2018). Review on motion capture technology. *Global Journal of Computer Science and Technology*, *18*, 23–26.

Rajhans, A., Cheng, S. W., Schmerl, B., Garlan, D., Krogh, B. H., Agbi, C., & Bhave, A. (2009). An architectural approach to the design and analysis of cyber-physical systems. *Electronic Communications of the EASST*, 21.

Rajkumar, R. R., Lee, I., Sha, L., & Stankovic, J. (2010, June). Cyber-physical systems: The next computing revolution. In *Proc. 47th Design Automation Conf.* (pp. 731–736). IEEE.

Raspberry-Pi-Zero-W. (n.d.). *Raspberry Pi Zero W*. Retrieved 2021, from https://www.raspberrypi. org/products/raspberry-pi-zero-w/

Rau, G., Disselhorst-Klug, C., & Schmidt, R. (2000). Movement biomechanics goes upwards: From the leg to the arm. *Journal of Biomechanics*, *33*(10), 1207–1216. doi:10.1016/S0021-9290(00)00062-2 PMID:10899329

Ridolfi, M., Van de Velde, S., Steendam, H., & De Poorter, E. (2018). Analysis of the scalability of UWB indoor localization solutions for high user densities. *Sensors (Basel)*, *18*(6), 1875.

Robert-Lachaine, X., Mecheri, H., Larue, C., & Plamondon, A. (2017). Validation of inertial measurement units with an optoelectronic system for whole-body motion analysis. *Medical & Biological Engineering & Computing*, *55*(4), 609–619.

Roca, D; Nemirovsky, D; Nemirovsly, M; Milito, R & Valero, M. (2016). Emergent Behaviors in the Internet of Things: The Ultimate Ultra-Large-Scale System. *IEEE Micro Journal, 36*(6).

Rodriguez-Perez, A., de Aranda, R. P., Prefasi, E., Pablo, J. S., Dumont, S., Rosado, J., Enrique, I., Pinzon, P., & Ortiz, D. (2020). Towards the Multi-Gigabit Ethernet for the Automotive Industry. *2020 IEEE International Symposium on Circuits and Systems (ISCAS)*, 1–5. 10.1109/ISCAS45731.2020.9180481

Roetenberg, D., Luinge, H., & Slycke, P. (2009). *Xsens MVN: Full 6DOF human motion tracking using miniature inertial sensors*. Xsens Technologies BV, Tech. Rep.

Roetenberg, D., Baten, C. T., & Veltink, P. H. (2007). Estimating body segment orientation by applying inertial and magnetic sensing near ferromagnetic materials. *IEEE Transactions on Neural Systems and Rehabilitation Engineering*, *15*(3), 469–471.

Rosenstatter, T. (2017). *A state-of-the-art report on vehicular security*. Academic Press.

Rouse, M. (2020). *Confidentiality, Integrity, and Availability (cia triad)*. https://whatis.techtarget. com/definition/Confidentiality-integrity-and-availability-CIA

Roy, A., Cruz, R. M., Sabourin, R., & Cavalcanti, G. (2018). *A study on combining dynamic selection and data preprocessing for imbalance learning*. Academic Press.

Sanchez, J. J., Morales-Jimenez, D., Gomez, G., & Enbrambasaguas, J. T. (2007). Physical layer performance of long term evolution cellular technology. 2007 16th IST Mobile and Wireless Communications Summit, 1–5. doi:10.1109/ISTMWC.2007.4299090

Sari, A., Lekidis, A., & Butun, I. (2020). Industrial Networks and IIoT: Now and Future Trends. In *Industrial IoT* (pp. 3–55). Springer. doi:10.1007/978-3-030-42500-5_1

Sari, T., Güles, H. K., & Yiğitol, B. (2020). Awareness and Readiness of Industry 4.0: The case of Turkish Manufacturing Industry. *Advances in Production Engineering & Management (APEM) Journal, 15*, 57–68.

Sathiyamoorthi, V., Suresh, P., Jayapandian, N., Kanmani, P., & Janakiraman, S. (2020). *An Intelligent Web Caching System for Improving the Performance of a Web-Based Information Retrieval System.* Academic Press.

Sayama, H. (2015). *Introduction to the Modeling and Analysis of Complex Systems.* Open SUNY Textbooks.

Schepers, M., Giuberti, M., & Bellusci, G. (2018). *Xsens MVN: Consistent Tracking of Human.* Xsens Technologies BV, Tech. Rep, 1-8.

Scheurer, S., Tedesco, S., Brown, K. N., & O'Flynn, B. (2017, May). Human activity recognition for emergency first responders via body-worn inertial sensors. *2017 IEEE 14th International Conference on Wearable and Implantable Body Sensor Networks (BSN)*, 5-8.

Seo, J., Kim, K., Park, M., & Lee, K. (2017). An analysis of economic impact on iot under gdpr. *2017 International Conference on Information and Communication Technology Convergence (ICTC)*, 879–881. 10.1109/ICTC.2017.8190804

Shannon, C. E. (1948). A Mathematical Theory of Communication. *The Bell System Technical Journal, 27*(3), 379–423, 623–656. doi:10.1002/j.1538-7305.1948.tb01338.x

Sharif, A., Li, J., Khalil, M., Kumar, R., Sharif, M. I., & Sharif, A. (2017). *Internet of things— smart traffic management system for smart cities using big data analytics.* Paper presented at the 2017 14th international computer conference on wavelet active media technology and information processing (ICCWAMTIP).

Shi, H., Xu, M., & Li, R. (2017). *Deep learning for household load forecasting—A novel pooling deep RNN.* Academic Press.

Shotton, J., Fitzgibbon, A., Cook, M., Sharp, T. F., Moore, R., Kipman, A., & Blake, A. (2011, June). Real-time human pose recognition in parts from single depth images. *CVPR, 2011*, 1297–1304.

Sinaeepourfard, A., Krogstie, J., & Petersen, S. A. (2018). *A big data management architecture for smart cities based on fog-to-cloud data management architecture.* Academic Press.

Sinaeepourfard, A., Krogstie, J., Petersen, S. A., & Ahlers, D. (2019). *F2c2C-DM: A Fog-to-cloudlet-to-Cloud Data Management architecture in smart city.* Paper presented at the 2019 IEEE 5th World Forum on Internet of Things (WF-IoT). 10.1109/WF-IoT.2019.8767226

Singh, G. (2013). A Study of Encryption Algorithms (RSA, DES, 3DES and AES) for Information Security. *International Journal of Computers and Applications, 67*(19).

Sinha, R. S., Wei, Y., & Hwang, S.-H. (2017). A survey on lpwa technology: Loraand nb-iot. *Ict Express*, *3*(1), 14–21. doi:10.1016/j.icte.2017.03.004

Siriwardhana, Y., De Alwis, C., Gür, G., Ylianttila, M., & Liyanage, M. (2020). The Fight Against the COVID-19 Pandemic With 5G Technologies. *IEEE Engineering Management Review*, *48*(3), 72–84. doi:10.1109/EMR.2020.3017451

Smith, C. (2016). *The car hacker's handbook: a guide for the penetration tester*. No Starch Press.

Solberg, R. T., & Jensenius, A. R. (2016). *Optical or Inertial? Evaluation of two motion capture systems for studies of dancing to electronic dance music*. Sound and Music Computing.

Souza, M. L. H., da Costa, C., de Oliveira, G., & da Rosa, R. (2020). A Survey on Decision-Making Based on System Reliability in the Context of Industry 4.0. *Journal of Manufacturing Systems*, *56*, 133–156. doi:10.1016/j.jmsy.2020.05.016

Stallings, W. (2017). *Cryptography and network security: Principles and practice*. Pearson Education.

Stallings, W., & Brown, L. (2015). *Computer security: principles and practice* (4th ed.). Pearson Education.

Stoltzfus, J. (2020). *Your car, your computer: ECUs and the controller area network*. https://www.techopedia.com/your-car-your-computer-ecus-and-the-controller-area-network/2/32218

Strohbach, M., Ziekow, H., Gazis, V., & Akiva, N. (2015). Towards a big data analytics framework for IoT and smart city applications. In *Modeling and processing for next-generation big-data technologies* (pp. 257–282). Springer. doi:10.1007/978-3-319-09177-8_11

Suciu, G., Vulpe, A., Halunga, S., Fratu, O., Todoran, G., & Suciu, V. (2013). *Smart cities built on resilient cloud computing and secure internet of things*. Paper presented at the 2013 19th international conference on control systems and computer science. 10.1109/CSCS.2013.58

Suma, S., Mehmood, R., & Albeshri, A. (2017). *Automatic event detection in smart cities using big data analytics*. Paper presented at the International Conference on Smart Cities, Infrastructure, Technologies and Applications.

Sundaram, J. P. S., Du, W., & Zhao, Z. (2019). A survey on lora networking: Research problems, current solutions, and open issues. *IEEE Communications Surveys and Tutorials*, *22*(1), 371–388. doi:10.1109/COMST.2019.2949598

Susmitha, K., & Jayaprada, S. (2017). *Smart cities using big data analytics*. Academic Press.

Tao, W., Liu, T., Zheng, R., & Feng, H. (2012). Gait analysis using wearable sensors. *Sensors (Basel)*, *12*(2), 2255–2283. doi:10.3390120202255 PMID:22438763

Taylor, L., Miller, E., & Kaufman, K. R. (2017). Static and dynamic validation of inertial measurement units. *Gait & Posture*, *57*, 80–84.

Tencent Keen Security Lab. (2019a). *Experimental security research of tesla autopilot.* https://keenlab.tencent.com/en/whitepapers/ExperimentalSecurityResearchofTeslaAutopilot.pdf

Tencent Keen Security Lab. (2019b). *Tencent keen security lab: Experimental security research of tesla autopilot.* https://keenlab.tencent.com/en/2019/03/29/Tencent-Keen-Security-Lab-Experimental-Security-Research-of-Tesla-Autopilot/

Thatcham Research. (2020). *Thatcham research consumer security rating.* https://www.thatcham.org/what-we-do/security/consumer-rating/

Theodoridis, E., Mylonas, G., & Chatzigian-nakis, I. (2013). Developing an iot smart city framework. *InIISA, 2013,* 1–6.

Thomas, P. (2019). *Thatcham releases the latest results of motion sensors in key fobs that block relay attacks.* Academic Press.

TINYTILE. (n.d.). *tinyTile.* Retrieved 2021, from https://www.element14.com/community/docs/DOC-82913/l/tinytile-intel-curie-based-miniaturised-adaptation-of-the-arduinogenuino-101-board

Tomasin, S., Zulian, S., & Vangelista, L. (2017, March). Security analysis of LoRaWAN join procedure for Internet of Things networks. In 2017 IEEE Wireless Communications and Networking Conference Workshops (WCNCW) (pp. 1-6). IEEE. doi:10.1109/WCNCW.2017.7919091

Tragos, E. Z., Angelakis, V., Fragkiadakis, A., Gundlegard, D., Nechifor, C.-S., Oikonomou, G., . . . Gavras, A. (2014). *Enabling reliable and secure IoT-based smart city applications.* Paper presented at the 2014 IEEE International Conference on Pervasive Computing and Communication Workshops (PERCOM WORKSHOPS). 10.1109/PerComW.2014.6815175

Trend Micro. (n.d.). *Industrial internet of things (iiot).* https://www.trendmicro.com/vinfo/us/security/definition/industrial-internet-of-things-iiot

TUBITAK-SAGE. (n.d.). *TUBITAK SAGE.* Retrieved 2021, from https://www.sage.tubitak.gov.tr/

Uhlemann, E. (2015). Introducing connected vehicles. *IEEE Vehicular Technology Magazine, 10,* 23–31.

Unity. (n.d.). Retrieved 2019, from https://unity.com/

Upstream. (2020). *Upstream security's global automotive cybersecurity report.* https://www.upstream.auto/upstream-security-global-automotive-cybersecurity-report-2020

van Andel, C. J., Wolterbeek, N., Doorenbosch, C. A., Veeger, D. H., & Harlaar, J. (2008). Complete 3D kinematics of upper extremity functional tasks. *Gait & Posture, 27*(1), 120–127. doi:10.1016/j.gaitpost.2007.03.002 PMID:17459709

VICON. (n.d.). *VICON.* Retrieved 2021, from VICON Products: https://www.vicon.com/

Compilation of References

Villela, L. (2018). *Arquitectura y Algoritmo de Gestión para Redes IoT Autonómicas* [Lexical Characteristics of Spanish Language] [Master Thesis]. Centro de Investigación y de Estudios Avanzados del Instituto Politécnico Nacional (CINVESTAV) Unidad Guadalajara, Guadalajara, México.

Virtanen, N., Schirokoff, A., & Kulmala, R. (2006). *Impacts of an automatic emergency call system on accident consequences.* Academic Press.

Von Scheel, H. (2020). *Henrik von Scheel – Industry 4.0 originator.* http://von-scheel.com/industry40/

Wagner, I. (2020, October 8). *Car costs - automotive electronics costs worldwide2030.* https://www.statista.com/statistics/277931/automotive-electronics-cost-as-a-share-of-total-car-cost-worldwide/

Wang, A., & Gollakota, S. (2019, May). Millisonic: Pushing the limits of acoustic motion tracking. *Proceedings of the 2019 CHI Conference on Human Factors in Computing Systems,* 1-11.

Wang, L., Ning, H., Tan, T., & Hu, W. (2004). Fusion of static and dynamic body biometrics for gait recognition. *IEEE Transactions on Circuits and Systems for Video Technology, 14*(2), 149–158. doi:10.1109/TCSVT.2003.821972

Wang, X., & Li, Z. (2016). *Traffic and Transportation Smart with Cloud Computing on Big Data.* Academic Press.

Waqas, A., Malik, H. A. M., Karbasi, M., Nawaz, N. A., & Mahessar, A. (2017). CLOUDSIS. *An Application of Cloud Computing for Smart School Management System.* Academic Press.

Wedd, M. (2020, June). *What is LPWAN and the LoRaWAN Open Standard?* Technical report, iotforall.

Wieclaw, L., Pasichnyk, V., Kunanets, N., Duda, O., Matsiuk, O., & Falat, P. (2017). *Cloud computing technologies in "smart city" projects.* Paper presented at the 2017 9th IEEE International Conference on Intelligent Data Acquisition and Advanced Computing Systems: Technology and Applications (IDAACS).

Wireless, S. (2018). *Lte-m vs. nb-iot: What are the differences?* https://www.sierrawireless.com/iot-blog/lte-m-vs-nb-iot/

Wittmann, F., Lambercy, O., & Gassert, R. (2019). Magnetometer-based drift correction during rest in IMU arm motion tracking. *Sensors (Basel), 19*(6), 1312.

Woo, Jo, & Lee. (2015). A practical wireless attack on the connected car and security protocol for in-vehicle CAN. *IEEE Transactions on Intelligent Transportation Systems, 16,* 993–1006.

Woo, S., Jo, H. J., & Lee, D. H. (2014). A Practical Wireless Attack on the Connected Car and Security Protocol for In-Vehicle CAN. *IEEE Transactions on Intelligent Transportation Systems,* 1–14. .2351612 doi:10.1109/tits.2014

Wouters, L., Marin, E., Ashur, T., Gierlichs, B., & Preneel, B. (2018). *Fast, furious and insecure: Passive keyless entry and start systems in modern supercars.* Academic Press.

XSENS. (n.d.). *XSENS.* Retrieved 2021, from XSENS Products: https://www.xsens.com/products

Xu, H., Hao, S., Sari, A., & Wang, H. (2018, April). Privacy risk assessment on email tracking. In *IEEE INFOCOM 2018-IEEE Conference on Computer Communications* (pp. 2519-2527). IEEE. 10.1109/INFOCOM.2018.8486432

Xueying, Y. (2017). *Lorawan: vulnerability analysis and practical exploitation.* Delft University of Technology.

Yang, C., Huang, Q., Li, Z., Liu, K., & Hu, F. (2017). *Big Data and cloud computing: innovation opportunities and challenges.* Academic Press.

Yang, X., Karampatzakis, E., Doerr, C., & Kuipers, F. (2018, April). Security vulnerabilities in LoRaWAN. In *2018 IEEE/ACM Third International Conference on Internet-of-Things Design and Implementation (IoTDI)* (pp. 129-140). IEEE. 10.1109/IoTDI.2018.00022

Yan, X., Li, H., Li, A. R., & Zhang, H. (2017). Wearable IMU-based real-time motion warning system for construction workers' musculoskeletal disorders prevention. *Automation in Construction, 74*, 2–11.

Yazdani, M., Zarate, P., Coulibaly, A., & Zavadskas, E. K. (2017). A group decision making support system in logistics and supply chain management. *Expert Systems with Applications, 88*, 376–392.

Ye, F., Qian, Y., & Hu, R. Q. (2017). *Big data analytics and cloud computing in the smart grid.* Academic Press.

Yin, C., Xiong, Z., Chen, H., Wang, J., Cooper, D., & David, B. (2015). *A literature survey on smart cities.* Academic Press.

Yukalov, V & Sornette, D. (2014). Self-Organization in Complex Systems as Decision Making. *Advances in Complex Systems Journal, 17*(3), 1450016.

Yu, Y., Li, H., Yang, X., Kong, L., Luo, X., & Wong, A. Y. (2019). An automatic and non-invasive physical fatigue assessment method for construction workers. *Automation in Construction, 103*, 1–12. doi:10.1016/j.autcon.2019.02.020

Zavala, L. E. V., García, A. O., & Siller, M. (2019, July). Architecture and Algorithm for IoT Autonomic Network Management. In *2019 International Conference on Internet of Things (iThings) and IEEE Green Computing and Communications (GreenCom) and IEEE Cyber, Physical and Social Computing (CPSCom) and IEEE Smart Data (SmartData)* (pp. 861-867). IEEE. 10.1109/iThings/GreenCom/CPSCom/SmartData.2019.00155

Zeng, H., & Zhao, Y. (2011). Sensing movement: Microsensors for body motion measurement. *Sensors (Basel), 11*(1), 638–660.

Compilation of References

Zhang, Q., D'souza, M., Balogh, U., & Smallbon, V. (2019). Efficient ble fingerprinting through uwb sensors for indoor localization. *2019 IEEE SmartWorld/SCALCOM/UIC/ATC/CBDCom/IOP/SCI Conference*, 140–143. 10.1109/SmartWorld-UIC-ATC-SCALCOM-IOP-SCI.2019.00065

Zhang, Y., Huang, T., & Bompard, E. (2018). *Big data analytics in smart grids: a review.* Academic Press.

Zhang, T., Antunes, H., & Aggarwal, S. (2014). Defending connected vehicles against malware: Challenges and a solution framework. *IEEE Internet of Things Journal*, *1*(1), 10–21. doi:10.1109/JIOT.2014.2302386

Zheng, P., Sang, Z., Zhong, R. Y., Liu, Y., Liu, C., Mubarok, K., ... Xu, X. (2018). Smart manufacturing systems for Industry 4.0: Conceptual framework, scenarios, and future perspectives. *Frontiers of Mechanical Engineering*, *13*(2), 137–150. doi:10.100711465-018-0499-5

Zhong, H., Zhu, W., Xu, Y., & Cui, J. (2018). *Multi-authority attribute-based encryption access control scheme with policy hidden for cloud storage.* Academic Press.

Zhou, H., & Hu, H. (2008). Human motion tracking for rehabilitation—A survey. *Biomedical Signal Processing and Control*, *3*(1), 1–18.

Zhuang, Y., Yang, J., Li, Y., Qi, L., & El-Sheimy, N. (2016). Smartphone-based indoor localization with bluetooth low energy beacons. *Sensors (Basel)*, *16*(5), 596.

About the Contributors

Ismail Butun received his B.Sc., and M.Sc. degrees in Electrical and Electronics Engineering from Hacettepe University; his M.Sc., and Ph.D. degrees in Electrical Engineering from the University of South Florida. He worked as an Assistant Professor in the years between 2015 and 2016. Since 2017, he has been working as a post-doctoral fellow for various universities (University of Delaware, Mid Sweden University, Chalmers University of Technology, Royal University of Technology). He has more than 47 publications in peer-reviewed scientific international journals and conference proceedings. His citations have passed 1,800 and counting, along with an H-index of 17. He is a well-recognized academic reviewer by IEEE, ACM, and Springer, who served for 50 various scientific journals and conferences in the review process of more than 190 articles. He is an editor of Springer Nature and IGI Global. His research interests include but not limited to; computer networks, wireless communications, WSNs, IoT, cyber-physical systems, cryptography, network security, and intrusion detection.

* * *

Çağlar Akman has been graduated from Middle East Technical University Electrical and Electronics Engineering Department in 2008. He completed his M.S. degree in robotics area in electrical and electronic engineering at Middle East Technical University in 2017. During his MSc. he has worked on system modelling, sensor arrays, array signal processing, beamforming, multi-object detection and sensor fusion. He is a PhD candidate at Middle East Technical University in robotics field in Electrical and Electronics Engineering department. He joined HAVELSAN Inc. as a system engineer and he is the senior engineer in the modelling and sensor technologies. He has been working on system architecture design, algorithm development for control systems, sensor networks, and sensor fusion as well as wearable system design in body motion capture, indoor/outdoor localization, and robotics projects. He has taken a role in several R&D projects as a project technical manager.

Åke Axeland is a master's student at Chalmers University of Technology, received a bachelor's in Computer Science in 2019, and is finishing up his master's thesis in the spring of 2021. He attends the master's program Computer Systems and Network where the focus has been on cybersecurity and distributed systems. He started as a student at Chalmers in 2016.

Joar Blom began studying at the Chalmers University of Technology in 2016 at the Department of Computer Science and Engineering. After receiving his bachelor's in 2019, the studies led to a specialization in real-time systems and cyber security at the Computer Systems and Networks master's program. He is now finishing his master's thesis in the spring of 2021.

Sagana C. is currently working as Assistant Professor(Sr.G) in the Department of Computer Science and Engineering, Kongu Engineering College, Perundurai, Erode. She has a work experience of 8 years in teaching. She is contributing towards research in the area of Cloud computing, Deep Learning the past 7 years. She has published around 8 research papers in reputed journals and presented 6 papers in National and International Conferences. Her areas of interest are Cloud computing and Deep Learning.

Magnus Carlsson started at Chalmers University of Technology in 2016 and took his bachelor's degree in computer science 2019. He is currently doing his last year in the master's programme Computer Systems and Networks, where his focus has been on distributed systems and cyber security.

Oscar Carlsson was born in Kristinehamn and moved to Gothenburg to study IT at the Chalmers University of Technology. Studies a master with a focus on cybersecurity and distributed systems.

Dennis Dubrefjord is enrolled in the Computer Systems and Networks Master's program at Chalmers University of Technology, where his main focus is information security.

Michel Folkemark is an MSc student in "Computer Systems and Networks" at Chalmers.

Qingyun Gu is a Master of Engineering student at Chalmers Tekniska Högskola.

Hayder Hadi is a master's student in the Computer Systems and Networks program at Chalmers University of Technology. He is focusing in Information security as well as Cloud Edge computing.

Henrik Hagfeldt began studying at Chalmers University of Technology in 2016 at the department of Computer Science and Engineering. Following his bachelor in 2019, the studies led to a specialization in distributed systems and computer security at the Computer Systems and Networks master's programme. He is now finishing his degree with a master thesis in the spring of 2021.

Myeong-jin Jang is a systems engineer who has a 6-year professional experience in combat systems at Hanwha Systems (South Korea) and is about to complete his master's degree in Computer Systems and Network at Chalmers University of Technology (Sweden).

Logeswaran K. received his M.E. degree in computer science and engineering from Anna university, Chennai, India, in 2011 and B.Tech degree in information technology from Anna university, Chennai, India in 2009. He is presently pursuing his Ph.D. in Information and Communication Engineering under Anna University, Chennai. He is currently working as Assistant Professor in the department of Information Technology at Kongu Engineering College, Perundurai, India. His research interests are in the areas of Data mining, Knowledge discovery and Networking. He has authored over 20 research papers in refereed journals and international conferences. He has received grants from various funding agencies like DRDO, SERB, and CSIR towards the conduct of seminars and workshops.

Sentamilselvan K. received BE Degree in Computer Science and Engineering from Anna University, Chennai, TN, India in 2010. He received M.Tech degree with specialization of Information Security from Pondicherry Engineering College, Pondicherry University, Pondicherry, India in 2013. He is currently working an Assistant Professor(Senior Grade) in the Department of Information Technology at Kongu Engineering College of Perundurai, Erode, TN, India. He is life member of Computer Society of India (CSI). His research interest is Hacking, Web application Security, Information Security, Predictive Analytics.

Stig Arne Knoph is an M.Sc. student in the Computer Systems and Networks program at the Chalmers University of Technology, Sweden.

Lina Lagerquist Sergel became a master's student at Chalmers University of Technology after receiving her bachelor's degree in Computer Science in 2019 and she is currently writing her master's thesis ending in spring 2021. She attends the master's programme Computer Systems and Networks where her focus has been on real-time systems and distributed systems. She started as a student at Chalmers in 2016.

Sangeetha M. is currently doing PhD degree in Anna University Chennai . She received her ME degree in computer science and engineering from the PSG College of Technology, Coimbatore, in 2010. She is working as senior assistant professor in Kongu Engineering College, Erode for past 10 years. Her research interests include web technologies, machine learning, data mining, and security privacy.

Olof Magnusson received his BSc and MSc degree from The Institute of Computer Science and Engineering at Halmstad University in 2019. He is currently studying at Gothenburg University at the Department of Computer Science and Engineering where his research interests include Cryptography, Computer Security and Embedded systems.

Oliver Otterlind is a last year M.Sc student in Computer Systems and Networks at Chalmers University of Technology.

Keerthika P. is currently working as Associate Professor in the Department of Computer Science and Engineering, Kongu Engineering College, Perundurai, Erode. She has a work experience of around 15 years in teaching. She has completed her Ph.D in Anna University, Chennai. She is contributing towards research in the area of Grid and Cloud Computing for the past 10 years. She has published around 30 research papers in reputed journals indexed by Scopus and SCI and presented 15 papers in National and International Conferences. Her areas of interest are Machine Learning, Cloud Computing and IoT. She is one of the recognized Supervisors in the Faculty of Information and Communication Engineering under Anna University, Chennai. She is currently guiding Ph.D scholars in the areas of Machine Learning and Cloud. She has received grants from various funding agencies like DRDO and DST. She is currently acting as Reviewer and Editorial Board member in reputed journals.

Suresh P. is currently working as Associate Professor in the Department of Information Technology, Kongu Engineering College, Perundurai, Erode. He has a work experience of 15 years in teaching. He has completed Ph.D in Anna University, Chennai. He is contributing towards research in the area of Grid and Cloud Computing for the past 13 years. He has published 30 research papers in reputed journals indexed by Scopus and SCI and presented 30 papers in National and International Conferences. His areas of interest are Networks, Cloud Computing and Big data. Currently he is working in the areas of Machine Learning and IoT. He has received grants from various funding agencies like DRDO, ICMR, and CSIR towards the conduct of seminars and workshops. He has received Best Faculty Award from Kongu Engineering College. He is currently acting as Reviewer and Editorial Board member in reputed journals.

Manjula Devi R. is currently working as Associate Professor in the Department of Computer Science and Engineering at Kongu Engineering College, Perundurai. She has a work experience of 14 years in teaching. She has completed her PhD (Information and Communication Engineering) from Anna University, Chennai. Her research interests are Machine Learning, Soft Computing, Computer Graphics, and Artificial Intelligence. She has published over 25 technical papers on Neural Network, Intrusion Detection System, Data Mining, Machine Learning and Cloud Computing. She is currently acting as Reviewer and Editorial Board member in many reputed journals. She has authored more than 20 books edited by Charulatha Publications, Chennai. She has been honored with the various award such as Best Faculty Award from Kongu Engineering College, Shri P. K. Das Memorial Best Faculty Award & Life Time Achievement Award–2015, Best Author Award from Charulatha Publication, GRABS Best Young Teacher Award, Young Woman Educator & Scholar Award, VIFA Young Faculty In Engineering, IARA Best Researcher Award, ASDF Best Computer Science Faculty, Dr.APJ Abdul Kalam Award for Teaching Excellence, etc., She has received grants from various funding agencies like ICMR and CSIR towards the conduct of seminars and workshops.

Viktor Rydberg is a Master student in Computer Systems and Networks at Chalmers University of Technology.

Alparslan Sari received the B.S. in Computer Engineering from Mersin University, Mersin, Turkey in 2006. He received three M.Sc degrees from University of Delaware (UDEL), Newark, DE, USA in Computer and Information Science(2012), Bioinformatics and Computational Biology(2014), and Software Engineering(2014). He worked as a graduate/research assistant between 2010 and 2014 at UDEL. He worked as an Applications Programmer in IT Web Development at UDEL between 2014 and 2019. Currently, he is a Ph.D. candidate in Electrical and Computer Engineering (Cybersecurity Research Group) at University of Delaware and he works as a Java Software Engineer at JPMorgan Chase. His research interests are Cybersecurity, Internet of Things, Privacy, and distributed systems.

Mario Siller is a Principal Investigator at Cinvestav Guadalajara, member of the Computer Science and Telecommunications Research Groups. During the period 2015-2016 he was Visiting Associate Professor at the MIT Media Lab and a Fulbright-García Robles Research Fellow. During his academic visit, he worked in the City Science area studying the emerging and aggregate complex behavior of cities, from the perspective of Complex Systems Theory. His research areas include City Science, Analysis and Modeling of Networked Systems, Distributed Systems, Computational Intelligence, and IoT in application domains such as Smart Cities, Health, Blockchain, Industry 4.0, Intelligent Transport Systems and Urban Agriculture.

Amanda Sjöö is a Master student in the Computer Science Department at Chalmers, School of Technology.

Tolga Sönmez graduated from Bilkent University electrical engineering department in 1995. He completed his M.S. and Ph. D. studies in University of Maryland College Park in electrical engineering. During his Ph.D. study he has worked on optimal sensor scheduling and tracking algorithms in sonar applications. After that, he worked in Advanced Acoustic concepts in USA then he continued to work in TÜBITAK Sage in Ankara to develop integrated navigation systems. He recently joined HAVELSAN Inc. as a signal processing and modelling manager to work on sensor fusion projects. His is interested in sensor fusion, sensor networks and integrated navigation systems. He has managed several research and development project in sensor fusion, navigation systems and acoustic signal processing.

Rikard Teodorsson received his BSc degree in Software Engineering at Chalmers University of Technology in 2019 and is currently studying to get a MSc in Computer systems and networks.

Sathiyamoorthi V. is currently working as an Associate Professor in Computer Science and Engineering Department at Sona College of Technology, Salem, Tamil Nadu, India. He was born on June 21, 1983, at Omalur in Salem District, Tamil Nadu, India. He received his Bachelor of Engineering degree in Information Technology from Periyar University, Salem with First Class. He obtained his Master of Engineering degree in Computer Science and Engineering from Anna University, Chennai with Distinction and secured 30th University Rank.He received his Ph.D degree from Anna University, Chennai in Web Mining. His areas of specialization include Web Usage Mining, Data Structures, Design and Analysis of Algorithm and Operating System. He has published many papers in International Journals and conferences. He has published many books and book chapters in various renowned international publishers. He has also participated in various National level Workshops and Seminars conducted by various reputed institutions.

M. C. Luis Eduardo Villela Zavala is a Sc.D student at Cinvestav Unidad Guadalajara, his research areas include IoT, Complex Systems, Autonomic Computing and IoT application domains such as Urban Agronomy, Smart Cities, Urban Mobility and Industry 4.0.

Index

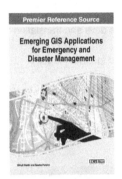
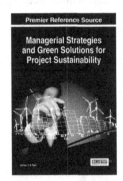

IGI Global Author Services

Providing a high-quality, affordable, and expeditious service, IGI Global's Author Services enable authors to streamline their publishing process, increase chance of acceptance, and adhere to IGI Global's publication standards.

Benefits of Author Services:

- **Professional Service:** All our editors, designers, and translators are experts in their field with years of experience and professional certifications.
- **Quality Guarantee & Certificate:** Each order is returned with a quality guarantee and certificate of professional completion.
- **Timeliness:** All editorial orders have a guaranteed return timeframe of 3-5 business days and translation orders are guaranteed in 7-10 business days.
- **Affordable Pricing:** IGI Global Author Services are competitively priced compared to other industry service providers.
- **APC Reimbursement:** IGI Global authors publishing Open Access (OA) will be able to deduct the cost of editing and other IGI Global author services from their OA APC publishing fee.

Author Services Offered:

English Language Copy Editing
Professional, native English language copy editors improve your manuscript's grammar, spelling, punctuation, terminology, semantics, consistency, flow, formatting, and more.

Scientific & Scholarly Editing
A Ph.D. level review for qualities such as originality and significance, interest to researchers, level of methodology and analysis, coverage of literature, organization, quality of writing, and strengths and weaknesses.

Figure, Table, Chart & Equation Conversions
Work with IGI Global's graphic designers before submission to enhance and design all figures and charts to IGI Global's specific standards for clarity.

Translation
Providing 70 language options, including Simplified and Traditional Chinese, Spanish, Arabic, German, French, and more.

Hear What the Experts Are Saying About IGI Global's Author Services

"Publishing with IGI Global has been *an amazing experience* for me for sharing my research. The *strong academic production* support ensures quality and timely completion." – **Prof. Margaret Niess, Oregon State University, USA**

"The service was *very fast, very thorough, and very helpful* in ensuring our chapter meets the criteria and requirements of the book's editors. I was *quite impressed and happy* with your service." – **Prof. Tom Brinthaupt, Middle Tennessee State University, USA**

Learn More or Get Started Here:

For Questions, Contact IGI Global's Customer Service Team at cust@igi-global.com or 717-533-8845

IGI Global
PUBLISHER of TIMELY KNOWLEDGE
www.igi-global.com

www.igi-global.com

Publisher of Peer-Reviewed, Timely, and
Innovative Academic Research Since 1988

IGI Global's Transformative Open Access (OA) Model:
How to Turn Your University Library's Database Acquisitions Into a Source of OA Funding

Well in advance of Plan S, IGI Global unveiled their OA Fee
Waiver (Read & Publish) Initiative. Under this initiative, librarians
who invest in IGI Global's InfoSci-Books and/or InfoSci-Journals
databases will be able to subsidize their patrons' OA article
processing charges (APCs) when their work is submitted and
accepted (after the peer review process) into an IGI Global journal.

How Does it Work?

Step 1: **Library Invests in the InfoSci-Databases:** A library perpetually purchases or subscribes to the InfoSci-Books, InfoSci-Journals, or discipline/subject databases.

Step 2: **IGI Global Matches the Library Investment with OA Subsidies Fund:** IGI Global provides a fund to go towards subsidizing the OA APCs for the library's patrons.

Step 3: **Patron of the Library is Accepted into IGI Global Journal (After Peer Review):** When a patron's paper is accepted into an IGI Global journal, they option to have their paper published under a traditional publishing model or as OA.

Step 4: **IGI Global Will Deduct APC Cost from OA Subsidies Fund:** If the author decides to publish under OA, the OA APC fee will be deducted from the OA subsidies fund.

Step 5: **Author's Work Becomes Freely Available:** The patron's work will be freely available under CC BY copyright license, enabling them to share it freely with the academic community.

Note: *This fund will be offered on an annual basis and will renew as the subscription is renewed for each year thereafter. IGI Global will manage the fund and award the APC waivers unless the librarian has a preference as to how the funds should be managed.*

Hear From the Experts on This Initiative:

"I'm very happy to have been able to make one of my recent research contributions *freely available* along with having access to the *valuable resources* found within IGI Global's InfoSci-Journals database."

— **Prof. Stuart Palmer,**
Deakin University, Australia

"Receiving the support from IGI Global's OA Fee Waiver Initiative *encourages me to continue my research work without any hesitation*."

— **Prof. Wenlong Liu,** College of
Economics and Management at
Nanjing University of Aeronautics &
Astronautics, China

For More Information, Scan the QR Code or Contact:
IGI Global's Digital Resources Team at eresources@igi-global.com.

Printed in the United States
by Baker & Taylor Publisher Services